SERVANT LEADERSHIP *for* CONGREGATIONS

Kent Halstead

Compass Books

SERVANT LEADERSHIP
for
CONGREGATIONS

Copyright © 2010 by Kent Halstead

All rights reserved
Printed in the United States of America
First Edition

Copyright exception
Although this work is copyrighted by the author, the publisher hereby authorizes for use exclusively within church congregations the right of reproduction of parts of the work in any form with author and title cited, without permission from the publisher. Reproduction for resale is not authorized.

Suggestions for improving this publication and contacting the author should be addressed to:
  Research Associates of Washington
  1200 North Nash Street, #1112
  Arlington, Virginia 22209

Web site
Portions of *Servant Leadership for Congregations* are currently available on the web site   (www.servantleadershipbook.org).

Ordering
This book may be purchased at www.amazon.com or through your local bookstore.

Cataloging Data
Dewey number 254.0
ISBN 978-1-883298-08-1

Published in the United States by Compass Books, a division of Research Associates of Washington, Arlington, Virginia

This book advances the responsibility of all congregations—pastors and laity together—to lead as servants of Christ, empowered by the Holy Spirit and guided by Scripture. The *servant* leader values and seeks the involvement of *all* in planning and deciding, to the very least person. Let no one doubt or be hesitant in this commission. Our strength resides in God's sovereignty over all and in our own inter-dependency and collective effort. Together we forge ahead, confident in this unity and inclusive Christian brotherhood.

The present author claims no creativity, the role being essentially that of review and compilation. The strength of what is said lies in the original sources, starting with the Bible and involving over 140 present day scholars. If in doubt, forge ahead, assuming that even modest success is superior to rejection proven wrong.

Servant Leadership begins with an explanation of the concept and spirituality of leading as a servant. The Bible guidance establishing the personal dimensions of the servant as leader is reviewed, together with the specific principles of Christian leadership. Then, how the church is structured and the various leadership opportunities and responsibilities are examined. The multiple elements of planning and leading are discussed together with the detail of effectively communicating and conducting meetings. Lastly, managing the various church functional areas—parish life, education, stewardship, community, and evangelism—as a servant leader are described. All the chapters can be read and taught as individual lessons. And use of the volume as a reference is an intended objective.

To ensure working use, we suggest this volume be kept in the church library and its importance and availability brought to the attention of as many present and future congregation leaders as possible. Include *Servant Leadership* in a recommended reading list and display with other notable titles. Most productive will be using the book as the subject text in an adult Sunday school class.

We close noting that success as servant leaders is always most dependent on prayer and Bible study.

"If any of you is lacking in wisdom, ask God, who gives to all generously and ungrudgingly, and it will be given you." (James 1:5)

Kent Halstead
Arlington, Virginia

Contents

Preface xv
Acknowledgements xvi

The Christian Servant Leader

1. Introduction 1
   Purpose 1
   Leadership Integral to Church Strategy 2
   Dependency on Congregational Acceptance 2
      –Special Note to Clergy and Seminaries 3
      –Promotion of the Concept 3
      –Dependency on Grace and Our Response 3
   Implementation and Benefits 4
   Presentation Style and Use 4
      –Format 4
      –How to Use 5

2. About Congregations 6
   The Word for Congregations 6
   Definition and Nature 7
   Emerging Conditions 8
   Meeting People's Needs 9
   Differences in Congregations 9
      –Traditions 9
      –Cultural Norms 10
      –Governing Structure 11
   Distinctions Among Members 12
      –Roles Played 12
      –Personal Orientations 12
      –Status Differences 13
   When are Congregations in Trouble? 13

Part I. CONCEPT AND SPIRITUALITY OF SERVANT LEADERSHIP

3. The Concept of the Servant as a Leader 15
   History of Servant Leadership 16
   Original Tenets 17
      What is Servant Leadership? 17

Ten Characteristics of the Servant Leader..................................18
      –Overall Responsibility...18
      –Attitude..18
      –Managerial Skills..19
   The Inner Resources of Leaders...20
   Application to Congregations...21
      Seekers and Prophets...22
      Vital Importance...22
      Distinguishing Servant Leadership from Christian Discipleship....23

4. **The Priesthood of All Believers**...25
   Priesthood Defined...25
   The Responsibilities of Priesthood...27
   The Office of Pastor...28
   The Holy Spirit...29

Part II. THE NATURE OF SERVANT LEADERSHIP

5. **Bible Guidance and Derived Principles**.......................................31
   Biblical Guidance for Servant Leadership...........................31
   Principles of Christian Servant Leadership........................34
      Love Jesus, Seek and Trust God's Will in All Things,
         Pray Constantly..34
      Be Loving, Kind to All..35
      See Things Whole, Seek the Truth.......................................36
      Commit to Excellence...37
      Encourage the Active Involvement of All..............................38
      Promote Democratic Action..39
      Commit to Lay Leadership and Its Development..................40
      Combat Domination, Build Diversity, Encourage Agreement........42

6. **Personal Dimensions of the Servant Leader** 45
   The Personal Nature of Leadership......................................45
      The Individuality of Leadership...46
      The Pre-eminent Qualities Needed......................................46
      Know That You Are Called to Discipleship...........................47
      Consider Your Discipleship a Responsibility to Lead............48
   The Leader's Commitment..49
      Identify with the Organization...50
      Commit to the Leadership Office..50
   Inner Resources of the Servant Leader...............................50
      Be Caring, Respectful, and Encouraging
         to the Very Least Person 51
      Embrace the Posture of Humility..52

  Be Joyful, Hopeful, and at Peace..53
  Be Calm, Patient, and Understanding...54
  Be Totally Honest, Open-Minded, and Fair................................55
  Be Confident, Resolute, Courageous...55
 Leadership Attributes/Skills...56

7. Peremptory Authority 58
 Forms of Management..60
 Peremptory Leaders, Indifferent Followers..................................61
  Faults of Leaders..61
   –Virtues of Rank..61
   –Self-Reliance..61
   –Self-Protection...62
  Weaknesses of Followers...62
   –Subservience..62
   –Over Sensitivity..63
   –Irresponsibility..63
  Destructive Social Mores..63
   –Discrimination..63
   –Tyranny of Tradition and Provincialism......................................64
   –Success in Human Terms..64
  Abuses of Authority...65
   –Bureaucratic Suffocation...65
   –Coercion...65
   –Manipulation..66
 Safeguarding Democracy..67
  The Threat Within..67
  Counter Measures..67
   –Biblical Guidance..67
   –Means of Correction..68

8. Core Elements for Leading/Managing..69
 Servant Leadership Defined for Congregations..........................69
 An Affinity for All Seasons..70
 Value of Servant Leadership..72
  –Advantages of Servant Leadership...72
  –Disadvantages of Servant Leadership..73
 How to Get Started...73
 The Servant Leader Model for Congregations............................74
 Management Functions, Organizational Structure,
 and General Strategy..75
  –Know the Operating Environment..76
  –Define the Organization's Mission and Goals.............................76

  –Set Forth Supporting Statements–Articles of Faith
    and Operating Principles..77
  –Establish the Organizational Structure and Job Descriptions........77
  –Select Appropriate Management Style; Recruit
    and Prepare Leaders...78
  –Develop a Plan of Action...79
  –Oversee/Direct and Coordinate Operations..........................79
Means of Leading..79
 Dependency on God and Prayer 81
 Persuade and Involve Others in a Unified Common Effort 81
 Provide Direction and Vision..82
  –Vision and Foresight...83
 Listen Attentively and Responsively................................83
 Focus on Priorities and Results......................................84
 Be Alert to Problems, Solving in an Orderly,
  Scholarly Manner..86
 Manage Conflict; Be Generous and Conciliatory....................88
  –The Nature of Disagreements......................................89
  –Sources and Severity of Conflicts..................................89
  –Means of Lessening Conflicts......................................90
  –Conflict Sources Within Congregations..........................91
  –Rules for Conflict Resolution......................................91
  –Location of Related Content..92

Part III. CHURCH STRUCTURE AND LEADERSHIP ROLES

9. Statements and Organization 95
 Church Statements..96
  Articles of Faith...97
  Emerging Conditions..100
  Mission Statement and Directional Concepts (Objectives).........102
  Operating Principles..106
  Church Policy...107
  Public Policy..108
 Church Constitution and Organization............................109
  Church Constitution..109
  Church Organization..110
  Job Descriptions..113

10. Leadership Roles..115
 A Common Binding Mission..115
  A Shared Ministry..115

    Democracy, the Foundation of the Servant-Led Congregation....116
    The Recruitment/Election Process..119
    Scripture for Leaders..122
Four Leadership Elements..123
    The Clergy–A Sacred Calling..124
        –United in Two Interlocking Roles.......................................125
        –The Key Role of Nurturing...126
        –Specific Responsibilities...127
        –Personal Qualities...128
    Role of Trustees..129
        –Mission and Authority..130
        –Membership and Officers...130
        –Diplomacy...131
        –Trustee Responsibilities..131
    Role of the Church Council...134
        –Council Mission and Authority..134
        –Council Membership and Desired Attributes.....................134
        –Council Modus Operandi...136
        –Council President..136
        –Council Responsibilities...138
    Committees–the Church's Working Force...........................140
        –Committee Missions...140
        –Committee Membership and Chairmanship.......................141
        –Committee Authority..143
        –Committee Strategy..143
        –Committee Responsibilities..144
        –Ad Hoc Special Task Forces...145

Part IV. LEADERSHIP IN PRACTICE

11. Communications and Planning......................................147
    Effective Communications..148
        The Art of Dialog and Receptive Listening...........................148
        Leading Group Discussion...149
        Encouraging Vision, Creativity, and Criticism.......................150
        The Ombudsman..153
        Open Forums/Critiques..155
    Long-Range Planning and Self-Study..................................156
        Nature of Long-Range Planning..157
        Self-Study...159
            –Self-Study Procedures...161

12. How to Conduct Meetings and Reach Decisions.........165
How to Conduct Meetings...165
Pre-Meeting Preparation...166
The Meeting Proper...168
–Deliberations...170
–Alternatives to Consensus.......................................172
Post-Meeting Follow-On...174
Role of Moderator..174
–Role of Moderator at Structured Meetings..........................174
–Moderator Duties..175
–The Philosophy of Christian Deliberations..........................175

Functional Responsibilities

PART V. WORSHIP

13. The Worship Service...177
The Nature of Worship..178
Role of Traditions..180
Attributes for an Effective (God-Focused,
People-Oriented) Service...181
Design Topics and Procedures.....................................183
Elements of Worship..185
The Setting..186
–Service Bulletin..186
–Symbols, Art, Color, and Ministerial Dress.....................187
–Sanctuary Design–Lighting, Sound, and Seating..............188
The Service..189
–Entering..190
–Reflection and Meditation..190
–Prelude and Postlude..190
–Words of Welcome...190
–Music and Processionals...191
–Liturgy...192
–Prayer..192
–Scripture Lesson...193
–Meditation...193
–Holy Eucharist..194
–Announcements/Offering Collection............................194
–Passing of the Peace..194

–Personal Intercessions and Laying On of Hands...................195
　　　–Personal Testimony..195
　　　–Benediction and Closure..195

14. New Needs, New Responses...199
　What are People Looking For?...200
　Our Response..202
　Derived Benefits of Attractive New Service Configurations........203
　Cautions in Implementation...203
　Implementation..204
　The Common round...204
　　　–Fundamentals...205
　　　–Hospitality..205
　　　–The Worship Place...206
　　　–Worship Construct..207
　Contemporary Innovations..207
　　　–Mission...208
　　　–Ambiance...209
　　　–Inclusiveness...209
　　　–Bulletin...210
　　　–Service Style...210
　　　–Music..211
　　　–Liturgy and Holy Communion..212
　　　–Spoken Word...212
　　　–Multi-Media..213
　　　–Facilities...214
　　Guidelines for Introducing and Developing
　　Contemporary Worship..214

15. The Spoken Word and Prayer.......................................221
　The Nature of Preaching..222
　　Definition..222
　　Importance of Preaching..223
　　The Preaching Domain...224
　The Interactive Elements...224
　　The Pastor-Congregation Bond..224
　　The Preaching-Listening Synergy..225
　　Partners in Proclamation..226
　　　–Attentiveness...227
　　　–Response..227
　　　–Advisement..227
　Pastoral Preparedness...228
　　Posture and Approach..228

Delivery Style and Skills...230
   –Ten Guides for Effective Delivery......................................232
Content Design..233
   Types of Sermons..234
   Principal Messages...235
     –What Are the Principal Bible Messages? 236
   Content Sources..238
     –Available Resources...239
     –Creativity and Citation..240
     –Search and Maintain..240
   The Planning/Writing Process.....................................241
     –The Enabling Retreat...241
     –The Topic Agenda...242
     –Supporting Mechanics..242
     –Guidelines for Content Preparation............................243
Leading Prayer...248

PART VI. DISCIPLESHIP

16. Parish Life..255
   Nature of the Christian Community..............................255
   The Meaning of Membership.......................................256
   The Embracing Mission of Caring and Involvement..........258
     The Essential Elements of the Christian Community.................259
     Means for Accomplishment...262

17. Small Group Ministries 265
   Definitions..265
   Role of Small Groups..266
   Small Group Formation...267
   Small Group Dynamics..268
     –Group Ambiance..268
     –Required Leadership..269
     –Mentor Training...270
   Responsibilities and Means of Mentoring.....................270
     –Mentoring Duties...270
     –Personal Temperament and Style................................271
     –Tools of Effective Mentoring.....................................272
   Special Need Response..273
     –Youth and Young Adults...273
     –Singles...274
     –Those in Need of Special Care...................................274

18. Christian Education 277
The Role of Christian Education 277
–The Special Opportunity of Adult Education 278
–Promoting Christian Education 279
Managing the Church School 279
Curriculum Design 281
–Curriculum Design Procedures 282
–Curriculum Taxonomy 283
Learning and Teaching Skills 284
–Creating Effective Learning Conditions 284
Reframing Confirmation 285

19. Our Call to Stewardship 288
The Nature of Managing God's Gifts with Charity 288
The Harsh Reality 291
Stewardship Committee Duties 292
Means of Gaining Everyone's Involvement 293
–Responding to God's Call 293
–Reaching Out to Embrace All 294
–Guiding and Supporting 294
–Ensuring Opportunities and Effective Employment 295
–Securing Commitment and Providing Recognition 296
–Financial Giving 298
Forms of Serving 298
–Outreach 298
–Nurturing 299
–Liturgical 299
–Management 299
Securing Financial Support 299
–The Reality of Our Wealth and Failure to Share 300
–A Permanent Condition of Faith and Self-Discipline 301
–Why People Give 301
–How to Become Charitable Givers 302
–Charting 305
–Special Fund-Raising Campaigns 309
–Hiring Fund-Raising Consultants 310
–Special Means 311

20. Evangelism—Basics and the Inreaching Responsibility 314
The Fertile Field 315
The Commission 316

    The Evangelism Committee...322
   The Inreach Responsibility...323
    The Embracing Congregation..323
       –An Inviting, Responsive Reception..323
       –A Compelling Service..324
       –Dynamic Preaching..325
       –Follow-up Ministry for Visitors...326
    The Sustaining Inreach Responsibility...327
       –Nurturing New Members..327
       –Ministry for Inconsistent and Inactive Members.................328

21. Evangelism—the Outreach Challenge..........................331
   The Calling..332
    A Hostile Environment...332
       –Recipient Barriers..332
       –Messenger Barriers...333
    A Task of Many Demands..334
    Recruiting and Training..336
    Prepared by Prayer and Empowered by the Holy Spirit............336
   Witnessing..337
    The Available Means..337
       –Media..338
       –Personal...338
    The Rudiments of Field Witnessing..341
    The Message..344
       –Pragmatic Content...345
       –Spiritual Content...345
       –Closing Prayer..348
    Follow-on Gatherings..349
    Pastoral Role...350
    A Responsive Congregation and Religious Service.....................350
    The Flyer Message..351

22. Community Ministry...355
    The Community Ministry Committee..356
    Setting Community Service Priorities...357
    Community Ministry Management..359

23. Administration Ministry 362
    Personnel Administration...362
    Finance Administration...363
       –Funding and Budget Comparisons..363
       –Salary Schedule...364

      –Budget Presentation...365
      –Salary Prorating..366
      –Investment Strategy..367
  Property Administration..367

APPENDICES:
A. Christian Music..369
    Selected Christian Music...371
B. Job Descriptions..377
    Senior Pastor..378
    Director of Music/Organist..381
    Congregation Council President..382
    Common Committee Elements...382
    Parish Life Committee...384
    Worship, Music, and Arts Committee.................................386
    Education Committee..388
    Stewardship Committee..389
    Evangelism Committee...390
    Community Service Committee...391
    Youth Committee..392
    Finance Committee..393
    Property Committee..394
C. The Challenge of Seeking Perfection......................................395
    The Commission and Our Enabling Strength.....................395
    The Leadership Challenge..395
    Strategies for Improvement..396
      –Proposal Review..397
    Challenges..398
      –Leadership...398
      –Management..400
      –Membership...401
      –Communications..402
      –Missions...403
D. The *Renewal* Reader 406

Preface

"I can do nothing on my own; I judge only as God tells me, so my judgment is right, because I am not trying to do what I want, but only what he who sent me wants." (John 5:30)

All Christians are called to serve. So commissioned, we must then each find those tasks most worthy, responding with our time and talent as we have been so blessed. In this instance, the author is guided to advance the principles of servant leadership as the exemplary means of Christian service. The claim is made with confidence for the concept itself is God-directed—all Christians being foremost servants. *You should look on us as Christ's servants who have been put in charge of God's secret truths.* (1 Corinthians 4:1)

The work of many scholars in the field of leadership has been studied in preparing this text. Over 140 authors are specifically quoted. The task has been primarily one of assembling, integrating, and interpreting their work in the context of advancing servant leadership as an instrument of faith. The perspective employed, however, remains that of a lay observer rather than scholar or theologian.

Confident that *Servant Leadership* will be of real value to congregations, we encourage as broad use as possible. Introduce the volume to others; include the title in a "recommended reading list." Most importantly, use *Servant Leadership* as the text in an adult Sunday school class. All the chapters can be read or taught independently. And, of course, use of the volume as a reference is an intended objective.

A copy of *Servant Leadership* should be retained in the church library and brought to the attention of present and succeeding congregation leaders.

As with all good things we are dependent on our heavenly Father and give thanks for his grace. We note with appreciation the pastors who have guided our steps toward righteous ways—Lyle C. Burns, John W. Rilling, Arnold F. Keller, Paul A. Wee, and Edward W. Bauman. And we give thanks to all good parents everywhere.

Those wishing to contact the author regarding servant leadership are strongly encouraged. Suggestions and new ideas are invited.

KENT HALSTEAD

January 2010
Arlington, Virginia

> Therefore I have undertaken this work ... not for the sake of speaking with authority about what I know but rather to know these subjects by speaking of them with reverence.
> St. Augustine, *De Civitate Dei [City of God]* (413 AD)

Acknowledgements

Every application of servant leadership draws heavily on the fundamentals pioneered by Robert K. Greenleaf, founder of the contemporary servant leadership movement. Among his many writings, the collection of essays, *The Power of Servant Leadership*, has proven most useful. Three other works—*On Becoming a Servant Leader*, *Seeker and Servant*, and *Servant-Leadership*—have furthered this dependency. As with all follow-on studies, we are entirely dependent on this seminal work. Much of Chapter 3 is devoted to reviewing Greenleaf's original ideas and their application to Christian congregations. To Robert Greenleaf then, this author as well as all society, owe immeasurable gratitude.

The author has also found great value in the works of a number of other inspired writers whose creative genius has vastly expanded our understanding of Christian service and leadership. Among these creators is Henri J. M. Nouwen and his spiritual studies, *In the Name of Jesus* and *Life of the Beloved*. The exceptional summary of congregational studies, *In Praise of Congregations: Leadership in the Local Church Today*, by Charles E. Bennison, Jr., et al, provides a wealth of practical advice. William Easum in *Dancing With Dinosaurs: Ministry in a Hostile & Hurting World*, warns us of the dangers of complacency and tradition in today's church and suggests new paradigms to solve old problems. In *Twelve Keys to an Effective Church*, Kennon L. Callahan identifies the characteristics of effective, growing churches in very specific instructional terms. His work is an exceptional treatise on strategic long-range planning for congregations. Finally, N. Gordon Cosby's book is inspirational throughout, *By Grace Transformed: Christianity for a New Millennium*. Among many notable accomplishments, Cosby is co-founder of The Servant Leadership School in Washington, D.C., where the author was first introduced and instructed in this transcending spirit. To all these creative writers the author is indebted.

In the area of homiletics, I have been primarily guided, as have so many practitioners, by two masters—Edgar N. Jackson, *A Psychology of Preaching*, and Edward W. Bauman, *God's Presence in My Life*, and a lifetime of listening to his inspired preaching.

From the field of management I am most indebted to John Carver and his masterful *Boards That Make a Difference*. His sweeping proposals reinvent the responsibilities of any senior management level of any type of organization, including churches, laying out a new forward-thinking, value-oriented, board-management partnership. His book guides leaders toward the big questions, a strategic visionary approach singularly suitable for church trustees and councils.

Extended quotations, and those where the original context is helpful, are fully footnoted. Short supplemental quotations are identified by author only. All scripture quotations are from the *Today's English Version* of the New Testament (American Bible Society) and the *New Revised Standard Version Bible* (National Council of the Churches of Christ in the United States of America), used by permission. Bible scripture is italicized; Jesus' words are further identified by quotation marks.

In the aggregate it is important to note that there is an untold amount of previously authored material used throughout this book, imbedded in the text in undistinguishable form. I have adapted freely from many sources, rewriting as necessary for continuity and style, the objective being always to surpass the abilities of a single author with the contributions of many. Our indebtedness is thus unusually great.

Finally, I cannot sufficiently express my thanks to my wife, Marjorie, who selfless support contributed to this project in so many ways, not the least of which being her invaluable editing.

The Christian Servant Leader

Chapter 1
Introduction

But you are the chosen race, the King's priests, the holy nation, God's own people, chosen to proclaim the wonderful acts of God, who called you from the darkness into his own marvelous light.
(1 Peter 2:9)

God commissions all who believe in him to serve and seek his will in all things. Faith makes this possible. So *faith* stands above all, enabling us through his grace to seek truth and serve as good leaders and followers. The intent here, in this work, is to strengthen this discipleship through the encouragement of *servant leadership.*

Purpose
Each of us, believing in Jesus Christ, are priests, each responsible for service as we are called, individually and collectively. The church laity and its pastors constitute Christ's kingdom on earth, the essential human element of all its successes and failures. This book is designed to foster the distinctive, loving brotherhood required, and promote the constructive service to which we are all commissioned.

The purpose here is to explain and promote the role of servant leadership in Christian congregations, and present related guidance in the various church functions. The aim is to engender a *philosophy* of individual importance and the value of each member's active involvement, however modest. In God's sight *all* are important, even to the very least one. His spirit enables us all to serve and be leaders. So we address not only existing officers, but more importantly, all followers as potential leaders. The message is also directed to pastors who as our spiritual counselors must be equally, if not more fully, informed and supportive of servant leadership if it is to be a viable central instrument of church management.

Perspective on our focus may be gained from the order of forces involved—God, human effort, skills and talents, guidance and direction. We are intent here on aiding the last fourth dimension, the responsibilities and training of leaders to guide and direct the congregation. Foremost, above all, is our heavenly Father, the creator and source of all goodness and strength, on whom all is dependent. Next in order are our own human efforts, large and small, made whole and worthy through Christ's sacrifice and teachings, and guided by the Holy Spirit. Third, supporting the second, are our human skills and talents, bestowed as gifts, each used according to his or her calling. So, the order is this—God leading, rank-and-file following armed with skills and talents, and lastly, disciple leaders from within.

Leadership Integral to Church Strategy

Servant leadership can be an effective means of direction in all manner of Christian service. It can become an integral infused dimension, a common overriding and bonding element of congregational life. Because of this permeation and breadth, each application is treated here as an aspect of servant leadership itself rather than a distinct functional entity. More commonly employed strategies, however, simply list servant leadership as a component part. For example, William Easum[1] provides one of the latest management guides as follows:

(1) Recognize the presence of multiple problems.
(2) Trust God. Pray constantly for guidance.
(3) Embrace the posture of *servant*.
(4) Look outside for answers.
(5) Be scholarly.
(6) Push through changes.
(7) Always strive for quality and effectiveness.

All these elements are included in this present work within the framework of servant leadership. We believe that the power of this means of leadership is so pervasive and encompassing that it warrants this overriding structuring.

Dependency on Congregational Acceptance

Every congregation is different and all will not equally respond to this message. Some will be receptive, others more cautious. Large churches may have problems associated with their structure, small parishes with limited resources. City congregations may face communication difficulties, rural churches problems of isolation. Readers will have to adapt what is presented to suit their circumstances, picking and choosing the most applicable and beneficial. For those with reservations, we encourage reasonable testing. Proof, we are convinced, will be found in the results.

No defense of the principles advocated is necessary. They are rooted in the writings of many respected authors, most notable the modern day founder of servant leadership, Robert K. Greenleaf. More recent voices are strongly supportive. The contributions of all are cited in the Acknowledgements. If there remains any hesitation regarding the great value involved, it is due to the present author's inability to convincingly express the true nature of servant leadership. Not an iota of reservation should exist regarding the concept itself.

Special Note to Clergy and Seminaries

Pastors play a pivotal role in servant leadership. Adoption and vitality are largely dependent on their acceptance and support. The precedent for acceptance is long standing. Consider one of the titles of the pope, "Servant of the Servants of God." Beyond scriptural and ecclesiastical admonition the change should, in fact, be welcomed by clergy. Transfer of an increasing share of duties to the laity affords pastors considerably more latitude and opportunity for spiritual guidance and counsel. Thus while this work is principally addressed to parishioners, it also, most assuredly, is meant for church pastors, whose position we believe will also be dramatically affected.

Congregations should always defer to their ordained clergy in spiritual matters. More encompassing, congregations should also continuously seek their pastor's advice in *all* church activities, for pastors are our shepherds, guarding and tending the congregational flock. There is no less pastoral involvement under servant leadership, just less management.

Greenleaf distinguishes **seminaries** at the top of the institutional hierarchy with a "unique opportunity to harbor prophetic voices that give vision and hope." He challenges them to provide "leadership of vision and inspiration that gives meaning, order, and light to those less able to generate these precious qualities for themselves." Specifically he tasks seminaries to "inspirit churches and equip them with the prophetic vision to become a forceful, society-building influence." Hopefully, this present work, directed specifically to this molding role of servant leadership as a vitalizing force in congregations will assist seminaries as well in this challenge.

Promotion of the Concept

Servant leadership is basically a management philosophy, in this application with strong religious overtones. We encourage its adoption through persuasive argument dependent on congregational prayer and bible study. The principles are advanced with confidence, details are left to congregational discretion. The intent is to get congregations *thinking* about the values involved, then how servant leadership can best be adopted to meet local needs. Once begun, the results will provide all the impetus and motivation required. Rooted in everyone's involvement, the concept will spring up and flourish.

Servant leadership, like any wellspring, tends to permeate all congregational activities. This infusion provides an opportunity in this volume to include many tangential matters. Some aspects may seem peripheral to the central focus, for example homiletics, but are in fact ingredients of the servant leadership whole.

Dependency on Grace and Our Response

We seek God's will in all things, diligently striving through prayer and supplication to discern his guidance. Christians have three means for this discernment: (1) prayer, (2) Bible reading, and (3) scholarly study.[2]

All endeavors should begin with prayer. It is the most powerful tool we possess, drawing God into the proceedings, evoking his counsel through his infinite love. Second, the Bible, the word of God, provides us his written guidance. Throughout this text we include Bible quotations as a continuing reminder of this ultimate source of enlightenment.

All must pray, all must read the Bible. In both spiritual matters we rely on our trained clergy for guidance. The third element–academic study–is somewhat different. Study by reading, observation, and research is primarily a nonsectarian tool of management, ably performed by self-directed congregational members. Although servant leadership in its universal application relies heavily on personal study, we, as Christians, recognize the preeminence of prayer and Bible study.

Implementation and Benefits

Not all ideas expressed in this book will "work" in every instance. Even some of the fundamental principles are not likely to be fully endorsed. Over time, however, it is expected that the gradual introduction and tailoring of servant leadership will eventually "tip" the congregation in its favor.

Robert K. Greenleaf in his *The Power of Servant Leadership* quotes Robert Frost, when asked the meaning of one of his poems, as saying, "Read it and read it and read it, and it means what it says to you." Greenleaf then explains that he thinks Frost was saying "...that meaning, that subtle signal that may shape one's future, is an elusive thing; it does not emerge, necessarily, as the logical end-product of a conscious analytical process. It fact, it may defy such an approach. It is more likely to come as a gift, as an insight, peripheral to the analytical process rather than the target of it." This is how congregations are likely to accept servant leadership, as an advancing adjustment in attitude engendered by a gradual perception of correctness rather than conscious decision.

Presentation Style and Use

This volume is designed as both a text and reference. We would, of course, like to see as much complete reading as possible, to fully grasp the totality of servant leadership and its many implications in church activities. Use as a reference, however, is more likely, looking up how servant leadership affects specific topics or problems.

Format

The text is limited to essentials. The writing is intentionally sparse and concise to emphasize the principles involved, rather than the encumbering details which are rightfully left to congregational design. Discussion and debate by users are an essential adjunct to the presentation. As with most guides, this endeavor should be approached with a watchful, discerning eye, cautionary values of servant leadership itself.

The presentation style is structured and cross referenced to facilitate selective use. Each section, devoted to a single topic, is largely self-contained, again to further selective use much in the way a "handbook" serves. Multiple headings and the resulting detailed table of contents should adequately assist readers in content location.

How to Use
This work, as with any guidance, is most productive when in the hands of potential users, not on a library shelf. It should first be reviewed and promoted by the pastor, then circulated among congregational leaders and members, finally, kept on-hand for ready consultation. Possibly the best "home" is with the current congregation president, passed from one incumbent to the next. These recommendations, however, require greater acceptance than is likely, so we encourage all readers to serve as promoters.

Church actions prompted from this or any source should be subject to group discussion and evaluation. Servant leadership strongly advocates that in every instance extended study be undertaken, concluding with democratic adoption or vote. Addition starting recommendations are presented in Chapter 8, Core Elements for Leading/Managing.

---

[1] William Easum, *Dancing with Dinosaurs, Ministry in a Hostile & Hurting World,* (Nashville, Abingdon Press, 1993) 128 pp.

[2] This triumvirate approach to discernment and problem solving was introduced to the author through a sermon by Bishop Theodore F. Schneider, then Pastor, Saint Luke Lutheran Church, Silver Spring, Maryland.

Chapter 2
About Congregations

All of you, then, are Christ's body, and each one is a part of it. (1 Corinthians 12:27)
"...you are all brothers of one another and have only one Teacher." (Matthew 23:8) *"If you have love for one another, than all will know that you are my disciples."* (John 13:35)

    This book is directed to Christian congregations, so it is appropriate to begin with the nature of the intended audience. The description is in the form of a series of brief interpretations from various perspectives, starting with a definition and emerging conditions, and concluding with congregational and member differences. More fundamental, however, and how we begin, is God's word concerning our discipleship together.

The Word for Congregations

    The essence of the Christian community is a Christ-serving ministry in which the members lovingly care for one another. These teachings specifically guide congregations as a "communion of saints."

- **Jesus loves us and we in turn are called to love and serve all our brethren in Christ's name.** *...love one another as brothers, and be kind and humble with one another.* (1 Peter 3:8)
- **Christ has bestowed on all believers a glorious priesthood, keeping us always in the presence of God.** *This is how we are sure that we live in God and he lives in us: he has given us his Spirit.* (1 John 4:13) *But you are the chosen race, the King's priests, the holy nation, God's own people, chosen to proclaim the wonderful acts of God, who called you from the darkness into his own marvelous light.* (1 Peter 2:9)
- **None is superior to another, all being equal brethren under God.** Treat every person with equal dignity, as if all were "little Christs," for there may be angels among us. *Suppose a rich man wearing a gold ring and fine clothes comes to your meeting, and a poor man in ragged clothes also comes. If you show more respect to the well-dressed man and say to him "Have this best seat here," but say to the poor man, "Stand, or sit down here on the floor by my feet." then you are guilty of creating distinctions among yourselves and of making judgments based on evil motives.* (James 2:2-4)
- **All things are possible through God. Be joyful, carry on the good work, never be discouraged.** *Be joyful always, pray at all times, be*

thankful in all circumstances. This is what God wants of you, in your life in Christ Jesus. (1 Thessalonians 5:16-18)
- **Our guidance comes from the Word and Holy Spirit.** *"If you obey my teaching you are really my disciples; you will know the truth, and the truth will make you free."* (John 8:31-32). *For we fix our attention, not on things that are seen, but on things that are unseen. What can be seen lasts only for a short time; but what cannot be seen lasts forever.*
(2 Corinthians 4:18)
- **The commission.** *Set your hearts on spiritual gifts, especially the gift of speaking God's message.* (1 Corinthians 14:1) *" 'You must love the Lord your God with all your heart, with all your soul, and with all your mind.' This is the greatest and the most important commandment. The second is like it: 'You must love your fellow-man as yourself.'"* (Matthew 22:37-39)
- **Be good stewards of the gifts God has given us.** *Each one, as a good manager of God's different gifts, must use for the good of others the special gift he has received from God.* (1 Peter 4:10)
- **Elect elders filled with the Spirit to positions of responsibility to direct the great work.** And they shall be known as servants to all people. *Be shepherds of the flock God gave you, and look after it willingly, as God wants you to, and not unwillingly. Do your work, not for mere pay, but from a real desire to serve. Do not try to rule over those who have been given into your care, but be examples to the flock.* (1 Peter 5:2-3)
- **Seek new ways.** *"Nor does anyone pour new wine into used wineskins. If he does, the skins will burst, and then the wine pours out and the skins will be ruined. Instead, new wine is poured into fresh wineskins, and both will keep in good conditions."* (Matthew 9:17) Christ is the wine, the church the wineskin which must adapt, applying the good news to a changing and often hostile emerging world.

Definition and Nature

"A congregation is a group of people who identify with each other under a certain name, share a particular set of basic assumptions, and meet regularly to communicate to one another those assumptions through language, story, rite, ceremony, or social behavior. In the case of religious congregations the shared basic assumptions are religious ones about God and about life in the world in relation to God."[1] This framework, while seemingly restrictive, is remarkably open-ended. The inherent complexity and multifaceted nature of congregations, plus the consequences of growth and change, result in great diversity, no two congregations ever being the same. What all churches have in common is "...the sharing and fostering of a certain set of fundamental understandings about God, the world, good and evil, and life itself."[2] Most important, all congregations are in God's protective care, all are brethren in Christ, all are commissioned to serve, and all are strengthened and guided by the Holy Spirit through prayer and the gospel. We are the family of God.

Emerging Conditions

These observations on the Christian scene by William Easum[3] are now seen dimly, possibly to emerge more clearly in the near future. But even if only partially true at present, they portend likely challenges and opportunities requiring planning and change in today's churches.

1. The United States is drifting away from Christianity, becoming a new mission field. If present trends continue, the unchurched will soon outnumber members two-to-one. And the transference is not neutral, but rather charged with a growing hostility toward Christianity.

2. The supremacy of the sovereign God is being increasingly questioned as modern society identifies truth and finds comfort in technology rather than faith. This dependency on material solutions promotes self-satisfaction as life's objective. Sin becomes outdated among people preoccupied with their own welfare.

3. An increasingly crowded and hostile world extends the need and difficulty for people to establish roots and identity. Congestion breeds disengagement and hostility as every change is seen as a possible threat to one's security. In the crowd, people seek out trusted and compatible friends and small secure groups for their socializing. Churches provide this sense of community, but have largely failed in reaching out to an increasingly disparate and isolated society.

4. Society is embracing new values and life-styles that emphasize personal fulfillment and meaning. This is manifest in the increased search for satisfying work, freedom to relax, and greater appreciation of the role of women in society and family life.

5. The distinction between clergy and laity is declining, as new responsibilities for community development require greater lay participation. The priesthood of all believers, holding all congregants accountable, will emerge as the dominant force in congregations. The clergy's effectiveness will be multiplied as their role shifts to that of equipping the laity to live their role as priests.

6. The decline in church membership may be directly contributed to the failure of congregations to adapt to changing needs and new delivery means. The substance of the Gospels is the same, the way in which it is proclaimed must be radically changed.

7. Inward looking congregations spend so much energy in self-ministering that they have little left for the unchurched and thereby fail to grow.

8. The sights and sounds of modern media and electronic music will dominate the way we perceive and assimilate knowledge and entertainment. A corollary is the future greater use of computers to process knowledge and aid in decisions, as opposed to our current primary reliance on experience and judgment.

Meeting People's Needs

People expect membership in a congregation to meet four of their needs:[4] **(1) To be understood**, that is, to be intimately known and cared for through close contact or long experience by member friends who are sympathetic and loving. **(2) To understand**, i.e., to perceive and comprehend the true nature and significance of God and God's relationship to man. **(3) To belong** to the church community as a distinctive yet integral member and as an essential contributing participant. **(4) To gain hope**, that is, to look forward with confidence and joyful expectation to God's will on earth and heavenly glory. In all of these personal relationships churches fall far short, with their fixation on groups as opposed to individuals.

Differences in Congregations

Congregations differ in many ways, the most readily observed being the common descriptors of parishioners' age, and congregation size,[5] location, wealth, and ethnicity. These external characteristics are largely mechanical in nature, more likely to influence the dimensions of church operations than the driving forces behind them. A small, rural church at the turn of the century, for example, faced essentially the same problems of defining its mission, generating commitment and participation, and creating a caring community as does today's large, financially wealthy, urban church, only the scale and time in history are different.

Far more important than physical traits is the congregation's mindset, for it is attitude and disposition that truly affect how we serve. We identify three sources within congregations that largely determine how members will interpret and respond to various situations: traditions, cultural norms, and governing structure.

Traditions

Traditions are modes of thought and behavior followed over the years that become accepted precedents. Traditions establish identity, promote continuity, and guide behavior. They permeate almost every aspect of church operations: how people dress, how they greet each other, the level of support and participation expected, how caring members are for one another, how democratic the leadership, even how robust the singing. All these conditions are largely governed by what is expected, i.e., "how we do things around here." When firmly entrenched, traditions can be very difficult to change

Time-honored traditions have a rightful and necessary role in every congregation, to preserve all that is good and productive. At the same time, congregations must be alert to adapting behavior patterns to a changing environment, and also be aware that, in some instances, a tradition may actually have been wrong in the first place. Congregations must not be pious regarding their practices, but rather openly honest, continually looking to God for guidance. *Jesus answered, "And why do you disobey God's command and follow your own teaching?"* (Matthew 15:3) A generous approach is to keep challenged traditions alive, in an altered more acceptable form by an innovative elastic adaptation.[6]

Cultural Norms

More telling than traditions are distinctions discerned from the **corporate character or "personality"** of congregations. Seven types of cultural conditions can be identified which form the interwoven web of beliefs and social patterns that constitute a congregation's distinct identity.[7]

Historical aspects of a congregation are its community memory and formal documents, evidence of the past that guide the future. They remind us who we are, a supportive heritage that encourages consistency and loyalty. Too great an allegiance to historical precedent can lead to stagnation and gradual loss in perception of changing realities. A futurist is probably more important to the development of a congregation than a historian.

The ***mission*** aspects of a congregation's culture are how members view their responsibilities and relationships to themselves, the local community and world, and the wider church. Missions reflect a congregation's orientation and priorities–inward versus outward, spiritual versus social, group versus individual, risk versus caution, demanding versus concessionary. Balances in these and other responsibilities are set by mission statements based on how a congregation understands its various roles. Frequently missions are too vague and comprehensive to provide any real guidance. Design of mission statements is addressed in Chapter 9, "Statements and Organization."

Liturgy and ***worship practices*** deal with how a congregation perceives it should interact with God in a generally formal group setting. The spiritual ethos (values), doctrinal expressions, and rituals of worship services are the purview of the clergy. But choice of "high" versus "low" forms and their attendant degree of connection between the sacred and secular worlds are a fundamental congregational responsibility. The selection will in large part depend on how the congregation recognizes its mission, one of a spiritual refuge or open hospitality. Design of the church service is addressed in Chapters 13, "The Worship Service," and 14, "New Needs, New Responses."

The ***stewardship*** aspects of a parish's culture are focused on defining the time and financial commitment expected of members and encouraging and building this level of participation and support. How a congregation goes about cultivating the time, talent, and treasure of its members speaks volumes of how it views the importance of each individual–reliance on a few or dependency on all. The rigor of the appeal, the performance levels sought, and the democratic coverage expected are all part of the stewardship equation. Stewardship is the subject of Chapter 19.

The *educational* pattern of a congregation provides great insight into the ethos exhibited toward member spiritual growth. Many factors are involved in designing a respectable program: attention to all age levels and special needs, curriculum development, instructional style, and possible overseeing of content. Promoting child and adult education is one of the most productive yet underdeveloped responsibilities of congregations. Adults can attend church services for years and seemingly never gain the understanding of God's word that is possible through church education programs. Chapter 18 deals with Christian education.

Ministry and leadership roles include the prevailing degree of hospitality and care for members and the community, the responsibilities of the pastor versus laity, leadership styles, and opportunities for lay ministry. Much of the present volume deals with this aspect of church culture, advancing servant leadership as the preferred management model. Part II presents servant leadership, principles through practice, in four chapters.

Demographic norms such as member age, race, location, and wealth, generally parallel those of the surrounding community. However, over time this similarity may change if a congregation favors and attracts one segment over another. This evolving identity is appropriate if it is supportive of democratically approved mission objectives. An older congregation, for example, would be expected in a church primarily serving a retirement community. But a diverse member population is more encompassing, has greater growth potential, and runs less risk of self-containment. Churches should conduct periodic surveys to gauge the homogeneity of the congregation and demographic trends. Surveys of this nature are discussed in Chapter 11, "Communications and Planning."

Governing Structure

Church management can range from autocratic to democratic. Strong willed, well-meaning, pastors along with dominant laity were guilty of some past authoritarian rule, but this has largely given way to democratic systems as congregations have become more assertive and self-reliant. Still, strongholds of control remain. Four countering dispositions tend to move congregations toward greater democratic leadership: (1) a church's structure that provides and encourages active member involvement and leadership, (2) commitment and enthusiasm, (3) receptivity to change, and (4) inward versus outward looking perspective. This book encourages growth in all four conditions, promoted through servant leadership. The fact that each posture is principally a matter of choice is providential, strongly encouraging to those who would establish greater democracy. In Chapter 7, "Peremptory Authority," we address some of the restraints involved. Documents for establishing a democratic supportive church structure are presented in Chapter 9, "Statements and Organization."

Distinctions Among Members

There is often greater diversity among members within organizations such as congregations than between organizations themselves. At the extreme, for example, are the few individuals who apparently oppose the majority's position regardless of the issue. These exceptions generally require personal counseling. More common are the broader distinctions between groups or segments such as old versus young. Problems arising here require extended discussion and understanding within the organization as a whole.

Distinctions between members and groups within congregations originate from three sources: roles played, personal orientations, and status differences.

Roles Played

The various ways in which congregational members participate in church activities are generally positive and uncontroversial. Three roles are typically played.[8] First, the **"saints"** by word and deed exemplify Christian behavior and lead and unify by example. Second, the **"organizers"** plan and manage activities, accomplishing the church's goals through its organizational structure. Third, the **"socializers"** enjoy and seek out companionship within the church, promoting interaction among members.

All members share these roles in various combinations, together with other personal traits and talents that make up the unique individual composites and group heterogeneity. Less common and tolerable are the rarer imbalances found. Thus a church might have an inordinate proportion of inward centered "socializers." Such a congregation would need to guard against inattention to the involvement requirements of its "saints" and "organizers." Member satisfaction surveys, discussed in Chapter 11, "Communications and Planning," can help identify trouble of this nature.

Personal Orientations

Not unexpectedly, congregations reflect the broad spectrum of **personal philosophies, attitudes, and expectations** of its members. Similar to the above "roles played," but more discerning, these distinctions classify people according to how they approach and are involved in congregational activities. Five such audiences have been identified:[9]

(1) *Socializers* seek fellowship allegiances through close contacts and friendships with members, often within small groups. This joining and acceptance is essential for sustained membership. Friendships, self-identity, and bonding all take place through the close associations fostered within small groups. Such groups must remain receptive to newcomers and also support the church as a whole.

(2) *Traditionalists* defend orthodox values and practices. They represent the backbone of the church and ensure continuity and cautious change. This very strength, however, may erupt in open hostility toward

those who challenge existing practices. This resistance, often subtly concealed in assigned authority and rules, constitutes a serious obstacle to servant leadership when it prevents open discussion and debate.

(3) *Academics* are members of the congregation who desire to learn more about their faith and how to live life accordingly. They frequently attend Sunday school and participate in study groups. They are open-minded and thus good candidates to support servant leadership.

(4) *Advocates* are issue-oriented and want to be agents of community change. They feel strongly about the rights and wrongs of society and seek to address perceived injustices.

(5) *Moderates* have multiple interests. They make up the majority of most congregations.

Status Differences

With respect to **relative influence and power**, congregational members fall into four categories defined by sociologist Melvin Williams[10] as "elite," "core," "supportive," and "marginal." Great care must be taken to ensure that this hierarchy remains as integrated and democratic as possible. Excessive reliance upon and authority given to any individual group is extremely detrimental to congregational cohesiveness and spirit.

Elite members have demonstrated their ability to organize and manage church operations. They are often "old-timers" with power based on their loyalty, long-time visibility, and rapport with the pastor. When receptive, they represent prime candidates for servant leadership. If entrenched, their autocratic authority represents a serious challenge.

Core members are the foundation stones of an effective church. They are committed to carrying out the church's missions and often hold key operating-level positions. They impart experience and insight to decision-making.

Supportive members make up the majority of most congregations. While attentive and contributive, they generally refrain, for one reason or another, from active participation. Some have demanding or exhausting jobs and seek a spiritual reprieve from the daily grind. Servant leadership recognizes the latent potential of these members and provides the supportive environment for greater involvement.

Marginal members, for a wide variety of reasons—age, infirmity, disenchantment, inability to relate, travel distance, etc.—generally refrain from church activities. This group, too often out of the main stream and neglected, are a great challenge, but not beyond a caring church.

When are Congregations in Trouble?

What evidence suggests a church's need for a full self-appraisal? Any one of the following nation-wide occurring conditions[11] may suffice: (1) declining or stable membership, (2) an aging congregation, (3) location in a largely unchurched and/or uncontacted neighborhood, (4) centralized leadership, (5) non-involved, underutilized parishioners, and (6) a majority of members having limited understanding of true Christianity.

---

[1] Charles E. Bennison, Jr. *et al.*, *In Praise of Congregations: Leadership in the Local Church Today* (Cambridge: Cowley Publications, 1999), pp. 24-25.

[2] *Ibid.*, p. 209.

[3] This commentary is adopted and summarized from William Easum, *Dancing with Dinosaurs: Ministry in a Hostile & Hurting World* (Nashville: Abingdon Press, 1993).

[4] Robert L. Randall cited in Bennison, *In Praise of Congregations,* pp. 149-150.

[5] About 80 percent of an estimated 400,00 churches in the United States have weekend attendance of less than 200.

[6] For a discussion of church traditions see Bennison, *In Praise of Congregations,* pp. 203-206.

[7] Briefly summarized from Bennison, *In Praise of Congregations,* pp. 65-81.

[8] Carl Dudley cited in Bennison, *In Praise of Congregations,* pp. 139-140.

[9] Restructured and re-titled from Warren J. Hartman cited in Bennison, *In Praise of Congregations,* pp. 136-138.

[10] Cited in Bennison, *In Praise of Congregations,* pp. 216-219.

[11] Adapted and altered from Easum, *Dancing With Dinosaurs,* pp. 38-39.

Part I.
Concept and Spirituality of Servant Leadership

Chapter 3
The Concept of the Servant as a Leader

> *"The servant-leader is servant first. It begins with the natural feeling that one wants to serve. Then conscious choice brings one to aspire to lead. The best test is: do those served grow as persons; do they, while being served, become healthier, wiser, freer, more autonomous, more likely themselves to become servants?"*
> — Robert K. Greenleaf, *The Servant as Leader,* 1970

The subjugation of one individual by another—servant and master—has demeaned society throughout human history. The idea that the relationship itself, *servanthood*, could, in some manner, be the foundation for a form of leadership would be deemed by most as utter fantasy. When this insight first occurred is not recorded. Certainly no one spoke more knowingly or commanded more adherence to servitude than Jesus Christ. *"Whoever wants to be first must place himself last of all and be the servant of all."* (Mark 9:35) Christ's teachings more than any other encourage and justify the present advocacy of this form of leadership for congregations.

In recent times, the observations and essays on servant leadership by Robert K. Greenleaf have led to what has become a growing worldwide movement of education and advocacy. Writing initially in the 1970s, Greenleaf's creative insight and clear vision of the servant as leader has masterfully detailed the subject beyond improvement. The present author, along with all Greenleaf's followers, are totally indebted to him for his powerful creative instruction.

This chapter attempts to summarize the essentials of servant leadership advanced by Greenleaf. Most of the material is adapted from his introductory content and that of respondents. The collection of Greenleaf's essays, *The Power of Servant-Leadership*, should surely be consulted. The excuse for not providing further detail here is that Greenleaf's guidance is employed throughout this volume in this congregational application. Greenleaf himself devoted a great deal of attention to advancing servant leadership in religious institutions. The dependency on his seminal work should be kept in mind.

History of Servant Leadership

It is amazing how often a fragile beginning turns into a colossus. But only when the original idea is totally sound. That beginning for Greenleaf was realization that the essence of leadership is service; being "the first person to make sure that other people's highest priority needs are being served." As common in so many lives, Greenleaf was strongly influenced by the life of another, in this case, surprisingly through a mythical tale. Here, from the *Preface* and Introduction[1] of *The Power of Servant-Leadership*, is the story.

> In 1970, retired AT&T executive Robert K. Greenleaf coined the term *servant-leadership* to describe a kind of leadership that he felt was largely missing from organizations. It was Greenleaf's belief that leadership ought to be based on serving the needs of others and on helping those who are served to become "healthier, wiser, freer, more autonomous, more likely themselves to become servants." Over the next 20 years, Greenleaf wrote a series of highly influential books and essays, which have helped lead the way for the emerging model in leadership and management.
>
> The idea of the servant-as-leader came partly out of Greenleaf's half-century of experience in working to shape large institutions. However, the event that crystallized Greenleaf's thinking came in the 1960s when he read Herman Hesse's short novel, *Journey to the East*–an account of a mythical journey by a group of people on a spiritual quest. The central figure of the story is Leo, who accompanies the party as the servant and who sustains them with his caring spirit. All goes well with the journey until one day Leo disappears. The group quickly falls into disarray, and the journey is abandoned. They discover that they cannot make it without the servant, Leo. After many years of searching, the narrator of the story stumbles upon Leo and is taken into the religious order that had sponsored the original journey. There, he discovers that Leo, who he had first known as a servant, was in fact the head of the order, its guiding spirit and leader.
>
> After reading this story, Greenleaf concluded that the central meaning of it was that the great leader is first experienced as a servant to others, and that this simple fact is central to his or her greatness. True leadership emerges from those whose primary motivation is a deep desire to help others.

In Greenleaf's own words, "First, I did not get the notion of the servant as leader from conscious logic. Rather it came to me as an intuitive insight as I contemplated Leo. Serving and leading are still mostly intuition-based concepts in my thinking."

Religious leaders. Over the course of his life, Greenleaf studied and met many people whose lives exhibited the inner strength and spirit of servant leaders and influenced his writing. Foremost among these "great spirit" images as he called them were a number of religious leaders. We credit them here briefly to document the religious heritage inherent in Greenleaf's work.

In a 1980's essay on the inner city church as a servant to its community, Greenleaf cites the lives of two pastors who invested over fifty years of their lives in building community institutions, Nikolai Grundtvig (1783-1872) known as the father of the Danish folk high schools, and John Frederic Oberlin (1740-1826) for whom Oberlin College is named. In a 1982 paper on church leadership of the United Methodist Church Greenleaf writes of John Woolman, an American Quaker who almost single-handedly rid the Society of Friends of slaves in the middle years of the eighteenth century. In a 1986 essay, he describes the spirit of Pope John XXIII "...that supported him as he became the disciplined, historically rooted seeker that his life so beautifully modeled–and that we who survive him have the option to emulate."

A personal friendship with Rabbi Abraham Joshua Heschel (1907-1972), theologian, educator, philosopher and author, evoked this evaluation, "He was ethical to the core of his being, in the deepest religious sense." The principal impact of George Fox, founder of the Religious Society of Friends in England in the seventeenth century, was "...upon ethical practice, immediately and permanently, in all walks of life." Lastly, in speaking of Martin Luther, Greenleaf describes his advocation of the priesthood of all believers as "...one of the great ideas of this millennium."

While others in different fields also influenced Greenleaf–Donald John Cowling in education and Robert Frost in poetry, for example–the religious sector seems dominant, interpreted here as exemplary lives of service through Christ.

Original Tenets

Greenleaf's "big idea" is "...that leadership, in the final analysis, must be about service." He covered this topic in four books and a series of essays now collected in one volume. He left for others the task of synthesis and summary, ably performed by a number of his admirers.

What is Servant Leadership?

In all of his works, Greenleaf discusses the need for a new kind of leadership model, a model that puts serving others–including employees, customers, and community–as the number one priority. Servant-leadership emphasizes increased service to others; a holistic approach to work; the promotion of a sense of community; and a deepening understanding of spirit in the workplace.

It is important to stress that servant-leadership is not a "quick-fix" approach. Nor is it something that can quickly be instilled within an institution. At its core, servant-leadership is a long-term, transformational approach to life and work–in essence, a way of being–that has the potential for creating positive change throughout our society.[2]

Ten Characteristics of the Servant Leader

Larry Spears does a most complete summary[3] in his "Introduction" to *The Power of Servant Leadership.* His ten characteristics, abbreviated and reordered here, are central to the development of servant leaders.

Overall Responsibility

Servant-leadership starts with a commitment to three fundamental responsibilities which form the basis for the subsequent attributes.

1. Stewardship: Robert Greenleaf's view of all institutions was one in which CEOs, staffs, and trustees all played significant roles in holding their institutions in trust for the greater good of society. Servant-leadership, like stewardship, assumes first and foremost a commitment to serving the needs of others.

2. Commitment to the growth of people: Servant-leaders believe that people have an intrinsic value beyond their tangible contributions as workers. As such, the servant-leader is deeply committed to the growth of each and every individual within his or her institution. The servant-leader recognizes the tremendous responsibility to do everything within his or her power to nurture the personal, professional, and spiritual growth of employees.

3. Building community: The servant-leader seeks to identify means for building community among those who work with a given institution. Greenleaf said that this could be accomplished "...by each servant-leader demonstrating his [or her] own unlimited liability for a quite specific community-related group."

Attitude

The servant-leader has two overriding intentions in interacting with others:

4. Empathy: The servant-leader strives to understand and empathize with others. People need to be accepted and recognized for their special and unique spirit. One assumes the good intentions of co-workers and does not reject them as people, even when one is forced to refuse to accept their behavior or performance. The most successful servant-leaders are those who have become skilled, empathetic listeners.

5. Healing: The healing of relationships is a powerful force for transformation and integration. Many people have broken spirits and have suffered from a variety of emotional hurts. Although this is a part of being human, servant-leaders recognize that they have an opportunity to "help make whole" those with whom they come in contact. In his essay, "The Servant as Leader," Greenleaf writes, "There is something subtle communicated to one who is being served and led if, implicit in the compact between servant-leader and led, is the understanding that the search for wholeness is something they share."

Managerial Skills
The management skills employed in servant leadership are commonly cited in many texts. Their potential is dramatically increased when interpreted within the responsibilities and attitudes listed above, and they are given a warmer, kinder, appeal. The present study applies these skills throughout, recognizing, however, that lasting success is ultimately more dependent on the leader's sense of responsibility and state-of-mind than managerial mechanics.

6. Listening: Leaders have traditionally been valued for their communication and decision-making skills. Although these are also important skills for the servant-leader, they need to be reinforced by a deep commitment to listening intently to others. The servant-leader seeks to identify the will of a group and helps clarify that will. He or she seeks to listen receptively to what is being said (and not said!). Listening also encompasses getting in touch with one's own inner voice, and seeking to understand what one's body, spirit, and mind are communicating. Listening, coupled with regular periods of reflection, are essential to the growth of the servant-leader.

7. Awareness: General awareness, and especially self-awareness, strengthens the servant-leader. Making a commitment to foster awareness can be scary—you never know what you may discover! Awareness also aids one in understanding issues involving ethics and value. It lends itself to being able to view most situations from a more integrated, holistic position. As Greenleaf observed: "Awareness is not a giver of solace—it is just the opposite. It is a disturber and an awakener. Able leaders are usually sharply awake and reasonably disturbed. They are not seekers after solace. They have their own inner serenity."

8. Persuasion: Another characteristic of servant-leaders is reliance on persuasion, rather than on one's positional authority, in making decisions within an organization. The servant-leader seeks to convince others, rather than coerce compliance. This particular element offers one of the clearest distinctions between the traditional authoritarian model and that of servant-leadership. The servant-leader is effective at building consensus within groups.

9. Conceptualization: Servant-leaders seek to nurture their ability to "dream great dreams." The ability to look at a problem (or an organization) from a conceptualizing perspective means that one must think beyond day-to-day realities. The traditional manager is consumed by the need to achieve short-term operational goals. The manager who wishes to also be a servant-leader must stretch his or her thinking to encompass broader-based conceptual thinking.

10. Foresight: Closely related to conceptualization is the ability to foresee the likely outcome of a situation, a characteristic that enables the servant-leader to understand the lessons from the past, the realities of the present, and the likely consequence of a decision for the future. It is also deeply rooted within the intuitive mind.

The Inner Resources of Leaders

Greenleaf ventures to say that servant leadership, at its highest level, needs to be in strong qualified hands. He identifies the strong as possessing "....the more ponderable qualities of competence, stability, resiliency, and values" and then adds three elusive ones, "...a sense of the unknowable, contingency thinking, and foresight." All seven qualities are intellectual in nature and interwoven. These inner resources of a leader,[4] support self-confidence that in turn builds confidence in followers.

Why would anyone follow the leadership of another unless one has confidence that the other knows better where to go? And how would one know better where to go unless one has a wider than usual awareness of the terrain and the alternatives, unless one is well armored for the unexpected, and unless one's view of the future is more sharply defined than that of most? Also, one's confidence in a leader rests, in part, on the assurance that stability and poise and resilience under stress give adequate strength for the rigors of leadership. All of the above stand on a base of intensity and dedication to service that support faith as trust.

One needs to have a sense for the unknowable, to be prepared for the unexpected, and to be able to foresee the unforeseeable. The leader knows some things and foresees some things which those one is presuming to lead do not know or foresee as clearly. This is partly what gives the leader his "lead," that puts him out ahead and qualifies him or her to show the way.

Sense of the unknowable—beyond conscious rationality. As a practical matter, on most important decisions there is an information gap. There usually is a gap between the solid information in hand and what is needed. The art of leadership rests, in part, on the ability to bridge this gap by intuition, by a judgment from the unconscious process. The person who is better at this than most is likely to emerge the leader because he contributes something of great value. Others will depend on him to go out ahead and show the way because his judgment will be better than most. Leaders, therefore, must be more creative than most; and creativity is largely discovery, a push into the uncharted and the unknown.

Contingency thinking. *Foresight* is anticipating what is likely to happen and taking precautionary steps. *Contingency thinking* relates to things that might happen but rarely do. Sometimes the latter appear as emergencies to which there is a preset response. Part of the confidence of followers in a leader rests on the belief that the leader will not be surprised by the unusual and will act promptly in response to it.

Foresight–the central ethic of leadership. One takes the rough and tumble of going out ahead to show the way in the belief that, if one enters a situation prepared with the necessary experience and knowledge at the conscious level, *in the situation*, the intuitive insight necessary for one's optimal performance will be forthcoming. One follows the steps of the creative process which require that one stay with conscious analysis as far as it will carry one, and then withdraws, releases the analytical pressure, if only for a moment, in full confidence that a resolving insight will come. The concern with the past and future is gradually attenuated as this span of concern goes forward or backward from the instant moment. The ability to do this is the essential structural dynamic of leadership.

Application to Congregations

Jesus called them together and said, "You know that those who are regarded as rulers of the Gentiles lord it over them, and their high officials exercise authority over them. Not so with you. Instead, whoever wants to become great among you must be your servant, and whoever wants to be first must be slave of all. For even the Son of Man did not come to be served, but to serve, and to give his life as a ransom for many." (Mark 10:42-45)

Servant leadership is applicable to all types of enterprises, none more so than church congregations. *Here is my servant whom I have chosen, the one I love, in whom I delight.* (Isaiah 42:1) In this Old Testament book, God describes through Isaiah the prophet the coming of the Great Servant, Jesus. Thus one of the earliest references to the coming Messiah speaks, not of a king, but a servant. And, throughout the New Testament, Jesus talks again and again of serving others. *"Whoever wants to be first must place himself last of all and be the servant of all."* (Mark 9:35)

Greenleaf noted this repetition, reporting that the term *servant* (along with *serve* and *service*) appear in the Bible more than thirteen hundred times beginning with the book of Genesis. He put churches along side of foundations at the very top as contemporary institutions with the highest potential for serving humankind. Two essays explain his position–"The Servant as Religious Leader" and "Seminary as Servant"–the only ones addressed to a specific type of organization..

Seekers and Prophets

In "The Servant as Religious Leader" Greenleaf adds two additional tests for religious leaders, that they must be seekers and prophets as well as leaders.

> Prophet, seeker, and leader are inextricable linked. The *prophet* brings vision and penetrating insight, The *seeker* brings openness, aggressive searching, and critical judgment–all within the context of the deeply felt attitude, "I have not yet found it." The *leader* adds the art of persuasion backed by persistence, determination, and the courage to venture and risk. The occasional person embodies all three. Both prophet and leader are seekers first.
>
> The effective religious leader, like other leaders, is apt to be highly intuitive in making judgments about what to do and what not to do. Such a leader also draws heavily on inspiration to sustain spirit. Careful analytical thought, along with knowledge and reflection, provides a check and a guide to intuition and inspiration, gives a solid basis for communicating with informed and prudent people, and offers a framework of assurance to those who would follow.[5]

Leadership versus management. Greenleaf is clear in distinguishing true leadership from management, especially in the context of religious organizations. Too often those in responsible church positions concentrate on and even belabor routine management and administrative problems common to any organization, and utterly fail to garner their deep inner resources and those of others in aggressive dynamic leadership that builds trust and confidence, attracting and holding followers. Church members tend to play it "safe." As Greenleaf once put it bluntly in an off-the-record session, "You seem not to believe in your own stuff."

Vital Importance

Now is the time to jettison old hierarchical models and replace them with new ones emphasizing persuasion and seeking consensus. No candidates should be more receptive than Christian congregations. The conversion, if we may be so bold to call it, may require only a slight blending here and there or a massive overthrow; it may be adopted quickly or gradually assimilated over many years, but it must take place. Greenleaf rightfully contends that "The strongest, most productive institution over a long period of time is one in which, other things being equal, there is the largest amount of voluntary action in support of the goals of the institutions."[6] Goals must be clear, comprehensive, understood, and enthusiastically supported. Then people believe in the things they are doing and take the necessary action without continual direction. Greenleaf believes institutions that achieve most of this kind of teamwork will be judged stronger than comparable institutions with less community involvement. Congregations can expect the same high returns.

Distinguishing Servant Leadership from Christian Discipleship

We conclude with a necessary distinction. Congregations are not institutions in the ordinary sense, but sacred commissions, the body of Christ on earth. Therefore the rules of man, however insightful and well motivated, are always a secondary source of guidance following prayer and scripture. This distinction, and the resulting alignment of servant leadership *within* the spirituality of Christianity, is explained at the beginning of the next chapter.

Servitude and leadership are true dimensions of Christian discipleship–active following of Christ. But in all things discipleship precedes, creates, and guides leadership and service, however admirably and humbly the later elements are carried out.

Robert K. Greenleaf[7] was an original and creative thinker to whom we are all indebted. His intuition derived the contemporary model of servant leadership, yet it is *not* the blueprint for this book, however dependent we are on his insight and writings. Our inspiration is Jesus Christ. We become servants and leaders in his name only and through his grace, not of our own free will. We must continuously remind ourselves that all good comes from our heavenly Father. *Not by might, nor power, but by my Spirit, saith the Lord of Hosts.* (Zechariah 4:6)

---

[1] Larry C. Spears, "Preface" and "Introduction" in Robert K. Greenleaf, *The Power of Servant Leadership* (San Francisco, Berrett-Koehler, 1998), pp. xix-xx, 3-4.

[2] *Ibid.*, pp. 4-5.

[3] *Ibid.*, pp. 5-8.

[4] Robert K. Greenleaf, *The Power of Servant Leadership*, pp. 124-126, 129-131.

[5] *Ibid.*, pp. 120-121.

[6] *Ibid.*, p. 51.

⁷ Greenleaf's writings provide some evidence of his personal religious posture. The distinction between his "spiritual search" and our conviction through faith warrants citation. "I consider myself fortunate that my early religious training, the little that I had, did not take very well. I arrived at my mature years with a sense of religion as something not yet found but, rather, something to be sought. It is something that will grow as I grow. I see belief or faith as a consequence, rather than a source. Such faith as I have is a consequence of my own experience framed in the religious feeling that is the light of my search. I am aware of and interested in what others have experienced and believe. But I prefer to see faith as Dean Inge defined it, the 'choice of the nobler hypothesis,' the kind of choice that only an experienced person can make." (*The Search and the Seeker*, pp. 287-288).

Greenleaf described himself as a "student of organization," his primary interest being "...in the quality of our society" which he judged to be far below what it could be. He believed that this shortfall could be corrected if churches and seminaries would reach for the best they can achieve. To this end he consulted with various religious organizations throughout his life ranging from individual churches to national judicatories and ecumenical groups. Despite his efforts, in later years he came to feel that the religious community was not fulfilling its obligations to society and to God. He felt the vast potential was largely untapped. "I have had more than 50 years of listening to and watching those who carry the leading and managing roles in institutions of all sorts, large and small. In all of this, I rarely hear reference to influence being wielded on these people's institutional roles by churches."

Greenleaf was "loving but tough and unsentimental." He was a person who got to the heart of things, questioning, for example, how church leaders could conduct conferences without speaking about God or the spirit, or the power of the Gospel to change and renew human life. One observer (Christ R. Klein, American church historian) said that Greenleaf made church leaders feel uncomfortable by his consistent framing of the question, either explicitly or implicitly, "Well, what difference does it make for you to say that you believe in God."

In pursuing Greenleaf's writings, the present author finds that Greenleaf makes direct reference to Jesus only once (In *Servant Leadership*, Greenleaf recites Christ admonishing his challengers, saying "Let him that is without sin among you cast the first stone." pp. 28-29). He continues, "I have come to see Jesus as a Jew living in the light of the Jewish law and carrying it forward by adding creativity to it through his own experience."

Apparently Greenleaf acted more out of *ethical sureness* that follows from the efficacy of religious feeling rather than by the power of *religious faith* itself. As we quoted him above, "I see belief or faith as a consequence, rather than a source. Such faith as I have is a consequence of my own experience." Later he wrote this poignant afterthought. "This search is a lonely affair. Beyond the few with whom I share individually, I have found it so. No group or movement carries me very far, although I value the 'lifts' they have given me." Oh that he knew Christ!

Chapter 4
The Priesthood of All Believers

Everything you do or say, then, should be done in the name of the Lord Jesus, as you give thanks through him to God the Father.
(Colossians 3:17)

This chapter presents a brief explanation, from a layman's perspective, of the doctrine of the priesthood of all believers. It is incumbent upon the servant leader to accept the responsibilities so bestowed. Martin Luther, the foremost herald of universal priesthood, makes this requirement clear. "In this way we are all priests, clothed and adorned with the same holiness of Christ. This is the beautiful and glorious priesthood of those who are always in the presence of God and serve Him with a true and holy service. Our priestly garments are nothing else than the beautiful, divine, and various gifts of the Holy Spirit."

The entry here into theology is a departure from our central focus on laity leadership. The exception is necessary because of the encompassing and authorizing nature of universal priesthood. Priesthood bestows on *every* believer discipleship, responsibilities, and dignity, deserving our utmost respect and servitude one to another. If we believe in this ordination, then all leaders are servants and all servants are leaders. Thus this chapter serves as the great defense of servant leadership as a living embodiment of the Christian spirit of universal priesthood and service.

Servant leadership in congregations may be deemed by some practitioners as an "application." We contend quite the opposite. Servant leadership, advanced by Greenleaf and others, is a modern continuing response to Christ's teachings, more derived than original, more dependent than distinct.

Our dependency on Christ's teachings in this as with all Christian writings is strong. The ties may be seen in the quoted scripture and the priesthood concept. Let no doubt remain, the philosophy of the servant as leader is more comprehensively and rigorously found in Christian doctrine than through any lay interpretation. Being a servant of Christ is all and more than being a servant leader per se.

Priesthood Defined

But you are the chosen race, the King's priests, the holy nation, God's own people, chosen to proclaim the wonderful acts of God, who called you from the darkness into his own marvelous light. (1 Peter 2:9) What does the "priesthood of all believers" mean? The dictionary definition of *priesthood*, "the office of a priest—one who is authorized to perform sacred rites," helps in one important respect. All believers receive the stature of an "office," meaning we are assigned duties, and an "authorization" of powers to perform these duties. This granting of stature and enabling power is freely given to every believer through God's grace, "grace" being defined as "the overflowing favor of God." (Oswald Chambers, 1874-1917, Scottish evangelical prophet) It means that God has freely entitled us to serve with strength through the Holy Spirit.

What are the inherent responsibilities of this entitlement? The ministry is defined in one instance as "a shared communal responsibility for prayer, proclamation, and service to all in Christ's name." A second congregation describes their mission as "a fellowship of Christian believers who touch people's lives as Christ does."[1] Martin Luther is even more succinct, "After all, what else does a priesthood require except the declaration of the works and word of God?"

There is something awesome and complete about the original expression, "the priesthood of all believers." There can be no real substitute however elaborate. Yet, an interpretive clause can be of value. "The priesthood of all believers is a shared ministry of communal prayer, proclamation, and service in Christ's name, bestowed on all faithful followers by the grace of God." This definition is instructive and workable. Five following supplements strengthen our understanding.

Every follower a priest.[2] Christ has bestowed on *all* believers a glorious priesthood, thus keeping us always in the providence of God. "Christ is indeed the only High Priest between God and us all. Nevertheless, He has bestowed this name on us, too, so that we who believe in Him are also priests, just as we are called Christians, after Him." (Martin Luther)

None is superior, all are equal brethren. This sacredness extends to the least one. *"...you are all brothers of one another..."* (Matthew 23:8) *"For he who is least among you all is the greatest."* (Luke 9:48)

Suppose a rich man wearing a gold ring and fine clothes comes to your meeting, and a poor man in ragged clothes also comes. If you show more respect to the well-dressed man and say to him, "Have this best seat here," but say to the poor man, "Stand or sit down here on the floor by my feet," then you are guilty of creating distinctions among yourselves and of making judgments based on evil motives." (James 2:2-4)

Before God we are all equal in dignity, all one in Christ Jesus who alone is our lord and master. There are no special privileges. Wealth, power, position, education, all earthly statures, convey no status in the kingdom of God. For we are all one together in Christ without distinctions. As St. Paul says, *...you are all one in union with Christ Jesus.* (Galatians 3:28)

One body, various offices. *We have many parts in the one body, and all these parts have different functions. In the same way, though we are many, we are one body in union with Christ and we are all joined to each other as different parts of one body. So we are to use our different gifts in accordance with the grace that God has given us.*
(Romans 12:4-6)

The Christian ministry can best be summed up by defining it as an office of grace. The office does not rest on our own merit but on God's divine love freely bestowed. Each then must serve according to the measure of strength God supplies, that in all service God may be glorified through Jesus Christ. *Each one, as a good manager of God's different gifts, must use for the good of others the special gift he has received from God.* (1 Peter 4:10)

Our guidance comes from the Word and Holy Spirit. *"If you obey my teaching you are really my disciples; you will know the truth, and the truth will make your free."* (John 8:31-32) *So we fix our attention, not on things that are seen, but on things that are unseen. What can be seen lasts only for a time; but what cannot be seen lasts forever.* (2 Corinthians 4:18) *This is how we are sure that we live in God and he lives in us: he has given us his Spirit.* (1 John 4:13)

Christ alone rules his congregation through the Holy Spirit. The Holy Spirit of the triune God–God's eternal and uplifting presence in all the faithful–is the great power behind all discipleship of which servant leadership is a part. We devote the last part of this chapter to emphasizing this dependency.

In service all things are possible. God strengthens us to the tasks at hand. Through him all things are possible. We can therefore be joyful in carrying on the good work, never discouraged for no task is too difficult, no service required beyond the gifts bestowed. Thus we all have the needed strength. Jesus said *"If you ask me for anything in my name, I will do it."* (John 14:14) *Be joyful always, pray at all times, be thankful in all circumstances. This is what God wants of you, in your life in Christ Jesus.* (1 Thessalonians 5:16-18)

In the subsequent two sections, we defer to Martin Luther to describe the responsibilities of Christian priesthood and the nature of the office of pastor.

The Responsibilities of Priesthood[3]

Of what does this priesthood of Christians consist? Teaching, sacrificing, and praying. Each one according to his calling and position, obtains the right and the power of teaching and confessing before others this Word which we have obtained from Him. Every Christian has the right and the duty to teach, instruct, admonish, comfort, and rebuke his neighbor with the Word of God at every opportunity and whenever necessary. If anyone will confess Christ, he must risk his property, honor, body, and life.

Mostly, the functions of a priest are these: to teach, to preach and proclaim the Word of God, to baptize, to consecrate or administer the Eucharist, to bind and loose sins, to pray for others, to sacrifice, and to judge all doctrine and spirits. All are splendid and royal duties. But the first and foremost of all royal duties on which everything else depends, is the teaching of the Word of God. For we teach with the Word, we consecrate with the Word, we bind and absolve sins by the Word, we baptize with the Word, we sacrifice with the Word, we judge all things by the Word. This Word is the same for all. The first office, that of the ministry of the Word, therefore is common to all Christians.

The Office of Pastor[4]

While all Christians are priests, only those who are called and hold the office are pastors. They became priests before they received their office, as do all of us, when they were baptized. They are specially chosen by the church only for the sake of the office–to proclaim the Word and administer the Sacraments. Pastors as well as other church leaders may have many additional duties including teaching, counseling, and management (as recorded in 1 Timothy, Chapter 3). The only difference between a pastor and other Christians is his office. Some must be selected who shall lead the others by virtue of the special gifts and training which God has given them for the office. Thus Saint Paul writes, *And His gifts were that some should be apostles, some prophets, some evangelists, some pastors and teachers, for the equipment of the saints, for the work of the ministry, for the building up of the body of Christ.* (Ephesians 4:11-12)

Every Christian has and practices priestly works. But above these activities is the communal office of public teaching. For this preachers and pastors are necessary. This office cannot be attended to by all the members of a congregation. Neither is it fitting that each household do its own baptizing and celebrating of the Sacrament. Hence it is necessary to select and ordain those who can preach and teach, who study the Scriptures, and who are able to defend the doctrine. They deal with the Sacraments by the authority of the congregation, so that it is possible to know who is baptized and everything is done in an orderly fashion. *You should look on us as Christ's servants who have been put in charge of God's secret truths.* (1 Corinthians 4:1) There is no other proclamation in the ministry of the Word than that which is common to all.

The authority and the dignity of the priesthood reside in the community of believers. Ministers should be treated as an equal among the brethren. And the guidance which pastors receive from the congregations should exceed that received by any civil administrators, since their ineffectiveness is less tolerable than a civil officer. The latter can be harmful only in matters of this life, whereas the former can be destructive of that which is eternal.

The concept of the universal priesthood of believers does not preclude the position that the ministry is ordained by God. The *spiritual* priesthood belongs to every Christian. The difference is not in the person but in the office.

The character of the ministry is service, the service of God, the work in which God is himself the chief subject. Keep in mind that the pastor is paid to do this work. The church has the right and duty to keep watch over the service of its pastors. If the church is the body of Christ, the call of the church is identical with the call of Christ, always presupposing the presence of faith.

The word requires a living proclamation, a living word, taught and preached. The office and the Word belong together, the office is an attribute of the Word. The office of pastor is thus the ministry of the Word.

The Holy Spirit

This is how we are sure that we live in God and he lives in us; he has given us his Spirit. (1 John 4:13)

The disciples were filled with joy at seeing the Lord. Then Jesus said to them again, "Peace be with you. As the Father sent me, so I send you." He said this, and then he breathed on them and said, "Receive the Holy Spirit." (John 20:20-22)

"I will ask the Father, and he will give you another Helper, the Spirit of truth, to stay with you forever. The world cannot receive him, because it cannot see him or know him. But you know him, because he remains with you and lives in you." (John 14:16-17)

This great gift from God, given to us through Christ, makes all faithful one with him, sacred parts of Christ's body, high priests in servitude. The Holy Spirit's living presence sanctions, guides, and enables us through God's powers to be his disciples. A wonderful way to describe this presence is that the Holy Spirit *overshadows* us in all things. Not only is the Spirit in our midst, but as Christ says, remains and lives within us. God in the Holy Spirit thus surrounds and resides in us all, making each disciple a sacred being in his great care. "The Holy Spirit doesn't help the pope. I'm simply his helper. He did everything." Pope John XXIII

The Holy Spirit of truth within enables us to seek God's will in all things. We are provided all that is necessary to seek God's truth–inner strength through the Spirit of Truth, guidance through prayer and bible study, and the community support of fellow Christians. Our response to these gifts is one of thanksgiving and discernment of what God is calling us to do.

God's peace is given to all in the Spirit. Knowing the Spirit lives within gives us confidence and peace–confidence through God's empowerment and guidance, peace through a sense of rightness and permanency. When we let go and empty ourselves of worldly things we receive in their stead the inner peace of God which passes all understanding. This enabling power allows us to dedicate ourselves to Christian service without concern for our own adequacy or wellbeing. *We know that in all things God works for good with those who love him, those whom he has called according to his purpose.* (Romans 8:28)

We conclude with this uplifting encouragement. Discipleship brings "fulfillment of the highest human possibilities...abiding peace, a life penetrated throughout by love, faith that sees everything in the light of God's overriding governance for good, hopefulness that stands firm in the most discouraging of circumstances, power to do what is right and withstand the forces of evil."[5]

---

[1] Part of the mission statement of Northridge Lutheran, Kalispell, Montana.

[2] We are gloriously not only *priests* (chosen to show others) but also *disciples* (students of Jesus) and *apostles* (messengers to spread the "good news").

[3] The words of Martin Luther (with reorganization and minor editorial changes) have been selected from many of his works dealing with the priesthood of all believers. Much of Luther's work was an attempt to overturn the hierarchy in the church, preaching that all should serve God according to their calling.

[4] Ibid.

[5] Dallas Willard, *The Great Omission*, (San Francisco, HarperSanFrancisco, 2006), pp. 9 and 12.

Part II.
The Nature of Servant Leadership

Chapter 5
Bible Guidance and Derived Principles

This chapter begins Part II, the core of this volume. All that needs to be said in this book about servant leadership for congregations is presented in this division. (The remaining Parts III-V primarily guide implementation.) Chapter 5 starts with Bible readings leading to eight principles that underlie and direct servant leadership. Chapter 6 continues with the personal dimensions or virtues required. Chapter 7 counsels against opposition and resistance to the concept. Chapter 8 concludes Part II, departing from this philosophical background to resulting practice, outlining the functions of management and involved leadership responsibilities. Chapters 5 through 7 orient the servant leader; Chapter 8 provides the "marching instructions." We recommend that readers pursue the entirety of Part II for completeness and mutual reinforcement.

We anticipate readers will be encouraged to adopt this remarkable philosophy and examine the full text. Conservatively, we believe that even token reading will engender adoption of some aspects of servant leadership, perhaps encouraging a partial trial run as an experiment. Congregations can expect to find such testing a rewarding experience, leading to greater if not full adoption of the servant as leader philosophy.

Biblical Guidance for Servant Leadership

The most persuasive argument for congregations to adopt and grow in servant leadership is to draw the parallel with Christ's teachings. We believe that servant leadership is embodied in the scripture. Christ was a servant leader in the perfect sense. *Instead, of his own free will he gave it all up, and took the nature of a servant.* (Philippians 2:7) We can, in fact, reasonably attribute the essence of modern day servant leadership to Christ's earlier teachings. Retracing these teachings shows the deep interrelationship and serves as strong encouragement to congregations questioning the wisdom of adopting servant leadership.

Relevant Bible quotations are interspersed throughout this volume[1] for no argument or justification is stronger. Here, in Chapter 5, we quote those passages most fundamental to the concept itself. In Chapter 6 we attend to the leader's dependency on the Holy Spirit for strength and guidance. The scripture cited there should be especially helpful to individuals seeking God's blessing as they venture on the path of servant leadership.

These then are the wonderful, encouraging, and supportive beliefs, typically employed in "articles of faith," that guide the Christian manner of doing God's work.

Jesus is preeminent. Jesus is the head of his body the church, source of its life, and its guiding light. (Colossians 1:18) Through prayer and bible study, and empowered by the Holy Spirit, each member must reach out to God in seeking to serve according to his will. And, in reaching out, we know that nothing in all creation can separate us from the love of God through his son Jesus Christ. (Romans 8:39)

Everything you do or say, then, should be done in the name of the Lord Jesus, as you give thanks through him to God the Father. (Colossians 3:17)

The congregation is the body of Christ and therefore sacred and commissioned. Each person is an object of God's love and therefore the object of our love for one another. We do not judge, but rather teach, support, and comfort one another. All should be made to think of their lives as a holy calling, an ordination to the ministry of God. Thus all church activities should be inclusive and democratic. *Christ is like a single body, which has many parts; it is still one body, even though it is made up of different parts. And so there is no division in the body, but all its different parts have the same concern for one another. If one part of the body suffers, all the other parts suffer with it; if one part is praised, all the other parts share its happiness. All of you, then, are Christ's body, and each one is a part of it.* (1 Corinthians 12:12, 25-27)

As one body we are no longer separate individuals. "We are meshed, we are intertwined, we flow into and out of one another and all others."[2] Every member is given different abilities to serve God, and since these are gifts from the Spirit none should be considered less than others. Everyone should contribute according to his or her own calling in which we all rejoice.

My brothers! As believers in our Lord Jesus Christ, the Lord of glory, you must never treat people in different ways, according to their outward appearance. (James 2:1)

God purposely chose what the world considers nonsense in order to put wise men to shame, and what the world considers weak in order to put powerful men to shame. He chose what the world looks down on, and despises, and thinks is nothing, in order to destroy what the world thinks is important. This means that no one can boast in God's presence.
(1 Corinthian 1:27-29)

"For he who is least among you all is the greatest." (Luke 9:48)

God's will is to be sought in all things, through prayer, bible study, and communal study and discussion. God is sovereign over all, the ultimate source of guidance. The purpose of servant leadership, as with all Christian undertakings, is to... *Get the Lord's road ready for him; make a straight path for him to travel!* (Mark 1:3) We are responsible to "straighten the paths" of the Lord, that is, do all within our power to allow Christ's message to reach all mankind. We are guided in this great crusade by the word and Holy Spirit. *"If you obey my teaching you are really my disciples; you will know the truth, and the truth will make you free."* (John 8:31-32)

To lead for Christ is to be a servant to all. It is wonderfully uplifting to know that through servitude leadership is open to all. The requirements then are minimal, love of God and service to all. *"If one of you wants to be great, he must be the servant of the rest; and if one of you wants to be first, he must be the slave of all. For even the Son of Man did not come to be served; he came to serve and to give his life to redeem many people."* (Mark 10:43-45)

You should look on us as Christ's servants who have been put in charge of God's secret truths. (1 Corinthians 4:1)

"Whoever wants to serve me must follow me, so that my servant will be with me where I am. My Father will honor him who serves me."
(John 12:26)

"...when you have done all you have been told to do, say, 'We are ordinary servants; we have only done our duty.'" (Luke 17:10)

As Christ's presence we are endowed through the Holy Spirit with unsurpassed capacity for worship and goodness. God's presence and support in our lives is beyond our comprehension. It is a wonderful blessed gift of strength through faith. To the father of the epileptic son who asks if it is possible to heal him, Jesus answered *"Yes, if you can! Everything is possible for the person who has faith."* (Mark 9:23). Pray that the reality of this capacity is made real in our hearts and minds.

"Remember this! If you have faith as big as a mustard seed, you can say to this hill. 'Go from here to there!' and it will go. You could do anything!" (Matthew 17:20)

We know that in all things God works for good with those who love him, those whom he has called according to his purpose. (Romans 8:28)

God is our refuge and strength, a very present help in trouble.
(Psalm 46:1)

...in Christ Jesus our Lord, in whom we have access to God in boldness and confidence through faith in him. (Ephesians 3:11)

...there is nothing in all creation that will ever be able to separate us from the love of God which is ours through Christ Jesus our Lord. (Romans 8:39)

Faced with all this, what can we say? If God is for us, who can be against us? (Romans 8:31)

"I do not call you servants any longer, because a servant does not know what his master is doing. Instead, I call you friends, because I have told you everything I heard from my Father." (John 15:15)

Principles of Christian Servant Leadership

The first objective of every Christian congregation is personal enhancement in Christ through belief, love, and service. To guide our service as leaders we set forth the following eight precepts or rules of conduct which underlie and govern all Christian servant leadership.[3] They prescribe a code for comportment, disposition, and reliance on God. All are within the power of each person through grace. Let there be no doubt, God is supreme over all, his Word, not any form of human leadership prevails. *"You must not be called 'Teacher,' because you are all brothers of one another and have only one Teacher. And you must not call anyone here on earth 'Father,' because you have only the one Father in heaven. Nor should you be called 'Leader,' because your one and only leader is the Messiah."* (Matthew 23:8-10)

Love Jesus, Seek and Trust God's Will in All Things, Pray Constantly

Jesus said *"I am the way, the truth, and the life"* (John 14:6) The most important thing in our lives is to love Jesus more than anything else. To put him first above all, even family and church. Then through this complete love God's great power is stirred up among us to provide all that is needed to serve him in humbleness and goodwill toward others. To love Jesus is to want to be with him, to obey him, to serve him, and to share him with others. To be *with* Jesus is to abide in him and he in us, to have a sense of his continual presence. In this togetherness we receive the Holy Spirit. *"If you love me, you will obey my commandments. I will ask the Father, and he will give you another Helper, the Spirit of truth, to stay with you forever."* (John 14:15-16)

From the Holy Spirit we gain hope which is evidence of faith. Hope looks forward with confidence through God's grace. *We must wear faith and love as a breastplate, and our hope of salvation as a helmet.* (1 Thessalonians 5:8) The opposite of hope is cynicism, disillusion, and despair, attitudes prompted by distrust. Hope believes all things are possible through a faithful heavenly Father who never leaves or forsakes us. So the Christian leader must view life with hope and confidence, the indispensable ingredients of leadership, seeing possibilities rather than problems, always seeking and expecting perfection. And, after we have done all that is possible to gain the vision, we must then be willing to leave it in the hands of God and simply wait his course.[4]

Loving Jesus, knowing God, and receiving the Holy Spirit are manifest in prayer. Prayer is forthcoming and evidence of our oneness with God through Christ. It is a personal spiritual conversation of listening, asking, receiving, and thanking. The relationship is like that of a child talking with his father. A friend of Horace Bushnell (leading American theologian of the nineteenth century), present when that man of God prayed, said that there came over him a wonderful sense of God's nearness. "When Horace Bushnell buried his face in his hands and prayed, I was afraid to stretch out my hand in the darkness, lest I should touch God." Oh that such presence and depth be part of all our prayers.

Be Loving, Kind to All

"We must delight in each other, make each other's condition our own, rejoice together, mourn together and suffer together....We must be knit together as one." –John Winthrop, first governor of Massachusetts.

Jesus gives us the great commandment, *"You must love the Lord your God with all your heart, with all your soul, and with all your mind."* And the second commandment like it, *"You must love your fellow-man as yourself."* (Matthew 22:37-39) We are then given this description: *Love is patient and kind; love is not jealous, or conceited, or proud; love is not ill-mannered, or selfish, or irritable; love does not keep a record of wrongs; love is not happy with evil, but is happy with the truth. Love never gives up: its faith, hope, and patience never fail.* (1 Corinthians 13:4-7)

Leaders must first and foremost follow Christ's great commandments, to love God with all our strength, and to love our neighbor as ourselves. All other guidance is derived from these two. Without love, leadership becomes simply a mechanical duty, shallow, and without heart. Love fosters democracy, personal involvement, fair hearings, and honest debate–all evidence of respect for others. And in all things, love seeks to enhance the individual in Christian spiritual growth.

The "communion of saints"—the essence of the Christian community, is a Christ-serving ministry in which the members lovingly care for one another, knowing that everyone is precious in the sight of God. *"If you have love for one another, then all will know that you are my disciples."* (John 13:35) Caring and nurturing, often occurring between individuals, can also be fostered within small groups which provide a Christ-oriented environment of intimate friendship and support. The basic operating element is attentive listening which develops a sense of belonging, building positive expectations. Listening conveys respect. It minimizes personal conflicts. So much can be accomplished in this regard by so little effort, simply listening to others with an open mind and loving heart. We address the involvement of individuals in church life and the role of small groups in Chapters 16, "Parish Life," and 17, "Small Group Ministries."

The task of church leaders is to establish caring communities that treat everyone as "little Christs." *Remember to welcome strangers in your homes. There were some who did it and welcomed angels without knowing it.* (Hebrews 13:2) Should we not believe that there are angels among us? Through faith we can be certain of things not seen. So believing, we treat all, even to the very least, as angels.

See Things Whole, Seek the Truth

Attention is directed here to two interrelated strategies. The first, that of seeing things whole in the context of their time, place, and circumstances, gains the perspective required for fair assessment. The second, and more encompassing, is that of always seeking the truth. Both perspective and truth are necessary for accurate evaluation. If we are not sure where we are and where we intend to go, it is hard to advance in the right direction. In contrast, an honest perception of the situation, greatly bolsters self confidence.

Leaders should be dedicated to making the *total* process work. Leaders must at times stand apart to view the entire enterprise in perspective. Where has the organization been, where is it going, and why? How do the various parts interrelate and support each other? The questions are more conceptual than operational. They may lead to setting new goals and plans, more often to reestablishing immediate direction. In all cases, however, looking at things whole is designed to find out one's current standing and the appropriateness of the actions being taking. We may not be sure of the precise goal, but we should always be certain the path is correct.

The discernment of direction and goals is often called vision, the capacity of foresight, to evaluate current status and see new possibilities. *Where there is no vision, the people perish.* (Proverbs 29:18) Vision is often impeded by the sheer dominance of problems being faced. Rather than attempting to continually adjust to these conditions, the visionary attempts to see the possibilities within for something that is utterly different. Insightful leaders gladly assume the responsibilities of visionary for the sheer joy of serving as a guide of God.

Then I heard the Lord saying, Whom shall I send? Who will go for me? And I answered. Here am I; send me. He said, Go, and tell this people . . . (Isaiah 6:8-9)

Truth is our main defense against evil. Truth is the first "armor of God" as a means to his mighty power. *So stand ready: have truth for a belt tight around your waist.* (Ephesians 6:14) Always seek the truth wherever it may lead. Honest, open, and unflinching discussion and scholarship, no matter how tough the issue, underlies the achievement of all ultimate quality and effectiveness. Face the difficult issues squarely. Reject rationalizations, lies, equivocations. Insist on the use of facts and evidence. "Truth never damages a cause that is just." (Mahatma K. Gandhi) "It is easier to live and fight for truth when we remember that the One who is the Truth is ultimately triumphant over all societal falsehood."[5]

Bold lies are seldom the real culprit. We live in a world of fabrications, exaggeration, shadings, evasive answers, and promises never intended. Even our personalities are often false, leading to artificial overtures, undeserved pride, imagined wrongs. In today's culture, pursuit of the truth is often difficult, unpopular, even viewed as destructive. So we must be wary of those who oppose truth or tolerate half truths. *Then we shall no longer be children, carried by the waves and blown about by every shifting wind of the teaching of deceitful men, who lead others to error by the tricks they invent. Instead, by speaking the truth in a spirit of love, we must grow up in every way to Christ, who is the head.* (Ephesians 4:14-15) Paul continues his letter telling the Ephesians that *...the truth...is in Jesus* (4:21) and that *Everyone must tell the truth to his brother, because we are all members together in the body of Christ.* (4:25). So in living lives inextricably connected with God, we welcome and seek truth as part of our holy being.

Commit to Excellence

Strive for perfection. (2 Corinthians 13:11) *You must be perfect, just as your Father in heaven is perfect.* (Matthew 5:48) The hallmark of a vigorous dynamic congregation is a continuous quest for excellence perfected through Christ. As Saint Paul writes to the Corinthians, we should *...run, then in such a way as to win the prize.* An enterprising congregation seeks quality and innovation at every turn, garnering great joy from a mission improved. A satisfied congregation, on the other hand, has lowered its goals resulting in slackened effort and eventual loss of vitality. *So let us not become tired of doing good for if we do not give up, the time will come when we will reap the harvest.* (Galatians 6:9)

Outside pressures and changes require adaptation and response from within. The congregation must be alert and flexible to new demands and new opportunities. "To live is to change; to live well is to have changed often." (John Henry Cardinal Newman, 1801-1890, a profound spiritual influence on the Church of England.) And, if the congregation is to successfully compete for people's time and attention it must be alert to changing personal and family needs as well. The responsible party here is the church council or other governing body which must devote more than passing attention to planning for the future (see Chapter 11, "Communications and Planning.").

One of the most difficult tasks in securing improvements is that of breaking the chains of tradition. Congregations are not immune. They need to cultivate a willingness, even desire to improve. Some have been known to dwindle to nothing, contending that everything is okay down to the last member. Accept the very real possibility that certain things being done are not working well, and then be sufficiently motivated to seek corrections in a spirit of compassion and understanding. The ideas and suggestions put forth by members may, in fact, improve conditions.[6]

A responsive encouraging attitude is critical to improvement, followed by dedicated study and sound implementation. Most importantly, all is proceeded and supported throughout by prayer and bible study. The whole process, if it may be labeled that, is discussed in Chapter 12, "How to Conduct Meetings and Reach Decisions."

Encourage the Active Involvement of All

The "...central impulse [of servant leadership] is its insistence on 'inclusion,' its boundary-shattering energy of love that excludes no one in the whole human family and, by implication, not even the smallest pulse and particle of life in God's cosmos." –Bennett J. Sims, *Servanthood: Leadership for the Third Millennium*

The church must go beyond egalitarian principles to seek the *active* involvement of *all* its members, not just the right to such engagement. However, too few congregations extend themselves sufficiently in this basic mission. "That's their business if they don't want to participate" is the usual justification. Wrong, wrong, wrong! Just the opposite, non-participation is a crucial church failure. The mandate is clear and unequivocal; seek out and encourage *every* person in Christian worship and service, to the very least one. *We urge you brothers: warn the idle, encourage the timid, help the weak, be patient with all.* (1 Thessalonians 5:14) All believers are so tasked, each according to his or her abilities. The church's call must be rigorous, persistent, specific, and compelling. If congregations would view their "calling" of members as important as that of securing a new pastor, the magnified effort and results would be momentous.

A major pitfall to extending involvement is the ease of relying on a few as opposed to the difficulty of cultivating the many. Such reliance is an easy trap and excuse. Availability becomes dependability. "We turned to the pastor and a few trusted members so often that no one else was considered." Congregations must continuously fight all such forms of exclusiveness. The assumed dependency, typically defended as necessary "staffing," is an all too common ruse. Fielding the "first team," the "best and brightest" is *not* a church requirement, fielding "everyone" is.

Opportunities to serve may also be restricted simply by unfair labeling. Keeping the "trouble-makers," and "unqualified" at bay seems to be more important to some members than extending opportunity. Such type-casting is discussed further in Chapter 11 in "Encouraging Vision, Creativity, and Criticism," page 150. Discrimination can, however, be avoided if we are sensitive to the danger. Above all, remember we are all *followers* of Christ, *servants* of one another, and *custodians* of our God-given talents. We strive to be *disciples*. None of these opportunities–follower, servant, custodian, disciple–are qualified by any personal, social, or economic requirements.

Encouraging and recruiting is then a constant challenge. Non-participants are either insufficiently motivated or feel they are not entirely welcome. The organizational structure may appear dominant, even intimidating. "How can I ever fit in?" Such perceptions, however, can be overcome by the encompassing love possible within congregations. The task of gaining participation generally falls within the stewardship province discussed in Chapter 19. The job is essentially that of extending involvement through one-on-one personal contacts, publicizing opportunities, and in inventorying member skills and interests. Individuals need to feel their talents are known, appreciated, and needed. Finally, church activities must always be open-door, an understood invitation of "visitors welcome." Only a very few meetings are so "sensitive" as to warrant privacy.

Promote Democratic Action

Do your best to preserve the unity which the Spirit gives, by the peace that binds you together. (Ephesians 4: 3) The servant congregation, seeking the will of God in all things, is necessarily a totally *democratic* institution. Such an institution trusts the spiritual integrity and moral judgment of its parishioners. We respect each other knowing all are equal before God. As Saint Luke writes, *I now realize that it is true that God treats all men on the same basis.* (Acts 10:34) We believe that the entire congregation–the body of Christ–is the primary source of governance, exercised through chosen pastors and elected lay representatives. As members, we are blessed and honored by this leadership. We extend to them our utmost respect, keeping them always in our prayers, and accord them all vested powers. In sum, the servant congregation, in God's grace, believes all things are possible through each member, to the very least person.

The definition of *democracy* is enlightening. Most sources include the descriptions "of or for the people" and "believing in or practicing social equality." These conditions are paramount in faith-based Christian organizations which espouse treating everyone as "little Christs." Such inclusiveness is not contrary to sound management, simply a little more burdensome and time consuming, increasing the possibility of taking some temporary wrong turns, but in the long run well-worth the accruing losses.

Unilateral and secretive decisions (however disguised as democratic) can never be tolerated. *"Whatever is hidden away will be brought out into the open, and whatever is covered up will be uncovered."* (Mark 4:22) Instead, all must be free to speak openly. *All of you may speak God's message, one by one, so that all will learn and be encouraged.* (1 Corinthians 14:31) The risk taken, that some "popular" decisions may be in error, is minimal. Errors can be corrected; loss of democracy is not so easily regained.

Christian democracy requires the congregation to respect and be attentive to the viewpoints of each member. This means that every member is encouraged to speak out and that such declarations be respectfully and attentively heard and acted upon. This positive response is extremely uplifting, making each member feel important and contributory. Lay officers and church staff should continuously seek out the ideas and positions of members in private as well as in open forum. Elected leaders are first and foremost representatives of the congregation, not their substitute. To act primarily on personal knowledge and preference without consulting those represented is irresponsible, yet too common. Church officers should operate as if they were continuously running for office, listening[7] and responding to the needs of their constituents (congregation). In practice, most members are never asked their opinion on church matters during their entire life. This failure is both a waste of talent and a personal indignity. In addition to open forum encouragement and private conversation, every church should have some form of recommendation system in place to encourage congregational input. An ombudsman (Chapter 11, page 153), is ideal for this purpose. The system must insure that submissions are properly presented, fairly evaluated, and acted upon, including non-acceptance with explanation and thanks. Without such policies, "suggestion boxes" will remain empty, for members soon recognize the futility involved. Other means by which democracy is thwarted within congregations are addressed in Chapter 7, "Peremptory Authority." A summary listing of ten "rules" for shared democratic leadership is presented in Chapter 10, page 117.

Commit to Lay Leadership and Its Development

Adopting servant leadership requires a commitment to individual growth and leadership for all. This encompassing mandate is based on the belief that each member has an intrinsic contributory value beyond basic worker duties. We know that every human soul is sacred, deserving our complete respect and attention. This great value, however, can only be fully realized if each individual is given the opportunity to reach his or her maximum potential, most commonly fulfilled in various forms of leadership. Getting everyone in leadership positions is accomplished in six ways:

1. Clergy and staff must surrender the necessary degree of sovereignty. Words of a failing church could well be, "Nothing was ever done here that didn't require the pastor's approval." The pastor should not be the church's CEO. Besides, the job is too big and diversified for any one person to effectively perform. Assuming CEO duties becomes a distraction from the principal mission of *spiritual* leadership. Martin Luther tells us the pastoral responsibilities include preaching, evangelizing, and administering the sacraments. In all such and allied matters the congregation defers to its pastors. Respect for the professionalism of other staff positions is also paramount for a harmonious, constructive atmosphere. These are our leaders by training and appointment, listen to them.

However, the interface between staff and laity should be interwoven with shared responsibility. Failure in this instance can be a great source of friction and a major deterrent to servant leadership. There is precious little space for autocratic rule in the Christian church. Our responsibilities to God so overlap that there is little requirement for absolute authority. A wise pastor and staff know the value of reliance on the congregation. Let members make most decisions, even stumble. Precious little will be lost but much gained from such self-direction. Is not the Holy Spirit as likely to act through the congregation as through its staff? We share being *Christians* first and foremost, all are disciples, all are accordingly leaders.

2. Create more leadership positions by flattening the organizational structure to lower and spread responsibility and related authority. Additional leadership positions can also be created by enlarging council and committee sizes and limiting office terms. For example, over a six-year span, a 16-member council serving two-year terms allows twice as many different office holders (48) as does a 12-member council serving three-year terms (24).

3. Assigning responsibility and authority at the lowest possible echelon with minimal vertical approval requirements. Continuous upward reporting is burdensome and demeaning. Give individuals as much autonomy as possible, exercising control through job descriptions, guidance, and encouragement rather than through reporting requirements.

4. Loosen position requirements to allow occupancy by less, even marginally qualified individuals. The most important requirement for any Christian position of leadership is love of God. All else is secondary. Thus the church council and committees do not require only the best and brightest. It is not the *first* team we seek to field, rather the *whole* team. The greatest virtues of lay leadership are integrity and a humble state of mind. Professional advice abounds, wisdom is in short supply. Christ asks only that we follow him. How can we add additional qualifications? Who among us can say with any certainty who will and who will not make a good leader? So the search should extend to the farthest recesses of the congregation knowing that God works in many hidden ways through all the faithful.

Nominating committees are especially prone to narrow office candidates to like-minded people. "The board members were all college graduates, and they nominated from their own ranks." Self perpetuation is safe and easy, but irresponsible. Also, restrictions, however well intended, stifle new insights and eventually lead to resentment among those repeatedly "overlooked."

5. **Conduct periodic personnel inventories** of member talents and interests, and match with church positions. *Each one, as a good manager of God's different gifts, must use for the good of others the special gift he has received from God.* (1 Peter 4:10) The church is obligated to call forth the special gifts of every individual. Let God lead us through the blessings he has bestowed.

6. **Conduct annual leadership training seminars and on-the-job training.** We address leadership in practice in Part IV.

7. **Identify young people of promise and cultivate their growth.** Youth, with their great potential for future contributions, need be specially singled out for extra encouragement. "Our very best influence needs to be brought to bear on our potentially best young people in the formative years from sixteen to twenty-five when the crisis of identity is being met." Greenleaf goes on to cite the example of Thomas Jefferson who as a young man lived and studied law with George Wythe, a fellow legislator. "The influence of George Wythe in maturing the Jefferson of history was incalculable, much greater than that of his parents."[8]

Combat Domination, Build Diversity, Encourage Agreement

Sisters and brothers...*Strive for perfection; listen to my appeals; agree with one another, and live in peace. And the God of love and peace will be with you.* (2 Corinthians 13:11)

Beware of the tyranny of the majority and vested few. It is seemingly paradoxical that power can be abused at both extremes, by the majority in ignoring the minority, and by an elected few who fail to share their authority. When power is vested in a few over extended periods, the beholders tend to become resistant to change, coveting their status and strength. It is extremely important that this accumulation of power be thwarted by frequent personnel rotation. Incumbents should be encouraged to continue serving as valued advisors.

One can readily tell when authority is getting out of hand. Recommendations are dismissed without explanation, shelved, or simply ignored. Meetings are closed, agendas unannounced. Secretiveness and hidden power prevails. Such domination and other negative elements must not be allowed. We devote the entirety of Chapter 7 to such combat. Church-wide hearings should be the norm. Other than sensitive personal matters, God's business is everyone's business. Visitors should be welcome at every meeting, never to feel as intruders in a private gathering.

Build diversity. Open the doors, welcome visitors, encourage dissent, promote debate, seek alternatives, uncover that which is concealed; and in this openness the truth will emerge and strengthen all. Yes, encourage the dissenting voice, promote lively discussion and debate, for God speaks to us in many hidden ways which may not immediately seem attractive. *Do not restrain the Holy Spirit; do not despise inspired* *messages. Put all things to the test: keep what is good, and avoid every kind of evil.* (1 Thessalonians 5:19-22) Other than certain core teachings, new doctrine should be possible as we gain insight and understanding. "Such an outlook dictates that questioning and challenging be respected as acts of faith, and that the hand of authority rest lightly on the pilgrims."[9] Churches should relish this eclectic and open approach.

This outlook dictates that the minority's position always be heard, never perfunctorily dismissed. It may represent something very dear, even sacred, to those so persuaded. Depending on the number of advocates and their level of support, the proper response to most reasonable alternatives is either trial testing, or partially or occasional employment. For example, if a few members favor a certain form of service, honor them with its occasional use, even if only once a year. Providing some proportionate response is far preferable to outright rejection. Be generous, accept with good grace positions strongly held. Establish a study group to gain perspective. Further study aids amicable resolution through additional information and improved understanding. Finally, trial testing may be used to demonstrate the feasibility of proposals, often satisfying both advocates and opponents. These and related issues of problem solving are addressed in Chapter 12.

Encourage agreement. The effective leader uses open discussion, negotiation, and persuasive reasoning to secure consensus. Persistent problems are resolved through compromise and trial testing. Personal authority is largely abandoned. Dependency on the group offers one of the clearest distinctions between servant leadership and traditional authoritative models. The servant led organization operates on consensus building, dependent on persuasion not coercion. While it takes more time for everyone to express their views, continued open discussion generally leads to a meeting of minds, a forging of some type of agreement or working resolution. This unity, however tenuous, then becomes a powerful force for successful implementation.

There are few administrative and operational issues in the church where right and wrong are crystal clear, yet we frequently argue as if such were the case. Amicable resolution commonly requires compromise. And there are often so many reasonable alternatives that competing positions can be simultaneously served. For example, advocates of contemporary music can enjoy it at one service while more traditional music is played at another, or the two may be interspersed. To settle by compromise is the correct response for many disputes.

---

[1] The idea of "servant" is deep in our Judeo-Christian heritage. The concordance to the Standard Revised Version of the Bible lists over 1,300 references to *servant* (including serve and service).

[2] Our unity in Christ is well developed by Gordon Cosby. See N. Gordon Cosby, *By Grace Transformed, Christianity for a New Millennium* (New York: The Crossroad Publishing Company, 1999), p. 26.

[3] Abstracted and adapted from many sources, most notably the observations and recommendations of William Easum. See William Easum *Dancing with Dinosaurs: Ministry in a Hostile & Hurting World* (Nashville, Abingdon Press, 1993).

[4] Cosby, *By Grace Transformed,* pp. 21-22.

[5] Marva Dawn, "Wielding truth," *The Lutheran,* February 2001, Vol. 14, No. 2, February 2001, page 6.

[6] Interwoven are many of the observations and recommendations of Easum, *Dancing with Dinosaurs*.

[7] An extreme example of listening for advice, exhibiting real confidence, are pastors willing to establish a pulpit team tasked to periodically critique sermons and advise on preaching (see Chapters 14, page 217, and 15, page 227).

[8] Robert K. Greenleaf, *On Becoming a Servant Leader,* (San Francisco, Jossey-Bass, 1996), p. 80.

[9] Jim Naughton, "Mass Protest–Men, women, authority and dissent at Georgetown's Holy Trinity Parish," *The Washington Post Magazine,* August 25, 1996, p. 15.

Chapter 6
Personal Dimensions of the Servant Leader[1] [2]

Be joyful always, pray at all times, be thankful in all circumstances. This is what God wants of you, in your life in Christ Jesus.

May the God who gives us peace make you holy in every way, and keep your whole being, spirit, soul, and body, free from all fault at the coming of our Lord Jesus Christ. (1 Thessalonians 5:16, 23).

The nature of a leader is a reasonable balance of mutually supporting talents. The combinations can be markedly varied, strengths countering weaknesses. Some leaders rely on their natural abilities, reducing the role of acquired skills. Others are mechanical in their approach, depending on careful study and preparation. Still others rely heavily on personal charisma and diplomacy. But all must maintain an adequate overall and integrated balance of talents and learned skills. And all, as Christians, must subscribe to the faith-based beliefs and principles of leadership outlined in Chapter 5.

Here in Chapter 6, we add to our belief foundation the personal dimensions sought in the servant leader, those characteristics that strengthen and distinguish such a person from others. We begin with the *commitment* required. What are the basic obligations of congregational leaders? Then we list the personal *virtues* necessary, the inherent moral goodness expected. To these moral aspects we add the personal *attributes* and *skills*, proficiencies necessary to effectively lead. These skills are so integrated into the practice of leadership that they are primarily discussed from that standpoint. Chapter 8, "Core Elements for Leading/Managing," performs this task, first listing the seven *functions* of leading, then the seven *means* by which such responsibilities are accomplished. The "Servant Leader Model for Congregations" section, page 74, presents an outline taxonomy.

The Personal Nature of Leadership

The servant leader is natural to the Christian church. Whenever God calls, the invitation includes accepting leadership–showing the way, guiding others to Christ. To not lead, to not take the forefront, is to evade an inherent responsibility that goes with discipleship. And Christian leading need not be greater than one's commitment and talents allow. It can be as modest, for example, as simply being kind to someone ignored by others. Whenever one goes ahead while others hesitate, whenever one sets an example for others to follow,[3] whenever one guides another, leadership is present. The summation of many such small acts can become a great leading force. So Christians inherit an obligation to lead, not of our own choosing, but as a requirement of discipleship.

The leadership we speak of is as a servant. Christ admonished, *"If one of you wants to be great, he must be the servant of the rest; and if one of you wants to be first, he must be the slave of all."* (Mark 10:43-44) The servant leader seeks to serve others before satisfying personal needs; responds to problems by first listening; and views the past, present, and future as one moving organic entity. This type of leadership builds strength in other people, creating new regenerative forces. Eventually it builds a strong permanent organization with a sense of mission manned by able, committed followers.

The Individuality of Leadership

Groups don't lead, individuals do.[4] This book about leadership is thus primarily directed to individuals, although we recognize, and address later in this chapter, the great advantage of sharing the hard tasks of discipleship. The charge, in fact, is extended to all, each a leader through God's grace. The call is ever present, the opportunities unlimited, only our acceptance remains.

Leadership is part and parcel of the individual, totally integrated, inseparable, and interdependent. So although we devote a considerable portion of this text to explain the cognitive skills involved, the character of the individual is most important. The intrinsic unavoidable burden of leadership is the personal responsibility conveyed. Such responsibility "...requires that a person think, speak, and act as if personally accountable to all who may be affected by his or her thoughts, words, and deeds." –Robert K. Greenleaf

Leadership can be pressure-ridden and personally taxing. Four defenses help meet the challenge: (1) be conspicuously yourself, "natural" in word and deed, (2) withdraw occasionally to cast off the burden, even for a short time, to refresh and regain inner peace, (3) recognize the nature of a continually changing world, (4) engage in a never-ending search for depth of understanding.

The Pre-eminent Qualities Needed

Henri J. M. Nouwen (spiritual writer) admonishes us to "think theologically with the mind of Christ." Yes, put on the mind of Christ! *I will instruct you and teach you the way you should go; I will counsel you with my eye upon you.* (Psalm 32:8) Yet we mostly think as enablers, facilitators, role models, and fathers and mothers, rather than first believers. Christian leadership is foremost a deep faith in God's real presence. It is saying "no" to the secular world, substituting the divine nature of God and listening to him in all things.

The Christian qualities of leadership may also be learned from Peter's second letter. *God's divine power has given us everything we need to live a godly life through our knowledge of the one who called us to share his own glory and goodness. For this reason do your best to add goodness to your faith; to your goodness add knowledge; to your knowledge add self-control; to your self-control add endurance; to your endurance add godliness; to your godliness add brotherly love; and to your brotherly love add love.* (2 Peter 1: 3-7) So we strive for these things: goodness, knowledge, self-control, endurance, godliness, brotherly love, and finally, greatest of all, love.

Greenleaf uses the wonderful term "spirit carriers" to describe those individuals who have the driving animating force that disposes one to be a servant of others. It is "...the quality in a leader that leads him or her into risk and venture; this is communicated to the timid and the less venturesome who are energized to follow." It also is a pervasive loving attitude toward all people. The very presence of spirit carriers communicates this kind of love. Greenleaf tells of Jack Lowe, Sr., a Dallas businessman and civil leader. At any civic meeting the blacks and Hispanics always gathered around him because they knew he loved them and understood them. Would that we all had this spirit of unequivocal love for others to be true spirit carriers. *The fruit of the Spirit is love, joy, peace, long-suffering, gentleness, goodness, faith, meekness, temperance.* (Galatians 5:22-23)

On the management side, the leader must have interpersonal skills to carry the organization along toward its objectives–understanding of the environment, experience, judgment, persistence, and related abilities required to conduct operations on a day-to-day basis. Of greater importance are the conceptual talents required that enable managers to see the organization (church) as a whole and guide it toward a long-range vision. Here the leader must be able to analyze and evaluate the changing scene, to foresee contingencies, and to adjust goals accordingly.

Know That You Are Called to Discipleship

Seeking the life of Christ we preach discipleship, embracing and spreading the good news. Jesus said, *"If you continue in my word, you are truly my disciples; and you will know the truth, and the truth will make you free."* (John 8:31-32) We cannot earn this favor through our own accord. We abide (reside) in Christ because he has given us his Spirit. *Do you not know that you are God's temple and that God's Spirit dwells in you?* (1 Corinthians 3:16)

We are all meant to use Christ's indwelling power to reach beyond ourselves and bear much fruit. As we deepen in unity with Christ and learn to receive this power, God lives in us and we become his disciples. *"Abide in me as I abide in you. Just as the branch cannot bear fruit by itself unless it abides in the vine, neither can you unless you abide in me. I am the vine, you are the branches. Those who abide in me and I in them bear* much fruit, because apart from me you can do nothing." (John 15:4-5) The vine is inseparable from the branches. One does not exist without the other. *"I am the true bread from heaven, the good shepherd, the resurrection and the life."* And, *"You are the light of the world, the salt of the earth, a city on a hill."* There is an explicit connection *"I am...you are," "abide in me, as I abide in you."* Thus we are all called to be one with Christ as disciples.

Consider Your Discipleship a Responsibility to Lead

Acceptance of discipleship is also a commitment to lead for the two are integrally bound together. Who can eagerly serve God without encouraging and guiding others? Follower-disciple-leader, are interwoven, interdependent parts of one whole. One cannot be a part without being all.

Becoming a leader. *Then I heard the Lord saying, Whom shall I send? Who will go for me? And I answered, Here am I, send me. He said, Go, and tell this people...* (Isaiah 6:8-9) To be called by God is a requirement to lead. The opportunities and needs are so great that leadership is an absolute, inherent, and continuous responsibility. Volunteer for almost any activity and you are soon expected to be in charge. Make the task more difficult or unattractive and the leadership is yours for the asking. Institute new action and the commission is automatic. To lead in most instances requires simply raising one's hand. Here am I, send me. If we are faithful to our calling we become leaders, for that is God's will for us, to go out in front for others to follow.

Despite this obligation, we all are somewhat reluctant to become leaders, either through lack of confidence, false sense of inferiority, or simple laziness. All can be overcome by God's call and enabling power. But some people want to escape accepting responsibility altogether. "I don't see myself as a leader, I just want to be a good follower." This is really saying, "Please don't burden me with any real responsibilities." Being selfish wastes our talents. *Each one, as a good manager of God's different gifts, must use for the good of others the special gift he has received from God.* (1 Peter 4:10) Our talents should be a door to leadership, confidence builders, invitations to acceptance. God will refine our skills, enabling us to do whatever is required. Remember, every person's calling and service is truly special and unique, however modest, and therefore worthy and pleasing in God's sight. So God will provide all the strength needed. There is no reason to fear anything in accepting leadership, only rejoicing.

> If there is anything good in us, it is not our own, it is a gift of God. But if it is a gift then it is entirely a debt one owes to love. And if it is a debt owed to love, then I must serve others with it, not myself. Thus my learning is not my own, it belongs to the unlearned and is the debt I owe to them. My wisdom belongs to the foolish, my power to the oppressed. My wealth

belongs to the poor, my righteousness to the sinner. For these are the forms of God of which we must empty ourselves in order to be a servant. It is with all these qualities that we must stand before God and intervene on behalf of those who do not have them. —Martin Luther

Leadership can be very modest. Servant leaders are all around us, often unrecognized because their service is a way of life without position or title. The wonderful story *Great Stone Face* by Nathaniel Hawthorne illustrates this commonness.

The story relates how the people in a small New England town, nestled in the mountains, see a profile in the nearby rocks resembling a great majestic face. They come to believe that someday a noble man will come whose own profile will be that of the great stone face. His presence will bring prosperity into their lives and all will be well. In the course of the story, a procession of people from outside the valley, people of wealth and status, come to compare their likeness. Each is heralded with great expectation, but always there is disappointment. None resemble the great stone face. Years pass by. The villagers grow old waiting with waning hope that the mountain image will become a reality in some visitor who will enrich them by his presence. Finally, one day, they see among their own people one who has that profile. He has been there all the time, enriching their lives, demonstrating all they had hoped for. Only in old age had his features grown to resemble that on the mountain.

If we look closely we can see this form of leadership all about us, typically unrecognized and unheralded. It is the great bottom rung of servant leadership, the wide base of the leadership pyramid on which the entire structure is built. And the character of all, from highest to lowest, is exactly the same. This nature, what we perceive as inner strength, is the product of how we live our lives. Robert K. Greenleaf consistently emphasizes this internal dependency. Christians live their lives according to the Gospel. The Christian leader is therefore, first and foremost, a fervent follower of Christ. Then one's heart and soul is blessed, leading to the exemplary behavior required of leaders. Apart from God's blessing, such virtues are of little value. We cannot train ourselves to be Christian leaders, rather, as Christians we become leaders through God's grace.

The Leader's Commitment

Effective leaders have a predisposition or mental readiness that allows them to receive and respond to problems in an effective, adroit fashion. The principles of servant leadership presented in Chapter 5 involve this preparedness; for example, a requirement to love Jesus, and to be caring and kind to all. In this context we address here the related personal *commitment* involved, that is, the emotional and intellectual binding of church leader and responsibilities. The first such requirement is necessarily that of living according to the above servant leadership tenets. The second and third are identification with the organization and dedication to the office.

Identify with the Organization

Underlying all leadership is respect for the organization and commitment to making the total process work. The leader must disassociate him or herself from provincial and transient factions and substitute intense caring for the whole enterprise and its success. Leaders don't take sides, they work out agreements. Their capacity to lead cannot be limited by too narrow a focus but rather expanded by a global outlook. The object is to enhance the whole, not one segment at the expense of others. To be so detached, leaders must at times stand apart to view the enterprise in its entirety, in the perspective of time and place. Organizational history helps provide this vantage point. How would our predecessors have voted on this issue? Are our goals consistent with the past and are they still primary? What changes should be taken into account? A sense of history and other conceptual insights represent the highest level of leadership thinking.

Commit to the Leadership Office

...let us run with perseverance the race that is set before us... (Hebrews 12:1) *So let us not grow weary on doing what is right, for we will reap at harvest time, if we do not give up. So then, whenever we have an opportunity, let us work for the good of all, and especially for those of the family of faith...* (Galatians 6:9-10)

No one can lead without being committed to the office, serving to the best of one's skills, knowledge, and ability. Candidates must know and accept the responsibilities involved. At the top levels they can be a heavy burden indeed. The weak, faint-hearted, and fearful should be encouraged to serve in lesser positions. Leaders at any level, however, must be alert to the requirements and obligations involved, and be willing to make the commitment of time and effort necessary. Hesitancy in this regard does not augur well for the future. Candidates should be excited about the job, consider it an opportunity, and look forward to the experience.

Inner Resources of the Servant Leader[5]

Caring requires not only interest and concern; it demands self-sacrifice and wisdom and tough-mindedness and discipline. It requires that an individual be personally dedicated to making the object of attention a thing of beauty. The church leader must personally feel that he or she stands as a symbol of institutional quality. The many virtues required, some seemingly small, together constitute a sum greater than the parts.

Roger Rosenblatt (essayist for *Time* magazine) wrote of the importance of such fragments in his remembrance of John F. Kennedy Jr., "The measure of a life is often taken in the smallest units."[6] He describes how a parking attendant in the garage that Kennedy used mentioned in a TV interview how Kennedy came over personally each year to wish him a merry Christmas. Rosenblatt writes, "From such fragments of evidence a whole life is constructed, or reconstructed." May all our lives be so blessed with such small fragments.

No one can be a servant leader without possessing, to a degree, the qualities required. All are obtainable through God's grace. However, the acquisition is not easy, far more difficult, for example, than learning the mechanics of leading. So the virtues must be taught and cultivated. This chapter can be of assistance in this regard in listing the perspectives and attitudes required. Follow-on training and personal counseling can assist in the acquisition, but ultimately our personal outlook is a gift from God, obtained through prayer and supplication.

These six **primary virtues** are the moral excellence sought by the servant leader, governing how he or she should think and behave as a leader:

1. Caring, respectful, encouraging, to the very least person
2. Humble as a servant
3. Joyful, hopeful, and at peace
4. Calm, patient, and understanding
5. Honest, open-minded, fair
6. Confident, resolute, courageous

Be Caring, Respectful, and Encouraging... to the Very Least Person

Christianity is altogether inclusive, every good deed counts, every word has power, everyone shares in redeeming the world. "Nothing we do, however virtuous, can be accomplished alone, therefore we must be saved by love." (Reinhold Niebuhr, 1892-1971, Protestant theologian.) This outward looking philosophy requires that above all other traits, the servant leader be a caring person, one who is deeply committed to the church, and the well-being and spiritual enhancement of each of its members. It is a selfless motive, yet one that should come easily to Christians guided by Saint Peter to *"...love one another as brothers, and be kind and humble with one another."* (1 Peter 3:8)

Caring requires interest, compassion, and concern. *Have the same concern for everyone.* (Romans 12:16) The caring person must be sensitive to the inner feelings and needs of others (sentience), and an abiding desire to be of assistance. This outgoing approach demands self-sacrifice, putting others before oneself. It is accomplished not through any self-directed effort or personal discipline, but rather as a spiritual gift, becoming a "good Samaritan" to all through Christ's example. A genuine affection for others is a mark of true Christian leadership.

So God grants to the seeking servant leader a spirit that is kind, generous, understanding, supportive, fair, and gentle. *He is able to deal gently with the ignorant and wayward, since he himself is subject to weakness.* (Hebrews 5:2) The servant leader makes people feel they are something special by exuding acceptance and looking for the good in each person. *...outdo one another in showing honor.* (Romans 12:10) When followers feel so loved, they tend to perform beyond the limits they set for themselves.

Embrace the Posture of Humility

As God's chosen ones, holy and beloved, clothe yourselves with compassion, kindness, humility, meekness, and patience. (Colossians 3:12) No trait is more elemental to servant leadership than humility. It creates the very being of the servant who leads. Paul writes, *May I never boast of anything except the cross of our Lord Jesus Christ...* (Galatians 6:14) Humble leaders are modest in behavior, attitude, and spirit; not arrogant or prideful. In practice this posture is evident in the leader's receptivity to advice, and encouragement of criticism as constructive rather than personal. Humble leaders are selfless, always crediting others and admitting failures. They understand there are no justifiable resentments. They seldom need to exercise their authority for they understand that servant leadership is persuasive not controlling, a common not individual effort.

Power can be a seductive license. There is always the temptation for misuse. One of the worst faults of leaders is to be so impressed with the authority that rank conveys as to not take seriously the dissent of outsiders or subordinates. (This is the chief reason churches are so often unresponsive to the non-traditional spiritual needs of non-members.) The servant leader, in contrast, seeks downward mobility, that is, opting for what "is small and hidden and poor." (Gordon Cosby, founder and pastor of The Church of the Savior, Washington, D.C.) Henri Nouwen (spiritual writer) in choosing to live among the mentally handicapped, experienced this great contrast with his former university life. The "descending way" as he describes it, transposes our orientation from climbing the rungs of personal success, to standing with the poor and excluded.

By embracing servitude we begin to lose ourselves to others, we are released, freed from our own needs. This denial of self brings about great peace of mind. Consider the advice of Thomas a' Kempis, a German monk (1379-1471). "Study to do another's will rather than thine own. Choose ever to have less rather than more. Seek ever the lower place and to be subject to all; ever wish and pray that the will of God may be perfectly done in thee and in all. Beyond such a man enters the bounds of peace and calm."

People love to serve under humble leaders for they know their ideas will be carefully heard and given full credit. Martin Luther added this observation, "But what a great virtue moderation of mind is in great men...but when a king, prince, noble, teacher, or rich man is humble, this is a most beautiful thing. Their humility shines like the sun and the moon."

The need for humility is found throughout scripture. *God opposes the proud, but gives grace to the humble.* (1 Peter 5:5) *He who is greatest among you shall be your servant; whoever exalts himself will be humbled, and whoever humbles himself will be exalted.* (Matthew 23:11-12) *Do nothing from selfish ambition or conceit, but in humility regard others as better than yourselves.* (Philippians 2:3) *Do not be proud, but accept humble duties. Do not think of yourselves as wise.* (Romans 12:16)

Only the servant leader, and particularly the Christian servant leader, is called to conduct him or herself so inconspicuously. In the corporate sector, and especially the military, a degree of swagger is considered a necessary accouterment of the position, manifestation of the confident leader. Under Christ, reverence for God and the congregation served dictates far more modest behavior. Apart from Christ we have no claim to power or stature. All that is good comes from our heavenly father. Martin Luther said it most boldly. "We are all equal and we are all nothing. If anyone feels that he is something and in fact is superior to another, and pleases himself in this, thinking highly only of himself, considering only his own advantage and not how he may serve others thereby—he is in fact deceiving himself and is nothing since then the gift of God is without effect in him."

Be Joyful, Hopeful, and at Peace

May God, the source of hope, fill you with all joy and peace by means of your faith in him, so that your hope will continue to grow by the power of the Holy Spirit. (Romans 15:13)

We know, of course, that true joy and happiness is found only in what is pleasing to God. Amidst all trouble and turmoil, the Christian leader, with the glory of God dwelling in him, steadfastly looks with joy at the things which are not seen. *So we fix our eyes not on what is seen, but on what is unseen. For what is seen is temporary, but what is unseen is eternal.* (2 Corinthians 4:18)

Be joyful, carry on the good work. Joy is contagious and inspiring. It embraces and encourages others. The Salvation Army tells its members "...we in the Army can tell if we're getting 'warmer,' getting closer to alignment with God's purpose for our lives, by the levels of joy we're feeling." Christian joy is a deep inner feeling of confident well-being and anticipation, knowing we are forever in the arms of Christ Jesus. In the sermon on the mount, Christ teaches that true happiness belongs to all those who *"...are my followers. Be glad and happy, because a great reward is kept for you in heaven."* (Matthew 5:11-12) Through God's grace we are made holy and set apart for holy use. This sanctification brings great joy. *Rejoice in the Lord always; again I will say, Rejoice.* (Philippians 4:4)

We can add here that a **sense of humor**, manifest of inner joy and peace, seems always present in great leaders. Greenleaf observes, "The few people I have known who were in the best contact with the deeper levels have been buoyant, fun-loving people with a light touch. One needs to be susceptible to spontaneous laughter, about everything and everybody, especially oneself. Purpose and laughter are the twins that must not separate. Each is empty without the other. Together they are the impregnable fortress of strength...to choose the right aim and to pursue that aim responsibly over a long period of time."

The servant leader is also always hopeful, a trust built on faith. Hope looks forward with confidence in God's grace. The opposite of hope is cynicism and disillusionment, when one feels there is no use. The Christian is not discouraged by what appears to be failures, setbacks, and hardship. These are temporary in God's great plan. Keep spiritually focused, striving steadfast for good with the vision always before us, and then, having done our best, simply wait for God's will to be done.

The peace from God, the grace of redemption, and the certainty of eternal life are the keys of Christian joy. *Do not worry about anything, but in everything by prayer and supplication with thanksgiving let your requests be made known to God. And the peace of God, which surpasses all understanding, will guard your hearts and your minds in Christ Jesus.* (Philippians 4:6-7) Truly believing that God is working in and through us greatly lessens our personal anxiety. His presence casts out fear, isolation, and despair because these are human frailties, and substitutes hope and confidence.

Be Calm, Patient, and Understanding

These three–calmness, patience, and understanding–are so often interlocking they may be treated as one. Thus we counsel responding to difficulty and provocation with calm, tolerant understanding, i.e., patience. Some detachment can be obtained by cultivation of an inner serenity. But one will always be dealing with people who can be immature, stumbling, inept, and lazy. The reality is that there are no perfect people. The fact that leadership is a shared rather than individual task makes the challenge easier. Shared work leads to cooperation, then to understanding and appreciation.

No matter how complicated and hectic matters become, God's presence provides overriding peace and tranquility. *"Peace is my parting gift to you, my own peace, such as the world cannot give. Set your troubled hearts at rest, and banish your fears"* (John 14:27) We know that God loves us unconditionally and is continually working for good within us. We also know that nothing can separate us from the love of God. (Romans 8:38) *Therefore, since it is by God's mercy that we are engaged in this ministry, we do not lose heart.* (2 Corinthians 4:1) So armed, Christian leaders are, in the words of Charles Bennison, Jr. (Episcopal Bishop of Pennsylvania), able "to separate themselves from the anxieties around them and remain a calm presence."[7]

Be Totally Honest, Open-Minded, and Fair

These characteristics are often summed up as "rock solid integrity," a term often used to describe General George Catlin Marshall. Few can match his strict ethical code, but we must all try to develop a natural drive in this direction–to be totally honest, to always seek the truth, and to fully respect the work and ideas of others. In many ways this objectivity requires us to step outside ourselves, to view things impassively, not filtered through the prisms of our own experiences, assumptions, and prejudices. This is very difficult since we bring a great deal of excess emotional baggage with us. But real leaders are personally detached, free of bias, self-interests, and fixed allegiances. The leader insists on the truth, believing that together the congregation can discern God's will in all things.

Be Confident, Resolute, Courageous

Do not lag in zeal, be ardent in spirit, serve the Lord. (Romans 12:11) *Have not I commanded thee? Be strong and of a good courage, be not afraid, neither be thou dismayed for the Lord thy god is with thee...* (Joshua 1:9)[8]

Put on all the armor that God gives you...have truth for a belt tight around your waist; put on righteousness for your breastplate, and the readiness to announce the Good News of peace as shoes for your feet. At all times carry faith as a shield...and accept salvation for a helmet, and the word of God as the sword that the Spirit gives you. (Ephesians 6:11,14-17)

The ability to lead rises from an inner personal confidence, independent of assigned authority. Leaders are usually people who early in their lives believe they are right[9] about something and have the gumption to contest those in formal authority with opposing viewpoints.[10] And they are usually men and women of courage, for a fighting spirit is often required. Ernest Shackelton, famed British explorer, sought these virtues among his men: optimism, patience, physical endurance, courage, and idealism. For today's church leaders the inner strength and confidence required is typically more moderate, gradually acquired through trust in God's calling and strengthened in day-by-day productive service. We gain the necessary strengths through Christ's blessings.

It is often surprising to learn how hard it is to go from deciding that something ought to be done to making it actually happen. Turning an opinion into a decision and a decision into results turns out to be a real skill. Thus leadership requires driving power to get things done and resolution in the face of inevitable disappointments. The response to failure and disappointment is prayer, study, rededication, and perseverance; not self-pity and disillusionment. Leadership is a continuous struggle, often against substantial odds. It takes inner strength and perseverance to get things done, an indefatigable spirit. Martin Luther advocated a "lively reckless confidence" in the Grace of God. Vince Lombardi (American football coach) put it in these terms, "The difference between men is in energy, in the strong will, in the settled purpose, and in the invincible determination."

Robert Greenleaf states this premise, "To lead is to go out ahead and show the way when the way may be unclear; difficult, or dangerous–it is not just walking at the head of the parade–and that one who leads effectively is likely to be stronger, more self-assured, and more resourceful than most because leading so often involves venturing and risking."[11] Congregational surroundings may temper these demands but not by much. Being a Christian leader is therefore an heroic adventure requiring discipline and courage. The individual must be willing to pay the cost of discipleship, to lead wherever God's truth dictates. *"Whoever serves me must follow me, and where I am, there will my servant be also."* (John 12:26) We must have the confidence in God to see us through all trial and tribulation as expressed by Virginia statesman John Page in writing to Thomas Jefferson after the Declaration of Independence was signed. "Do you not think an angel rides in the whirlwind and directs this storm?"

Leadership Attributes/Skills

Leaders must have certain personal attributes and skills. By *attribute* we mean those mental and emotional qualities that allow individuals to effectively function. By *skills* we mean facilities acquired or developed primarily through training and experience. Attributes generally include intelligence, knowledge, stability, resilience, and other mental characteristics commonly found in adequate measure in most adults. Skills include effective listening, awareness, and persuasion, together with conceptualization and foresight. However, the distinctions are not as clear as labeled. Perhaps a better encompassing term would be personal *abilities* contributory to leadership.

    1. Intelligence
    2. Knowledge
    3. Stability and resilience
    4. Listening capacity
    5. Awareness
    6. Persuasiveness
    7. Conceptualization and foresight

These capacities were introduced and explained as managerial skills in Chapter 3. They can also be viewed as management functions, Chapter 8, and as elements of communications and planning, Chapter 11.

¹ This chapter is substantially indebted to the works of Robert K. Greenleaf, particularly *Servant Leadership: A Journey Into the Nature of Legitimate Power and Greatness* (New York: Paulist Press, 1977); Henri J. M. Nouwen, *In the Name of Jesus* (New York, Crossroad, 1989); N. Gordon Cosby, *By Grace Transformed: Christianity for a New Millennium* (New York, Crossroad, 1999); and Charles E. Bennison, Jr. et al., *In Praise of Congregations: Leadership in the Local Church Today* (Cambridge, Cowley, 1999).

² A number of references list the specific qualities required of servant leaders. For example, David Young, *Servant Leadership for Church Renewal* (Scottdale, PA, Herald Press, 1999), cites these seven attributes:

(1) Servant leaders feel a *sense of calling*, a calling to serve God.
(2) A personal and *humble manner*.
(3) A *heart of peace*.
(4) The servant leader has *a clear vision*.
(5) The servant also *listens*.
(6) The servant does not have a dazzling appearance.
(7) The servant leader experiences *power in weakness*.

Note, we would probably cast #6, non-dazzling appearance, with #2, but Young makes a persuasive case for its unique contribution.

³ I remember walking with a friend who occasionally stopped to pick up discarded trash, usually small items, pieces of paper and the like. This gentle conscientious housekeeping has stayed with me and I occasionally remember to do the same. Leading by example can be this simple.

⁴ The army has a saying "Eagles don't flock" which recognizes the distinction and isolation of command,

⁵ This section includes many recommendations from William Easum, *Dancing With Dinosaurs: Ministry in a Hostile & Hurting World* (Nashville, Abingdon Press, 1993).

⁶ Roger Rosenblatt, "The Measure of a Life," *Time,* August 2, 1999: p. 56.

⁷ Bennison, *In Praise of Congregations*, p. 225.

⁸ This Old Testament passage was engraved on the back of Army Captain Russell B. Rippetoe's identification tags, age 27, killed in action in Iraq, April 3, 2003.

⁹ While one's own intuitive processes should be respected, the possibility that one may be wrong should always be understood.

¹⁰ Howard Gardner, *Leading Minds: An Anatomy of Leadership* (New York, Basic, 1995), p. 184.

¹¹ Greenleaf, *The Power of Servant Leadership,* p. 114.

Chapter 7
Peremptory Authority

"Systems succeed because they cherish their members and speak the truth. Systems fail because they exploit their members and practice concealment and deceit." –The Institute for Servant Leadership

"Some bear fruits of stagnation–apathy, indifference and the perfunctory discharge of duties or neglecting them altogether."[1]

–Craig A. Satterlee, assistant professor of homiletics at the Lutheran School of Theology at Chicago.

We know that all manner of love and goodness flourish within congregations guided by the Holy Spirit. God strengthens and encourages us at all times in fervent love for one another and in Christian service. Yet, without exception, we fail to live the life Christ sets before us. We are sinful unto ourselves and towards one another. Even within the congregation family we are weak and selfish, never fully trusting our fellow members. We depend on ourselves rather than seeking God's help. We may even interfere, obscure, and block what we do not understand or personally favor. For all of us then, some harsh words are necessary to guide us in straight paths. *In all your ways acknowledge him, and he will make straight your paths.* (Proverbs 3:6)

It is far easier to develop a sense of equality and respect between individuals on a personal one-to-one basis than within the community at large. Thus while we may convince some members of the value of servant leadership, it is far more difficult to advance the theory against the usually strong inertia and resistance of the congregation as a whole. The corporate structure may be likened to a suffocating molasses. When too powerful, it dominates rather than liberates, contains rather than inspires, rejects rather than enrolls.

The purpose of this chapter is to warn congregations of the dangers from within that interfere or preempt the democratic and servant-led process, and suggest means whereby the offending parties may be admonished so as to constructively repair and buildup as supportive participants. Knowledge of such infractions also helps us better understand the basic nature of servant leadership as an opposing force.

We must all, especially leaders, heed the words from Paul to Timothy, *Hold the standard of sound teaching that you have heard from me, in the faith and love that are in Christ Jesus. Guard the good treasure entrusted to you, with the help of the Holy Spirit living in us.* (2 Timothy 1:13-14) *...be strong in the grace that is in Christ Jesus.* (2 Timothy 2:1) So we must all be strong in guarding "the good treasure" of discipleship given us by Christ, letting no barrier arise that bars or restricts our Christian growth. This chapter responds by directing attention to the negative ways in which congregations and individuals may discourage and prevent servant leadership from within, and suggests constructive responses. However, we must always keep foremost in mind that Christ is at the heart of *every* person ever created. Christ within us is a *uniting* presence, a countervailing force breaking down the walls of enmity and hostility and fostering reconciliation.

Some readers will not like this book and this chapter in particular. The harshest critics of servant leadership are generally those in power. The admonitions become too personal. Church leaders typically enjoy their authority and are proud of their service. This is natural and good if self-contained. It is always pleasing to serve God, but only as humble servants doing what the master has commanded. *"...when you have done all you have been told to do, say, 'We are ordinary servants, we have only done our duty.'"* (Luke 17:10) We are servants first, leaders second, and then only as servant leaders. The authority exercised is from God thereby defining our stewardship as a *gift* of discipleship.

Nature of transgressions. The transgressions addressed here are not deliberate, intentional disobedience to God's will. For as *Christian* congregations, the body of Christ, we are sacred, loved and cared for by our heavenly Father who protects us from all evil. The sins that slip by, if they may be so labeled, are typically of a more hidden nature, often so mundane and prevalent as to be commonly tolerated, even accepted as part and parcel of church business as usual. For example, imputing unimportance because of limited popular support, sidestepping the real issue, and repeated delays, all seemingly reasonable yet devious responses.

The apparently benign nature involved makes identification and rooting out such transgressions all the more difficult. We are focused on subtle, illusive, concealed, even disguised shortcomings arising from human frailties. Although harmful, the actions are seldom malicious, more often self-serving. Any pain inflicted is usually borne stoically in private by the offended party. Thus seemingly minor and evasive, the infractions involved are made palatable by a mistakenly tolerant membership. This very latitude, however, makes the task of correction all the more difficult, requiring courage to step forward against the majority's acceptance.

Modest as they may appear, the obstacles addressed here are, in fact, insidious, and over time are effective against servant leadership and all forms of democracy, always a fragile structure. Thus they must be addressed. It doesn't take much counterbalancing to tip the scales in favor of autocracy. This chapter, unpleasant as it may be to some, is thus essential to encourage a supportive rather than hostile environment that nurtures rather than impedes the introduction of servant leadership. We have no excuse for not perfecting our receptivity in this manner.

Special word about the interface with pastors. Our pastors are usually a congregation's only full-time professional church leader. By training and sense of personal responsibility some may be as inclined to manage as guide. And the respect they deserve may inadvertently foster this extended role. We argue here, and again in Chapter 10, "Leadership Roles," that the pastor's principal managerial responsibility is to train and guide the congregation in self-governance. "Taking charge," other than in the most exceptional instances, should be avoided, however compelling the immediate reasons. We admonish pastors therefore to be alert to excessive intervention, always encouraging and expanding lay leadership; to, in effect, "work themselves out" of church management. Pastors who insist on being chief executives are among servant leadership's toughest barriers.

Forms of Management

There is a wide range in the manner in which organizations can and should be directed, dependent primarily on the degree of centralized authority required, the importance and speed of decisions, and the necessary qualifications of leaders.

An exceptional level of centralized authority is required when:
  (1) decisions are critical and difficult and must be made quickly and authoritatively; plans must be as free of error as possible; coordination is essential.
  (2) the leader must be exceptionally well qualified and specially trained, while the rank-and-file may be strictly nescient followers.
  (3) few alternatives are possible, dictating a single one-time solution to most problems.
  (4) operations are primarily impersonal and mechanical in nature.

An exceptional level of democratic latitude is possible and desirable when:
  (1) operations consist of a number of relatively stable, independent, and simple elements requiring minimal management and coordination; operations are flexible with considerable latitude for creativity, autonomy, and error, and can be pursued at a relatively leisurely pace.
  (2) leadership opportunities abound with minimal skill and training requirements; individual growth is paramount; rank-and-file are diversely qualified.
  (3) compromise and trial-and-error are real alternatives in problem solving.
  (4) operations deal primarily with people and their social, economic, and physical needs.

The **military** is a good example of conditions favoring centralized authority. Combat decisions are urgent matters of life and death with no luxury for discussion; soldiers must be ordered into battle; senior officers are highly trained and experienced; compromise opportunities are rare; and key factors are non-personal (terrain; weather; enemy position, strength and arms; etc.). At the other extreme are church **congregations** where all members are considered equal and precious in God's sight; decisions involve fairly routine matters that can be pursued at a relatively leisurely pace; leaders are selected as much by their willingness to serve as qualifications; and the viewpoint of minorities is seriously considered with compromise an often workable solution.

Thus we may conclude that the activities of church congregations are likely the most attractive grounds for servant leadership among all organized human endeavors. Christ is the ultimate servant leader. We endeavor only to follow in his footsteps.

Peremptory Leaders, Indifferent Followers

Overly self-assured leaders and apathetic followers are an unfortunate combination that can lead to authoritative rule limiting congregational growth. Servant leaders, on the other hand, continuously encourage followers, promoting involvement and stimulating development. How we combat one and foster the other is introduced at the end of this chapter, and is, of course, the subject of the entire book. Initially, however, we need to understand the nature of the foe itself. What are the personal traits and organizational structures that lead to and maintain peremptory or assertive authority? We address four: (1) the mindset of insistent leaders, (2) the disposition of subservient followers, (3) social mores discouraging democracy, and (4) abuses of power.

Faults of Leaders

Leadership, by its very nature of directing others, tends to cultivate personal ego and its attendant negative traits.

√ Virtues of Rank

Positions of authority tend to prompt, in those so susceptible, a certain degree of arrogance and self-assumed importance. Officials that know better are gripped by hubris. The opinions of subordinates and outsiders are not taken seriously or simply ignored. Even pastors are susceptible, most commonly in not recognizing the professionalism of members. This vanity distorts self-perception. More destructive are its consequences on others. Aloofness and superiority destroy trust and confidence. And enhancing the identity of a few leaders invariably diminishes that of the majority. The servant leader, in contrast, parks his or her ego at the door and soon forgets its very existence in the common effort. The fact that God, the supreme authority, is *always* open to *all* our thoughts and prayers, shows the absurdity of imposed human barriers.

√ Self-Reliance

Authoritative leaders often adopt a secretive, insular posture, relying more on their own intellect and abilities than those of subordinates and sometimes even God. There is little soul-searching; a tendency not to hear anything that suggests one might be off course. Prayer and Bible reading are left to others. They appear to not understand how little they know. Such leaders act as if they are on intimate terms with certainty. They control meetings by being so forceful that everyone else backs down. They are myopic, doing little homework and ignoring advice. Decisions are made on personal preference rather than factual analysis. They don't take dissent seriously. Their rationale often is the perceived need to get the job done correctly and in a hurry. In reality they are more motivated by impatience and self-rewards than effectiveness. Plus they find that control is far easier (and self-serving) than democracy.

√ Self-Protection

The mind of the autocratic leader is invariably defensive, resentful of the critic too often right.[2] Dominating leaders fear unfettered access for it increases the risk of disclosure and all manner of possible negative consequences. "The less light shed on our performance the better." They seek safety in the crowd while fearing the individuals that compose it. Congregations can be controlled, individual members cannot. To this end they employ all sorts of protective measures—isolation, evasion, secretiveness, and an apparent loss of hearing for all but the most comfortable inputs. Defensive leaders like consistency that avoids any need for accommodation or personal sacrifice. Yet all organizations must change to grow and all leadership must be challenged to govern well. Be warned. Retreat from those who fear change and are averse to dissent for they cast a shadow over progress, their only goal being that of preservation.

Weaknesses of Followers

It is not just the faults of leaders that hold back congregations. Members themselves who consciously tolerate such leadership and fail at the rank-and-file level must share the blame.

√ Subservience

Obeying authority is an essential obligation of responsible citizenship. In fact, obedience is so ingrained from childhood that it remains largely unquestioned in later life. Most adults find it difficult to challenge any form of authority, actual or perceived. Church hierarchy especially engenders fidelity. Of course we owe the utmost respect to governing authorities. But devotion and caring are not the same as subservience. Dogmatic, unquestioning adherence to authority is what must be avoided. "Go-along-to-get-a-long" is not a rule for productive involvement. It is the antithesis. Holding one's views in check is tantamount to a betrayal of our gifts. We are obligated as Christians to always do our very best, unrestrained, regardless of difficulties.

Authoritative leaders know well the advantage of a submissive congregation, faithful to the organization. Such leaders espouse the creed "My church, right or wrong." They challenge, "Who are you to question church policy?" And a submissive membership, overly guided by allegiance, dutifully agrees, thereby vanquishing all opportunity for correction and creativity.

√ **Over Sensitivity**

Inter-personal relations among friends and neighbors are usually more stable and temperate than within congregations where deeply held beliefs may quickly engender hurt feelings, and, too frequently, retaliatory flare-ups. Leaders must be aware of what others hold dear, but not to the point of capitulation. When issues become too personal, the alert leader backs off, allowing time for objective rephrasing. But there must be balance. Catering too often to the sensitivities of a small minority can be detrimental to the majority. We talk of the role of compromise in such situations in "Alternatives to Consensus," page 172.

√ **Irresponsibility**

Too many congregational members are indifferent to the vitality of the church, always relying on others to serve and lead. Laziness, procrastination, neglect, however labeled, prompts too many individuals too often to take refuge in the status quo and proven few. "We've always relied on these people and they do a good job." Negligent congregations inadvertently allow authority to gradually shift to a responsible few, as much by default as by intent. It becomes a vicious cycle. The more power is concentrated, the less involved dependent members become, shifting the balance even more. Irresponsibility is thus a most corrosive, destructive element. Fortunately, servant leadership has at its very heart the intent to invest *everyone* as leaders thereby effectively countering congregational detachment.

Destructive Social Mores

We have described the faults of leaders and the weaknesses of followers. Now we add the actions of *groups* destructive to others. What makes this foe especially formidable is its cloak of apparent general acceptance, forcing tolerance by individuals fearful of ostracism.

√ **Discrimination**

Discrimination within congregations is usually well concealed. It seldom involves acts of outright prejudice or bias, more often it is manifest in lack of hospitality and neglect. Discrimination in any form is totally against God's will in love for all. In its more discreet forms it involves observing and holding in greater esteem certain social and economic differences within society. It accords greater honor and respect on those of position and wealth. It forms prejudicial opinions not on the merits of a person, but rather by the characteristics of the group to which the individual belong. "Not 'our kind' of people." It is the old-boy network. It is social cliques. For some, it is simply a matter of holding on to first impressions.

Churches are on the front line in attacking and dispelling the more obvious and blatant forms of discrimination. Subtle, hidden prejudices, however, may too often be tolerated; for example, failure to extend an invitation, harboring resentment, irritation, distrust, and bullying the critic. The kingdom of God tolerates no such prejudices, however concealed and untraceable. Among Christians there is no second class, no outcasts, all are one in Christ to the very least. Christians are prejudiced only against the devil.

√ Tyranny of Tradition and Provincialism

The church is God's temple on earth. It is a holy structure in which we are privileged to worship and serve in reverence and humbleness. But we also know that the church, although under God's care and shielded from evil, is not without human faults. Two problems in particular plague modern day congregations. Both discourage change and growth. The first is the **tyranny of tradition**, that is, unequivocal reverence for perceived value and excessive allegiance to the past. This, of course, is not in reference to the sacraments, liturgy, church calendar, and other sacred rituals of Christian worship. Rather it addresses the stubborn adherence of congregations to the status quo, consistent practice without review or challenge, reluctance to change no matter how persuasive the argument. The sense of order becomes an overriding restraint. "If it was good enough for our forefathers, it is good enough for us." But we serve a living God in a modern world. How God speaks to us today through prayer and the Bible must override all else in guiding our actions, our conscience is to be held captive by the word of God. If today's message counteracts yesterday's conformity and customs, the old must give way to the new. *"No one sews a piece of unshrunk cloth on an old cloak, for the patch pulls away from the cloak, and a worse tear is made. Neither is new wine put into old wineskins; otherwise, the skins burst, and the wine is spilled, and the skins are destroyed; but new wine is put into fresh wineskins, and so both are preserved."* (Matthew 9: 16-17)

The second allied problem is **provincialism**, the narrow self-centered approach to problems that limits perspective and narrows alternatives. Our Christian attitude should be just the opposite, wide open, examining everything with a positive outlook. What is new and different outside the church should be evaluated and the good gathered in and employed. There should be no lack of attention to change and progress. *Do not stifle inspiration or despise prophetic utterance, But test them all; keep hold of what is good and avoid all forms of evil.* (1 Thessalonians 5:19-22)

√ Success in Human Terms

Congregations may be misguided in striving for popular, socially recognized goals as opposed to seeking God's will. Can our most popular churches with brilliant preaching, quality music, and a multitude of programs be sure of their direction? Only if so guided by prayer, Bible study, and scholarship. So congregations must continuously review their course. We address this self-study of mission in Chapter 9, pp. 102-106.

Abuses of Authority

"Great leadership honors the freedom of the human spirit. It uses power to inspire, enroll and organize—never to manipulate or subjugate."
–Bennett J. Sims, retired Bishop of Atlanta.

What happens when we award a title and bestow authority? In most instances favorably responsive service, but occasionally the power granted is too great or becomes abused. The leader goes from caring to ruling, from mindful to inattentive. The sin involved is the leader's increased unwillingness to see value in others. Abuse of authority in this fashion is difficult to root out. "Those who have power in their hand will not give it up while they can retain it." –George Mason, chief advocate of a constitutional bill or rights.

Peremptory authority of this sort generally comes about through gradual acquisition of unwarranted influence, whether sought or not. Older, long-term office holders are particularly susceptible. The remedies include counseling, written job descriptions, and an attentive membership.

In the following sections we distinguish three kinds or dimensions of power: the suppressive capacity of the organization as a whole, outright pressures applied to force conformity, and last and most pervasive, subtle but effective influences used to discourage individuality.

√ Bureaucratic Suffocation

The structural design and administrative procedures of an organization itself can be extremely intimidating and burdensome. A dysfunctional bureaucracy is inevitably multi-layered, limiting vertical communication and contacts, and overworking top executives. At its worst, procedures are in place that allow those in power to evade and obfuscate, while they decide what, if anything, to do. Artificial barriers and complex and inflexible regulations and procedures abound to confuse and discourage. Activities appear in bewildering complexity to hide the true nature of what's going on. "It's so complicated everybody is afraid to raise their hand and say, 'I don't understand it.'" –Louis B. Gaghardi, analyst, commenting on Enron's employees' reaction to the corporation's financial reports.

Churches normally attempt to hold procedures and red tape to a minimum and generally succeed. And even what may appear to be chaos, typically breeds vitality and creativity. We draw attention to the extremes here simply to dramatize the dangers involved. Most important, red tape nonsense is intolerable at any level and can generally be avoided.

√ Coercion

While some bureaucracy can be tolerated as a necessary evil, congregations must always outlaw all forms of coercion. It is a danger that must be fully understood to be avoided. Coercive behavior compels others to act or think in a certain way by use of pressure, threats, or intimidation. In its most powerful form it is arrogant, forceful, suppressive, and impatient. Congregations seldom have the rogue bullies or aggressive cliques capable of such extremes, but coercion is possible in subtle, masked forms. Less extreme examples include a distaste for being questioned, suppression of critical and creative expression, tabling of controversial issues, and unexplained delays. All are intended rebukes, all are forms of coercion. None must be tolerated.

√ Manipulation

Manipulation in the negative sense used here is the shrewd, even devious, influencing or managing of others for special gains. It is usually supported by plausible rationale rather than any outright threat or sanction as with coercion. The "special gain" may be no more than that of silencing critics. This nearness to "making sense" makes manipulation especially difficult to identify and root out. Not only is it the most concealed form of power abuse, it is also the most pervasive. It is so common and subtle that it has become a generally accepted part of the fabric of much of our society. Yet manipulative behavior is devious and degrading, tending to perpetuate divisiveness, partisanship, and gridlock.

Congregants are likely to recognize from experience some of the following **manipulative behavior** used to discourage dialogue and democracy:

1. Unannounced or closed door meetings, or meetings held at inopportune times to prevent or discourage participation.
2. Meetings held without advance notice of issues and related information.
3. Meetings shortened to prevent or discourage full expression, limit debate, and restrict study.
4. Isolated, inaccessible leaders and committees.
5. Elections limited to pre-selected screened candidates, and stacked committees.
6. Restricted communications including failure to solicit suggestions, field complaints, and employ surveys.

Also helpful in the struggle against manipulation is knowledge of the **benign ways ideas and suggestions may be thwarted** by clever, dysfunctional responses. All such evasive maneuvers must be aggressively fought.

(1) Issues framed to insure approval without fair presentation of alternatives.
(2) Rejection of recommendations by bogus counter arguments, refusal to address issues,[3] dismissal out-of-hand.
(3) Hollow approval allowing proposal to die of neglect.
(4) Extended and torturous approval action, delaying or postponing decisions indefinitely.
(5) Added restrictions and requirements, hollowing out the core idea.
(6) Compromise responses or alternative substitutions that appears similar but miss the key intention.

(7) Initiator made to feel guilty, by, for example, providing only a partial response as a personal undeserved favor.
(8) Failure to assist in promoting idea.

Safeguarding Democracy

The next two divisions of this book–*Part III. Church Structure and Leadership Roles* and *Part IV. Leadership in Practice*–present the details of how congregations may effectively oppose the difficulties cited in this chapter. Here in Chapter 7, in summarizing the negative forces at work, we describe the general nature of possible adversities and briefly list the servant leader's counter measures.

The Threat Within

The weaknesses cited in this chapter are not unduly common in Christian congregations. They represent more risk than reality. However, they evolve from our human nature, represent a real potential, and must be confronted when present in seeking perfection through Christ. It seems natural to want to order others about, to relax when following, to "go-along" with the crowd, and to adjust to wrongdoings. These tendencies restrain otherwise good and able people from being fully receptive to democracy and servant leadership. Our mindset is that less able people need to be led rather than self-motivated, that forceful direction provides security. When this inclination is combined with the weight of tradition and habit, it can be a very formidable opponent indeed.

Autocratic power is actually seldom vested; it is rather gradually acquired in the absence of democratic safeguards and protective leadership. Power fills a void. Once secured, it is not easily released. Forceful leaders believe they are doing the right thing, for the good of all. And they often are, but at a high cost. The combination of power and some good is extremely difficult to combat. The very process represents a challenge to existing authority and a presumption of questionable practices, an awkward posture from which to begin. Thus church "politics" must be handled very carefully in true Christian fashion.

Countermeasures

All congregational problems can be resolved, simply enough, if members are sufficiently attuned to the Christian spiritual life. We turn then first to the Bible for guidance.

Biblical Guidance

We must not confuse guidance with judgment in combating dominance. *"Do not judge others, so that God will not judge you."* (Matthew 7:1) We do not stand in judgment of our Christian brethren; rather we guide and admonish one another as fellow servants in the faith. All are sinners, all require God's grace. So we are to be merciful and forgiving. *"Be merciful, just as your Father is merciful."* (Luke 6:36).

We must also put away all manner of falsehood and speak the truth in our admonitions. *Let all of us speak the truth to our neighbors.* (Ephesians 4:25) *Do not use harmful words in talking. Use only helpful words, the kind that build up and provide what is needed, so that what you say will do good to those who hear you.* (Ephesians 4: 29) Truth itself is sufficient. No rebuke, no reproach need be added. *Get rid of all bitterness, passion, and anger. No more shouting or insults. No more hateful feelings of any sort. Instead, be kind and tenderhearted to one another, and forgive one another, as God has forgiven you in Christ.* (Ephesians 4:31-32)

Means of Correction

The servant leader shows by example how difficult, often deeply ingrained, problems can be resolved in a peaceful, amicable way by respectful listening and studied resolution. The details of how this is accomplished are presented in the "Manage Conflict; Be Generous and Conciliatory" section of Chapter 8, page 88. One of the most serious oversights of congregations is failure to root out their difficulties. Leaders must go to extraordinary lengths in this regard, concurrently soliciting advice on problem resolution. Eventually most problems can be corrected passively over time, if not by leader replacement.

Corrections are particularly difficult when personal feelings and long held allegiances are involved. The approach must always be that of persuasion and concern for the individual. In sensitive matters the situation should be discussed openly and frankly. Members should be advised of the reasoning behind the change or correction. Disagreements should be met with love and understanding, compromise and trial-testing available options. Admonishment is always a last resort. If reprove is necessary it should be done gently and constructively in private. As Oswald Chambers (1874-1917, Scottish evangelical prophet) reminds us "The critical faculty is an intellectual one, not a moral one." We remain always disciples together in shared faith.

---

[1] Craig A. Satterlee, "From being fruit to bearing fruit," *The Lutheran*, August 2002, pp. 20-21.

[2] One cannot be right too often and not create enemies. Leonard Mosley referring to the successful air war strategy of Hugh Dowding, British Air Marshall during World War II, versus his adversaries in the House of Commons, writes, "...having committed the major crime of being too hard-mindedly right too often against the wrong people." *The Battle of Britain* (Alexandria, VA, Time-Life Books, 1977), p. 146.

[3] Possibly one of the most stinging and humiliating rebukes is that of being ignored. Leonard R. Klein labels it "dysfunctional politeness" which silences many voices. See Leonard R. Klein, "What you really can't say in the ELCA," *The Lutheran*, October, 2002.

Chapter 8
Core Elements for Leading/Managing

This chapter is somewhat mechanical in nature, combining the philosophy of the preceding three chapters with modern business theory to achieve a set of practical guidelines for day-to-day church management from a servant leader perspective. It should not be read apart from the preceding chapters, yet it may frequently be referred to as an outline of leader responsibilities. Perspective on the entirety of Part II can be gained from the taxonomy on pages 74-75.

It is appropriate to begin with a definition of servant leadership, then describe the special attractiveness of the congregational application. We then argue the value of servant leadership with its overwhelming advantages over traditional schools of management. This introduction is followed by two central messages–the basic management responsibilities of the leader, and the specific means or actions involved in providing direction.

Servant Leadership Defined for Congregations[1]

Servant leadership is defined here from the writings of its modern advocate, John Greenleaf.[2]

Servant leadership is a democratic philosophy of guiding stewardship that values the responsibilities, interests, and abilities of all affected parties, and actively encourages their full involvement in planning and decision-making through study and open discussion toward consensus.

In the present application to Christian congregations, we add this inclusive theological preface adapted from Oswald Chambers.[3]

The Christian servant leader is one who, recognizing God's sovereign will over all, leaps to do that will with the help of the Holy Spirit.

Thus, seeking God's will in all things, the servant leader enthusiastically marshals the congregation to strive toward perfection, actively engaging together in prayer, study, and decision-making.

The leader's focus underlies all. The servant leader views the enhancement of members as important as the successes of the organization itself. He or she also devoutly believes in the organization's mission and strives mightily to advance toward agreed-upon goals. The two–enhancement and mission–are mutually supporting. Both are implemented by the tools of servant leadership–perceptive guidance and the creation of pathways for involvement by all. The servant leader's aim is to relinquish authority to the majority, substituting foresight, encouragement, and guidance for control.

Institutions function better when the idea, the dream, is in the forefront, and the leader is seen as servant to the idea. As Greenleaf explains, "To lead is to go out ahead and show the way when the way may be unclear, difficult, even dangerous—it is not just walking at the head of the parade." Real leadership requires vision, resourcefulness, and risk-taking. Without this foresight we have simply routine management, preservation of the status quo rather than advancement.

"When the leader leads well, the people will say, 'We did it ourselves'" (ancient Taoist proclamation). This apparent scission is accomplished by leaders who encourage wide discussions that draw out new directions as individuals find creative ways to solve problems and move forward. And this full involvement is fortified and strengthened by the Holy Spirit which guides all things.

Planning and study. We draw attention to the terms *planning* and *study* in our definition of servant leadership, elements of management alluded to by Greenleaf throughout his work, but not given this prominence in his defining statements. These two "academic" components of management are of critical importance to the success of any organization, and are especially well developed when subject to the give-and-take and multiple inputs encouraged by servant leadership. Planning and study functions are discussed in Chapter 11.

An Affinity for All Seasons

The servant leader is natural to the Christian church. Christ admonished us, *"If one of you wants to be great, he must be the servant of the rest; and if one of you wants to be first, he must be the slave of all."* (Mark 10:43-44) The servant leader seeks to serve others before satisfying personal needs; to respond to problems by listening first; and to view the past, present, and future as one moving organic entity. This type of leadership builds strength in others, originating new regenerative forces. Eventually it also builds strong permanent organizations with a true sense of mission manned by able, committed followers.

Faith-based institutions, in their universal love and equality, present a unique opportunity for servant leadership. In reality, however, Christ's teachings both precede and exceed the principles of servant leadership expressed by modern man, so that the latter is already within the former, albeit seldom so explicitly associated. Thus, while we speak here, for purposes of emphasis and clarity, of "applying" the principles of servant leadership to congregations, in reality they are already present, inherent and fundamental in Christ's teachings. Servant leadership, in every respect, is dependent and derived from the Bible, whether recognized or not by Greenleaf and other modern practitioners. This congruence affords the present author the greatest possible latitude and confidence in advocating servant leadership to all congregations, for it can be interpreted as God's will for leaders to so serve.

Servant leadership for congregations has many similarities with applications to secular organizations. But there are also substantial differences, the greatest being our dependency on God in all things. Congregations also have unique missions of administering the sacraments, serving others, bonding in brotherhood with Christ, and most challenging, evangelizing. Profit is not a motive. Productivity and efficiency, hallmarks of commercial enterprises, are, at best, ancillary considerations. Ultimately, God, not man, dictates the course, our good works being dependent on his grace.

Embodying Christ's teachings, servant leadership for congregations should be the most promising of all applications. And that promise will exceed all expectations because of God's love and guidance. So make no mistake, servant leadership is part and parcel of God's sanctified power for congregations. Apart from this sacred use, it is simply another tool of management.

Congregational practitioners of servant leadership must always recognize the Gospel as the underlying and ultimate message and source. This spiritual dependency and other distinctions from secular applications should be recognized:

(1) The universal priesthood of all believers makes us *all* one in Christ. *All of you, then, are Christ's body, and each one is a part of it.* (1 Corinthians 12:27)

(2) God's will is sought in all things in which we take great strength, joy and comfort. We strive first for the righteous reign of God.

(3) Our ultimate guidance comes through the Holy Spirit. Prayer and Bible study are our chief counsel. The eternal presence of God through his spirit guides and protects us. We must always reach out to receive this grace.

(4) The pastor role, above all, is that of spiritual leader and counselor.

(5) Congregations generally have the opportunity to operate at a fairly leisurely, but steadfast pace. This latitude allows time for extended discussion and study, essential elements of servant leadership. The congregation must not allow this deliberate pace to be rushed by impatient observers. Interaction is productive, not "wasted" time.

(6) Christian beliefs make congregations receptive to servant leadership. This natural affinity and the generally monolithic nature of congregations eases acceptance of the democratic requirements imposed. When members believe they are equal in God's sight, they tend to act responsibly together.

(7) Church operations are philosophical in nature, sometimes eliciting strong emotional involvement with potential for personal abrasion and conflicts. Thus the emphasis on kindness, understanding, and compromise espoused by servant leadership are particularly relevant and counterbalancing.

Value of Servant Leadership

The supreme value of servant leadership is that it follows Christ's teachings of servitude one to another. In embracing humbleness we are actually strengthened. God blesses the servant-led congregation.

Advantages of Servant Leadership

Servant leadership is the best means of securing active participation, and is also the surest means for gaining informed consensus.

Servant leadership:

- **Cultivates and extends spiritual growth through increased participation.** Sharing in God's commissioned service is a rightful responsibility and duty of all the faithful, to be nurtured to its fullest.

- **Improves the sense of community and belonging within congregations** through broader sharing of responsibilities and interaction.

- **Attracts greater resources for mission tasks.** The laity bring many special skills to Christian missions, collectively far more than possessed by the church's professional staff alone. In cultivating this great resource, servant leadership not only helps each member in their personal Christian growth, but also serves the congregation as a whole in building its programs and services.

In addition to occupational skills, the laity have several distinct operating advantages over the clergy. The congregation is generally more comfortable within its own sphere. Lay leaders can ferret out commentary that members might otherwise feel uncomfortable revealing to their pastors. And open and frank criticism is more easily expressed among peers than shared with the congregation's pastor, often elevated beyond reproach. Lastly, members rub shoulders with the unchurched every day, providing numerous invitational opportunities unavailable to pastors. However, this evangelistic potential usually remains largely untapped. (See Chapter 20 on evangelism)

- **Provides safety in numbers.** Increasing the number of informed participants improves the odds of better decision-making. Reliance on a single or few individuals can be disastrous. President Kennedy's "best and brightest" advisors repeatedly deceived themselves regarding intervention in Vietnam. Servant leadership promotes large-scale democratic involvement and cultivates the critic, both measures serving to preclude unilateral one-sided decision-making.

- **Promotes constructive improvements and creative ideas.** The congregation best knows its own and community needs. Drawing out and careful listening taps this source. Congregants are also sensitive and knowledgeable about church shortcomings and failures. They are the recipients of poor sermons, inattentiveness, member cliques, and simple neglect. They must be free and encouraged to speak up. If anyone wants to know what's wrong with a church, ask the congregation.

- **Relieves the pastor of many management duties** freeing him or her for more appropriate spiritual responsibilities.

Disadvantages of Servant Leadership

Servant leadership:

- **Requires more time and is more difficult to initiate and maintain than autocratic rule.** It is far easier to simply let a few qualified individuals take over and run the show than devote the time and effort required to build participation and share leadership.
- **May discourage exceptional leaders who simply want to "get things done."** Servant leadership requires patience that must be built on trust.
- **May reportedly "waste time" trying ideas for the sake of testing.** Servant leadership advocates trial testing of ideas to demonstrate their possible value, occasionally even proposals lacking majority support. "Trial-and-error" is a necessary but taxing ingredient of growth. Progress is seldom a straight path.
- **May be inherently conservative.** Democracy is dependent on a majority vote. Contesting every issue in this manner makes introduction of new, and certainly radical ideas difficult. Humble congregations recognize and value exploration, dissent, and minority positions. Respect permits new ideas to be tested, not always with advance approval.

How to Get Started

Because the Gospel message supports servant leadership, most churches are well into this means of leading in Christian spirit if not by outward choice. Consequently, this volume is more likely to expand and perhaps formalize servant leadership in congregations than to initiate its adoption. Robert Greenleaf, modern originator and principal advocate of the concept, notes that it is not a quick fix gimmick to be applied by management, but rather involves adoption of a potentially encompassing philosophy which eventually permeates and flavors the whole organization. He cautions that instigators embrace a disposition of *gradualism*, "...being comfortable with a slow pace that accepts taking opportunities when they come, rather than trying to batter down offending walls that are not ready to give way." Although existing injustices and other shortcomings are difficult to accept, they frequently must be temporarily tolerated to prevent incurring consequential distress and long-term side effects as a result of too abrupt action. Ultimately healing will take place as converts are persuaded in their own hearts of the value involved.

The surest way for an idea or reform to be started and have a lasting effect is for it to be embraced by the current leader. What the pastor is and does as a servant leader speaks louder than any instruction. The congregation president and other laity may also set an example. Identification of potential leaders, provision of coaching and support, and progressive congregational instruction and involvement, combine to bring about acceptance. This volume will hopefully encourage and strengthen the necessary individual efforts, training, and transitions involved. And the odds for adoption are improved as more readers become advocates. We recommend as many church members as possible be encouraged to read at least portions of this volume. Then all should engage in responsive group discussions and prayer as a first step. Even a modest change toward servant leadership is viewed here as a constructive beginning toward eventual full adoption. Congregations will find all responses rewarding, no matter how seemingly small.

Major rites of passage include an inventory of members to identify untapped talents and promote greater use of existing skills. Thought should be given to flattening the church structure to reduce approval requirements and spread authority. Increasing open forum discussions begins a more democratic process. These early steps are discussed in Parts III, "Church Structure and Leadership Roles," and IV, "Leadership in Practice," of this volume.

Over time a combination of small changes will result in big effects. The aim is to reach the "tipping point"[4] when the shift toward greater servant leadership becomes permanent. Initial instigators need not be discouraged. If, as we contend, servant leadership follows Christ's teaching, then we have God's blessing on all who attempt and welcome this change.

The Servant Leader Model for Congregations

Servant leadership applied to congregations can be described as a model of three mutually supporting, integrated, yet distinct parts. The first element, the basic **principles of servant leadership** or guiding doctrine, is presented in Chapter 5. The second component, the **personal dimensions**, identifies the commitment, virtues, and skills required (Chapter 6). The third, the **responsibilities of management and leadership practice**, involves many traditional management duties. Some may be marginally affected by servant leadership, but are nevertheless part of the model whole. The details of this third element–management functions and means–interpreted in the servant leadership context, are presented in this chapter, with further interpretation later in the book.

The taxonomy of the servant leadership model for congregations is as follows:

Principles of Christian Servant Leadership (Chapter 5)
1. Love Jesus, seek and trust God's will in all things
2. Be loving, kind to all
3. See things whole, seek the truth
4. Commit to excellence
5. Encourage the active involvement of all
6. Promote democratic action
7. Commit to lay leadership and its development
8. Combat domination, build diversity, encourage agreement

Personal Dimensions of the Servant Leader (Chapter 6)
  −**Commitment**
   1. Commit to the principles of servant leadership
   2. Identify with the organization
   3. Commit to the leadership office
  −**Primary Virtues**
   1. Be caring, respectful, and encouraging...to the very least person
   2. Embrace a posture of humility
   3. Be joyful, hopeful, and at peace
   4. Be calm, patient, and understanding
   5. Be totally honest, open minded, and fair
   6. Be confident, resolute, courageous
  −**Attributes/Skills** (Chapters 3, 8, and 11)
   1. Intelligence
   2. Knowledge
   3. Stability and resilience
   4. Listening capacity
   5. Awareness
   6. Persuasion
   7. Conceptualization and foresight

Basic Guidelines: The Practice of Leadership and Management (Chapter 8)
  −**Functions/Responsibilities**
   1. Know the operating environment
   2. Define the organization's mission and goals
   3. Set forth supporting statements−articles of faith and operating principles
   4. Establish the organizational structure and job descriptions
   5. Select appropriate management style; recruit and prepare leaders
   6. Develop a plan of action
   7. Oversee/direct and coordinate operations
  −**Means of Leading**
   1. Depend on God and prayer
   2. Persuade and involve others in a unified common effort
   3. Provide direction and vision
   4. Listen attentively and responsively
   5. Focus on priorities and results
   6. Be alert to problems and solve them in an orderly, scholarly manner
   7. Manage conflict, be generous and conciliatory

Management Functions, Organizational Structure, and General Strategy

Servant leadership is a selected form of management. *Management* may be distinguished as a broader dimension of directing and supervising, employing conventional forms and procedures common to commerce and industry. The entire scope of management, however, can be influenced by the servant leadership philosophy. Thus all aspects of church management are part of the concept present here, albeit some areas are rather material in nature. The first building block of the servant leadership model therefore, consists of the commonly cited basic management responsibilities introduced in this chapter. Further information on how these functions are performed is presented in Parts III and IV as previously referenced.

Servant leadership is not simply a day-to-day operating tool. In place, its power and influence extend upward to an organization's highest level of direction and planning and downward to the lowest participant, guiding all aspects of management and operations. Therefore, we begin in this overview chapter with the commonly cited strategy and general management principles applicable to *all* organizations, interpreted and modified here for their role in servant lead congregations.

Too often, congregations, immersed in the fast tempo of daily operations, ignore higher level study and development, contributing in many instances to the day-to-day difficulties being experienced. For example, challenged by too many primary missions. So it is important that church leaders review strategy at least yearly, maintaining a record of their deliberations and conclusions for subsequent review. Institutions must document what they are all about.

The means for organizing and leading Christian congregations differ from that of other enterprises. The principles of management generally apply, but are modified and supplemented in application by scripture. Also, being non-profit frees the church from the aggressive policies born of competition. Most important, congregations defer to the supreme authority of God not man. God takes the place of the CEO. No action should be taken without invoking his guidance and blessing.

We identify seven interactive components of overall nonsectarian strategy and management as follows:

1. Know the Operating Environment

Leaders must identify and record their congregational operating environment–to respect what deserves honor, cultivate what may be developed, and challenge what may be improved. Geographical conditions include the demographic characteristics of the congregation, the neighborhood, city, and region. However, in this context, we are more concerned with operating norms that may aid or hinder effective leadership such as church traditions, existing power structure, and role of the pastor. Through the years most members become well aware of these unwritten conventions. It behooves any leader to tread carefully, for these conventions often have strong advocates among long-term members. All protocols, however, must eventually be investigated and changed if proven a hindrance.

2. Define the Organization's Mission and Goals

Mission statements and related goals identify what an organization is attempting to do and provide benchmarks for judging their accomplishment. They help develop a strong sense of purpose and clear vision. Goals must be well articulated. Vagueness and doubt are present when such directions are lacking. If the goal is right, the rest of leadership strategy falls into place naturally. If it is wrong or inadequate, leadership lacks a compass and wanders aimlessly.

Evangelism, spreading the good news, is, of course, the principle mission of all Christian congregations. No congregation is exempt, however modestly the commission is interpreted. Yet, circumstances may dictate other emphasis–spiritual enhancement, Christian education, community service, and mission support. Some missions may be pursued and accomplished in relatively short order while others become permanent priorities as the church grows and matures. But all are subject to reassessment. Mission statements and goals must be written out and reviewed annually. More detail on constructing mission statements and goals is provided in Chapter 9, "Statements and Organization."

3. Set Forth Supporting Statements–Articles of Faith and Operating Principles

The mission statement indicates what is being attempted while the supporting statements indicate the why and how of the activities involved. Most organizations place too much emphasis on personal abilities and neglect preparation of supporting statements, particularly operating principles. But "why we are doing this" and "how do we get there" are important defining elements. Congregations should start with written **"articles of faith"** which state what the church believes in. The articles constitute the basic premises upon which all that follows is dependent. An example list of such precepts is presented in Chapter 9, page 97.

Operating principles may be defined as "rules of the game," i.e., predetermined policies or modes of action. For example, we advance the *principles* of servant leadership (Chapter 5, page 34) as rules for effective Christian leadership. Operating principles may and should be devised for essentially all church activities–education, financial management, physical facility use, etc. However, they are sometimes difficult to identify and may be too confining. Some congregations may consequently shy away from such rigorous guidance. On the other hand, proven principles are excellent guides. We illustrate various known operating principles in their respective functional areas in the second division of this book, *Functional Responsibilities* (Parts V and VI).

4. Establish the Organizational Structure and Job Descriptions

An organization is an orderly arrangement of various functional parts to systematically work together in the business at hand. Church organizations should be as flat as possible to encourage and give visibility to ground-level operations and facilitate upward communication. Two layers minimize the chain and are generally feasible–a council overseeing the various operating committees. Broadly distributing authority in this manner can actually minimize the control leaders must exert, even though the span involved may be wide. Given sufficient independence and latitude, each element becomes self-directing and autonomous. More about the organizational structure is presented in Chapter 9 "Statements and Organization."

Job descriptions assign and distinguish worker responsibilities, thus clarifying and avoiding duplicating responsibilities. Good job descriptions insure work coverage, properly link associated tasks, and provide necessary coordination. They greatly reduce misunderstanding and conflict. Every "job" in the church should have a description, from pastors and staff, through the church council and its officers, down to committees. The Sunday school superintendent should have one also, as well as a general description for teachers.

Full descriptions set the ground rules for operations including essential division of duties. Without such detail, responsibilities are vague and overlaps are sure to cause problems. Experience dictates that job descriptions be continuously reviewed, especially before a new appointee is assigned. Setting clear, comprehensive rules before an individual takes office gets everyone off on the right foot from the start. Job descriptions should be published in a church handbook. How jobs are described is presented in Chapter 9, page 113, with examples in Appendix B.

5. Select Appropriate Management Style; Recruit and Prepare Leaders

We advocate servant leadership as the appropriate management style for all Christian congregations. This volume (especially Parts II and III) can serve as a training reference. However, democratic leadership is time consuming and occasionally cumbersome for practitioners, who might prefer to "simply get on with it." So most congregations expediently adopt various "textbook" forms that members learned in college or on the job, with little knowledge or appreciation of more suitable alternatives. The result is a range of practices, from close to autocratic dominance by a single or few individuals, to near orderless laissez-faire. Generally the most common form of governance is a high degree of authoritarianism, however subtly employed, and we devote Chapter 7 to its potential evils.

Every congregation should recognize that church management typically can be improved. The whole structure should be reviewed and critiqued on an annual basis asking, "Is this the most effective organization and leadership style of which we are capable?"

Candidates for elected church offices (trustees and council) are typically identified by appointed nominating committees. The considerable responsibilities involved are discussed under the "Recruitment/Election Process" heading, page 119, in Chapter 10. Candidate selection is a considerable entrustment, never left to personal judgment alone, but always also including the application of explicit qualification criteria.

Orienting new officers prepares them to immediately participate with minimal disruption or regression. Appointees should be "walked through" their job description and "shown-the-ropes" by a seasoned member. Even before election, candidates should understand and accept the terms of office. As John Carver, noted writer on board leadership, says, "Orientation is important enough to be a mandatory step rather than an optional exercise." No one wants a surprised and dismayed appointee, least of all the individual himself.

6. Develop a Plan of Action

Planning (establishing goals and designing the means for their attainment) is the principal intellectual exercise of leadership. It establishes the organization's operational roadmap. It must be fairly continuous as new conditions and opportunities arise, requiring refocusing. Yet some organizations, including churches, are entrenched in what they believe is a static situation, barely plan at all, repeating the same agenda year after unquestioning year. Is a plan really required to carry out God's will? Most certainly, because worldly conditions are continuously changing offering new opportunities and requiring new responses. The importance of planning is addressed in Chapter 11.

7. Oversee/Direct and Coordinate Operations

While performing all of the above functions, leaders must also attend, however perfunctory, to day-to-day operations to ensure they are being conducted in a reasonably effective manner. The pastor, or preferably an appointed staff manager, may have this overall responsibility. Fortunately, well-structured and staffed church organizations are largely self-directing. The council, however, must independently keep informed. Representatives should periodically attend staff and committee meetings without appearing intrusive or judgmental. Monitoring in any form is not always easy, but better to awkwardly learn of troubles early than to be unpleasantly "surprised" later. And showing consistent interest through this participation fosters a team rather than "us versus them" approach. Most "direction" by the church council, when necessary, takes the form of *advice* thereby preserving the integrity of delegated authority.

Means of Leading

Give your servant therefore an understanding mind to govern your people, able to discern between good and evil; for who can govern this your great people? (1 Kings 3:9) *But you do not live as your human nature tells you to; you live as the Spirit tells you to–if, in fact, God's Spirit lives in you.* (Romans 8:9)

As in all things, the leader begins his or her duties with prayer, "on our knees."[5] This is the first and greatest *means* of leading. All other actions are dependent and responsive.

Exactly *how* the seven management responsibilities presented in the previous section are carried out is too often sidestepped in favor of the more easily perceived desired results. For example, "high morale," is touted as opposed to explaining *how* to improve morale. The basic question is, "What *personal actions* must be taken by the leader to guide the organization effectively forward on course?" The specifics involved have more to do with procedure and mechanics than with personal attributes. However, ultimate success also depends on the leader's individual character as well as his or her ability to guide and direct. Thus the means of leading are, to a large degree, cognitive in nature, i.e., they can be studied and learned as opposed to gradually acquired as part of one's persona.

Leaders guide and encourage the organization *forward* to improved productivity and quality. The job is to advance, not maintain, the status quo. If your organization is marking time, you basically have no real leaders. Unfortunately, some churches may not want to run the risk of having such challengers, they simply want maintenance personnel to comfortably continue the past. Thus leaders may have to begin by convincing others of the need for change and improvement.

The major shortcoming of leaders is, of course, failure to *lead,* to prepare for and be willing to undertake the hard and high-risk task of building a better institution. Real leaders provide an insistent motivating force that obligates the institution to move forward. And the aim is to move forward to *distinction* not mere adequacy. Thus the means of leading presented here constitute an essential element of this book if not its pivotal guidance.

A good way to begin is by quoting the master, Robert K. Greenleaf, who had this to say about the requirements of leadership.[6]

> Why would anyone follow the leadership of another unless one has confidence that the other knows better where to go? And how would one know better where to go unless one has a wider than usual awareness of the terrain and the alternatives, unless one is well armored for the unexpected, and unless one's view of the future is more sharply defined than that of most? Also, one's confidence in a leader rests, in part, on the assurance that stability and poise and resilience under stress give adequate strength for the rigors of leadership. All of the above stand on a base of intensity and dedication to service that supports faith as trust.

Based on these fundamentals, we list seven leadership actions that constitute the essence of what the individual must *do* as a leader:
1. Depend on God and prayer
2. Persuade and involve others
3. Provide direction and vision
4. Listen attentively and responsively
5. Focus on priorities and results
6. Be alert to problems and solve in an orderly, scholarly manner
7. Manage conflict, seek harmony

Dependency on God and Prayer

Not by might, nor by power, but by my spirit, says the Lord of Hosts. (Zechariah 4:6) *We know that in all things God works for good with those who love him* (Romans 8:28) These old and new testament passages tell us all we need know of God's abiding love and support for us as our heavenly Father. *If God is for us who can be against us?* (Romans 8:31) Thus, all good is possible through God, all evil overcome. So strengthened, the task is to discern through prayer and bible study where we are being led, knowing we will be enabled to confidently pursue whatever the calling. *...because God is always at work in you to make you willing and able to obey his own purpose.* (Paul writing in Philippians 2:13)

We, of course, are not the source of this strength, simply the conveyers. Our source is always God through Christ. *Christ Jesus our Lord, in whom we have access to God in boldness and confidence through faith in him.* (Ephesians 3:11-12) Prayer enables us to position ourselves in God's line of sight. So advantaged we can, as Oswald Chambers writes "...pray with our eyes on God, not on the difficulties." And in his vision we gain the faith and trust necessary to confidently wait for his will to be done after we have done all we can.

Our total dependency on God and his fulfillment of every good purpose and act prompted by faith is beautifully express by Father Thomas Merton (1915-1968, Cistercian writer) in this beautiful prayer.

> My Lord God, I have no idea where I am going. I do not see the road ahead of me. I cannot know for certain where it will end. Nor do I really know myself, and the fact that I think I am following your will does not mean that I am actually doing so. But I believe that the desire to please you does in fact please you. And I hope that I have that desire in all that I am doing. I hope that I will never do anything apart from that desire. And I know that if I do this, you will lead me by the right road, though I may know nothing about it. Therefore, I will trust you always, though I may seem to be lost and in the shadow of death. I will not fear, for you are ever with me and you will never leave me to face my perils alone.

Persuade and Involve Others in a Unified Common Effort

We must delight in each other, make each other's condition our own, rejoice together, mourn together and suffer together... We must be knit together as one. – John Winthrop, first governor of Massachusetts.

The Lord your God will raise up for you a prophet like me from among your own brothers. You must listen to him. (Deuteronomy 18:15)

A leader must comprehend the ways of those being led, and through this knowledge make them understand him by addressing problems in their language. This means that in order to readily engage others, one must share common concerns and anxieties and gain trust. Then he who steps forward is able to induce others to follow by his willingness to confront what others know but are hesitant or unwilling to undertake. The great advantage of servant leadership is that by sharing responsibility one increases the talents and energy involved, thereby lessening the demands on one's own abilities and capacity.

James MacGregor Burns (biographer and student of leadership in American politics) calls the interaction involved *transcending* leadership "...in the sense that the leaders throw themselves into a relationship with followers who will feel 'elevated' by it and often become more active themselves..." He writes that it is also "transformative" in engaging others in such a way that all "raise one another to higher levels of motivation and morality...and thus it has a transforming effect on both leader and led."[7]

Involving others in leadership roles demands accompanying delegation of authority. Responsibility always requires associated authority which should be given and received joyfully, not hesitantly, without any false sense of possession.

Moving forward, while usually launched by an individual, can often be more readily advanced by a like-thinking team. The originator, the catalyst, should always keep in mind the strength that may be gained through enlistment of others as soon as possible to forge ahead as a group. The lone individual's idea may be mistrusted simply because of the apparent lack of support. "If others are not convinced, why should we?" Often the wisest course is to begin with the support of at least a few others, thereby establishing some initial validity.

Provide Direction and Vision

At its highest interpretation, direction means having a vision of the future and persuading others of the path to be taken. Intermediate levels involve setting goals and designing the means for their accomplishment. At the lowest working level, direction is in the form of assistance in problem solving. Each in turn requires less prescience, or foresight, the ability to make a good guess or estimate of what is going to happen and when. At all levels, however, direction should be as *proactive* as possible, preparing in advance to deal with expected opportunities and problems rather than reacting to the immediate present. And direction, regardless of level, must always be accompanied by encouragement and inspiration. The exceptional leader has a relentless intent to visualize the future while at the same time accomplishing the current mission. It is not only determining where to go but the enthusiasm of getting there that matters.

The highest order of leadership can only be obtained if the leader has a burning desire for improvement. It means having the exceptional ability to get people to see what they have never seen—and get them to like and want it. Providing direction also lessens fears and anxieties, drawing people to the provider. So we strive for this perfection in Christ, for all things are possible through him.

Vision and Foresight

Where there is no vision, the people perish. (Proverbs 29:18) "What is now proved was once only imagin'd." —William Blake (1757-1827), British poet, painter, visionary, mystic, and engraver.

The "lead" that the leader has is vision and foresight, the past, present, and future being viewed as one organic whole. "One is, at once, in every moment of time, historian, contemporary analyst, and prophet—not three separate roles." (Robert Greenleaf) The leader must keep alert to God's hope for us and continually ask for his will to be done. Leaders are "...people with enough imagination to pursue a new vision, value adventure over personal safety, and be challenged by situations that make most people anxious."[8] "God is a God of the present and reveals to those who are willing to listen carefully to the moment in which they live the steps they are to take toward the future."[9] Leaders ask, "What is the real future of this organization? Do present conditions offer any possibilities of doing things differently? What are our greatest unfilled opportunities? Have I assessed the widest possible range of choices?" As Greenleaf describes it, "Vision is the ability to see potential worthwhile possibilities. And these possibilities must then be taken on as a challenge. So the visionary must not only see new things but must also act on them, assuming the responsibility for their investigation and initial cultivation. New things must be actually started, not just dimly conceived. Interest must be generated, and this is often the hardest part with unreceptive audiences."

On a more immediate front, vision takes the form of *foresight*, the ability to anticipate what is likely to happen in the near future and take appropriate preparatory action; to try, if you will, to "peer around the corner" to see if any trouble lies ahead that can be avoided. Greenleaf calls this "contingency thinking, ...anticipating what is likely to happen and taking precautionary steps." Foresight gives leaders sufficient perspective to not be surprised by the unusual and to be prepared to respond promptly.

Church trustees are generally charged with fashioning the congregation's dream of the future. It is important that this be an *assigned* systematic duty not merely an option (see Chapter 10, "Leadership Roles," for assigned trustee duties, page 129).

Listen Attentively and Responsively

Many people are looking for an ear that will listen. They do not find it among Christians, because these Christians are talking where they should be listening." —Dietrich Bonhoeffer

Leaders should be eager to listen, generous with their time, and appreciative of everyone's ideas. One of the worst faults is for office holders to be so impressed with the wisdom and virtue that rank conveys as to not take the dissent of subordinates and outsiders seriously. Leaders must understand the absolute need to surround themselves with capable subordinates and *listen to them*. The reasons are numerous. God speaks to us through what others think and recommend. Open forums are democratic, involving all in leadership. Discussion leads to understanding and consensus among participants. Careful listening results in new creative ideas, problem solutions, and constructive criticism. Finally, it is surprising how many issues advocates drop once they believe they have been properly heard. In fact, listening is one of the most critical elements of a healthy organization. Organizations that don't listen are headed for trouble. We discuss effective listening in Chapter 11, "Communications and Planning."

Focus on Priorities and Results[10]

Note: Setting organizational priorities and designing programs based on demonstrated performance are parts of a larger rubric of mission definition and program planning and monitoring, topics of *Part III. Church Structure and Leadership Roles*, and *Part IV. Leadership in Practice*.

The Christian church exists to love, obey, and serve God and spread the "good news." These are the *priorities* and reason for our very being. How can such focus come about? First we must fully recognize and accept our responsibility to God alone as an external commitment transcending all human boundaries. This holy devotion gives true understanding of the church's mission and meaning to all its endeavors. Thus in Christ we seek real converts, not improved attendance; inspirational guidance, not polished rhetoric; true sharing, not re-distribution; joyful giving, not funding; and so on. Then, in this holy context we are able to adjust our efforts in terms of both ends and means, directing our efforts towards Christian goals, and succeeding through his guidance and grace.

Mission selection. We know that all good works are commendable in God's sight apart from any dependent returns. Is the number of converts counted on two hands not worth a lifetime of mission? We therefore seek first obedience to our commission, always joyful in knowing God blesses our calling. For Christians, *service* is the operative word, the harvest provided by the Lord. *Then he said to his disciples, "The harvest is plentiful, but the laborers are few." "I am the vine, you are the branches. Whoever remains in me, and I in him, will bear much fruit; for you can do nothing without me. This is how my Father's glory is shown; by your bearing much fruit; and in this way you become my disciples."* (John 15:5,8)

The principal management responsibility of the church council is that of establishing mission priorities (see Chapter 9, page 102). Some councils are comfortable simply listing every commission without priority, "covering all the bases" so to speak. But in reality, congregations typically gravitate toward their strengths and favoring conditions.

Resources are invariably limited, opportunities often are location dependent. Consequently, congregations gradually establish their agendas as much by assimilation as deliberate decision. And the alignment is invariable reasonable, if not optimal. However, rethinking priorities must follow as a yearly refining exercise and to accommodate changing conditions (see following "Program Evaluation" section).

Entrusted to do our best. Our dependency on God does not allow us to waste our time and talent in idle fashion. That would be foolish and negligent. Good intentions, well meaning actions, need to be accompanied by productive effort. Beyond fostering spiritual growth, the most important work of any church council is to see that the congregation effectively serves the Lord, that is, engages all in achieving Christ-oriented results. *"The man to whom much is given, of him much is required; the man to whom more is given, of him much more is required."* (Luke 12:48) Thus church activities must be "rigorously weighted against the standard of purpose." (John Carver) Choice of how we do something (means) is then determined chiefly by whether it produces the expected results (ends).

Means mistaken for ends. As W. A. Kirk charges, governing boards too frequently "become so engrossed in doing an infinite variety of discrete things, pursuing an endless number of routines, that they lose sight of the results, if any, that the activities are supposed to accomplish."[11] "An organization can become so permeated by the belief that well-intended or reasonable actions (rather than the results) are the reason for existence that no one realizes something is awry. Services and programs are often treated as if they have value in themselves...rather than means to some end." (Carver) G. S. Odiorne (management consultant and author) describes the confusion this way, "People tend to become so engrossed in activity that they lose sight of its purpose...and the activity becomes a false goal, an end in itself."[12] Thus both observers warn of "insidious counterfeits," activities associated with good intentions accepted as legitimate endeavors without demonstrable achievement.

Program evaluation. The most neglected management responsibility of church councils is the evaluation of ends. "How are we doing?" is simply never asked. Perhaps the all-too-possible negative consequences put everyone ill at ease. And, admittedly, challenging program value can be a risky, disruptive business if done in a sporadic, haphazard manner. It must be done in as "precise, systematic, non-intrusive, and criteria-focused" manner as possible. (Carver) Special assessment sessions can be held between the involved actors and observers in a non-threatening, supportive, and constructive context. Subject individuals should feel invigorated and replenished by a properly conducted performance audit.

In practice, program evaluation requires the church council and committees to be constantly vigilant to the effectiveness of each and every sponsored activity, i.e., that they are actually accomplishing what they intend to do and are not merely ends in themselves. The value of each activity in terms of desired outcomes, must then be weighed against alternative resource use. "Is what we're doing, serving the Lord as best we're able?" Such "outcome" testing should be applied in detail, down to, for example, selection of individual Sunday school class content. There is no excuse, for example, in teaching a younger group "Comparative Religions" when they would welcome and benefit more from a class on "Contemporary Ethics."

Outcome measurement is not easy; however, evidence of some sort is almost always present. One can well begin with available physical counts–attendance, contributions, enrollment, contacts, distribution, etc. Over time, such indicators may reveal significant trends. But counts are only indicative of quantity. What we really seek from service programs are spiritual and psychological understanding and growth. And this information can be gained by carefully interviewing the involved consumers. "How did you like the sermon?" "What music would you prefer?" "Why didn't you attend?" Whenever possible, participants should be invited to complete an evaluation questionnaire. The tabulated responses can then be converted into permanent "lessons learned" instructions for planning future similar events.

Evaluation should also consider returns relative to their cost, primarily in terms of alternative human assignments. Thus the third "greeter" would probably be better employed talking with members after the Sunday service. The rule is simple, the next best alternative use must be inferior to that selected. Often the subject individual best knows the relative importance of the assignments involved.

Be Alert to Problems, Solving in an Orderly, Scholarly Manner

With respect and trust, parishioners of differing viewpoints should reason together toward common goals. This means engaging in logical, rational, and analytical thought. Study and analysis play a far more important role in problem solving than most people understand. No matter how dynamic the leader, or knowledgeable, the complexity of today's world and problems demand study. The leader's role is to ensure that such study includes deliberate open hearings; informed and frank discussion of issues; encouragement of minority viewpoints; and the seeking of expert testimony. At the start, the leader should require that problems be clearly and cogently stated along with possible solutions and their relative merits. All investigation should be done with the involved parties' agreement and participation. This preparation gets everyone off on the same informed footing. Problem solving procedures are discussed in Chapter 12, "How to Conduct Meetings and Reach Decisions."

Seek the truth always. Leaders should have "a lively, disinterested, persistent liking for the truth." (Henri Frederic Amiel, 1821-1881, Swiss philosopher) Christians, are specially aided in this endeavor, enabled to see God's truth through the Holy Spirit. Jesus said *"When the Spirit of truth comes, you will be guided into all the truth."* (John 16:13) With this invincible aid the church servant leader seeks to solve problems through prayer, Bible reading, and intellectual study.

As we have emphasized elsewhere, initially getting the situation straight is critical to successful problem resolution. Part of every controversy is misunderstanding of the facts[13] involved and the opponent's position. Appointing an independent study group generally separates hard information from opinions and allows time for participants to "cool off" as well.

Pursue all sources of guidance and information. Those involved are always a primary source of information. Obviously, the vast bulk of knowledge required in problem-solving resides not in any single individual, leader or not, but in the substantial numbers of people being led. Thus it is important to tap this immediate source through personal and group discussions, and study groups. Contacts may then be expanded by interviews, surveys, and site visits. References should be studied. Finally, if additional help is required, consultants may be employed. Throughout, Bible study and prayer are a constant aid. Pursuing these multiple sources is discussed in Chapter 11 as part of communications.

It should be clear that involving everyone in problem study does not lessen the leader's control or responsibility. Quite the opposite, extending involvement insures that the leader's position is brought forward, not as a personal directive with possible negative connotations, but rather as one of a many advanced alternatives. Edmund Burke wrote "...a representative owes the people not only his industry, but his judgment, and he betrays them if he sacrifices it to their opinion." So the leader must advance his or her own ideas, rigorously if necessary, but always in the context of competition with others. To do this willingly, leaders must have confidence in their own status and ideas, and be prepared to surrender credit to the group. This is what the *servant* aspect of leadership is all about.

Problem awareness extends to trustees and council operations. Problems originating within an organization's own governing structure are often least subject to scrutiny. Trustees and councils are not immune to flaws, often with the most serious consequence. As Peter Drucker (writer and consultant in business strategy and policy) has famously observed, boards have one thing in common, "They do not function." The irony, pointed out by John Carver, is that where opportunity for leadership is greatest, study and guidance for board leadership is poorest. Thus the focus here on the church's governing structure.

In *Boards That Make a Difference*, Carver cites various debilitating conditions[14] common to a degree in almost every senior governing board. Church councils are especially susceptible to these four:

Vague authority lines. Whenever authority is not clearly defined in coordinated job descriptions, items in question will invariably be shuffled upward to the highest authority. Such overburdening transfer must quickly be dispelled by establishing to whom the decision properly belongs, preferably at the lowest echelon possible.

Time spent on the trivial. While board members understand the need to deal with first things first, they may not agree on how to or even begin to order their agenda. In this confusion, they often lapse into grappling with small details with which they are familiar leaving unaddressed items of importance and possible complexity. As the old story goes, "The board spent 15 minutes discussing the multi-million dollar bond issue which was apparently beyond their grasp, and two hours on the location of the company's bicycle racks in which they felt quite confident." Such misfocus can be minimized by distributing pre-meeting information sheets, agenda ordering, and strict meeting control, all topics discussed in Chapter 12.

Short-term bias. Immediate "pressing" problems invariability supersede distant broader concerns. This close focus is so frequently necessary and time-consuming that we recommend church councils transfer, if appropriate, the visionary role to appointed trustees (see Chapter 10, pages 129-133). This delegation ensures that oversight and long-range planning are always attended to.

Monitoring and reactive stance. Senior boards are inclined to spend far too much time reviewing what the organization's operatives are doing and too little time proactively creating their own agenda. Church committees must be well staffed, given firm "marching instructions," and then largely weaned from further supervision. Our recommended governance model also encourages delegation of long-range studies to the church trustees, further freeing the council for large issues, external focus, and similar forward thinking.

Manage Conflict; Be Generous and Conciliatory

...all of you be in agreement and that there be no divisions among you, but that you be united in the same mind and the same purpose.
(1 Corinthians 1:10)

Some form of conflict is almost inevitable in a parish of different people with different needs and ideas how to fulfill those needs. Such conflict arises from the varying life experiences of individuals, differences in education and reasoning processes, and, perhaps most importantly, the resulting values held. Whatever the cause, leaders must strive to prevent the divisiveness and hostility likely to emanate from such factions. Discussions should always be kept on an academic level and impersonal, opposing views honored. Debate should be constructive not antagonistic, with petty arguments promptly dismissed. *But stay away from foolish and ignorant arguments; you know that they end up in quarrels.* (2 Timothy 2:23)

Harmony is easy to advise, but difficult to accomplish when each side is convinced they are right. To prevent these occurrences, the leader must personally remain calm and unflappable, concentrating on fostering understanding and resolution. Meetings should start and end with prayer, beseeching God's guidance and recognizing that all good things come from him. Opponents should be encouraged to relax and recognize value in the others' position. Summarizing the advantages and disadvantages of both sides helps and may lead to compromise solutions. Deadlocks can be resolved by trial testing or delaying decisions until further information is provided.

The Nature of Disagreements

We tend to agree with others when hard facts are readily available and in highly technical areas beyond our grasp. Thus few are sufficiently knowledgeable to debate issues in the hard sciences, economics, law, and medicine, fields requiring specialized education. On the other hand, everyone has an opinion on religion, politics, and the arts, matters close at hand and generally understood. The lesson here is that disagreements are common in personally encountered *subjective* areas, where "Bias and impartiality is in the eye of the beholder." –Lord Barnett, British Conservative politician.

Disagreement thus commonly occurs in matters of style, priorities, and direction, areas readily subject to personal interpretation and judgment. As comic strip character Charlie Brown says, "I'm best at matters of opinion." At the other extreme are long held, firmly entrenched, personal values essentially immune to outside influence. The cognitive distinctions involved can be defined in five degrees, listed here in descending order of frequency encountered and increasing order of severity of disruption:

1. **Style and taste**–personal preferences for distinctive features of expression, execution, and performance.
2. **Relative emphasis**–special attention or priority attached to something singled out.
3. **Direction**–a course of action toward a perceived end or goal such as vision and mission statements and expressed expectations.
4. **Principles**–rules and policies guiding behavior.
5. **Beliefs**–something accepted as true and fundamental, often without proof.

Sources and Severity of Conflicts

Disagreements often occur during the creation of new programs when numerous alternatives are possible and everyone has an opinion. They are also common when programs go astray, and criticism abounds. In-between, when operations are running smoothly, few are sufficiently concerned to raise questions. Common problem **sources** include:

(1) Lack of a clear vision and purpose. Multiple expectations tend to conflict and frustrate the various advocates leading to dissatisfaction and irritation.
(2) Operations go bad. Conflict often accompanies failed activities or expectations not met. It is important to realize that the reality of ideas and projects may emerge only when they are tested under the worst possible conditions. Judgment should accordingly be reserved
(3) Controlling pastoral or laity authority, typically evident in invasive involvement at all levels and prohibiting approval procedures.
(4) Choice of liturgical and musical style.
(5) Growth and change versus stability and preservation. This conflict can also be identified as a clash between visionaries and those more practically responsible.[15]

The **severity** of disagreements largely depends on the degree of difference involved, and the emotional attachment present. Modestly held matters of style and emphasis, for example, can usually be easily accommodated. Changing cherished rituals, on the other hand, is likely to arouse strong feelings of resentment.

Means of Lessening Conflict

Disagreements are a natural and healthy part of progress. Conflicts, on the other hand, are disagreements gone astray.

Distinguish and encourage constructive criticism. "We must not confuse dissent with disloyalty." –Edward R. Murrow (1908-1965), U.S. broadcast journalist.

The most unwelcome communication is criticism, and congregation leadership is no exception. Everyone wants to be comfortable, balanced, unchallenged. As Oswald Chambers characterizes, "criticism is love turned sour." Consequently, in the spiritual life there is no room for adverse criticism except against sin. We substitute instead constructive advice, lovingly given as an intercession, entreat, or petition. The means for its delivery include a receptive staff and congregational leaders, deliberate inclusion and study of alternatives, open discussion forums, annual evaluations, ombudsman, surveys, and suggestion systems. And, less this seem too soft and yielding, let there be no doubt that on occasion constructive advice must be delivered with vigor to maintain pressure and vigilance, disrupt complacency, ferret out ills, and provide new challenging options.

The value of compromise. While compromise solutions are not perfect and seldom fully satisfy either side, they are workable and can be improved with experience. Often the answer to controversies lies somewhere in the middle. The advantage of a compromise solution is that it can be repeatedly revised until all, or most everyone, are satisfied. So leaders must be generous, proportioning some return to the minority, and acquiescent in small matters.

The potential for disagreement is greatly lessened by the amount of associated work involved. Arguments flow freely when there are no strings attached. On the other hand, issues are often resolved amicably if dissenters know they will face the task of implementing whatever changes they advocate. It is surprising how quickly problems are resolved favoring the path of least personal commitment. Consider your own response to these challenges. "If you want to do it that way we'll make you chairman of the task force." "Would you like to teach the course you prefer?" "To clarify your position, please prepare a short position paper." The old euphemism "talk is cheap" is too often true. Real dissent is constructive and substantive with an implied service commitment.

Conflict Sources Within Congregations

Unresolved conflict within congregations is disruptive and unacceptable. Associated roadblocks must be discovered and remedied. Personal obstructionist behavior typically requiring individual counseling includes:
   1. Stubbornness, simple unwillingness to listen to opposing views and accede to the majority regardless of proposal merit.
   2. Disagreement arising out of personality conflicts or personal animosity. .
   3. Excessive pastoral or council authority.
   4. Control by a small clique of powerful members.

Other hindrances to problem resolution related to personal outlook that may occasionally be amenable to outside influence and pressure include:
   1. Long held imbedded opinions, concepts, and allegiances, possibly so ingrained as to be immutable, beyond any force of reason or persuasion.
   2. Differences in fundamental philosophy such as practical and expedient versus challenging and visionary.
   3. Entrenched positions on controversial social issues such as abortion, death penalty, homosexuality, immigration policy, war.

Rules for Conflict Resolution
<u>Preparatory and safeguards</u>
   1. In sensitive issues, commit to dealing only with first-party information.
   2. Affirm with all participants the brotherhood of all in Christ and commitment to working constructively together.
   3. Review the rules of working together in good faith with all deliberations to be performed in a respectful conciliatory manner. Dissenters are loyal members also.
   4. Explain that conflicts are a normal, inevitable part of doing business and can be effectively and systematically resolved through open discussion and cooperation.

5. Establish a safe and fair listening environment, open and responsive to all. Explain the importance of careful, patient listening.
6. If encountered, caution, then disengage chronic troublemakers and individuals harboring personal animosities. Divisiveness and personal ego must not be allowed to lead participants

Analyses
1. Make sure from the beginning that there is a clear accepted understanding of the goals involved.
2. Identify and examine any assumptions made to ensure their applicability and validity.
3. Gather facts and supporting information. Share findings with all. Listen with fairness and patience to all viewpoints. Note that some highly relevant information may involve perceived injustices and past personal hurts. This content must be treated with sensitivity and discretion.
4. Agree on the order of priority in working on issues. Work on one issue at a time.
5. Begin by identifying the central conditions and/or reasons for disagreement. Look first for strengths in each position and common ground. Focus on developing areas of understanding and agreement that may subsequently resolve or encompass areas of disagreement.
6. Use tools such as negotiation and brainstorming to come to an agreement. A willingness to compromise is essential. To resolve conflicts, exact positions must first be clarified, then attempt to find a shared resolution, followed lastly by some form of compromise.

Decision and implementation
1. The problem/conflict resolution process consists of fact-gathering, study/analysis, discussion, and decision. When consensus is not obtained, decisions may be reached by majority rule or resolved temporarily by postponement to allow continued study or trial-testing. Mediation by a neutral trained third party is typically the last resort.
2. The choice should be implemented with respect for any existing opposition, but not subjugation.

Location of Related Content
The nature of conflict and its resolution are dealt with in other contexts in additional locations within this book:
Promote Democratic Action, p. 39.
Combat Domination, Build Diversity, Encourage Agreement, p. 42.
Safeguarding Democracy, p. 67.
Manage Conflict; Be Generous and Conciliatory, p. 88.
Democracy, the Foundation of the Servant-Led Congregation, p. 116.

Encouraging Vision, Creativity, and Criticism, p. 150.
The Ombudsman, p. 153.
The Meeting Proper–Deliberations, p. 170.
Alternatives to Consensus, p. 172.

---

[1] Three recent books address servant leadership for congregational laity: David Young, *Servant Leadership for Church Renewal* (Scottdale, PA, Herald Press, 1999), referenced in Chapter 6; Harold E. Bauman, *Congregations and Their Servant Leaders,* (Scottdale, PA, Mennonite Publishing House, 1982), cited in Chapters 11 and 12 ; and Bennett J. Sims, *Leadership for the Third Millennium* (Boston, Cowley Press, 1997), quoted in Chapter 5. All three volumes are excellent.

Sims' work is especially relevant and supplemental to the present chapter. Some selected observations warrant quotation.

This, then, is the work of the servant leader as I now define it, "... *to honor the personal dignity and worth of all who are led, and to evoke as much as possible their own innate creative power for leadership.*

...a servant leader concentrates on building up the people, not on polishing the system or the leader's self-importance.

Servant leadership defines success as giving, and measures achievement by devotion to serving.

The servant leader...thinks: I am the fellow human whose *responsibility* it is to love and guide this family, to serve and lead the parish, to point the direction for this company, to stimulate the learning process in the classroom.

The important lesson for leadership here is that real power rises from authenticity, not from appearances or manipulation. Real leadership is never wizardry. It always springs from unpretentious humanity. What this means is that an easy humanness is the foundation of servanthood.

[2] The content of this chapter is heavily indebted to Robert K. Greenleaf, *The Power of Servant Leadership*, Chapter 5, "The Servant as Religious Leader" (San Francisco, Berrett-Koehler, 1998).

[3] Oswald Chambers, one of the great Christian thinkers of our time. During his short life (1874-1917) Chambers served as founder and principal of the Bible Training College in Clapham, London, and later ministered to Australian and New Zealand troops in Egypt during World War I. Throughout the twenty years of his ministry he wrote continuously, authoring 29 books still in print, including the classic *My Utmost for His Highest.* His belief is characterized by a child-like trust in God and self-discipline. Perhaps the best introduction to Chambers is to read *Oswald Chambers: The Best From All His Books* (Nashville, Oliver-Nelson Books, 1987).

[4] The "tipping" concept was introduced by Malcolm Gladwell. See Malcolm Gladwell, *The Tipping Point: How Little Things Can Make a Big Difference* (Boston: Little, Brown, 2000).

[5] Making decisions "on our knees" is attributed to Pope John Paul II (1920-2005). "I am so busy," Martin Luther said at the height of the Reformation "that unless I pray more hours every day I won't get my work done."

[6] Greenleaf, *The Power of Servant Leadership*, p. 31.

[7] Cited in Charles E. Bennison, Jr. et al., *In Praise of Congregations: Leadership in the Local Church Today* (Cambridge: Cowley Publications, 1999), p. 222.

[8] Bennison, *In Praise of Congregations*, p. 225.

[9] Henri J. M. Nouwen, *In the Name of Jesus* (New York, Crossroad Publishing Company, 1998), p.3.

[10] This section is highly indebted to John Carver, Chapter 4, "Focusing on Results," *Boards That Make a Difference* (San Francisco, Jossey-Bass Publishers, 1997).

[11] W. A. Kirk, cited in Carver, *Boards That Make a Difference*, p. 53.

[12] G. S. Odiorne, cited in Carver, *Boards That Make a Difference*, p. 54.

[13] Use of facts always reminds me of the delightful Charles Dickens quotation from *Hard Times*. "Now, what I want is, Facts. Teach these boys and girls nothing but Facts. Facts alone are wanted in life. Plant nothing else, and root out everything else. You can only form the minds of reasoning animals upon Facts: nothing else will ever be of any service to them. This is the principle on which I bring up my own children, and this is the principle on which I bring up these children. Stick to the Facts, sir!"

[14] Carver, *Boards That Make a Difference*, pp. 9-10.

[15] The role of visionary versus practitioner is well illustrated by this story. Stephen T. Mather, Superintendent of Parks, selected George Goodwin as his highway engineer to design the central access road to Glacier National Park. He also employed Thomas Vint, a leading architect to provide counsul. There was bitter disagreement between the two men regarding the road's location. Goodwin proposed a practical expedient route along the lower reaches of the Park. Vint's location was high up on the mountain side, scaling Logan Pass at the Continental Divide, involving great engineering difficulties and cost. The three men rode on horseback along the proposed higher route to Logan Pass. Vint won out. Completed in 1932, the "Going to the Sun" road is now one of the world's most beautiful, a lasting tribute to visionary thinking and making the right choice.

Part III.
Church Structure and Leadership Roles

Chapter 9
Statements and Organization

Come as living stones, and let yourselves be used in building the spiritual temple, where you will serve as holy priests to offer spiritual and acceptable sacrifices to God through Jesus Christ. (1 Peter 2:5)

This chapter begins Part III, which together with Part IV, "Leadership in Practice," constitute the working components of this volume. Saint Peter says we should be like living stones to be built together into a spiritual house. This chapter explains how this temple of believers fits form to function by its guiding statements and organizational structure.

The church on earth is the living body of Christ, sacred, commissioned, ever changing, subject to man's building and tearing down. It has three intra-functioning parts—members, leaders, and structure. The last component, the organization structure, establishes how we work together. Structure plays a larger role in our success than generally understood because it guides individual performance, utilizes specialization, and multiplies effort through marshalling and grouping. Poor organization is a great detriment. Sin can actually be involved, inhibiting and restricting by form and function, either accidental or intended. So, as William Easum says, congregations must be "designed and structured to introduce people to Christ in a language that they can understand and respond to with integrity." The purpose of this chapter is to assist in this design and structuring. Each church, however, as a complex and unique multifaceted entity, must tailor its own design.

This chapter is divided into two divisions—church statements, and church constitution and organization. The two are interrelated in the sense that some statements such as articles of faith and mission are usually contained in the church's constitution. However, our division treats the various statements collectively as matters of outlook and *philosophy*, and the operational aspects of constitution and organizational structure as separate aspects of church *management*.

Church Statements

The purpose of church statements is to establish firm evidence of the congregation's beliefs and intent. They focus and guide church activities. They are written as "articles of faith," church "constitution," "goals," etc., each of which will be described in this chapter. All are living entities, interlocking and mutually reinforcing. Such statements should be placed in a "documents" booklet, distributed to members. As an act of reaffirmation, the statements should be periodically reviewed, updated, and approved with rededication and confidence. Statements transient in nature, such as church goals, should be reviewed frequently, perhaps even yearly during changing conditions. Certain guidance related to operations, consistently employed, such as job descriptions, authority lines, and coordination and approval procedures, may also require separate earmarked periodic distribution in addition to inclusion in the collective documents volume.

The updating of church statements requires care and discernment. God continually speaks to us. We must be alert to hear. *"And what I say to you I say to all: Keep awake."* (Mark 13:37) Congregations must pray to have "eyes to see, ears to hear, and a mind that may know God's will." Typically, a special group must be convened to conduct the review. Their mission, to seek God's true calling for the congregation. The review must be both introspective and outward looking. A thorough inquiry requires study, reflection, reading, interviews with congregational members, discussions, and drafting and redrafting. To discern what God wants a congregation to do and how he wants it done is altogether a difficult and time-consuming task. Prayer, bible reading, and diligent reordering are the keys. *Prepare the way of the Lord, make straight his paths.* (Matthew 3:3)

We must also add that church statements must in no way establish any hierarchy, authority, or procedure that discourages joyful entry into the body of Christ and enthusiastic service. Such restraints are what we referred to earlier as a "sin" of the organization.

The statements presented in this chapter are as follows in order of their dependency, i.e., each succeeding statement is based upon and engendered by its predecessors:

*Articles of faith**
Emerging conditions
Mission statement and directional concepts*
<u>Operating principles</u>
<u>Church policy</u>
Public policy

While the list of entries may seem excessive to some, few churches in fact have all six, each is distinctive and supportive of the whole. The two italicized statements–*Articles of faith* and *Operating principles*–are underlying and generally subject to little change. The two underlined statements–<u>Operating principles</u> and <u>Church policy</u>–have the greatest affect on day-to-day operations. The asterisk indicates statements typically contained in the church constitution.

Articles of Faith

Organizations based on faith must necessarily begin their corporate existence with the beliefs on which they are founded. Christians take great comfort from these articles, for they transcend all human frailties and misery, promising eternal life for all believers. They reaffirm the theological basis for us to join together and serve as a church entity. In all things the congregation returns again and again for comfort and strength to these underlying precepts.

The confession of faith should be written in simple language for all to understand. While expressed in words suitable for each congregation, the statements are based on denominational creeds and sanctions. Bible passages are usually referenced for each article. Model articles may be obtained from the various denominations, actual articles from individual congregations.

The most common articles can be stated as follows:

1. <u>HOLY TRINITY</u>

We believe that there is one true God, eternally existing in three persons–the Father, the Son, and the Holy Spirit–three-in-one.

The grace of the Lord Jesus Christ, the love of God, and the fellowship of the Holy Spirit be with you all. (2 Corinthians 13:13)

2. <u>CHRIST'S ADVENT</u>

Jesus Christ is the eternal Son of God, the Living Word, who came into the world that he might manifest God to men, fulfill prophecy, and become redeemer of the world. He is the perfect deity and true humanity united in one person. Jesus lived a sinless life on earth and voluntarily atoned for the sins of men by dying on the cross as their substitute, thus satisfying divine justice and accomplishing salvation for all who trust in Him alone. We believe that, He arose from the dead in the same body, though glorified, and ascended into heaven and now sits at the right hand of God the Father, where He is the only mediator between God and man, continually making intercession for His own. Jesus Christ is the head and authority of the Church.

The Word became a human being and lived among us. We saw his glory, full of grace and truth. This was the glory he received as the Father's only son. (John 1:14) *For Christ himself died for you; once and for all he died for sins, a good man for bad men, in order to lead you to God.* (1 Peter 3:18) *"For the Son of Man came to seek and to save the*

lost." (Luke 19: 10) *I write you this, my children, so that you will not sin; but if anyone does sin, we have Jesus Christ, the righteous, who pleads for us with the Father. For Christ himself is the means by which our sins are forgiven, and not our sins only, but also the sins of all men.*
(1 John 2:1-2)

3. SCRIPTURE
The Bible is the inspired word of God leading to Jesus Christ and designed for our practical instruction.

For all Scripture is inspired by God and is useful for teaching the truth, rebuking error, correcting faults, and giving instruction for right living, so that the man who serves God may be fully qualified and equipped to do every kind of good work. (2 Timothy 3:16-17) *For I have complete confidence in the gospel: it is God's power to save all who believe, first the Jews and also the Gentiles.* (Romans 1:16)

4. HUMANKIND
Man and woman were created in God's image yet are now burdened with original sin as a result of Adam's first act of disobedience. Man is therefore unable to please God except by renewal through divine grace. Through faith we are forgiven and healed as a gift from God.

So God created man in his own image, in the image of God created he him; male and female created he them. (Genesis 1:27) *...and all men have sinned and are far away from God's saving presence. But by the free gift of God's grace they are all put right with him through Christ Jesus, who sets them free.* (Romans 2:23) *For I am certain that nothing can separate us from his love: neither death nor life; neither angels nor other heavenly rulers or power; neither the present nor the future; neither the world above nor the world below–there is nothing in all creation that will ever be able to separate us from the love of God which is ours through Christ Jesus our Lord.* (Romans 8:38)

5. SALVATION
The world is redeemed through our savior Jesus Christ's death and resurrection. The assurance of salvation is not based on any kind of human merit, but is produced by a new birth of the believer which comes through the Holy Spirit.

"I tell you the truth," replied Jesus, "that no one can enter the Kingdom of God unless he is born of water and the Spirit." (John 3:5) *Now that we have been put right with God through faith, we have peace with God through our Lord Jesus Christ. He has brought us, by faith, into this experience of God's grace, in which we now live.* (Romans 5:1-2) *I write you this so that you may know that you have eternal life–you that believe in the name of the Son of God.* (1 John 5:13)

6. THE HOLY SPIRIT

The Holy Spirit, the third person of the Trinity, lives in every believer as Spiritual counselor, and is the source of all power and acceptable worship and service.

The Helper will come—the Spirit of truth, who comes from the Father. I will send him to you from the Father, and he will speak about me." (John 15:26)

7. THE CHURCH

The church is the Body of Christ composed of all believers who have been joined to Him through saving faith. God has ordained the church to proclaim the Good News of Jesus Christ throughout the world, to conduct worship services, and to gather the faithful together for mutual encouragement and support.

God put all things under Christ's feet, and gave him to the church as supreme Lord over all things. The church is Christ's body, the completion of him who himself completes all things everywhere. (Ephesians 1:22-23) *"Go, then, to all peoples everywhere and make them my disciples."* (Matthew 28:19)

8. THE FINAL JUDGMENT

The prophecy will be fulfilled. Jesus Christ will come again to the earth to receive to himself into Heaven his own.

There will be a shout of command, the archangel's voice, the sound of God's trumpet, and the Lord himself will come down from heaven! Those who have died believing in Christ will be raised to life first; then we who are living at that time will all be gathered up along with them in the clouds to meet the Lord in the air. And so we will always be with the Lord. (1 Thessalonians 4:16-17)

9. SATAN

There exists a personal spirit of evil, Satan, enemy of God and the people of God. Satan, our adversary, carries on continuing opposition to the Kingdom of God, seeking the demise of all men. At the end he will suffer ultimate and total defeat at the hands of Jesus Christ.

How art thou fallen from heaven, O Lucifer, son of the morning! How art thou cut down to the ground, which didst weaken the nations! (Isaiah 14:12) *Be alert, be on watch! Your enemy, the Devil, roams around like a roaring lion, looking for someone to devour.* (1Peter 5:8)

10. ETERNAL LIFE

The saved will live with Christ forever in his glory.

"Then the King will say to the people on his right: 'You who are blessed by my Father: come! Come and receive the kingdom which has been prepared for you ever since the creation of the world.'" (Matthew 25:34)

Articles of faith are often expressed in simpler terms for general use as follows:[1]
1. God, the creator of all things, lives and governs all.
2. Jesus Christ, the son of God, teaches us the good news of spiritual living and brings forgiveness and healing through his death and resurrection.
3. Faith underlies and brings about all good. We believe, trust, and are confident in God's love and goodness.
4. Through prayer, and directed and empowered by the Holy Spirit living within us, we reach out to God in seeking to serve according to His will.
5. The Bible is the Word of God, our source of inspiration, and the ways of Christian living.
6. The peace from God, the grace of redemption, and the certainty of eternal life are the hallmarks of the Christian life.
7. Each person is an object of God's love and therefore the object of our love for one another. We do not judge, but rather teach, support, and comfort one another.

And, in simplest form, typically for broad distribution, articles of faith dealing with the church's relationship with people are often expressed as "**core values**." Consider this example:
- People matter to God and to us.
- The Gospel message transforms people's lives.
- Evangelism must be conducted in a meaningful manner relevant to every person.
- All people must be treated gently and respectfully.
- People need to be connected to a caring community.
- Every Christian has spiritual gifts for ministry.
- We seek excellence in all things.
- We must cultivate and value Godly leadership.
- Risk taking with faith is necessary for growth.

Emerging Conditions

People generally take most things for granted, reasonably assuming that day-to-day circumstances will remain essentially the same. Altogether different is the difficulty of seeing some distance ahead. Of such skills, fortunes have been made. The church also "profits" from such insight, not from any riches gained, but in new knowledge and awareness of emerging opportunities. Yet congregations place surprisingly little importance on the assessment of trends and forecasting, partly because most changes are so gradual that increments appear negligible and unimportant. "We kept losing a few members each year, until suddenly we realized we had no congregation!" No church wants to undergo disappointments or forego opportunities because of lack of foresight

Every few years a special task force should be convened to review the church environment in light of changing world, national, and local conditions. Their findings and implications should be presented to the congregation followed by any necessary response.

William Easum's list of "emerging conditions," reported in Chapter 2, page 8, illustrates the nature of such statements at the national level. At the local level, the church's changing environment may be examined in three ways:

(1) The **changing demography of the immediate surrounding community** may be examined in terms of past trends and short-term projections. What's happening to the neighborhood is of great consequence to church membership. Inner city churches in particular must be sensitive to their often rapidly changing surroundings. "We once were the center of activities in a long-standing older community; now we compete for the attention of younger, more transient and detached residents." Factors involved are population, family characteristics, racial composition, wealth, movement, and religious affiliation.

Most important to the church's outreach mission are local demographics of poverty, homelessness, crime, and immigrant population. The degree to which related needs are being met by others has a strong bearing on the church's selected role. Information to help in these analyses is generally available through published city demographic studies and local newspaper reports.

(2) The **changing status and composition of the congregation** itself is revealing. Where do new members come from and why did they join? What are the circumstances of departures? Is the membership aging? Are commuting distances increasing? And often most important, how is the membership talent pool and financial capacity to support the church changing? The answers need to be studied over time. Priorities may be revised, for example, if it is discovered that families now join for the children's program whereas they previously became members because the church was nearby. Information on the congregation can only be gained through a member survey.

(3) Evidence of **changing community mores and values** will help the church design appropriate responses. Examples of discernable attitudes include evidence of growing distrust of leaders, rising uncertainty and stress, increased division and polarization, decline in denominational allegiance (people simply want to be Christians), and greater concern for "spirituality" as opposed to organized religion. Many of these sociological changes are national in nature and their prevalence in a given community can be ascertained by limited polling, published studies, and newspaper accounts.

Mission Statement and Directional Concepts (Objectives)

The great commandments are to love God with all our heart, soul, and mind (Matthew 22:37), and to love our neighbor as ourselves (Matthew 22:37-39). We are further commissioned to go forth and make disciples of all people everywhere (Matthew 28:19). To do this we must be spiritually prepared which is also a commandment. *But you do not live as your human nature tells you to; you live as the Spirit tells you to–if, in fact, God's Spirit lives in you. Whoever does not have the Spirit of Christ does not belong to him.* (Romans 8:9) These are the mission responsibilities of all Christians. They are well summed up by Dietrich Bonhoeffer. "The first demand which is made of those who belong to God's Church is ....that they shall be witnesses to Jesus Christ before the world. It is for this task that the Holy Spirit equips those to whom He gives Himself. It is, of course, to be assumed that this testimony before the world can be delivered in the right way only if it springs from a hallowed life in the congregation of God." Note, first the outward look then the inward preparation. An evangelistic outreaching church always receives more than it gives, however generous in its benevolence. (See Chapters 20 and 21 on evangelism as an inreaching responsibility and outreach challenge.)

So commissioned, church mission statements might appear largely a settled matter. And in the highest sense they are, for in all things we seek God's will. But every congregation is also bound up in a unique set of circumstances and opportunities allowing, even mandating, special responses. This means that the congregation must discover for itself its own distinct calling. To do so involves an integration of scriptural guidance, member needs and talents, and community and society needs. The essential components are *who* is to be served, and secondarily *what* are their needs. We then respond in *how* these needs are to be satisfied.

But a church's mission is principally tied to *who* it seeks to serve. The choice depends primarily on spiritual calling, proximity and depth of need, and practical feasibility. Most churches develop their mission from local community needs. Discernment is important to avoid carbon copies. The mission must also naturally have the wholehearted endorsement and support of the congregation. It must inspire support and enrich the lives of members. Its distinction should engender pride. Strong mission statements also strengthen a church's boundaries and set its members apart. I know of one church whose evangelistic calling is so strong the pastor warns members that as a result they may often feel personally neglected and that this must be accepted as a necessary sacrifice for the mission. What an enrichment this mission!

Missions must not be left apart to become overly settled and latent. Sometimes goals are even lost sight of and must be chosen again. Congregations become distracted by what William Easum observes is a constant merry-go-round of meetings and taking care of facilities until we lose sight of our original mandate. Part of any misdirection may stem from a lack of specificity. Supporting policy statements provide this detail as a second echelon to the mission statement itself. They may include general courses of action, goals, priorities, and objectives, all introducing realism.

Multiple missions require ordering. Ordering awakens and motivates. It is critical when resources are limited. Spread too thin, the congregation's efforts are diluted, leading to marginal performance. Better to do a few things well than sacrifice the quality of all in undertaking too much. Ordering focuses and unifies the congregation's energy. It identifies those combinations of opportunities and abilities that result in the greatest overall member involvement and productive service. The smaller the congregation the greater the requirement for such concentration. Time is also an ordering factor. In some instances, special attention may be focused for a relatively short duration, sufficient only, for example, to bring a faltering program up to par.

Mission statements must be realistic. However receptive and enthusiastic a congregation may be to new challenges, much of what is hoped for may be limited by apparent or real restrictions. Historical precedent, geographical location and surrounding community, and congregational size and financial strength may all act to limit what appears possible. Sometimes a new set of circumstances intervene to alter and improve prospects. The arrival of a new pastor or completion of a capital building program, for example, can renew energy and free resources. Without such stimuli, congregations must simply stay positively alert to all potential challenges, believing in God's power to direct and marshal all that is required. As with Abraham and Moses, we must listen for God's voice and not fear to plunge into uncharted waters.

Most congregations begin their mission statement with a vision preface, a perceived image of a preferred future or promising outcome that guides and motivates. Together the two–vision and mission–can and should be stated simply as in the following example:[2]

Our Vision

That every person and community will discover and respond to the Kingdom of God embodied by Jesus Christ.

Our Mission

To nurture, equip, and embolden individuals and communities to:
— grow into the likeness of Jesus Christ,
— discover God's purpose for their lives, and
— respond in faith and through sacrificial action.

Substantially more detailed mission statements often include *directional concepts* (identified by • below) of intentions or objectives which add specificity. They may go so far as to quantify objectives such as a physical count of new members. Obstacles likely to be encountered may also be included. The resulting concepts/objectives combination introduces real intentions, reality that increases the likelihood that the congregation will take the mission seriously.

Mission and concept/objectives statements are illustrated as follows:[3]

A house of worship and prayer (to experience the living presence of God).

Jesus said, "Worship the Lord your God and serve only him!" (Matthew 4:11) *"God is Spirit, and those who worship him must worship in spirit and in truth."* (John 4:24) *Set your hearts on spiritual gifts, especially the gift of speaking God's message.* (1 Corinthians 14:1)

A transforming relationship with God through Jesus Christ is nurtured through an inward journey of prayer and study along with an outward journey of worship.

- Administer the sacraments of Holy Communion and Baptism.
- Establish a pulpit of excellence in the proclamation of the gospel of Jesus Christ.
- Provide opportunities for prayer, quiet meditation, discussion, and reconciliation in a faith context.
- Design the service to enhance the experience of every member and provide alternative services to meet the special needs and preferences of groups such as young people and newcomers.
- Preserve and enhance the architectural, musical, artistic, and cultural ministry.

A house of nurturing and involvement (a life-sharing fellowship community).

But continue to grow in the grace and knowledge of our Lord and Savior Jesus Christ. (2 Peter 3:18) *Each one, as a good manager of God's different gifts, must use for the good of others the special gift he has received from God.* (1 Peter 4:10)

Life is best lived and call genuinely discerned within a community of faith, support, and accountability.

- Assist every member in their spiritual journey, promoting life-long growth in discipleship. Use small groups to establish a sense of fellowship and mutual concern for one another.
- Instruct and encourage all to become involved in service, consistent with personal abilities and interest. Direct members to be faithful stewards of their talents and resources.
- Direct special attention to the well-being of children and young adults by providing a safe and nourishing environment, especially for those at risk. Strengthen family bonds.
- Develop new leaders by seeking out potential candidates, conducting training programs, and providing opportunities to lead.

A house to spread God's word (sharing God's power and love).

"Go, then, to all peoples everywhere and make them my disciples: baptize them in the name of the Father and of the Son and of the Holy

Spirit, and teach them to obey everything I have commanded you."
(Matthew 28:19-20)

Jesus Christ came to save all people and challenges us to pursue the challenge of spreading the Gospel message for all to hear.
- Go forth in the immediate community proclaiming God's good news boldly to bring residents into the folds of the church
- Sponsor domestic and foreign missions.

A house of Christian education (searching together).

Do not be like children in your thinking, brothers; be children so far as evil is concerned, but be mature in your thinking. (1 Corinthians 14:20) *Parents, do not treat your children in such a way as to make them angry. Instead, raise them with Christian discipline and instruction.* (Ephesians 6:4)

We are sustained and directed as we ground ourselves in biblical scripture.
- Expand programs of Christian education to include curriculum development and increased youth and adult participation.
- Train instructors how to teach. Use modern technology and the media to optimize the learning experience.
- Create opportunities for dialogue on national and international issues in a faith context.

A house of Christian service to others (serving to the very least one).

All the believers continued together in close fellowship and shared their belongings with one another. They would sell their property and possessions and distribute the money among all, according to what each one needed. (Acts 2:44-45)

God has a purpose for everyone and invites each of us to discern and live out that call.
- Develop a responsive social service presence concentrating on the local community.
- Maintain mutual support and sharing relationships with congregations and institutions in the area.
- Meet the ecumenical responsibilities inherent in membership of the greater church as a whole.
- Continue to play a role in interfaith dialogue, understanding, and cooperation.

From a different perspective, these six essential responsibilities commonly represent exceptional opportunities for quality church performance:
  (1) **Preaching effectiveness.**
  (2) **Music selection and performance.**
  (3) **Sunday school curriculum and teaching.**
  (4) **Member friendliness including personal attention to every individual and small group membership.**

(5) **Opportunities to serve others.**
(6) **Program of evangelism.**

Operating Principles

Principles are generalizations gained from experience that describe observed functional relationships in patterns of behavior. They are the apparent *natural processes* which underlie how humans work and function together. Principles are generally stated as a cause and effect, e.g., a smile conveys friendliness; harsh and unkind words create pain and lasting resentment. They indicate our understanding of the dynamics involved in human relations.

Principles pertaining to church operations are not easy to identify, but their importance to understanding *how* things can be most effectively accomplished warrant making an attempt. However, we must keep in mind Oswald Chambers' warning, "The authority we blindly grope after is God Himself, not a tendency making for righteousness, not a set of principles."

The following list of principles for effective human interaction relevant to congregational life is illustrative rather than definitive:

People respond to overtures of kindness and expressions of concern.

- Recognition and credit encourage performance.
- People are motivated by clear-cut reachable goals or sought end-results.
- Personal contributions are maximized when individual talents and skills are recognized and employed.
- Caring groups establish emotional involvement and honest communication.
- Small group discussions are most effective in fostering openness, self-examination, and in changing people's attitudes and values; a straight lecture is least effective.
- Conviction of the mission's importance creates cooperative wholeness for change and concerted effort.
- A singular and simple focus facilitates communication, e.g., the single "take-home" sermon message.
- The more vivid and intense the impression, the greater the chance of retention.
- Effective communication requires accessibility and listening receptivity.
- Written instructions and training greatly improve performance.
- Decentralization of authority and leadership encourage involvement, increasing productivity.
- A flat organizational structure distributes responsibility and authority, allows specialization, and facilitates vertical communication.

— Flexibility and adaptability are essential for success in new undertakings.
— Continuous evaluation and corrective feedback leads to improvement.
— Control and micro-management overloads operating units and stifles self-initiative and creativity.
— Sharing concerns with the neighborhood demonstrates the spirit of serving.

Church Policy

Policy is a *declaration of intentions*, the "rules of the game" if you will, the map and compass of operations. Policy statements are designed to *guide* operations in a harmonious and productive manner. They often implement approved operating principles (stated above). Church policies encourage cooperation, understanding, and patience, and recognition that the church's mission is a common task, not an individual one. With this important role, preparation of policy statements should never be neglected. Example statements of this type are:

It is the policy of the (church name) congregation to:

(1) Foster love and a caring covenant among members to the very least one. People matter to God and to us.

(2) Treat every congregational member gently and respectfully, knowing that each is equally important as a child of God and has a God-given ministry.

(3) Ensure that every member is encouraged to join one or more of the church's study, service, or fellowship groups.

(4) Promote stewardship through personal counseling and suitable advertisement of opportunities and needs.

(5) Encourage every member in personal evangelism.

(6) Promote personal spiritual growth by requiring periodic participation in church education programs.

(7) Design and conduct a comprehensive program of Christian education that meets the needs of all members.

(8) Provide a range of participation and leadership opportunities to all members, encouraging universal involvement according to individual abilities and calling.

(9) Facilitate attendance by holding meetings at convenient times and places.

(10) Encourage attendance at all meetings by an announced "open-door" policy.

(11) Begin every meeting with prayer, seeking God's guidance to do his will.

(12) Elect leaders who collectively represent the whole congregation.

(13) Seek excellence in all things by enlisting all available talents and remaining flexible and adaptable to new ideas and changing conditions.
(14) Always be receptive to new and creative ideas and suggestions. Be willing to step out in visionary faith and take risks for God.
(15) Solve problems through prayer, bible study, and scholarly inquiry and discussion.
(16) Earnestly seek pastoral guidance from God's emissary.
(17) Foster improvement in the spoken word through a lay pulpit advisory group.

Public Policy

Christian churches are always vitally concerned with social justice and public issues affecting human dignity and well-being. The involvement may be documented in a prepared position statement that responds to the issues from a biblical and theological foundation. Such papers are intended to be both instructive and persuasive, within the framework of individual interpretation. One indirect advantage of such dissemination is that it greatly lessens the need for contemporary politics from the pulpit. Below is an outline of public policy areas for which position statements have been prepared by the United Methodist Church[4]:

I. THE NATURAL WORLD
    A) *Water, Air, Soil, Minerals, Plants*
    B) *Energy Resources Utilization*
    C) *Animal Life*
    D) *Space*
    E) *Science and Technology*
    F) *Food Safety*

II. THE NUTURING COMMUNITY
    A) *The Family*
    B) *Other Christian Communities*
    C) *Marriage*
    D) *Divorce*
    E) *Single Persons*
    F) *Women and Men*
    G) *Human Sexuality*
    H) *Family Violence and Abuse*
    I) *Sexual Harassment*
    J) *Abortion*
    K) *Adoption*
    L) *Faithful Care of the Dying*
    M) *Suicide*

III. THE SOCIAL COMMUNITY
    A) *Rights of Racial and Ethnic Persons*
    B) *Rights of Religious Minorities*
    C) *Rights of Children*
    D) *Rights of Young People*
    E) *Rights of the Aging*
    F) *Rights of Women*
    G) *Rights of Persons with Disabilities*
    H) *Equal Rights Regardless of Sexual Orientation*
    I) *Population*
    J) *Alcohol & Other Drugs*
    K) *Tobacco*
    L) *Medical Experimentation*
    M) *Genetic Technology*
    N) *Rural Life*
    O) *Sustainable Agriculture*
    P) *Urban-Suburban Life*
    Q) *Media Violence and Christian Values*
    R) *The Internet*
    S) *Persons Living with HIV & AIDS*
    T) *Right to Health Care*
    U) *Organ Transplantation and Donation*

IV. THE ECONOMIC COMMUNITY
   A) Property
   B) Collective Bargaining
   C) Work and Leisure
   D) Consumption
   E) Poverty
   F) Migrant Workers
   G) Gambling
   H) Family Farms
   I) Corporate Responsibility

V. THE POLITICAL COMMUNITY
   A) Basic Freedoms and Human Rights
   B) Political Responsibility
   C) Freedom of Information
   D) Education
   E) Civil Obedience and Civil Disobedience
   F) Criminal and Restorative Justice
   G) Military Service

VI. THE WORLD COMMUNITY
   A) Nations and Cultures
   B) National Power and Responsibility
   C) War and Peace
   D) Justice and Law

Church Constitution and Organization

This chapter division briefly discusses the nature of church constitutions, church organizational structures of trustees, council, and committees, and the critical importance of job descriptions.

Church Constitution

Constitutions set forth an organization's governing system, describing its nature, functions, and structure. Denominational models are typically available. Certain provisions are generally required within religious affiliations. Specific internal details, applicable to a given congregation, are covered in bylaws and continuing resolutions.

A typical model constitution provided by the Evangelical Lutheran Church in America has these chapter components:

Preamble
1. Name and Incorporation
2. Confession of Faith
3. Nature of the Church
4. Statement of Purpose
5. Powers of the Congregation
6. Church Affiliation
7. Property Ownership
8. Membership
9. The Pastor
10. Congregation Meetings
11. Officers
12. Congregation Council
13. Congregation Committees
14. Organizations within the Congregation
15. Discipline of Members and Adjudication
16. Bylaws
17. Amendments
18. Continuing Resolutions
19. Indemnification
20. Parish Authorization

Constitutions, by-and-large, are mechanical in nature, underlying but minimally affecting day-to-day operations. The "constitutionality" of certain matters may occasionally be checked, but otherwise the document itself is seldom referred to. It remains an unseen church "backbone." Far more important in guiding behavior are the church's operating principles and policies. We emphasize their preparation and broadcast. Even articles of faith, though sacred and fundamental, are more likely to be viewed as reaffirmation of scripture than as working tools. Operating principles and church policy, on the other hand, whether documented or not, are what "moves and shakes" congregations. No congregation should be without both.

Church Organization

Leadership and organization are the ultimate collaborative effort between the congregation, the clergy, and God. Man and system work together, enjoined with the Holy Spirit to do God's will. It can be a very effective partnership. How we organize establishes how the work is shared. It plays a large role in the effectiveness of each individual. In military terms it is a "force multiplier." Therefore, every congregation should continuously seek to improve its organizational structure.

Organization starts with a church's mission statement and objectives, for we organize to achieve these purposes. Organization is also based on the principles of division of labor and specialization. Horizontal divisions are created to group like activities for reinforcement and coordination, and to marshal the special skills and talents required. Vertical division is created to allocate duties and responsibilities of control and management to provide direction and oversight.

For congregations, the organizational dimensions generally consist of two vertical operating levels,[5] the *council* with elected church officers, and a number of *standing committees* and temporary task forces creating the horizontal level. In addition, we recommend church "trustees" be named to provide senior level guidance and conduct special studies. Because of the involved complexity, it is always advisable to chart the church's organizational components together with brief descriptions.

An additional organizational dimension less often recognized is the *number* of leadership opportunities involved. Terms of office become a factor. Consider, for example, that a 12-member council with two-year terms has more than twice the number of individuals involved over a six-year period (total = 36) as an eight-member council with three-year terms (total = 16). Congregations should keep count and continuously seek to expand their leadership positions.

Several principles are involved in organizational structuring. First, *bureaucratic layering* of organizational levels should be kept to a minimum to facilitate vertical control and communication. Second, *delegation of responsibilities* should be made to the lowest level possible, consistent with recipient capabilities. This means giving properly staffed committees as much responsibility in their assigned area as their expertise permits. Third, *transfer authority equal to responsibility* since the two must work in tandem. Congregational committees should be given big jobs and told to run with them. Fourth, the *span of control* should not extend beyond what the involved authority can manage. This simply means don't overload the boss. The congregation president and council should oversee not micro-manage.

Some churches may feel the need to establish executive committees, deacons, and other high level offices. Some have intermediate levels between committees and the council. We believe such senior positions and organizational layers create or at least imply a hierarchical structure incompatible with the democratic nature of Christianity. Servant leadership advocates a minimal vertical dimension. "Layering" stifles initiative, creativity, and energy. It inhibits and slows upward communication. "We always felt the deacons were looking over our shoulder and it was inhibiting." "There were so many approvals required, we simply quit making suggestions." "Our division director always reported for us, so we felt out of the loop." Thus in the recommended church structure, committee chairs report to the church council, or, possibly, directly to the congregation.[6] (See Chapter 10, "Leadership Roles," pages 134-145, for council versus committee authority.)

Horizontal span of control can also be a problem, but is greatly lessened when committees are well staffed and left to work out their own problems. The design and advantages of the committee arrangement are also discussed in Chapter 10. In evaluating any church organization, keep in mind that the intent of the structuring is always twofold: (1) to identify and group similar core activities so that the necessary skills and talents can be assembled together for a collective, mutually supporting effort, and (2) to provide guidance (control) and coordination through a vertical overseeing structure.

Church Staff. The duties of the professional and operational church staff are generally supervised by the congregation pastor or, in very large churches, shared with a full-time administrative officer. Pastors may appropriately manage all routine staff duties, if so assigned, including day-to-day direction. However, the general functional responsibilities of key employed staff members should be overseen by the related congregational committees acting in an advisory role. Thus the church Director of Music also "reports" to the Worship and Music Committee; the Sunday School Superintendent to the Education Committee; the Church Treasurer to the Administration/ Property/Finance Committee and so on. This oversight may not sit well with some controlling pastors, but is essential if the congregation is to be fully interwoven in church operations and take greater responsibility. And, importantly, such commissioning, when employed, is at all times tempered by interwoven pastoral guidance, *always* essential, *always* sought.

Congregation Trustees. Trustees are an option, but one strongly recommended to perform broad oversight duties normally beyond the immediate concerns of the church council. Four important purposes are served: (1) to care for and support the council president/members and occasionally advise, (2) to conduct special studies and prepare general guidance papers, (3) to mentor potential young leaders, and (4) to provide additional honored opportunities for members to serve (as trustees). The role of church trustees is discussed in detail in Chapter 10, page 129.

Congregational Council. The church council has general oversight over the spiritual life and activities of the congregation seeing that everything is done in accordance with the Word of God. Its specific functions advised here are those of setting goals and priorities; staffing; monitoring, evaluating, and guiding activities; and long-range planning (sometimes referred to the trustees). The council guides the congregation in developing its mission and ministry and ensures peace and goodwill among members. Program administration and solving most operating problems are delegated to the church's committees. Council members are elected by the congregation. Council officers are elected by the council. All members should exemplify the Christian life. Details on council actions are presented in Chapter 10, page 134.

Congregational Committees. The church's standing committees (variously called teams or ministries) focus on individual church functions and attract members with corresponding skills and interests. Committees serve as clearinghouses for debate, analysis, planning, and management. Their jurisdiction is mandated by the church council. All assigned responsibilities should be related. Too diverse combinations are difficult to oversee, frustrating leaders and members. Too focused specialization, limits interest and possible participation.

Committees are generally sufficiently dedicated and capable to be semi-autonomous, dealing directly with problems largely independent of higher level approval. Committees are the "work horses" of the congregation in terms of guiding day-to-day performance and recommending improvements. Each committee has a job description outlining duties and authority. The role of committees is discussed in detail in Chapter 10 page 140.

...by speaking the truth in a spirit of love, we must grow up in every way to Christ, who is the head. Under his control all the different parts of the body fit together, and the whole body is held together by every joint with which it is provided. So when each separate part works as it should, the whole body grows and builds itself up through love. (Ephesians 4:15-16)

All committee structuring stems from eight distinct Christian and support responsibilities:
— **Parish Life** (responsible for the encouragement of communications, fellowship, and the well-being of all members of the congregation)
— **Worship & Music** (oversees the conduct and promotion of worship services and musical presentations)
— **Evangelism** (oversees the outreach program of witnessing for Christ in the community and welcoming church visitors)

- **Stewardship** (responsible for the promotion and encouragement of Christian service through one's time, talent, and wealth)
- **Christian Education** (oversees the conduct and advancement of the church school and other education activities)
- **Youth Ministry** (oversees the conduct and development of special programs of fellowship and service for young people)
- **Social Ministries** (oversees the mission programs which seek to broaden the vision of the congregation toward serving Christ at home and throughout the world)
- **Finance/Property** (responsible for the church's financial integrity, annual budget, and maintenance of the building and grounds)

Job Descriptions

Job descriptions spell out specifically and concisely, the activities and responsibilities of a job, and the manner and circumstances in which they are to be performed. They include authority, accountability, coordination, and reporting responsibilities. Over time, job descriptions should be extended and refined to ensure coverage and coordination of *all* church positions. They are an essential tool in training new office holders. They promote continuity and effectiveness. Finally, job descriptions are a sign of respect for the subject offices.

Jobs have to be made as attractive and seemingly important as possible to attract new appointees and hold incumbents. Leadership responsibilities, however slight, add prestige to any job. Descriptions should never be written in such a manner as to deter creativity and innovation. Jobs are often what individuals make of them. Resourceful people, closest to the action, should always have latitude to make new job boundaries. Descriptions should be upgraded based on such findings whenever possible.

All church job descriptions should be written, maintained in a church documents omnibus, and appropriately distributed. Job descriptions are presented in Appendix B.

---

[1] Primarily adapted from William Easum, *Dancing With Dinosaurs: Ministry in a Hostile & Hurting World* (Nashville, Abingdon Press, 1993).

[2] The Festival Center and The Servant Leadership School, Washington, D.C., 2004.

[3] Format and some content adapted from the "strategic directions" and related planning statements of the Washington National Cathedral, Washington, D.C. Other content from The Festival Center and The Servant Leadership School, Washington, D.C.

[4] The United Methodist Church, *Social Principles, The United Methodist Church: 2001-2004* (Washington, DC, The General Board of Church and Society, 2002).

[5] The organization may also have "trustees" assigned to manage the church endowment, "deacons" to serve with the pastor in performing pastoral ministry tasks, and "elders," governing officers having pastoral, teaching, or music functions. The pastor is generally responsible for managing full-time staff members such as assistant pastors, day care director, office secretaries, and custodians.

[6] The Boards (committees) of Our Savior Lutheran Church (Chippewa Falls, Wisconsin), for example, are autonomous, reporting directly to the congregation. "Our church council makes no decisions. That's a big change from the old tradition. The job of that group is to totally look forward, to plan. So there aren't any three-hour council meetings about the hole in the roof or problems with ushering. The Boards (committees) all make their own decisions and build their own budgets. They're responsible directly to the congregation. Our council asks questions." Roger R. Skatrud, Our Savior Lutheran Church, Chippewa Falls, Wis.

Chapter 10
Leadership Roles

May our Lord Jesus Christ himself, and God our Father, who loved us and in his grace gave us eternal courage and a good hope, fill your hearts with courage and make you strong to do and say all that is good.
(2 Thessalonians 2:16-17)

This chapter describes the altered roles of pastors and lay leaders under servant leadership. The first section, "A Common Binding Mission," begins with the shared nature of church leadership, followed by "rules" for establishing the necessary supporting environment. Recommended staffing/election procedures are then presented, concluding with scripture guidance. The second section, "Four Leadership Elements," the chapter's main division, begins with the new and more challenging role of clergy under servant leadership. Then the responsibilities of each of the three principal lay leader positions–trustee, council member, and committee chairman–are presented under the servant leadership concept.

This chapter is the first to deal with servant leadership in practice, converting the preceding philosophy into "hands-on" procedures. The remainder of the book continues this operational guidance, all of which should be critically reviewed in terms of practicality for any given congregation.

A Common Binding Mission

A Shared Ministry

How congregations are organized and led is often a matter of circumstances and personalities. A strong pastor and staff may direct more than guide. Long-standing appointees may be firmly entrenched. Special talents may be quickly recognized, while lesser abilities remain largely untapped. Whatever the conditions, the natural tendency for any organization is to gravitate toward its immediate strengths and opportunities, assigning responsibilities to individuals of proven ability. Churches are no exception, necessarily exploiting its best resources, often extending to excessive reliance on those most talented and energetic. Such practices are occasionally necessary and acceptable so long as the same confident callings are extended to *all* members as equally bound disciples, however modest their credentials. For we know that our strength comes as a gift of the Holy Spirit, not from any human enterprise. Jesus our Savior had no titles, no recognized training, no station in life, and no writings.

By his example, therefore, we are called to approach *every* individual in a universal calling, pleasing in God's sight.

Christian congregations can best be described as **communities of shared discipleship**. Everyone is asked to embrace and spread Christ's teaching. There are no exceptions. All must be disciples, all must be ministers, and all must be Christian leaders, distinguished only by the gifts and grace bestowed by God. This holistic calling dissolves differences, basically erasing our own identity, substituting oneness in Christ.

If then we are one with Christ there is no need to individually prove oneself by personal accomplishments. Jesus wants us to feed and care for his sheep, not as "professionals" but as vulnerable brothers and sisters always dependent on his guiding light. We are, after all, universal *followers* of Christ, not leaders in our own right but only lead through his bestowing grace. Thus we are all the same without distinction, servants in shared discipleship. Rejoice in our common bond.

Democracy, the Foundation of the Servant-Led Congregation

Servant leadership builds upon, while being dependent on, a strong supportive underlying democratic environment. Only faith itself is more essential. Democracy means the common people (congregation) are the primary source of governing power. Democracy exercises the popular vote. Democracy practices social equality. It seeks variety and criticism. Christian democracy goes even further, believing that *all* believers are *equal* in God's sight, obligated to lead and serve as one and the same, thereby providing all manner of opportunities and encouragement.

This generous receptive approach should not be construed as conflicting with principles of sound management. Quite the contrary, a servant-led democratic enterprise, by extending leadership (and sound management) to a broader segment of the governed, is actually stronger than any commercial counterpart. God does not frown on man's use of his own intelligence. Democratic methods should not be interpreted as conflicting with our subservience to God's will. We employ society's methods of discussion, debate, study, research, election, etc., certainly, but always subservient to God's will, our actions dependent first on faith guided by prayer.

Earlier, in Chapter 7, we directed attention to the evils of autocratic rule. Preemptive leadership is often more a matter of circumstances and personalities than deliberate intent. Long-standing members become firmly entrenched and overreaching. A strong pastor may, for example, gradually become the focal point of decisions. Whatever the cause, the natural tendency is for organizations to gravitate toward their strengths, assigning increasing responsibilities to the ablest or incumbent members. Such abdication of responsibility and concentration of authority must be continually fought to preserve democratic rule. Congregations, be alert!

Representative leadership is obtained not so much from structural form as by practical principles of democratic governance. Below are 10 "rules" for establishing and maintaining shared church leadership:

1. Assigned authority and professionalism must be respected. Our pastors are our beloved spiritual *leaders*. Martin Luther tells us the pastoral responsibilities include preaching, evangelizing, and administering the sacraments. In all such and allied matters the congregation defers to its pastors. Respect for the professionalism of other staff positions is also paramount for a harmonious, constructive atmosphere. All designated offices including those of the laity deserve our greatest respect and cooperation. The crucial alliance between pastor and congregation is discussed in detail later in this chapter in "The Clergy–A Sacred Calling" section.

2. The interface between staff and laity should be interwoven with shared responsibility. Too much friction comes from failure to *share* leadership. There is precious little space for autocratic rule of any sort in the Christian church. Our responsibilities to God so overwhelm and overlap that there is little need for any absolute authority. Wise church staffs recognize the primary governing role of the congregation and encourage self-direction. When the congregation stumbles in such freedom, precious little is likely to be lost, but much gained in internal growth. Is not the Holy Spirit as likely to act through the congregation, even to the least member, as through any of its appointed officers? Our shared dependency humbles us all, superseding all imposed structuring.

3. Church organization should be designed to foster democratic action. Democracy requires first that governing bodies represent their constituency. Nominating committees should avoid narrow slates of similar background or like-minded candidates. Special interests should be assigned a spokesperson. Oversights foster resentment and undermine the diversity and balance inherent in representative government.

Second, governing structures should be as flat as possible, closely interrelating leaders and electorate. A minimal hierarchy promotes vertical communication and strengthens the lowest operating level. In fact, standing committees should be as autonomous as possible, allowed to deal directly with most problems independent of higher approving authority. The church is, after all, not a conglomerate corporation, but a single entity of the faithful.

4. Church officers should be visible and accessible. The names and means of contact of all church officers should be publicized. Officers should wear special nametags with their position identified and be generally accessible to members, for example, during designated after-service coffee hours.

5. Practice "transparent" leadership. The church holds no secrets, no hidden power. Other than personal matters, most church activities may and should be openly discussed and debated, without pretense or rancor. Church business should be conduct much like a town forum, with a posted agenda and invited open-attendance. Visitors are too often made to feel as intruders in a private gathering. Who said God's business is the right of a select few? Open the doors, welcome guests, encourage dissent, prompt debate, uncover that which is concealed; in this way the truth is revealed.

Keep the congregation informed at all times. Minutes should be kept and publicly reported. Explain the "why" of decisions, the most perennial unanswered question. It is dumbfounding how a church council or committee can debate an issue at length, and then turn around and report the resulting "decision" without explanation. The congregation should be considered part and parcel of such deliberations and so kept informed. The minority's position is also part of such documentation.

In fact, most complex issues could well profit from extended deliberations and delayed action. Detailed broadcast of proceedings often surfaces new information and additional proponents. Sometimes a larger audience may even draw out new and original solutions, an altogether positive outcome of publicizing issues.

6. Create opportunities and encourage everyone to lead. It is far easier to rely on a few individuals than cultivate the involvement of many. It seems safer too, sometimes even expected. We naturally feel a bit more comfortable being led by those in whom we are most confident. Such dependency, of course, is never actually necessary, for all are called to discipleship. Yet church responsibilities may seem overwhelming, the recommendations of those in authority persuasive. Why take a risk? So congregations often feel pressured to depend on a favored proven few, or are at least more comfortable with such reliance. Eventually something akin to paternalism evolves, the very antithesis of distributed responsibility.

To combat such dependency on a few, congregations must go well beyond egalitarian principles to actively seek the involvement of all, not just the right to such engagement. Non-participants are seldom sufficiently interviewed and encouraged. "We talked with John about joining our group and he didn't appear interested so we apparently forgot about him. Later we learn he was an accountant and would have gladly served on the finance committee." To some members the church may appear overwhelming, even intimidating. Others may feel apart, excluded. Under such circumstances, expecting everyone to volunteer is totally unrealistic. Participation must be carved out individual-by-individual. The disinclined and hesitant can be recruited only if singled out and personally approached. Everyone, in fact, needs to feel recognized and needed as one of God's special servants. Without such personal treatment most congregational resources will remain largely untapped. The Stewardship Committee is responsible for successful recruitment (see Chapter 19).

7. Christian democracy requires that the congregation not only respect and be attentive to the viewpoints of others, but go beyond in seeking out such contributions in a spirit of common responsibility. The congregation must have the philosophy that *every* member's ideas and viewpoints are an important part of the overall democratic process. Elected lay officers must understand they *represent* the congregation, and are not its substitute. To act exclusively on personal knowledge and preference, without consulting those represented, is a dereliction of duty. Elected officers should continuously test the congregational waters by sympathetic and responsive *listening*.[1] The rarity of such attentiveness can be is found in answering how often your own opinion has been sought by an elected church official.

Henry J. Kaiser, industrialist, was once asked the key to his success and he reportedly responded, "I surround myself with people that are smarter than I am, and *I listen to them*." (italics added) Would that congregation leaders acted likewise.

8. Rigorously encourage scholarly study and debate. Build diversity, cultivate the dissenting voice, encourage criticism and debate. Church officers should rely on academic study as much as personal opinion and experience. Relish an eclectic approach to matters. Beware of the tyranny of the majority. Seek consensus through compromise, not unilateral one-time solutions. Balance the long-term corporate good with the immediate needs of the least member.

9. Decide important and controversial issues by plebiscite. Never allow the congregation to relinquish its voting privilege to a governing body. Even when issues are clear, voting should be accorded as a respected part of the democratic process. Persistent topics should be tabled for further study rather than debated to distraction. Councils often appear reluctant to bring controversial matters to a vote, due often to the unlikely possibility that something questionable might actually be approved. But indecision fails to conclude troubling issues, leaving proponents and objectors alike to stew in frustration. A negative vote at least allows some respite from debate, and time for proponents to rethink their position. A vote count should always be reported.

10. The position of the minority should always be acknowledged and hopefully receive some degree of accommodation. Always look for what is good in the minority position, and work to incorporate some of that which is acceptable in approved solutions. No one wants to continuously be on the wrong side of issues. Persistent "trouble makers" invariably are at least partially right some of the time. And sometimes one must look below the surface to see the real issues involved.

The Recruitment/Election Process

"Recruitment," as used here in the church context, is the process of identifying candidates for leadership positions and the procedure for their appointment/election. Few topics involve more controversy or policy differences. Two means are at hand–most common is simply announcing a handpicked selection, tantamount to an appointment. The rarer opposite is a slate of candidates, with possible embarrassment for those not elected. Each has advantages and disadvantages. We hope to strike a favored middle ground.

Congregations, as the body of Christ, operate under a different set of rules than sectarian politics, most notably the need to preserve human dignity. The rough and tumble of government politicking has little place in the church fabric. Rather than foster competition, we advocate increasing service opportunities through additional positions and limited terms of office. More jobs allow the possibility of limiting candidates to the number of available vacancies. Competition takes the form of stronger individuals venturing forth as volunteers.

The typical church structure has three lay leadership levels–trustees, council president and members, and committee chairpersons. In addition, there may be permanent special purpose groups and temporary ad hoc task forces. The total number of offices involved may not exceed three dozen. All recorded congregational members are eligible. In a congregation of say 250 members, 36 officers will allow one-in-seven to serve at any one time. If two-year terms are practiced, every member could then serve once every fourteen years. This illustrates how rare church leadership opportunities generally are, making increasing their number singularly important. Note that council members are invariably elected, committee chairs frequently appointed.

Encouraging volunteer candidacy. *I heard the voice of the Lord, saying, Whom shall I send, and who will go for us? Then said I, Here am I; send me.* (Isaiah 6:8) Before any nominating group is formed, a strenuous public effort should be made to encourage all members to consider their responsibilities and volunteer as called. Qualifying experience such as service in a lesser capacity may be cited as desirable, but the emphasis should be on personal response to prayerful meditation and inner reflection. We cannot over-emphasize the importance of an open-door policy, relying first on volunteers. In effect, seeing how God provides before our intervention. Volunteerism is the church's substitute for political competition. Note that other than under exceptional circumstances, the names of all volunteers should be placed on the candidate slate undistinguished from committee nominees.

Selection of nominees. Our commission to serve is a Christian entrustment, the essential element being not the mechanics of the appointment, but rather its sanctioning by the Holy Spirit. *Lord, you know the hearts of all men. And so, Lord, show us which one of these two you have chosen to take this place of service...* (Acts 1:24-25)

Nominating committees should consist of a representative sample of informed non-office holding congregation members. The committee should be completely reconstituted each year to avoid any possible criticism of "stacking the deck." Their assigned task is to canvas the entire congregation to ensure that all are given leadership opportunities consistent with interest and abilities.

The procedure for nominating members for principal church offices, notably council members, may be outlined as follows:

1. <u>Screen member records</u>. The church should maintain a confidential spiritual gifts inventory and service record of all congregation members, listing skills and talents, office appointments, other positions held, service dates, and possibly evaluative commentary. The service record should be used, in particular, to avoid excess reliance on a few by identify those as yet unasked to serve.

2. <u>Consider qualifying experience</u>. Identify desirable experience from available job descriptions. Compare any such prerequisites with candidate qualifications. Some church positions are a natural progression from subordinate service, e.g., from a committee chair-elect to the chairmanship. However, as recognized earlier, Jesus had no formal credentials, so beware of placing too much weight on human "ticket punching."

3. <u>Try for representation</u>. Review the congregation's makeup to see if representation may be improved. Factors that may be considered include age, sex, marital status, ethnicity, and as important, character and outlook. Too much homogeneity among officials restricts perspective and creativity. Remember that...*God chose the poor people of this world to be rich in faith.* (James 2:5) We honor all by including the least among us.

4. <u>Interview subjects</u>. Potential candidates should be informally interviewed to determine their interest in and dedication to the intended position. Subjects should be encouraged to express how they visualize the role and what possible "agenda" or "ideas for improvement" they might attempt if elected/appointed. A job description should be used to ensure mutual understanding of the entailed responsibilities.

The number of nominees plus volunteer candidates should generally not exceed the count of positions available. In some instances a larger slate, representing distinctive choices, may be appropriate, even desirable. The fact that some candidates will lose should not be construed as an intolerable consequence of the democratic process. Defeated individuals may be accorded alternate positions held open on their behalf.

Floor nominations are typically spur-of-the-moment impulses that seldom have any chance of election, and may cause embarrassment. A well-prepared slate developed from a total canvas of church membership usually minimizes the possibility of such offhand nominations. Individuals still seeking to nominate from the floor should secure the subject's approval in advance.

Election mechanics. Church leaders must be appointed *legitimately*, i.e., selected only from among those who honestly seek office, are qualified and fairly elected, and who are expected to validate the process by forthcoming exemplary service. Elections should be announced in advance with a handout of candidate backgrounds and qualifications. The date and time should be as convenient as possible with absentee balloting permitted.

Installation of officers. Installation and consecration of laity into their called ministry is a sacred commissioning that seeks God's blessing on those entering service. It is desirable and appropriate that we begin always by recognizing our dependency on God and the need for his continual guidance. We strongly recommend this sanctifying initiation.

Training of appointees. Each year incumbent and newly elected church officers should sit down together with the staff for an annual "year-in-review" to jointly examine what has been accomplished, lessons learned, necessary coordination, and new ventures. This is a good time to also review and update job descriptions. All should understand the countervailing power of the multiple-leader arrangement. This early "clearing of the air" goes a long way toward creating a harmonious similarly focused start. This session may take the form of a spiritual retreat including family participation, although for such a gathering it may be necessary and certainly courteous to invite the entire congregation as guests and observers.

Scripture for Leaders

Throughout this text as in all things we seek God's will. In three instances a special section is reserved to explain this singularity in purpose. The first, in Chapter 2, provides guidance for the congregation as a Christian community. In the second, in Chapter 5, we see how Christ's life and teachings set the example of the servant as leader. Here, in Chapter 10, our third listing focuses on Christ's guidance for church leaders.

Rabbi Meir Ben Yitzchak, the great 11th century liturgical poet, wrote that no number of words would be enough to describe the power of God..."Even if the heavens were parchment, the forests were quills, the oceans and all gathered waters were ink, and the Earth's inhabitants were scribes." So we must always recognize and profess our total dependency on our heavenly Father.

1. We can do nothing ourselves, but through Christ all things are possible. *"I can do nothing on my own; I judge only as God tells me, so my judgment is right, because I am not trying to do what I want, but only what he who sent me wants."* (John 5:30) *"And I will do whatever you ask for in my name, so that the Father's glory will be shown through the Son. If you ask me for anything in my name, I will do it."* (John 14:13-14)

2. Each has received from God special gifts to be used according to the grace that has been given us. *There are different kinds of spiritual gifts, but the same Spirit gives them. There are different ways of serving, but the same Lord is served. There are different abilities to perform* *service, but the same God gives ability to everyone for their service.* (1 Corinthians 12:4-6) **And each receives God's power.** *I ask God, from the wealth of his glory, to give you power through his Spirit to be strong in your inner selves, and that Christ will make his home in your hearts, through faith.* (Ephesians 3:16-17)

3. Be good stewards of the gifts God has given us. *Each one, as a good manager of God's different gifts, must use for the good of others the special gift he has received from God.* (1 Peter 4:10) *Since you are eager to have the gifts of the Spirit, above everything else you must try to make greater use of those which help build up the church.* (1 Corinthians 14:12)

4. We have the Spirit for guidance, unmerited divine assistance through God's grace. *This is how we are sure that we live in God and he lives in us: he has given us his Spirit.* (1 John 4:13) When we receive the Holy Spirit, God expects the work of the Spirit to be manifest in us.

5. Seek God's wisdom. *If you indeed cry out for insight, and raise your voice for understanding; if you seek it like silver, and search for it as for hidden treasures—then you will understand the fear of the Lord and find the knowledge of God.* (Proverbs 2:3-5)

6. Let God transform you. *Do not conform outwardly to the standards of this world, but let God transform you inwardly by a complete change of your mind. Then you will be able to know the will of God—what is good, and is pleasing to him, and is perfect.* (Romans 12:2)

7. Be shepherds of the flock. *Be shepherds of the flock God gave you, and look after it willingly, as God wants you to, and not unwillingly. Do your work, not for mere pay, but from a real desire to serve. Do not try to rule over those who have been given into your care, but be examples to the flock.* (1 Peter 5:2-3)

8. Work diligently. *...let us run with determination the race that lies before us...so that you may not grow weary or lose heart. Therefore lift your drooping hands and strengthen your weak knees, and make straight paths for your feet...* (Hebrews: 12:1, 3, 12-13) *Remember this: the man who plants few seeds will have a small crop; the one who plants many seeds will have a large crop.* (2 Corinthians 9:6)

9. Strive for mature thinking. *Do not be like children in your thinking, brothers; be children so far as evil is concerned, but be mature in your thinking.* (1 Corinthians 14:20)

10. Be always joyful. *Be joyful always, pray at all times, be thankful in all circumstances. This is what God wants of you, in your life in Christ Jesus.* (1 Thessalonians 5:16-18)

Four Leadership Elements

Paul, in his second letter to the Thessalonians, gives this hope and strength to the leaders of the young churches...*we always pray for you. We ask our God to make you worthy of the life he called you to live. May he, by his power, fulfill all your desire for goodness and complete your work of faith. In this way the name of our Lord Jesus will receive glory from you, and you from him, by the grace of our God and the Lord Jesus Christ.* (2 Thessalonians 1:11-13)

Church leaders must keep in mind that the church is totally Christ centered, spirit guided, not institutionally led by man. As church leaders we are to be instruments and servants of Christ. With Christ as our beacon we can be of good cheer, rejoicing in Christian fellowship and grace, free of concern knowing we are always directed by and in his care.

Identification. The servant led congregation readily identifies its leaders to increase their accessibility and encourage interaction. We recommend that the names and photos of church trustees, council members, and committee chairs be prominently posted and published in conjunction with a church organization chart (see church organizational structure, Chapter 9, pages 110-113). The chart should further contain a brief outline of the responsibilities of each organizational component, opportunities to serve, and telephone number contacts. The names of key officers may also occasionally be reported in the Sunday church bulletin. This publicity helps the congregation know and contact their leaders. Officers should also be encouraged to wear distinctive nametags with their title and periodically be available for contact after Sunday services.

The four leadership elements described in this section are–pastors, trustees, council members, and committee chairs. In small congregations the role of trustees may be subsumed by the council; however, the distinct functions assigned here, argue for a separate entity.

The Clergy–A Sacred Calling

The Holy Spirit guides the coming *together* of congregation and pastor. In simplest terms the procedure is that of matching needs and strengths, guided by prayer. The congregation calls on the basis of what it is, what it hopes to do, and the leadership desired. The candidate accepts largely on the challenge and opportunities provided. The bonding is strengthened from the beginning if all parties clearly understand and agree on the pastoral job description detailing both authority and responsibilities.

But clearly, the office of pastor is far more than the simple mechanics above. It is necessarily a *spiritual* undertaking. We gain a deeper understanding from this description by Dietrich Bonhoeffer (1906-1945, German theologian and Protestant resistance leader).

> The preacher is not the spokesman of the congregation, but if the expression may be allowed, he is the spokesman of God before the congregation. This office is instituted directly by Jesus Christ himself; it does not derive its legitimacy from the will of the congregation but from the will of Jesus Christ. It is established *in* the congregation and not *by* the congregation, and at the same time it is *with* the congregation.

The congregation which is being awakened by the proclamation of the word of God will demonstrate the genuineness of its faith by honoring the office of preaching in its unique glory and by serving it with all its powers; it will not rely on its own faith or on the universal priesthood of all believers in order to depreciate the office of preaching, to place obstacles in its way, or even to try to make it subordinate to itself.

All authority is in God and through God. "Pastors must always remember, beyond any shadow of a doubt, that the flock belongs to Christ and that they are, at the fullest, 'undershepherds' of the Good Shepherd. They are stewards of the flock, not owners." (Theodore F. Schneider, Bishop, Evangelical Lutheran Church in America.) Likewise, there is but one sole mediator of holy authority between our heavenly Father and humanity, Jesus Christ. Jesus is the head of the church and the congregation his body. All human structure is subservient to this centrality and supremacy. Pastors must always seek to lead in humbleness; parishioners to follow likewise. This recognition of God's supreme authority and our common discipleship bonds clergy and parishioners in servitude far exceeding earthly distinctions. So what is common governs–allegiance to God–refraining from all manner of personal sovereignty, seeking agreement in all things.

United in Two Interlocking Roles

The roles of pastors and congregation have become increasingly unified in recent years, more interlocking than interfacing. Under the best of circumstances the pastor and congregation unite in working together as God's servants, forging bonds of mutual trust, affection, and appreciation. Distinctions properly remain, primarily those of professional training and commission. The clergy, ordained and called, are given *spiritual* charge as shepherds of the congregation, living exemplary lives and setting before members the vision bestowed by God, and authorized to perform the sacred responsibilities of their office. From this consecrated charge we respond with allegiance, according our deepest respect and gratitude. However, pastors and parishioners alike are foremost *disciples*, active *followers* of Christ, spreading the good news. And all, together as believers, enter into a common *priesthood of sanctity with Christ*, the dominant equalizing force emerging in today's congregations. (See also Martin Luther's description of the office quoted in Chapter 4, "The Office of Pastor," page 28.)

The pastor is always the spiritual conscience of the congregation. His or her wisdom is sought in all matters, a cordially invited defacto member of all church deliberations. However, a self-governing congregation frees the pastor from the mundane tasks of management, allowing concentration on matters of the spirit. The pastor should *not* be an ex officio member of the church council. Wearing two hats is a distraction, possibly fractious, and the congregation deserves and should welcome all the responsibility it can handle. The object is not to have a church organization designed according to the preferences of the staff, but rather uniquely formed based on the collective nature of the whole congregation, each member contributing according to his or her calling. The most effective staff is one that motivates the entire congregation in service, each according to his or her calling.

Loving dependency. We all share God's grace in humble gratitude. We all seek redemption through devotion and prayer. Life is not what we achieve but what God gives us. This dependency means that no one is essential, there being no need for individual heroics. Ministers need not attempt to hide their own sins and failings but rather join with the congregation in seeking comfort and consolation. Only then can they really love and care for the flock as an inherent part. And this belonging generates the affection and friendships that ministers so vitally need.

Transcending Leadership. Transcending leadership transforms and exceeds what is humanly possible through God's grace. It is leadership in which "...leaders throw themselves into a relationship with followers who will feel 'elevated' by it and often become more active themselves, thereby creating new cadres of leaders."[2] An effective pastoral ministry succeeds in its transcending mission when it knows where to draw the line between allowing parishioners to be who they are and encouraging Christian growth. The exact line is seldom clear as God's message is continually reinterpreted. The task is to be faithful to a congregation's traditions while also bringing in new challenges.

No pastor, however dedicated, can be expected to meet all congregational expectations. Conflicts, hurt feelings, and departures are inevitable. The response, in love and kindness, is to encourage flexibility and openness. The pastor may well serve as mediator. Doubtful ventures can be tested, experiments undertaken, errors tolerated, all with good grace. Such accommodation keeps problems in public discussion allowing the involved parties to work on and eventually transcend their differences. Problems should never be allowed to become politicized.

The Key Role of Nurturing

Of all the interactions between pastor and congregation and among parishioners, the most fundamental responsibility is nurturing, passionately seeking personal Christian growth in all. To *nurture* is to develop and mold into a new being. Unless this underlying devotion to building-up is manifestly present, the pastor will always remain more a symbol than leading light. Charles Bennison, Episcopal Bishop of Pennsylvania, uses the term *valency*, "the capacity for the instantaneous, involuntary combination of one individual with others for the purpose of acting out the parish's myth." He also calls it *sentience*, "...that quality whereby a person feels genuinely what others are feeling in order to be 'with' them in the deepest sense of the word." William Easum, church consultant and author, calls for pastors to enlarge their role from that of broad leadership to that of "*equipping* the laity to minister to one another and take responsibility for their own ministry and evangelism." However titled, to nurture the congregation in Christian growth requires understanding and caring for each member individually, cultivating his or her unique personal development in an environment of openness and support.

A nurturing pastor is foremost a sensitive listener, seeking out the reality of the speaker without any form of prejudice. Good listening requires one to be inquisitive, supportive, and collegial, totally responsive to the speaker's needs. Such ministry is "client-centered" as opposed to "audience focused," common among so many public services. The congregation should always be viewed as a number of individual members, each distinct, multifaceted, growing, but never viewed in the collective group sense.

The nurturing pastor, and similarly long-term church leaders, must realign themselves from primary doers to trainers of others to do. The congregation then increasingly graduates from receivers to ministers. Such a transfer requires a secure, confident servant-oriented pastor who realizes that the clergy's full potential can only be realized by a shared and commissioned discipleship with the laity. This *equipping* function is clearly implied in Christ's admonition, *"I chose you, and appointed you to go and bear much fruit, the kind of fruit that endures."* (John 15:16) The sheer number of laity and the sizable activities now being attempted by so many churches further advances this ecclesiastical shift in focus from pastors to parishioners. The realignment is also buttressed by the congregation's usual diverse skills and energy. Thus the congregation as a whole, the body of Christ, gradually becomes, as it should, the basic working force of Christianity.

Specific Responsibilities

"God our shepherd, grant our pastors the holy gift of wisdom that they may serve your people with humility, preach your truth with clarity, and lead your people in worship with simplicity of heart."[3] The principal responsibilities given congregational pastors as a sacred trust are:

1. Preach, teach, and interpret the Word of God.
2. Administer the sacraments.
3. Evangelize and expand and extend opportunities to serve.
4. Create a community of "belonging" in which people are called out of loneliness and isolation into caring, supportive relationships with others. As pastor be especially attentive to the presence and needs of visitors and new members.
5. Provide pastoral care, counseling, and nurturing to all. Know and care for all members individually and personally as a shepherd.
6. Mobilize the laity for ministry. Install and equip church leaders and members to serve faithfully as called. Provide continual

pastoral guidance and encouragement, the cornerstone on which a strong church is built.
7. Represent, as pastor, the church publicly.
8. Interpret and promote affiliation doctrine and programs.
9. Administer the church staff.
10. Remain fresh, enthusiastic, and prepared by properly attending to personal family life. Welcome self-imposed/sanctioned rest, opportunities for study, and periodic sabbaticals.

Personal Qualities

Pastors should be "vessels of transforming power" through Christ.[4] To be so embodied, what the pastor *is* as a person is more important than what he or she says or does. Deep personal faith and rock-solid integrity are absolute essentials. The special skills required—preaching, teaching, care-giving, and leadership—all stem from these two underlying strengths.

The nature of these services requires that pastors have a loving, caring nature. This concern for others brings the pastor and congregation together as one, engendering affection, friendship, and counsel. Pastors cannot hide their own sins and failings, but must join with the congregation in seeking comfort and consolation. They need affection, support, and true friends, as do we all. Then, and only then, as truly one of us, can the pastor really love and care for the flock.

We are bold to suggest the required disposition or temperament of pastors in eight character attributes:

1. Deep faith and spiritual commitment to a life of Christian love and dedicated service.
2. A firm belief in the priesthood of all believers and the importance of every individual to the least one.
3. Personal integrity of the highest order.
4. Skills in sharing and transmitting the faith through preaching and teaching the Good News, mindful that the channels of God's grace are always made real, not by a particular pastor's hand, but by the true presence of the Holy Spirit.
5. Respect for and trust of others, openness to ideas, discernment of needs, generosity with time. Recognition that the pastoral role is more to nurture and guide others than to personally manage.
6. Sensitivity and interpersonal skills in caring, comforting, and protecting.
7. Understanding that no one is essential, that your contribution is not what you achieve, but what God gives you. (M. Craig Barnes) Pastors should be considered members of the congregational team at work. If pastors allow themselves any pride it should be in the involvement and Christian growth of the congregation.
8. Knowledge and appreciation of the culture and history of those served. Allowing parishioners to be who they are.

In addition to this litany of responsibilities, it may be as useful to cite areas of possible greatest deficiency. This abbreviated list of **"lessons our mistakes teach us"** by William Easum, can add to the awareness pastors have to critical needs:
1. Have a consuming vision and passion for transforming people
2. Fully understand the power of prayer in making disciples and decisions.
3. Provide enough staff and fully utilize the membership in assigned responsible duties.
4. Think of evangelism as a principal mission responsibility.
5. Dream big and have patience for its realization. (Yet, pastors are seldom too harshly critical, restraining their advocacy to ensure reasonable stability and congregation comfort. "Risky" ventures are best undertaken with the full support of all involved.)
6. Focus on the mission statement, never losing sight of its directive influence.
7. Develop and sustain small groups as an essential tool of changing people's lives.

Role of Trustees[5]

"Institutions need two kinds of leaders: those who are inside and carry the active day-to-day roles, and those who stand outside but are intimately concerned, and who, with the benefit of some detachment, oversee the active leaders. These are the *trustees*." (Robert Greenleaf) Here, we similarly recommend that church trustees serve to oversee and strengthen leadership rather than their more common employment of simply holding title to and directing church funds. Despite such oversight potential, church trustees are seldom given much to do and may be absent altogether. The aim of this section is then, quite obviously, that of persuasively arguing their resurgence.

Founded on spiritual faith, the principal attributes sought in trustees are integrity and a rigorously inquiring mind. Integrity seeks the highest quality without compromise, thus necessitating the willingness to risk change. Seeking the right answers is bound up in asking the right questions. Both attributes are enhanced by the trustee's unique environment: (1) freedom from the responsibilities, pressures, and minutia of day-do-day operations, creating a relaxed, supportive environment, (2) detachment affording an impartial perspective, and (3) unrestricted time to seek out and develop a variety of information sources and conduct reasonably paced thorough studies. If trustees are basically qualified, and devote sufficient time to fully exploit these advantages, their judgments will well serve and merit respect in any congregation.

In small churches, the trustee's role can be subsumed by the council, but this exception is not recommended for the two functions involved–overseeing versus directing–are distinct, requiring different outlooks and approaches not easily combined in one body. However, the actions involved are interrelated, applying, to a degree, to each entity. Thus trustees and council members must work together, albeit from different perspectives. From a strictly practical standpoint, having both trustees and a church council affords congregations the advantage of adding twice the number of top-level leadership opportunities. Trustees also lessen the need to appoint special task forces by subsuming most special study requirements.

Mission and Authority

The mission of congregational trustees defined here is to attend to the church as an institution through observation, study, and assistance that materializes in helping each component in reaching its optimum potential through Christ. It is an evaluative, advisory, and visionary responsibility of the highest order. It is performed through diligent attention, inquiry, prayer, and recommendations, the trustee's only "marching orders." Trustees focus on the large picture, scrupulously avoiding any intrusion in the operational jurisdiction of the church council and committees. They act strictly as an independent oversight and advisory body without managerial, administrative, or approval authority. This autonomy and freedom from operating details and pressures allows trustees the opportunity to become what Greenleaf calls "originators of new regenerative forces."

While largely self-directing, trustees should also be responsive to outside commentary and requests. Though accessible, most requests are likely to be referred to more immediately responsible lower echelons. Again, trustees must not usurp the responsibilities of the church council or committees. Any pretense of infringement or meddling must be avoided. Otherwise, trustees are given remarkable latitude. They report but are not subject to the council and congregation. They operate independently with minimal, if any, subject and time restraints. This latitude allows freedom of thought and reflection, rare but necessary requisites for in-depth study.

Note that the tangible assets of the church and all legal and charter responsibilities should be vested in the church council or governing board. However, as a historical and often pro forma matter these responsibilities may be held by the trustees for legal simplification.

Membership and Officers

Trustees and council members are elected offices (see this chapter's earlier section "The Staffing/Election Process," page 119). Above all, trustees should be individuals of vision, always seeking a sense of the direction to be taken. They are expected to work hard. There is no nominal or honorary aspect to this appointment.

Trustees need not have served in any "preparatory" leadership positions. Membership doesn't require "eligibility" or "qualifying" service in the typical sense. Rather, candidates must possess an inquiring mind, a sustaining spirit to challenge the status quo, and unqualified dedication and commitment to the Lord. Trustees need not represent constituencies in the church. They are *not* a political body as is the governing council; rather, they are custodians of the *quality* of the church.

Trustees act as a *team* with an elected *primus inter pares* (first among equals). This shared or attenuated leadership tends to balance responsibility and encourage a unified approach. The role of the trustee chair is to see that the group directs its attention to substantive issues, sustains a common purpose, and effectively develops and employs its findings. Meetings are invariably informal, in the order of a group of scholars. The chairman questions, guides, tasks, and encourages. This modest direction is basically one of unfettered intellect, likely the least fatiguing, free and satisfying "leadership" position in the whole church structure.

Diplomacy

As designed here, church trustees are an inconspicuous lot. They advise behind the scenes complementing the council, never confronting, always constructive. They should conduct themselves with quiet dignity commensurate with their office, always humble in God's sight. Gentle persuasion is the operative word. They are respectful to all, for the trustees themselves are the most expendable of church officers.

While few churches are likely to be persuaded to allow non-members to serve as trustees, the advice of "outsiders" with their distinct perspective should be readily sought. How can a church effectively serve the community without the neighboring resident's active involvement? First-hand ground-level knowledge is an essential input to most undertakings. Trustees consequently should never be reluctant to ask congregational members, or, for that matter, any source for help. The resources available in most reasonably sized congregations are staggering, yet too frequently neglected.

Trustee Responsibilities

Trustees must intensely care for the congregation and church, and their success in serving Christ. They seek no recognition or reward for themselves as peripheral agents, but rather take satisfaction from seeing the church council and committees perform well. Their work typically materializes in counsel, distributed papers, and occasionally open-forum discussions. We emphasize again, church trustees should be an inconspicuous lot.

As defined here, the trustees are *not* the court of last resort. That responsibility along with all authority resides with the elected church council.

Church trustees are generally responsible for the following duties:

• **Continuously seek God's guidance** through prayer, bible reading, and study. Separated from the cares of day-to-day operations, the trustees, more than any other church office, have the opportunity and obligation to seek obedience to God's will.

- **Set personal standards of exemplary Christian behavior.** As their name implies, trustees must have the vision, values, and staying power that engender congregational trust. Trust underlies their effectiveness. Over time, worthy trustees are recognized as *symbols* of trust.
- **Mentor church leaders** as a principle duty. Mentoring is..."sustaining the faith of able people to persevere and to be effective in their caring and serving, and giving support when (they) get discouraged or confused." (Robert Greenleaf) Leadership positions can be lonely at times, needing a supporting hand. Each church leader, including the pastor, will value a trustee or other church member as a confidant friend.
- **Create a powerful persuasive vision of the church**, a perception of the desired future, a move to distinction, which immediate managers are either not likely to have or are too busy to pursue. Visioning is the trustee's second principal responsibility. *Where there is no vision, the people perish.* (Proverbs 29:18)

Lack of vision is endemic in our churches, which are seemingly content to serve the present membership in unchallenged fashion. Trustees must try to visualize the growing edge of the church that will lift the sights of all parishioners and give them a great goal to strive for. Living out a great dream coalesces the congregation behind its leaders who are seen as servants of the idea. They in turn must direct the hard work of extracting reality from concept.

- **Attend to the organizational structure** by annually reviewing the church mission statement, goals, and organizational design. This monitoring is the trustee's third major responsibility. The mission statement should be clear and compelling. Goals should be set slightly higher than what everyone feels is achievable, thereby becoming more fully dependent on God's grace. The objective always is to move the church to *distinction* in God's service. Advice may also be proffered regarding the criteria by which performance may be judged.

Trustees have an advantage over the council in regard to all structural dimensions by their detachment and likely greater objectivity. The council is typically too involved to have the perspective required concerning their own role and that of church committees.

- **Monitor and periodically assess the *major* elements of church performance.** Trustees advise the council president and members on remedial action and possible adjustments. They should be especially attentive to the necessary *interaction* within and between the council and committees. The level and detail of study undertaken should be far less than that normally performed by the council itself. It is the *objective* approach expected of the trustees that justifies their involvement. Recommendations pertaining to committees should, of course, be made to the council.

Trustees will gain the confidence of council and committee members as they demonstrate wisdom and impartiality. The interface will be far less prone to difficulties if trustees keep in mind that the council and committee chairs are the *executives* of the church, not the trustees. Trustees, for their part, must be gifted in the art of *persuasion* as opposed to direction. In a sense, trustees should be viewed as providing the oil and balm necessary in a common effort. However, trustees bear an indirect responsibility for church management through their advisory role, and should not hesitate to counsel and even admonish church leaders when such measures are called for. Periodic oversight and intervention provides the check-and-balance necessary in every organization. Robert Greenleaf goes so far as to admonish that "No one, *absolutely no one*, is to be entrusted with the operational use of power without the close oversight of fully functioning trustees."

- **Seek to build optimally serving lives**. Identify good, able people and encourage their nomination/appointment for appropriate positions. Cultivate and mentor young potential leaders. Churches too often provide insufficient room for gifted people to grow. The more growth that occurs the more opportunity to release incumbent office holders for important work elsewhere.

- **Do a lot of attentive listening**, attempting to discern the true nature of problems and opportunities. Trustees ask, more than answer questions. As a listening organization, they will invariable have representatives periodically attend council meetings and, on occasion, committee meetings, always as invited supportive guests, never as intrusive suspected critics. Occasionally a canvas of members may be necessary to gain background information. But attentive listening, both to discern and resolve problems, remains the trustee's basic tool.

- **Conduct special studies and surveys**. Trustee studies should be characterized by four attributes: (1) detachment from personal involvement and pride, (2) use of a broad array of information sources, recognizing that insightful voices are speaking cogently today as they have in the past, (3) design couched in the context of church history, past-present-future, and (4) supportive of the ultimate purposes of the congregation. The role here is that of study, not advocacy.

- **Be alert to the church's place in a changing social and economic environment**.

- **Entertain the unexpected and seemingly impractical**, regardless of source, for God sends his messages in various hidden ways to test man's spiritual allegiance. Ideas of potential, however enthusiastically endorsed, should be field-tested on a modest scale. Such "experiments" may generate additional requirements/improvements, further trial, or rejection. Such "lessons learned" are valuable in themselves and generally satisfy the project's initiators.

Role of the Church Council

The church council is the senior lay governing authority of the church. With the spiritual guidance of the pastor and under the ever-watchful eye of the congregation and trustees, the council oversees and directs the church's organizational structure. It is responsible for staffing and management. It defines the mission and guides the church's committees that oversee and conduct actual operations. Together with the committee chairs, the council members constitute the *executives* of the church, i.e., those with management authority. Lastly, the council is the court of last resort for the resolution of problems and conflicts not resolved directly by the involved parties.

Council Mission and Authority

The council's mission is essentially that of "...developing systems that ensure people are received into fellowship, guided and encouraged in their spiritual growth, and supported as they live out their lives as Christian disciples." (Mount Olivet, Arlington, VA) This ultimate authority and responsibility cannot be delegated. Council members must therefore be good *stewards* of the congregation entrusted to their care and protection. Each council member must be a servant leader, continuously striving to serve the needs of others, always open to suggestions, never harshly controlling. A properly commissioned council guides the committees in their operative role and planning requirements. They ask and are aided by the trustees in answering "How are we doing now?" and "Where should we be going and how do we get there?"

Throughout this volume, servant leadership argues for maximum delegation of authority to the lowest possible echelon. And further, delegated as broadly as possible, thereby creating an abundance of leaders closest to the action, in touch with reality. To this end, the church council should continuously strive to work itself out of much of its peripheral responsibilities by greater and greater delegation. As their management role decreases it is replaced by greater involvement in strengthening existing programs and planning new ones. The committee's side of this relationship as entrusted functionaries is explained in this chapter's next division, "Committees–the Church's Working Force," page 140.

Council Membership and Desired Attributes

Elect elders filled with the Spirit to positions of responsibility to direct the great work. And they shall be known as servants to all people. *Be shepherds of the flock God gave you, and look after it willingly, as God wants you to, and not unwillingly. Do your work, not for mere pay, but from a real desire to serve. Do not try to rule over those who have been given into your care, but be examples to the flock.* (1 Peter 5:2-3)

Membership and Offices. The church council should be large enough to be representative and small enough to encourage full participation of every member and allow in-depth discussion. Twelve to 16 people seem a reasonable balance. Individuals cannot be on the church council and also serve on committees. They should be too busy with their senior position responsibilities. Also, the pastor should not be an ex officio council member, for he or she serves the distinct, separate role of spiritual leader. Committee chairpersons may appropriately be invited to council meetings for special hearings. And council meetings should, of course, always be open forums with everyone welcome.

The council elects its president. The duties of the office are detailed in a following section. The appointed *secretary* has the responsibility of recording council and congregational meeting minutes and publicizing actions taken. The secretary also informs council members of meeting dates and prepares advance handout materials. The council's treasurer office handles routine check disbursements. Overall record keeping and finances are the responsibility of the church finance committee.

Member Attributes. Council members should be studious, energetic, resourceful, likeable, and, above all, spiritual. Each should exemplify Christian virtues. The calling is at once the most responsible, demanding, and rewarding, in the church structure. When we say *responsible*, we mean that each council member should "...think, speak, and act as if personally accountable to all who may be affected by his or her thoughts, words, and deeds." (Robert Greenleaf) Such responsibility requires great strength, a willingness to choose the right aim among alternatives, and pursue that choice with confidence. Only through the Holy Spirit are we so enabled.

In apparent conflict with the above qualifications, Saint Paul admonishes us to seek out the weak in recognition of God's power through the least person. *For God purposely chose ...what the world considers weak in order to put powerful men to shame.* (1 Corinthians 1:27) This means that church nominating committees must make every effort to be as inclusive as possible in their recommendations, including critics, minorities, old and young, male and female, weak and strong, as well as those most able. A truly representative council so chosen will benefit greatly from the resulting diverse and sensitive thinking, all favored in God's sight.

Members of the council need not be as visionary or creative as trustees. But they should abhor mediocrity, believing that the church is capable of accomplishing all within its power. Such optimism requires faith and the knowledge that through God all things are possible. *May the God of hope fill you with all joy and peace in believing, so that you may abound in hope by the power of the Holy Spirit.* (Romans 15:13)

Finally, church council members should be good *listeners*, an often neglected responsibility of those once gaining office. This topic, attentive and receptive listening, is discussed in Chapter 11, "Communications and Planning," page 148.

Council Modus Operandi

How does the principal laity office of the church—the council—effectively *lead* the congregation in seeking God's will? Such essential duties can be performed well only with the help of the Holy Spirit that sustains us all. Through prayer and Bible reading we receive the required wisdom and strength. The writings of modern day scholars are also spiritually inspired. The breadth and importance of their advisory work is evident throughout this study in the numerous quotations and references cited. Church leaders are strongly encouraged to pursue the original works.

We earlier alluded to **the importance of delegating authority**. In the servant-led congregation, this commissioning, this investment in others, is a richly rewarding experience, reflecting both our confidence and joy in those so empowered. The church council with its extended responsibilities must be particularly observant of this rule. Positioned between the visionary mission of trustees and the management operations of committees, attenuates some of the load. But the council must still carve out its own distinct intermediary role, delegating secondary and peripheral matters to others. And, not surprisingly, a very full schedule remains as indicated by the remarkably large and diverse slate of core responsibilities suggested, page 138. Thus we admonish councils to concentrate on these tasks, leaving to the trustees and committees their distinct supporting assignments, thereby creating both suitable differentials and an encompassing composite whole. Councils run no greater risk of impairment than failure to share leadership, thus becoming overburdened and neglectful.

It would be naive to believe that entrenched, empowered councils will necessarily abdicate authority voluntarily. In stubborn instances, they must be encouraged by persuasive argument. The obstacles to delegation most often expressed include: (1) loss of necessary authority and respect, (2) perceived deficiencies of subordinates, and (3) increased potential for disabling errors. All three contentions are, in fact, baseless. First, increased sharing of leadership raises responsibility at every level according greater respect for all. Second, few church tasks exceed the capabilities of even the lowest, least qualified, echelon. Third, with the possible exception of certain major irreversible commitments, most church errors can be readily corrected, terminated, or absorbed as a learning experience. So, in bold trust in the Lord, we are to be confident in all servants to the very least. *Each one, as a good manager of God's different gifts, must use for the good of others the special gift he has received from God.* (1 Peter 4:10)

Council President

The council president is elected by the council from its membership. Like the trustee primus, the council president is first among equals, a *team* builder, responsible for the effective performance of the council as a whole through each individual member. One could call the president the "caretaker of the council's integrity." The position deserves our greatest respect as instructed by Saint Paul. *We beg you, brothers, to pay proper respect to those who work among you, those whom the Lord has chosen to guide and instruct you.* (1 Thessalonians 5:12)

Foremost, the council president must be a faithful Christian who cares deeply for the church and congregation. Then the president must have effective interpersonal skills, especially the ability to persuade others while being open-minded. Third, the president should be able to reason logically and exercise critical judgment. Also helpful, although less important, are skills in public speaking. Finally, the council president must have courage to risk doing what God is saying to the congregation, to take action against possibly daunting obstacles.

Responsibilities. The managerial responsibilities of the office of council president and similarly, although less formally, that of committee chairs include:

1. Work closely with the pastor.
2. Ensure that all council members are fully informed in advance of topics currently subject to council deliberations. (Ignorance of subject matter is the most disabling of deficiencies.)
3. Chair council meetings (see Chapter 12, "How to Conduct Meetings and Reach Decisions).
4. Be an effective group leader (see Chapter 12).
5. Be proactive, that is, anticipate and act in advance to deal with expected difficulties.
6. Serve as chief laity representative of the church.
7. Train the president-elect.
8. Provide for yearly council and committee retreat training sessions to orient new members, review job descriptions and coordination measures, and develop tentative priorities.

And then there are, of course, the overriding *leadership* duties of the council president which, in generic terms, constitute the thesis of this book. We bring to your attention Chapters 5, 6, and 8 in particular. And the presidency position in itself may offer unique leadership opportunities, those of continuously challenging the process and status quo, inspiring others with vision, enabling and encouraging, and serving as a model of Christian service.

Power. Whether sought or not, a certain degree of power accompanies the office of council president. By *power* we mean the strength associated with an office that allows the incumbent to exercise control and exert pressure. Make no mistake, it exists and can be used effectively if cautiously controlled. The office must never be allowed to ascend to the top of a pyramid of subordinates. A "...pyramid structure weakens informal links, dries up channels of honest reaction and feedback, and creates limiting chief-subordinate relationships." (Robert Greenleaf)

The correcting counter-balancing influence of close colleagues of parallel stature must always be present. Yet, even with safeguards, the chief governing office conveys respect and authority to the beholder, however modestly evident. The effective council president uses this advantage to be heard above the uproar. Power also accredits one's position, helping the leader convince others of the rightness of the chosen course of action. And authority can be used to gain access to a wider range of information sources.

Council Responsibilities

The church council serves with the pastor to guide the congregation. The council delegates specified operations and related planning to the various church committees, always with accountability. No church entity should be entrusted with operational authority without being subject to some oversight. Committees report to the council which in turn is monitored by the trustees and vice versa. All are responsible to the congregation. Once authority is assigned, the council's role reverts to advising, assisting, and evaluating committee work. The council serves the broadest needs of the church–structuring, overseeing, and planning–activities generally extending beyond the purview of individual committees. The objective is to design and improve the corporate role of the church, present, and future.

The responsibilities of the church council may be organized under three headings–structuring, setting goals and planning, and overseeing and guiding operations. The communications, planning, and problem solving aspects of performing these functions are covered in Chapters 11 and 12.

Structuring:

• Appoint and contract the church pastor and staff. Pastoral selection may be assisted by a special "call committee" under the auspices of the church council.

• Periodically review and revise as necessary the church articles of faith, constitution, and bylaws.

• Establish the church's organizational structure and approve staff and committee job descriptions. Ensure that new trustees and committee chairs are personally instructed on their duties. Job descriptions should be written and updated by office holders subject to council approval.

• Elect, or nominate for congregational approval, the council president and appoint committee chairpersons based on member recommendations.

• Ensure that all trustee, council, and committee meetings are announced and open door. Proceedings should be documented and published.

• Find, encourage, and train new leaders. (The strongest support possible should be given the committee chairs. The council should continually ask, "How can we help you do your job?")

- Assist the trustees and committees in their recruitment.
- Appoint a church ombudsman to independently review and critique church operations and process recommendations/complaints. This individual is a key interface between the church council and congregation, although all council members should be attentive listeners. See ombudsman section in Chapter 11, pages 153-155.
- Ensure adequate human and monetary resources are available to committees. Provide technical support such as references, consultants, computers, etc.
- Serve as the laity representatives of the church.

Setting Goals and Planning:
- Continuously observe and listen to the congregation and community to sense needs and opportunities.
- Study the corporate church in the context of the past, present, and future. Generate responses to new opportunities and means for strengthening programs.
- Yearly update the church mission statement and operating premises (emerging conditions, operating principles, and policy statements). Establish a strong clear sense of mission within the congregation. This responsibility may be carried out with the assistance of the church trustees.
- Work with committees to set goals and long-range plans for their achievement. Ideas are sought from every source.
- Work with church trustees in identifying and developing special study requirements and projects.

Overseeing and Guiding Operations:
- Interact with the pastor in assigned church personnel areas (typically excluding theological positions). The council always "works with" the pastor in the shared ministry of the church. The council or pastor is the immediate supervisor of contracted staff members and volunteer office laity as designated in associated job descriptions.[6] Ensure proper introductory training for all new staff, trustees, council, and committee appointees.
- Delegate new work to appropriate operating committees. The church office and staff should serve as a clearinghouse to route material to the appropriate committees.
- Monitor and oversee church operations, providing assistance and guidance as required and encouraging new resourceful directions. Observe trustee and committee meetings. The task of the council is to encourage excellence, not preserve respectable, comfortable, time-sanctioned adequacy.
- Evaluate performance. No matter how able, committees seldom have the ability to consistently perform at a high level of excellence, or set goals for their own performance and judge it objectively. Sometimes those most competent are least able (or willing) to examine the assumptions

under which they operate. While committees must be positive in what they are doing, the council must sometimes be critical in its evaluative role, not harshly but constructively. The committee chairs in particular should be graded. The process extends upward from the committees, to the council itself, and to the trustees who should never be considered above such appraisal.

• Recognize and celebrate the contributions of the committees and their members and all who serve. Announce and fete, as appropriate, new appointments, accomplishments, and departures.

• Speak up for the minority and underrepresented. Ensure that the unpopular position is welcomed, expressed, and fairly heard.

• Coordinate work of the various committees as required and resolve conflicts.

• Prepare and meaningfully present the annual church report to the congregation.

• Advise and task the church trustees regarding special studies and survey as may be required.

• Serve as the court of last resort in resolving problems in peace and goodwill.

• Arrange appropriate sabbatical leave for pastors and professional staff.

Committees–the Church's Working Force

Program direction is vested in the church's standing committees. Oversight and some approval authority may remain with the council, but by-and-large as much independence should be given the various committees as possible, commensurate with their demonstrated capacity. This decentralization properly aligns authority with responsibility, multiplies the number of leaders possible, and takes full advantage of specialized skills. Strong, focused committees are the basic building blocks of effective church operations. Each committee/chairperson tandem should have a job description.

Committee Missions

Standing committees are the principal means of service for a majority of the congregation. Eight committees of eight members each, for example, immediately engage 64 individuals in direct program responsibilities according to their calling. No other church entity creates such a wealth of opportunities.

Committees plan, oversee, and are responsible for activities in their respective areas. Their focus is fairly narrow, confined typically to one of eight or so distinct major church functions, e.g., worship and music, education, stewardship, etc. Large churches, with a broad spectrum of activities, usually require more committees, but they are essentially subdivisions of the "big eight" identified here. These eight divisions are sufficiently important and distinct to warrant separate organizational formation in almost every instance:

Parish Life (builds the Christian community of faith among members, Chapter 16. This most important committee cares for every member and cultivates each individual's Christian growth.)

Worship, Music, and the Arts (the religious forms expressing our love of God, Chapter 13)

Christian Education (teaches the word of God, Chapter 18)

Stewardship (promotes involvement of all members in service and Support, Chapter 19)

Evangelism (outreach to spread the Good News, Chapters 20 and 21)

Youth Ministry (special attention to young people, Chapter 17, page 273)

Social Concerns (serves the needs of mankind, Chapter 22)

Administration–Finance, Property, Staffing (handles business aspects of the church, Chapter 23)

Committee designations and responsibilities are established by the church constitution and detailed in written job descriptions (Appendix B). This documentation ensures full coverage and minimal overlap. Written descriptions also establish a coherent rationale for the entire structure so there is no confusion as to who should be doing what.

There has been a recent proliferation of church committees. "Beware of Christian *activities* instead of Christian *being*." (Oswald Chambers, Scottish evangelical prophet.) Argument can be made in either direction. More committees allow greater specialization and increase leader opportunities. Too many, attending to the unessential, reduce committee importance and erode strength. The rule is simply to have only strong viable committees, even though some may be slightly overloaded.

Committee Membership and Chairmanship

From the beginning there should be a tacit understanding that committee membership involves real work and personal responsibility. Committees are where the "tire meets the road" as the saying goes. Members must have sufficient experience in committee responsibilities to ensure competence, although a single residing "expert" may provide sufficient creditability for the entire group. It is surprising how many professional church members seem to check their skills and acumen at the door. Committees are where such expertise is most needed, teachers to plan the Sunday school curriculum, musicians to help design the worship service, accountants to develop the church budget, and so on.

Committees should ideally number eight to ten individuals, enough to be inclusive, yet sufficiently small for close interaction. Membership should also reflect, at least in spirit if not actual representation, the congregation's diversity. Finally, prospective committee members should be interviewed by the committee chair to ensure propriety of motive and acceptable commitment.

Terms of office can be flexible, but rotation should be encouraged to enable all to serve. The problem with extended tenure is that the incumbent frequently becomes such a fixture that he or she is difficult to dislodge. "Jane was *the* altar committee for so long that nobody had the temerity to ask her to step down." In such instances, the individual might be respectfully asked to train a replacement, serving as an adviser, or given an attractive new assignment. Entrenched membership may gravitate to cliques and "old timers," difficult to join or disperse. Such encumbering difficulties can be minimized by written "terms of service" to be reviewed by all new members and office candidates prior to appointment. Individuals may, of course, rejoin a preferred committee after an appropriate hiatus. And requirements for special skills and adequate membership allow existing tenure policies to be liberally interpreted. Church "rules" are always subject to immediate interpretation.

Committees are the chief vehicles of congregational service. Eight ten-member committees, for example, affords everyone in a 240 member congregation a chance to serve at least one two-year term every six years. Adding the other typical services of teaching, visitation, teller, choir, etc, results in a large diverse set of opportunities generally sufficient for even the most eclectic congregation. The problem is generally not one of insufficient positions, rather an absence of applicants. Thus recruitment must be unceasing. Discipleship is a way of life, not a temporary duty.

Committee chairs must understandably have a keen interest in the discipline involved. Such interest is typically demonstrated and observable during any apprentice period. Chairs should also be action "can-do" people, excited and challenged by the mission. Interest and energy, in turn, should be tempered by a keen awareness of the overriding responsibility of effectively engaging all in discipleship. Effective committees operate principally as a group. Marshalling and guiding the group is accomplished during committee meetings which the chair oversees (see "How to Conduct Meetings and Reach Decisions," Chapter 12). In this role the chair must *lead*, controlling the discourse rather than allowing it to drift aimlessly. The most common complaint among committee members is that of frustration over the perceived ineffectiveness involved.

Chair duties are similar to those of the council president as previously listed. Perhaps one unique opportunity is available, i.e., the appointment of an understudy chair-in-training. This duality, typically for a single year, lessons the chair's load, trains and tests the future chair, and perhaps most important, minimizes risks associated with appointing individuals of lesser ability by ensuring thorough apprenticeship.

Committee Authority

One of the most controversial aspects of church management is the degree to which authority is delegated. Conservative councils run a tight ship, requiring committees to seek their approval at every turn. Supportive councils understand that committees are the church's operating arms and encourage their independence, requiring only that they understand their mission and are properly staffed. We recommend this later choice as one leading to a stronger, more resourceful and creative whole. And the chance of possible missteps is generally so small and correctable that any claimed risk is largely without merit.

Delegation raises the focus of both the receiving and entrusting office. Committees gain higher level responsibilities allowing the council to attend to more senior duties. In contrast, councils who retain authority often receive credit for work actually performed by committees. Despite these negatives, it is often difficult to wean councils away from their preoccupation with control and detail. They must be reoriented to higher demands, which, in itself, should be attractive to at least the stronger members.

At the extreme, full autonomy, committees report directly to the congregation in their functional area.[7] This confidence may take years to develop, but is a worthy goal. Whatever their degree of independence, no intervening authority should ever be imposed between the church council and committees. Such imposition impedes vertical communications and reduces lower echelon status and pride. What we seek are self-governing semi-autonomous committees fully capable of independently carrying out their demanding commissions. Keep in mind that committees know their subject matter better than anyone else. This strength alone should justify their largely self-rule.

Committees must keep the council informed of their activities and plans, particularly those warranting broader perspective. Surprises are not a welcome occurrence in any enterprise, particularly churches steeped in tradition. Committee as well as council decisions should always be explained and justified, not simply announced as a *fait accompli*. An informed congregation is a safeguard against faulty leadership, whereas ignorance allows questionable practices to go unchallenged.

Pastoral guidance at the committee level is, of course, essential, although it is not unusual for pastors to sometimes overlook committees in favoring the church council. There are, naturally, just so many meetings an individual can attend. But each committee should be honored by at least an occasional pastoral visit to consecrate and encourage their work.[8] And pastors should seek out committee chairs for periodic informal briefings.

Committee Strategy

The committee arrangement is tremendously advantageous. Quality is invariably improved by the focused attention and integrated judgment of each group's assembled experts. The only caution is that too much specialization can lead to lack of perspective. One can only imagine, for example, how a worship service might be altered if designed exclusively by the church choir, senior's club, or any other special interest party. Therefore, committees must strive for balance.

As envisioned under servant leadership, church committees serve as functional line units in their specialty, subject only to certain restrictions as may be imposed by the church council, and always attentive to pastoral guidance. This means, for example, that design of the worship service is established by the Worship and Music Committee with pastoral and music director approval, the Sunday school curriculum is set by the church Education Committee, and so on. The necessary check and balance required is inherent in the spread of authority among committee members operating essentially as self-monitoring "teams," and the ever-watchful eyes of the congregation's pastors, trustees, and council. Most important, the congregation itself exercises the greatest protective influence by its tacit approval. Frankly, there is very little a committee can do seriously wrong for long without hearing about it from someone. Congregations should have little concern about giving their committees too much responsibility.

Committee action is also safeguarded by rigorous job descriptions detailing scope of authority and appropriate approval requirements. Such guidance typically includes the following recommended policies:

(1) Committee members must strive for expertise in their functional area by engaging in scholarly reading, visiting other churches to witness exemplary practice, and through extended dialog with the congregation. Members owe the congregation their industry and sound judgment. Individuals who consistently base their approval on personal preference should be admonished to engage in more studied assessment.

(2) Issues will be systematically investigated using all available resources, including outside consultants as may be required. Discussion, analysis, and debate are the working tools of committee deliberations. Dissent should be treated honorably as an act of faith. The trustees and council will be kept informed and their assistance/approval requested as needed.

(3) Controversial proposals will be trial-tested to assist in determining their feasibility.

(4) Committees will endeavor to appoint non-members to administer programs under their auspice whenever such action is expeditious.

Committee Responsibilities

These nine duties constitute the principal responsibilities of church standing committees:

    1. Staff and manage day-to-day activities in the committee's mandated functional specialty, always seeking perfection through Christ.

2. Delegate operational responsibilities among committee members, preferably extending roles to the congregation.
3. Recommend and conduct necessary inter-committee coordination.
4. Seek advice and assistance from the pastor, church council, and trustees as appropriate.
5. Obtain council approval of major new undertakings as may be required, or voluntarily as a privilege and courtesy.
6. Train new committee chair person, typically the chair-elect.
7. Continuously recruit new members employing the stewardship committee as needed.
8. Prepare an annual operational plan of activities and objectives. Prepare a yearly committee report and critique. Maintain a record of "lessons learned."
9. Review and recommend changes in committee/chairman job description.

Ad Hoc Special Task Forces

Appointment of special task forces arises when projects are so unique or require special skills or time beyond the capacities of current staffing. Calling a new pastor or a large construction program often qualify for such treatment. In lesser instances, care must be taken for such an appointment may convey a certain lack of confidence in the current organizational structure. Standing committees, as the backbone of the church, should never be arbitrarily sidestepped without their involvement in a negotiated agreement. Associated committee members should be among the first asked to serve in any specially formed group. The committee chair, in particular, with the most to lose, should be extended a sincere invitation. The creditability and honor of standing committees must always be carefully preserved.

---

[1] An example of confident listening are pastors willing to establish a pulpit team to periodically critique sermons and advise on preaching, see page 227.

[2] James MacGregor Burns, cited in Charles E. Bennison, Jr., et al, *In Praise of Congregations* (Boston, Cowley Publications, 1999), p. 222.

[3] Common congregational prayer for its pastors.

[4] The letters to Timothy and Titus are the only books in the New Testament written primarily for Christian ministers. Both letters are generally attributable to Paul. Paul first advises great care in selection of church leaders. Then three ministerial functions are deemed especially important: (1) care in preaching with vigor and enthusiasm, (2) setting an example "...in speech and conduct, in love, in faith, in purity," and (3) control of worship emphasizing prayer and explanation of Scripture through preaching and teaching.

[5] This section is highly dependent on the work of Robert K. Greenleaf, who, perhaps more than any other observer of management, saw the great, largely untapped, potential of trustees to lead organizations to higher institutional performance and to their own personal satisfaction. In the church, trustees best serve in an *advisory* capacity, with authority vested in the elected representative council. This arrangement differs from that of most public and corporate sector applications, which Greenleaf primarily addresses, where trustees retain final authority. Greenleaf's recommendations have been modified accordingly. See Robert K. Greenleaf, *Seeker and Servant* (San Francisco, Jossey-Bass, 1996), pages 231-273, and Greenleaf, *Servant Leadership* (New York, Paulist Press, 1977), pages 49-133.

[6] Staff positions that may report directly to the council (generally through the appropriate committee) include the pastor, Director of Arts and Music (Worship and Music), and Sunday School Superintendent (Education).

[7] The Boards (committees) of Our Savior Lutheran Church, for example, are autonomous, reporting directly to the congregation. "Our church council makes no decisions. That's a big change from the old tradition. The job of that group is to totally look forward, to plan. So there aren't any three-hour council meetings about the hole in the roof or problems with ushering. The Boards (committees) all make their own decisions and build their own budgets. They're responsible directly to the congregation. Our council asks questions." Roger R. Skatrud, pastor, Our Savior Lutheran Church, Chippewa Falls, Wis.

[8] One reason pastors don't often visit committee meetings is because so little real authority is involved that non-attendance is inconsequential. Assign actual responsibility for the Sunday service to the Worship and Music Committee and see how attendance increases!

Part IV.
Leadership in Practice

Chapter 11
Communications and Planning

This chapter presents two essential elements of management–communications, attentive listening and providing direction; and developing a plan of action. No one can lead without communication skills, and no progress can be made without self-study and planning. Church management is no exception.

Attention is focused on informal discussion and receptive listening, fundamentals of effective communications. More formal deliberations, e.g., council meetings, and the special persuasive elements involved are presented in Chapter 12, "How to Conduct Meetings and Reach Decisions." Part of informal communications is encouraging creativity and dissent, emphasized here as essential for full understanding and eventual unity, yet too frequently avoided as "troublesome." The role of ombudsman is also reported as a liaison of special value in resolving controversial issues.

The second part of the chapter discusses planning with special attention to its first step, self-study. Formulating the path ahead seeking God's will in all things is the essence of the Christian pilgrim.

Effective Communications

Communications is the exchange of thoughts, messages, or information by speech and writing and, to a lesser degree, by personal behavior. A "wink," for example, can be a very effective means of communications under certain circumstances. The interaction is to inform and become informed, as well as to please, comfort, care for, and, indeed, convey all manner of human emotions. Communications is always a dual affair, between two or more people, transmitter(s) and receiver(s). The critical component is achieving acceptance and response, not simply providing information.

We communicate to inform, instruct, or influence action. It is the basic means for all human interactions. Good communications ensures that everyone is operating from the same information base, circulates ideas and viewpoints, raises and answers questions, and exposes and reconciles differences. Good communications also develops teamwork through understanding and unified effort. The exact purposes involved are generally dependent on the needs or goals of the source. Receivers, on the other hand, may typically perceive the communication in terms of their own interpretation as opposed to its original purpose. The effectiveness of communications is thus highly dependent on the receiver's understanding and acceptance as well as the transmitter's intent.

Rather than being taken for granted and neglected, communications within churches, as with all organizations, should be periodically evaluated to test for effectiveness, distortion, and transmission failures. Does the system keep everyone informed, encourage interaction and debate, and cultivate new approaches? Regular channels must be in place to achieve each of the many purposes involved. Deficiencies can be determined through informal surveys. Upward communications, in particular, must be encouraged. Individuals in the congregation are the single best source of creative new ideas. They are most sensitive to church shortcomings. They are the recipients of poor sermons, unending meetings, and dominating leaders. They must be free of rebuke and encouraged to speak up. The next division of this chapter, "Encouraging Creativity and Dissent," focuses on this role.

The Art of Dialog and Receptive Listening

The subject here is earnest *dialog*, intentional discourse, as opposed to simple casual conversation. The distinguishing features are *substance* (meaningful content) and *exchange* (giving and receiving reciprocally). Open dialog precedes and is a source of information for subsequent analysis (methodical examination), the latter often performed by a specially assigned group. Dialog is spoken conversation, exchanging thoughts, expressions, and feelings. Its purpose is to gain understanding and examine differences and similarities. It is built on respect and connective thinking which focuses on participant strengths not weaknesses, tapping into the wisdom of each individual to develop understanding and common ground. Persuasion and debate are not part of dialog. Consensus is not sought. What is encouraged is sharing and inquiry based on genuine interest and intent to learn. The basic rules of dialog are guaranteed attentiveness, receptivity, interaction, and response.

Underlying all effective dialog is receptive listening. The two–speaking and listening–are integral, necessary to establish the duality of the conversation, i.e., the *exchange* required. The great power of listening is the rapport it establishes with the speaker thereby creating opportunities for interaction. To a degree, the listener must be willing to abandon control of the direction the conversation takes, to follow rather than lead, to recognize one's vulnerability and seek strength in others.

"Listening might be defined as an attitude toward other people and what they are attempting to express. It begins with attention, both the outward manifestation and the inward alertness. It includes constructive responses that help the other person express both thoughts and feelings. The good listener remains in a position to assess the relationship among facts, opinions, attitudes, and feelings being expressed and is therefore able to respond to the total expression of the other person."[1]

Henry Kaiser (1882-1967), father of modern shipbuilding, was reported as saying, when asked his key to success, "I surrounded myself with people smarter than me, and I listened to them." Calvin Coolidge understood this importance in commenting, "No one ever *listened* himself out of a job."

Leading Group Discussion

We define *group discussion* as an informal discourse on a particular topic, generally involving little or no preparation or recording. (The distinction of presiding over official meetings is reported in Chapter 12.) Any discussion leader, however informally appointed, should be perceptive of what's going on to ensure a positive outcome. The posture must be primarily that of seeing and listening while keeping one's own analytical apparatus quiet. We're talking about "...sensitive, empathetic, concentrated listening to discover what people are really trying to communicate."[2]

These rules may be employed by group leaders and participants to promote effective group discussion:

(1) **Be inquisitive, eager for knowledge.** Convey to others a real interest in what they are saying and a readiness to positively respond. This "attentive" listening requires trying hard to really understand what the other person is saying. It requires undivided focused attention without being preoccupied by one's own thoughts or distracted by surrounding events. Attentiveness may be shown through eye contact, head nodding, and encouraging expression.

(2) **Ask questions to clarify and ensure understanding.** Questions show interest and build confidence and trust in the speaker. "Grant that I

may seek not so much to be understood as to understand." –Saint Francis of Assisi (1181-1226) founder of the Franciscan Order.

(3) **Encourage all to be heard** beyond the most articulate or forceful. Interaction and the give-and-take of group discussion may, in fact, encourage many hesitant individuals to join in. Accommodate the malcontents as well as the creative. Appreciate the diversity and value of everyone's contributions. If notes are taken, be sure the minority position and rejected arguments are recorded.

(4) **Strive for honesty.** Candor–frank, sincere, impartial expression–underlies all effective communication. Without honesty, speech is hollow and distracting. In early discussions in particular, encourage diversity and dissent by an informal atmosphere of support. In addition, it is surprising how much honest communication can take place during "breaks" and other "off-the-record" conversation.

(5) **Avoid judgmental intrusions.** One of the greatest barriers to communications is the automatic tendency of the receiver to evaluate the content in his or her own frame of reference, including impressions of the speaker. Who is speaking may influence what is believed as much as what is being said. We never want to prejudice or polarize ourselves in this way. Information gathering should be a neutral activity. Interpretation and evaluation are reserved for later more detached sessions of study and analysis. As fellow Christians we must remain unified, respectfully seeking the truth together as one spirit.

(6) **Build positive expectations.** Inform participants of how the discussion content will be employed and how they may be further involved in the process. Schedule follow-on discussions for topics requiring continuation. Thank people for their contribution.

(7) **Assess what has transpired**. Critique your discussion session, asking participants if they felt they were able to get fully involved and were honestly heard. Appointment of a "recorder" to take notes will help your review. Schedule follow-on discussions if required.

Encouraging Vision, Creativity, and Criticism[3]

Forget the former things; do not dwell on the past. See, I am doing a new thing! Now it springs up; do you not perceive it? (Isaiah 43:18-19)

Saint Paul wrote: *Do not put out the Spirit's fire; do not treat prophecies with contempt. Test everything. Hold on to the good. Avoid every kind of evil.* (1 Thessalonians 19-22)

"We have to have respect for people with unusual talent." Observation on John Nash, Nobel Prize winner in economics, 1994.

The visionary, or prophet, sees into the future what later proves to be true. The creative person brings about new things. Critics judge and evaluate to change and improve. All three types of advice are powerful instruments to discern and carry out God's will. They must be encouraged for we know that God speaks to us in many new and different ways. No matter the conflicts or turmoil, we remain comforted knowing that we are being led where the spirit of Jesus wants to lead us.

Need for extremism. All three forces–vision, creativity, and criticism–require great effort and conviction, sometimes labeled "extremism" especially by mistrusting souls. But extremism, defined here as advocacy resorting to measures beyond the norm based on firm conviction, can and should be viewed in a positive manner. In this sense all three temperaments–visionary, creator, and critic–are typically extremists, commonly resorting to assertive and persistent efforts in order to bring about change against what is commonly perceived as disfavoring odds and even hostility.

Many great men and women have been "extremists" in this sense. The case is elegantly made by Reverend Martin Luther King Jr. in a letter from Birmingham city jail.

> But as I continued to think about the matter (Negro birthright of freedom) I gradually gained a bit of satisfaction from being considered an extremist. Was not Jesus an extremist in love? "Love your enemies, bless them that curse you, pray for them that despitefully use you." Was not Amos an extremist for justice–"Let justice roll down like waters and righteousness like a might stream." Was not Paul an extremist for the gospel of Jesus Christ–"I bear in my body the marks of the Lord Jesus." Was not Martin Luther an extremist–"Here I stand; I can do none other so help me God." Was not John Bunyan an extremist–"I will stay in jail to the end of my days before I make a butchery of my conscience." Was not Abraham Lincoln an extremist–"This nation cannot survive half slave and half free." Was not Thomas Jefferson an extremist–"We hold these truths to be self evident that all men are created equal."

The church has a long history of duty and respect for authority that is now being increasingly tested against new notions of popular sovereignty and dissent. Some of this challenge stems from our increasing awareness of "the basic principles of Americanism–the right to criticize. The right to hold unpopular beliefs. The right to protest. The right of independent thought." –Margaret Chase Smith (1897-1995) U.S. Senator and Representative. Congregations are prompted to take advantage of these rights by what they perceive as the immutable status of churches in a dynamically changing world. Thus the task has become one of balancing the multiple and often conflicting interests involved in such a manner as to "promote and protect and defend the integrity and the dignity of the individual,...essentially the meaning of religion."

–David Lilienthal (1899-1981) father of public power.

Visionaries. "In each class there are born a certain number of natures with a curiosity about their best self, with a bent for seeing things as they are, for disentangling themselves from machinery, for simply concerning themselves with reason and the will of god, and doing their best to make these prevail...and this bent always tends to take them out of their class and to make their distinguishing characteristic their 'humanity.' They have, in general, a rough time of it in their lives." –Matthew Arnold (1822-1888) English poet and critic, *Culture and Anarchy*.

Visionaries, in carving their own path, seek to see farther and probe deeper than other people. Too often they are prematurely evaluated, often in great error. Consider these rejections:

"The wireless music box has no imaginable commercial value. Who would pay for a message sent to nobody in particular." –Associates of David Sarnoff (1891-1971) pioneer in American communications, in response to his urgings for investment in the radio in the 1920s.

"Who the hell wants to hear actors talk?" –Harry M. Warner (1881-1958) pioneer of the sound film industry, 1927.

"I think there is a world market for maybe five computers." –Thomas Watson, chairman of IBM, 1943.

Rather than be labeled "trouble-makers," visionaries should be recognized as sources of God's revelations, to be empowered, not dispelled. Too often, instead, caution prevails. We "play it safe," going with the proven, staying within our capabilities, limiting our choices, whereas the real risk is not being led by the Spirit. Through prayer we learn God's mission for us, the true reality.

The critic. "...the demonstrators...are undertaking the time-honored, indispensable mission of democratic crowds; to crack a wrongheaded consensus, to energize actual and potential reformers on the inside, to polarize opinion and goad laggards, to precipitate public debates that have been suppressed by establishments or pursued only by experts in closed rooms where inertia and groupthink overwhelm dissent." –Todd Gitlin, professor of journalism and sociology, Columbia University, editorial, *The Washington Post*, April 16, 2000. "... jarring wake-up calls are rarely greeted with thankful smiles." –Carl Rowan (1925-2000) syndicated newspaper columnist.

In any group there are always a few individuals opposed to the majority position, or, at least prefer an alternative. They are often original or non-conventional thinkers. And sometimes they are dead right. Even when wrong, this creative aspect serves as a natural counter-balancing element that should always be welcome as a potential check on the possible lock-step consistency of the majority. A moderate degree of conflict is typically evidence of vitality, awareness, and interest—healthy conditions enabling change and growth.

Critics view speaking up for the minority, the underrepresented, the unpopular position, as a shining moment. They prefer debate and controversy as opposed to polite conversation. They strive for an open, egalitarian, and collegial relationship among church members rather than a hierarchical structure. Often, a profound feeling of isolation from the decision-making process affects their church life, a frustration born of a sense of powerlessness. However, by their nature, those that tend to find faults with others are generally remarkably tough themselves, able to ignore insult and outlast exclusion, to remain steadfast and upright. They may take refuge in knowing that "the Holy Ghost alone is in the true position of a critic...able to show what is wrong without wounding and hurting." –Oswald Chambers (1874-1917) Scottish evangelical prophet. Critics then should be guided by the Spirit in making strategic and deliberate decisions about how and when and for how long to promote a cause.

While encouraging constructive criticism, we must duly note that being constantly negative is wrong-headed and destructive. It tears down rather than builds up, drains our energy, adds tension, and arouses feelings of frustration and anger. Individuals so driven must be advised, yea admonished, to recognize common ground, observe protocol, be supportive, and seek honest resolution of differences.

The Ombudsman

House critic, inspector-general, arbiter, advocate, ombudsman, however termed, this position is a unique and important office indeed. The ombudsman position is a vital link between any organization's rank-and-file and management, religious institutions being no exception. Yet the role is rare within churches because of the encompassing parental care expected of pastors presumably precluding the need for any alternative avenue. But this reliance is deceptive, evident in the considerable turmoil and dissatisfaction within many churches. An ombudsman, in response, serves as a continuous dependable intermediary, providing an independent and neutral means for resolving problems. This liaison must be provided apart and quite distant from any response or failure to respond by staff and lay leaders, for they may, in fact, be part of the problem. Having said this, it is also proper to recognize that truly receptive pastors and responsible lay leaders, caring what the congregation thinks, largely negates the need for any supplemental envoy.

An ombudsman is appointed to field and investigate complaints, report findings to the appropriate parties, and, occasionally, when assigned, mediate settlements. The office may be so demanding as to require a team approach. However organized, the position must have the confidence and trust of all concerned. Congregation members should view the position as a receptive, effective channel to those in authority; church leaders similarly as a source of constructive assistance.

When needed. Problems are often so awkward to those involved that a detached mediator is a welcome relief. If questioned, the ombudsman position should be at least tested on a trial basis. In most instances the need is clear. Church leaders may be remote and insensitive, occasionally even lofty and possibly arrogant in their positions. Left on their own they become inclined to rely more and more on a kind of "in-house" mentality that typically defends and explains rather than questions. When questions are raised they are sidetracked. From a member standpoint, individuals may feel "uncomfortable" in expressing dissatisfactions and possibly even fear reprisal. However modest such conditions may be, they tend to thwart critical commentary from all but the most stalwart parishioner. Hence the need, in most instances, for the ombudsman.

Position duties. At its expanded scope, the ombudsman position includes the following responsibilities:

1. **Careful, first-hand, discerning observation to fully understand operating conditions and personnel.** The ombudsman must be fully informed to be able to knowledgeably respond to queries. While not an initiator, the informed ombudsman may tell others what to think about without conveying judgment. This broadcast of topics may include disclosing information the congregation needs, but what others may wish be kept secret for self-interest purposes.

2. **Encourage congregation members and staff to express their personal opinions and observations.** Most congregation members fail to realize their influence within their own church. It simply never occurs to them that anyone actually cares about what they think, much less welcomes what they may have to say. So encouragement is required at all times. This especially is the ombudsman's responsibility—to convey that everyone's ideas are valuable. Sometimes the individual thinking of one person can illuminate and guide us better than all the panels and commissions the church might convene.

3. **Field and present new ideas and criticism constructively** in such a manner as to prompt reform rather than spur resentment. This central function begins with *soliciting* congregational ideas not merely passively waiting for inputs. Suggestions and questions must then be put forth in a constructive, positive manner, typically requiring involvement in the response process.

Information and persuasion to rethink situations are the tools of the ombudsman. Actually, in most instances, there is likely to be very little difference between what the ombudsman may point out and what church leaders already know they should do. In reality, the principal function of the ombudsmen is to make leaders think about who they represent and serve, their standards, and the quality of service they seek. This is all that should be expected of the job. The ombudsman cannot force an issue. He or she must rely on convincing those in power of their responsibility to honestly and diligently attend to issues as they surface.

4. **Hold church leaders accountable to the congregation.** The toughest duty of the ombudsman is to get church leaders to acknowledge their responsibility as elected representatives to honestly listen and respond to *all* reasonable advice and criticism. This is part of our belief

that all Christians are at once both humble servants before our Lord and favored disciples.

What must the ombudsman avoid? The ombudsman should never be the source of actions. To maintain the office's independence and detachment, the ombudsman must only represent others, never initiating action, always a neutral, unaffiliated intermediary, seeking only honest presentation and open examination. Thus the ombudsman is never an advocate except for openness, truth, and God's will.

The ombudsman position should never be a substitute for direct dealings between involved parties. Quite the contrary. The ombudsman promotes direct contacts, never interfering, serving exclusively as liaison, and, if need be, a court of last resort. The ombudsman needs to convey to the congregation this limited role thereby promoting rather than circumventing normal lines of communication and authority.

Personal traits of the ombudsman. This is not a position for the timid or weak of heart. It requires courage, energy, and diplomacy, a rare combination. At his or her best, the ombudsman has:

(1) a profound sense of what is fair and the courage to pursue the hard and unattractive position.
(2) a willingness to step outside one's own assumptions and prejudices.
(3) a healthy skepticism that things are not as perfect or simple as they appear.
(4) the receptivity to intently listen, to encourage open discussion and ferret out underlying conditions.
(5) the ability to express positions accurately, well, and constructively without bias.
(6) an unlimited capacity to delve into facts and figures and the stick-to-itiveness to achieve final resolution.
(7) a willingness to occasionally look beyond the rulebook to see if the higher missions of the church are in fact being served by present imposed restrictions.

Suggestion systems have one advantage over the ombudsman, anonymity and therefore immunity to the initiator. However, an ombudsman is much preferred, substituting human interaction with all its flexibility and sensitivity for the mechanics and limitations of written commentary. Also, anonymously authored suggestions may too often be reduced to petty grievances and unfounded accusations, harmful in their own right. Typically, the suggestion box remains empty, testimony to its ineffectiveness.

Open Forums/Critiques

Group discussions can be structured or, as more commonly practiced, informal. Open forums and critiques tend to be structured. Both are suitable for congregation use. Forums typically involve expert or staff discussion of designated topics with audience participation encouraged.

Or they may be more loosely designed as an open session with minimal agenda other than a theme or series of related topics. Forums, however, are distinguished from open discussions in typically having an intended purpose, specific invitees, a leader, and democratic procedures. The rules of effective group discussion (pages 149-150), of course, still apply.

Critiques are largely a neglected form of communications because, quite frankly, their purpose is generally perceived as criticism. While this is partially true, positive elements are also addressed and negative observations can and should be expressed *constructively* as a means for improvement. Not a meeting, class, sermon, or any principal church assembly should take place without arrangements for a following-on candid review, however minimal. A qualified participant may simply be asked to perform this task, rendering a brief written or oral response privately at the end of the session. It is amazing how much improvement is possible by simply responding to another's observations, if we would only be willing to listen. *Where there is no guidance, a nation fails, but in an abundance of counselors there is safety.* (Proverbs 11:14)

Long-Range Planning and Self-Study

Do not be conformed to this world, but be transformed by the renewing of your minds, so that you may discern what is the will of God—what is good and acceptable and perfect. (Romans 12:2) *"For I know the plans I have for you," declares the Lord, "plans to prosper you and not to harm you, plans to give you hope and a future."*

(Jeremiah 29:11)

"If no plans are made to discern where God is leading, the congregation will keep on doing what it has always done and likely with declining meaning."

–Harold E. Bauman, *Congregations and Their Servant Leaders.*

Planning is a matter of formulating a scheme or program for the accomplishment of a specific task or attainment of a given objective. Planning day-to-day affairs is relatively routine and automatic. As the scope of activities expands and is projected, however, planning becomes much more complex and difficult. Such so-called "long-range" planning is systematic and extended, involving greater potential and higher risks. Plans of this nature often cover a five, even a ten-year period. They attempt to spell out the future, designing the proper aggressive response to changing conditions and challenges. Yet despite this great value, congregations often neglect extended planning. They are too willing to let well-enough alone, content with the status quo, unwilling to risk what God may ask. Much prayer is thus required to reach out to find God's calling. Christian planning is a very noble venture indeed, an intimate relationship with God's will, serving with joy and thanksgiving.

The breadth of planning requires some focusing for church application. Consider this typical scope:

1. Define and continuously re-define mission.
2. Identify major programs/activities required for mission accomplishment.
3. Set program priorities and/or order of performance.
4. Secure and align required resources.
5. Determine appropriate program methodology.
6. Coordinate programs.
7. Set performance measurements/benchmarks and evaluate.
8. Reallocate resources based on program evaluations.

Most congregations include planning activities 1 through 4 as part of their long-range planning. The remaining four activities are generally left, by default, to the respective operating elements. Setting performance standards and program evaluation are generally minimal, with all work considered "good" however questionably needed or performed. See step #3 below, "Evaluate and prioritize."

Who does long-range planning? The basic responsibility for long-range planning rests with the church council. However, planning may well be delegated to the church trustees who have both the time and inclination required. In fact, councils may serve best by maintaining a long-range mentality while standing just outside the planning process itself performed by trustees. And trustees generally have the semi-detached collegial relationship essential for impartial planning.

A real stumbling block to planning is hesitant councils, too busy or too imbedded in the given path, yet unwilling to relinquish responsibility to others. If planning is absent it is probably not because of any lack of need. Therefore, councils and trustees must be aware that discerning God's will in all things is the church's greatest responsibility.

Nature of Long-Range Planning

The mechanics of planning appear simple enough. Once the decision to plan is made (and it is a continuous process), four principal steps described below are involved. A complete written plan includes presentation of all four elements for they are sequentially interdependent. (Note, *implementation* of the plan is a distinct follow-on management function.)

(1) Gather and study information.

This first step identifies and attempts to understand <u>what the church is doing and why</u>. It is primarily descriptive, but must not get engrossed in detail.[4] What are the church's present activities and their justification? Where do the real strengths lie, where are weaknesses? What is happening in the community and its implication to church responsibilities? This step also attempts to look ahead, to visualize future developments and opportunities. Such intelligence gathering is often referred to as "self-study," presented in some detail in the next section.

A significant component of information gathering and examination is the encouragement of new ideas and programs. Perceiving God's will as he guides us toward our future is the essence of Christian planning. Without prayerful creative thinking, planning is pretty much a redundant exercise. Planners therefore must be prayerful, inventive, able to visualize opportunities and receptive to new ideas. "Regardless of the stress of circumstances, institutions function better when the idea, the dream, is to the fore... Dreams should be articulated by whomever is the ablest dreamer, and leaders should always be open to persuasion by dreamers." –Robert Greenleaf (1904-1990) father of modern servant-leadership.

Another important dimension in gathering information is through use of surveys. The questionnaire should rigorously deal with all elements of church operations under investigation. The intent is to securing honest, frank responses, preferably with proffered recommendations. Accompanying personal interviews often ferret out feelings and opinions that might otherwise remain unexpressed. Often more can be learned by talking with one disgruntled member than a host of satisfied parishioners. The source and use of all sensitive material must, of course, be vigilantly restricted, preferably by a single appointed investigating officer. The survey dimensions may also include site visits to other churches to identify means by which others have solved their problems. All such evaluation efforts may benefit greatly from employment of an outside trained enabler, knowledgeable in survey design, testing, and interpretation.

(2) Develop program objectives and goals.

The intent of every program, old and new, must be known. This is a time to be realistic about what should and can be accomplished. And be as specific as possible. An evangelism goal of 20 new family members (based on last year's 15-member accomplishment), for example, adds realism, encouragement, and reasonable pressure. Goals are typically worked out with the assistance of the subject committee.

(3) Evaluate and prioritize.

This most difficult third step decides which programs to maintain, expand, contract, initiate, or delete. It is diagnostic in its focus. In theory, the idea is to equate marginal returns, an economic concept, thereby ensuring the most productive use of resources. In practice this amounts to ranking the expected returns from adding dollars and staff to each program, then supporting those activities where the results appear most productive. Comparisons are, of course, typically a matter of judgment. This should not be too disconcerting for most decisions are, in fact, matters of evaluation. If, for example, a small contingent of evangelists encourages a dozen or so new families to join the church, strengthening this group would likely be a better use of personnel than adding additional members to an already seemingly adequate Sunday school staff. In simplest terms then, programs should be expanded where the highest returns relative to costs are expected, and curtailed where additions appear unwarranted. Often incremental funding is most productive with small programs where a few additional dollars can produce big results.

Kennon Callahan, church management consultant, reminds us that a church's strengths "...are present precisely because God has enabled His people to develop them. A church that decides to claim its strengths affirms that the power of God has been at work in the congregation, enabling it to develop these specific strengths."[5] He then adds, "The art of long-range planning is to decide those few strategic new strengths that it makes sense to add in the coming five to seven years. Successful churches work smarter, not harder."[6] Thus the most critical element of planning, this second step, is essentially that of determining not only which key programs to expand, but also, as important, which promising new ones to add with the rest expected to carry on as usual.

(4) Design ways and means to accomplish plan directives and goals.
This final step spells out how the plan and goals are to be accomplished in terms of budget, staffing, procedures, and progress benchmarks. The typical Who? What? Where? When? basics. (Note, actual implementation is carried out by the involved operational officers and thus is *not* part of planning.) Operators, of course, will have participated in some of the planning work, yet must be fully briefed on implementation. Their understanding and cooperation is obviously essential if the plan is to succeed.

A complete plan also recognizes the importance of early success in its implementation. Reasonably straightforward likely successful actions should be scheduled first, building confidence and capability. Also, existing programs are easier to expand than starting new ones. Finally, new programs are strengthened if they are part of a mutually reinforcing complementary set. Recruitment of young couples and expanding child-care is an obvious example; cultivating lay leadership while concurrently offering training and apprenticeships another.

Budget and staffing may initially be "roughed-in" to be detailed later as experience dictates. New ventures especially require ensured funding and resourceful initial leadership.

Self-Study
The will of God is not a system of rules which is established from the outset; it is something new and different in each different situation in life, and for this reason a man must ever anew examine what the will of God may be. The heart, the understanding, observation and experience must all collaborate in this task. Our knowledge of God's will is not something over which we ourselves dispose, but it depends solely upon the grace of God, and this grace is and requires to be new every morning.

–Dietrich Bonhoeffer (1906-1945) German theologian and Protestant resistance leader.

If we could first know where we are, and whither we are tending, we could better judge what to do, and how to do it. −Abraham Lincoln, the "House Divided Speech."

Some things go wrong and change is okay. Leaders must always recognized, and consider as a challenge, the very real possibility that some of what is going on in the organization may not be working. Such skepticism is offset by the remedy, a healthy respect for new ideas and constructive debate. The very nature of leadership is to advance the cause, so newness and change are actually evidence of leadership. Without new goals, new ventures, there is no leadership only maintenance. Therefore leaders must always ask, "How can we improve this situation?"

We should all appreciate the fact that change is not an admission that something is necessarily wrong; rather that improvement, progress, growth, or development is possible. Yet many in authority are reluctant to make changes, claiming it is too disruptive, potentially harmful. One of the hardest tasks of leaders is to convince others that change provides at least the opportunity if not reality to improve. And even when mistakes are made they are often minor and readily corrected. Failures should be considered learning lessons. *Do not stifle inspiration or despise prophetic utterance, but test them all; keep hold of what is good and avoid all forms of evil.* (1 Thessalonians 5:19-22)

Finally, making improvements should be recognized as a tough business requiring determined leadership. Optimism (expecting the best possible outcome), enthusiasm (excitement and interest in the cause), and resolution (firm determination) are all called for. Changes must often be pushed through in the face of hostility and unexplained rejection. Still, pushing should always be done with a light hand. Sometimes one must resort to a church-wide hearing to overcome a persistent negative minority. Too often weak leadership succumbs, thus we return to the necessary prerequisites: optimism, enthusiasm, and resolution.

The philosophy of self-study is one of communal examination and reflection in joyous celebration of determining God's will. The basic elements are continuous prayer and scripture reading, recognition of change as a Christ-derived precept, and purposeful investigation. The task may initially appear daunting because of the breadth of programs and activities involved. But some simplification can be added by recognizing that all church activities can be investigated in terms of three underlying qualities:

(1) **Does the church honor and uplift the Lord Jesus Christ** through a spirit of worship, and love and devotion to him in all gatherings and in its ministry? Is this evident in commitment to the Bible and dependency on the Holy Spirit's work among us?

(2) **Is the congregation warm, friendly, and caring**, inviting one and all to belong to and share in Christian brotherhood?

(3) **Is the church supportive of growth and change**, recognizing the talents and creativity of members and constructively responding to new ideas and suggestions?

Besides this focus, the list of self-examination topics may be reduced by relatively cursory examination of many long-standing church activities that have been refined over time to efficient routines needing little further study.

Self-Study Procedures[7]

Self-study is basically gathering and analyzing subject information with resulting recommendations. Every viable source of information should be considered to include: (1) existing reviews, studies, and reports, (2) interviews with church pastors, leaders, members, and visitors, (3) open forum discussions, (4) surveys, (5) library references, (6) observations from visiting other congregations, (7) local community contacts and employment of consultants, and above all (8) prayer and scripture reading.

Personal interviews with members are often the surest means of identifying congregational strengths, weaknesses, and problems. An informal yet structured design is preferred, administered by trained personnel in strict confidence. Be sure to ferret out the ideas and positions of all parties, particularly the young, old, minorities, and discontent. Listen to the experience of former office holders. If the broadest possible canvas is sought, questionnaires will likely be required. They should always be pre-tested with special attention to establishing a systematic means of analysis. *...bringing every thought into captivity to the obedience of Christ.* (2 Corinthians 10:5)

The key to self-study remains identification of real problem areas and improvement opportunities without delving into what's working right or inconsequential details. The first step is that of establishing a systematic diagnostic approach. We recommend concentration on seven central characteristics of successful churches developed by Kennon Callahan[8], church management consultant. Numerous other listings are possible, but Callahan's seem most focused and suitable as a prototype guide. Reading the original source is strongly recommended. Again note that the intent of the self-study guide is to ask discerning questions that will eventually lead to significant improvements.

1. Specific, Concrete Missional Objectives

• Is the church concentrating on a few major missions developed through prayer and extended study of opportunities, needs, and resources?
• Is evangelism one of these missions for it surely cannot be neglected?
• Is both the efficiency and effectiveness of our means of delivery considered in mission selection and continuation? • Are the selected missions fully understood and approved by the membership? • Is delivery performed "...in a competent, compassionate, committed, and courageous manner..."[9]

2. Visitation and Outreach

• Does the church maintain a balanced program of visitations to members and newcomers and those in hospitals or homebound? • Is the number of visits per week acceptably proportional to the congregation size? • Is there an appropriate balance between pastor and lay visitations? • Are outreach visitors trained in "sharing and shepherding, relating and reaching, and winning and working," the major stages of visitation?

3. Corporate, Dynamic Worship

• Is there a strong sense of belonging, togetherness, and warmth within the congregation before, during, and after the service that conveys a sense of Christian love and fellowship? • Does the sense of grace and community that members share also find its way genuinely and authentically to visitors? • Is the music dynamic, inspirational, and high quality? • Does the preaching lead people to live their lives more fully and richly in the spirit of the New Testament message? • Is there a strong interconnected progression in the power and movement of the liturgy to an appropriate summit?

4. Significant Relational Groups

• Are there ample opportunities for congregational members to seek real community in meaningful groups in which significant sharing and caring can take place? • Is there a long-range plan for establishing new significant relational groups?

5. Strong Leadership Resources

• Do church leaders lead the congregation forward to accomplish substantive objectives or merely enable through nondirective guidance? • Is leadership balanced with complementary skills in analysis, support, encouragement, organization, and direction? • Is the church focused on a few specific, realistic, concrete, and achievable objectives? • Is the focus on activities or performance and accomplishment? • Are leaders selected first for their competency as opposed to commitment? • Are leaders allowed sufficient tenure in their position to achieve strong continuity? • Is the number of leadership opportunities appropriately proportional to the number of reasonably active members, say at least 1 to 15? • Are the pastor and staff properly focused on major issues and objectives and not details? • Is a positive recognition and reward system in place to nurture effective leadership? • Are key lay leaders encouraged to focus on mission rather than merely maintenance activities? • Are key leaders given the necessary authority to fulfill their responsibilities?

6. Streamlined Structure and Solid, Participatory Decision-Making

• Does the decision-making process contribute to the development of wise decisions that focus on important priorities? • Is the decision-making process participatory in being openly conducted with informal lead-time for discussion?   Is the end product decisions rather than endless discussion? • Do leaders properly focus as much on the decision-making process as the decisions themselves? • Does the church have the capacity to resolve rather than repress conflict? • Is a streamlined organizational structure in place that succeeds in involving people in the church's mission and not just committee meetings? Is decision-making delegated to the lowest level possible? • Do church meetings foster community, i.e., sharing with one another a sense of friendship and fellowship? • Do meetings have a stated agenda shared in advance?

7. Several Competent Programs and Activities
 • Does the church conduct one or two, perhaps three, major programs respected in the community as being solidly competent[10] and outstanding services? • Is a program evaluation system in place?

---

[1] Robert K. Greenleaf, *On Becoming a Servant Leader* (San Francisco, Jossey-Bass, 1996), p. 70.

[2] John Mallison, *Mentoring to Develop Disciples and Leaders* (Adelaide, South Australia, Openbook Publishers, 1998), p. 129.

[3] The rebel element in society is a very popular dimension and we avail ourselves of many quotations on the subject of dissent from observers in all walks of life.

[4] I am reminded of the perhaps apocryphal story of planning the design of the ill-fated Titanic. "We spent two hours deliberating on the carpeting for the First Class cabins and fifteen minutes discussing the ship's lifeboats." Alexander Carlisle, managing director of the shipyard on conferring with J. Bruce Ismay, owner of the White Star Line, 1911.

[5] Kennon L. Callahan, *Twelve Keys to an Effective Church* (San Francisco, Harper & Row, 1983), p. *xvi.*

[6] Ibid. p. *xviii.*

[7] For detailed guidance on self-evaluation see, among other sources, Harold E. Bauman, "Self Study" section, Chapter 11, "Nature of Long-Range Planning," *Congregations and Their Servant Leaders* (Scottdale, PA, Mennonite Publishing House, 1982).

[8] Callahan, *Twelve Keys to an Effective Church,* p. *xii-xiv.* Callahan lists five additional characteristics (not reported here) of effective churches related to their physical functionality–physical accessibility; community visibility; adequate parking, land, and landscaping; adequate space and facilities; and solid financial resources.

[9] Source unknown.

[10] Such acclaimed programs generally serve multiple groups and require leaders skilled in the involved function as well as management. Further, the function is usually directly related to one of the church's primary mission objectives.

Chapter 12
How to Conduct Meetings and Reach Decisions

"All the activity of the disciples is subject to the clear precept of their Lord. They are not left free to choose their own methods or adopt their own conception of their task. Their work is to be Christ-work, and therefore they are absolutely dependent on the will of Jesus. Happy are they whose duty is fixed by such a precept, and who are therefore free from the tyranny of their own ideas and calculations."
    –Dietrich Bonhoeffer (1906-1943) German theologian and Protestant resistance leader.

This is the second functional or technical chapter of *Part IV Leadership in Practice*. Here we discuss the seemingly simple, yet too often bungled job of conducting formal meetings and reaching agreement. A trained moderator is the solution.

How to Conduct Meetings

The subject at hand is *formal* meetings, pre-announced official assemblies of selected participants and guests responding to a prepared agenda that is primarily directed to church-wide issues requiring deliberation. This focus is made possible by restrictive programming, i.e., attending to routine matters through written reports, and by substantial advance preparation. These arrangements allow concentration on critical matters–problem solving and planning–tasks requiring disciplined attention and energy without impediment by distractions and fatiguing delays. The above definition is also restrictive in other aspects. It excludes discussion gatherings and meetings to issue orders and instructions, coordinate actions, or simply disseminate information. Also excluded are extended assignments involving protracted problems and long-range planning. What remain are real immediate problems requiring analysis, interaction, debate, resolution, and implementation. This then is the proper focus and major responsibility of senior level governing bodies.

In most instances, formal meetings of the type described are conducted principally by the church council. However, the guidance prescribed applies, to a degree, to all planned assemblies, especially those involving problem resolution.

Council meetings typically follow, in loose fashion, the Robert's Rules of Order. Real performance, however, regardless of structure, lies in leadership rather than procedure. And the responsibility is substantial in terms of both achieving desired objectives and in the effective involvement of participants. Because of these demands and challenges, meeting leadership should be rotated among truly qualified council and committee members, preferably those trained as facilitators.

The strategy of conducting effective meetings is organized here in sequential order under three headings–pre-meeting preparation, the meeting proper, and post-meeting follow-on. The rules recommended, and/or other suitable accepted guidance, should be studied by *all* leaders at the beginning of the church year with a clear understanding that they will be followed as best able. And all church officers should reaffirm their understanding that beyond these mechanics, the overarching purpose of all Christian gatherings is ultimately that of forming disciples for Christ.

Pre-Meeting Preparation

Pre-meeting steps are absolutely essential for a successful meeting. They include ensuring an assembly is required, setting the agenda, preparing participants, assigning a facilitator and recorder, and setting time and location. Most neglected is assurance that a meeting is actually necessary, and secondly, insufficient preparation of attendees. "Most of the time we simply heard reports requiring no group action." "We knew nothing of the agenda so spent most of the meeting familiarizing ourselves with the problems rather than their solution."

Responsibility for planning church council meetings rests with the council president, an "executive committee" of three or so key council members, and the church professional staff. The assigned moderator should also be present to ensure the legitimacy of each candidate topic and the agenda length. In fact, the highly visible moderator is most likely to be held responsible for the "success" of any meeting. In reality, of course, this responsibility rests with the entire seven-or-so-member planning group identified above. Their responsibilities include:

(1) Determine meeting necessity and required participation. Is a meeting absolutely necessary or can the tasks at hand be accomplished through individual or lower echelon contacts? Is there a real *issue* involved requiring *deliberation* or is the matter simply one of conveying information or perfunctory approval? Has the appropriate homework been performed with resulting information in place? These requirements deserve restatement for their neglect often overburdens and dulls too many senior-level assemblies. To be considered a legitimate agenda item, topics must meet three criteria: (1) involve a scope and/or echelon of activity requiring *council level* engagement,[1] (2) involve *issues* requiring *collective deliberation* and interactive judgment, and (3) have received appropriate *preparatory study* and investigation. When thus orchestrated, meetings become primarily "working sessions" devoted almost exclusively to problem solving and related planning.

This first preparatory step also calls for the identification of any special guests or congregational members whose presence is judged important or whose involvement would likely be helpful.

(2) Prepare agenda, announce meeting, and secure advance inputs. An agenda, in outline form, should be carefully prepared with exact statements of the issues or problems to be addressed together with alternative proposals, pros and cons, and relevant supporting material as available. Topics should be limited to what can be completed in 1 to 1 1/2 hour's time with appropriate pre-meeting preparation. Sorting out what actually needs to be accomplished focuses attention and saves everyone's time. The planning group should study the issues attempting to distinguish the large from the small, then set priorities of exactly *what* needs to be decided and the appropriate *level* of detail required. The church council, as the senior governing body, should be tasked only with broad overlapping problems that appear irresolvable at lower echelons. In addition to issue selection, the planning group should endeavor to secure appropriate supporting information for all scheduled topics. This task may be delegated to parties associated with an issue. So armed, the planning group can be confident in announcing a meeting.

Upon completion of the above preparation, the agenda, meeting time, and location may be posted. This announcement should be broadcast to all church members at least two weeks prior to the meeting date. Congregational meetings are the Lord's business so, naturally, all should be encouraged to attend. The scheduling should be convenient.[2] Between services or immediately after a single shortened mid-morning service is likely to be most suitable and encourage parishioner attendance. Lead-time should be sufficient to allow participants to arrange their calendar and prepare. Telephone contact with participants, even for regularly scheduled meetings, is also good insurance. It shows we care about each individual's involvement.

The announcement should request congregational members seeking to respond to agenda topics to do so in writing in advance, as little time will be available during the meeting for such commentary. It must be understood by all that meeting times are for deliberation primarily based on *previously prepared inputs*. Having so emphasized, it is still necessary and understood that a limited time will be available for floor inputs, a few minutes per speaker. While saving time, written inputs are generally more deliberate and substantive than those that may be encountered in offhand oral deliveries.

(3) Prepare and distribute supporting materials to participants. Meeting planners should prepare all relevant handout material, including received member commentary. Informed participants are effective participants. Preparation provides the running start. Of particular value is knowledge of known alternatives solutions and their respective pros and cons. Being able to evaluate in advance this aspect of possible solutions is likely to greatly expedite eventual resolution. However, securing this information is particularly demanding, requiring real homework. The planning group may wish to assign such responsibility to knowledgeable individuals familiar with the problem at hand. When collected, all preparatory material should be e-mailed or faxed to participants at least one week before the scheduled meeting.

(4) Verify or appoint a meeting moderator, recorder, and time-keeper. We strongly recommend appointment, in most instances, of a trained moderator/facilitator (not the council chair) to conduct the central deliberations portion of the meeting. Leading congregational meetings is *not* the same as guiding and leading the congregation as its chief elected officer. Moderating is an exceptional skill requiring training, impartiality, a high level of personal "objectivity and toughness," and a good sense of humor, qualities the congregational president may not have to the degree required or wish to exhibit. Exercising such qualities also may distort the desired persona of the presidential role. And, most important, the council president should be free to lead, to be an advocate when necessary, not curtailed by the restrictions imposed on the moderator's role.

A recorder should be designated and instructed in advance. Most conspicuously absent in meeting records is the justification of actions taken. The moderator may thus appropriately indicate to the recorder such content and all material to be a matter of **record. In addition, a visible record of key ideas may be recorded on large** mounted sheets of paper to assist participants in keeping track of what is occurring.

A time-keeper may be appointed to help keep the agenda on schedule and program speaker deliveries.

(5) Prepare meeting room. Name cards of participants should be in place on the conference table. Different colors may be used for council and committee-level positions. Seating attending officers at a large conference table with guests occupying the periphery concentrates attention on the voting body where it belongs. All chairs facing the center allow full eye contact. Post a door sign announcing the agenda and inviting attendance. Stack handout materials with an identifying sign near the entrance.

The Meeting Proper

The congregational president is commonly the presiding officer. Here dual qualities of warmth and understanding to promote good feelings and reduce tensions must be accompanied by strength to control proceedings and rigorously pursue agreement. The presiding officer is at once, moderator, prime mover, and consensus seeker. This breadth can be substantially lessened by employing a trained moderator (page 174) to guide the deliberation phase (#5, #6, and #7) of the meeting design which follows. The council president preferably will, at a minimum, call the meeting to order, make introductions, review the agenda and previously distributed materials (#2, #3, and #4 below), and provide added guidance as appropriate. During the deliberations the president should encourage free-flowing discussion, differing views, and be quick to appreciate suggestions, praise efforts, and push for even more. And he or she must surely help the moderator, if not lead in attempting to secure consensus (#7).

The design of meetings is important to ensure as favorable a start and process as possible. The strategy of opening and conducting a successful meeting include:

(1) Open with prayer and a short period of silence. As with Saint Francis of Assisi, let us be "bold to pray" for God's intervention and guidance. *"Again, truly I tell you, if two of you agree on earth about anything you ask, it will be done for you by my Father in heaven. For where two or three are gathered in my name, I am there among them."* (Matthew 18:19-20) *"When, however, the Spirit comes, who reveals the truth about God, he will lead you into all the truth."* (John 16:13) All church meetings should begin and end with corporate and individual prayer, acknowledging the comforting and guiding presence of the Holy Spirit.

(2) Introduce participants and recognize visitors. Welcome attending participants, with pleasure, identifying by name council officers and invited participants. Recognize guests and indicate that limited time will be available for their possible commentary. It is likely that the hospitality of those assembled will not rise about that shown by the meeting's leader. Therefore, from the beginning, the presiding officer should convey a sense of joy and well-being in God's service, a collegial supportive atmosphere. Even humor has its place, as a way of creating fresh bonds and new unity.[3]

(3) Review agenda, restating the task(s) at hand and parliamentary rules. With advance announcement and handouts, the agenda need be only briefly reviewed. However, the main issues and objectives should be restated clearly and succinctly so that all in attendance are reminded from the beginning of the real business at hand. "This evening we are scheduled to select one of three bids received to reconstruct the church organ. The main considerations are cost, functionality, and demonstrated contractor expertise." Do not repeat introductory content to someone who comes in late. That person will have to "catch up" on their own or be briefed during a following break.

The moderator (if appointed) should be introduced at this time, who in turn should briefly cite the parliamentary procedures that will be observed, notably time restraints, rules for participation, and perhaps, most important, intervention when necessary to maintain focus.

(4) Review previously distributed materials. For a very brief period, attention may be directed to previously distributed reports and handout material. Since the content should be known by all attending officers, this review need only highlight key points and briefly respond to possible questions.

(5) Proceed systematically, stay focused. It is the responsibility of the moderator to preside over the deliberations. This entails guiding, prioritizing alternatives, and summarizing toward conclusion, all within a reasonable time frame. Agenda items should be addressed in order, each completed before moving on. Once started, sticking to the subject requires rigorous yet sensitive and perceptive control. The objective always is to arrive at a reasoned *conclusion*. Non-essentials may and should be postponed for later handling by implementing personnel. Such focus requires that content never be allowed to bog down on minutia or be distracted by extended and peripheral rhetoric. The moderator must be alert and firm, for wandering dialogue is the hobgoblin of productive discourse. Control should be exercised kindly and respectful, yet promptly and firmly.

Spur-of-the moment floor petitions must not be allowed to alter or water-down well-prepared proposals. Participants are too often swayed by immediate, apparently popular, suggestions. Ensure that a careful review is first undertaken.

(6) Control discussion, emphasize deliberations. *All of you may speak God's message, one by one, so that all will learn and be encouraged.* (1 Corinthians 14:31) In sharp contrast to informal gatherings where everyone is encouraged to participate (see Chapter 11, "Leading Group Discussion," page 149), unlimited open-forum discussion cannot be allowed during most formal meetings. The agenda must be accomplished in a reasonable time. Commentary from non-officers must primarily be restricted to earlier written submissions which are included in the preparatory distributed materials (see preceding pre-meeting preparation #2 and #3). If time permits, audience response may be allowed for an allotted period. The duration must be strictly controlled. If thirty minutes is available, then ten speakers, for example, may be allowed three minutes each. This limitation must be exercised, kindly but firmly.

Deliberations[4]

Thoughtful discussion of issues and careful, fair, consideration of alternative responses, possibly reaching conclusion, is the heart of any formal meeting. At this juncture the role of the moderator becomes paramount. The exact duties involved are outlined in the last section of this chapter.

The issues at hand should be clearly restated at the start. Then the facilitator must rigorously guide the ensuing discussion, drawing out and clarifying, while remaining focused. Sticking to the subject requires rigorous yet sensitive control. Pseudo issues must not be allowed to interfere. Dissent also can be disruptive if allowed to degenerate into time-consuming debate. Tangential matters need only be briefly reviewed.

If the issue is where and when, then the who, what, and why should be of concern only in their bearing on location and time. Finally, council members repeatedly expressing personal opinion should be reminded of their *representative* responsibilities.

Periodically the chair/moderator should summarize, noting the elements agreed upon and the status of remaining issues, together with appropriate encouragement. If the moderator or pastor sees evidence of the need for prayer or spiritual guidance along the way, it is always a most welcome reprieve. Pastors should never be hesitant to intercede for is not God our most important advisor?

(7) Strive for consensus allowing for other options. *...all of you be in agreement and that there be no divisions among you, but that you be united in the same mind and the same purpose.* (1 Corinthians 1:10)

Elected officers must first accept that they alone are responsible for decision-making and not shirk from this duty because of conflict, confusion, or opposing pressures. Second, seeking consensus is a worthy process in itself, whether or not successful. Third, other means of resolution are acceptable should consensus fail. Fourth, a major alternative solution, albeit temporary, is employment of a proposal on a trial basis, the resulting performance assisting in appraisal.

Consensus refers to a meeting of minds in which all parties are persuaded to accept a common point of view, either as the right or best solution or one that can be supported as reasonable in light of current conditions. Each individual must recognize that the decision is the best option for the entire group. The underlying assumption is that a cautious discussion of the issues allows such a conclusion to emerge. All members need not agree on the details, only the essentials. Seeking this unity is based on the premise that each person has some part of the truth and no one has all of it. Therefore, only in total combination can the highest quality decision be made.[5] This belief establishes the respect and trust that allows parishioners of different viewpoints to reason together toward common ends.

The tools for securing consensus are those of developing understanding of the relative merits of alternatives, melding and revising to gain the advantages of each, and developing an effective compromise. Sometimes it is helpful to restate the unified purpose of all the proposals so there is at least agreement on the ends sought. The exact differences and concerns involved should then be spelled out. Lastly, a combination or synthesis should be attempted, a "third way" discovered, or trade-offs negotiated. However achieved, securing a compromise requires careful sympathetic listening, patience, and creative thinking.

Considerable responsibility for reaching consensus rests with the dissenting minority. Certain assurances must be secured, often best obtained in private with the objecting parties. The dissenting group should first be asked if they have exhausted all their compromise solutions. Then, as with all participants, they should be asked to assure themselves that they are acting out of strong belief, supported by prayer, and not out of self-interest, bias, or other personal negative feeling. They must feel that allowing the decision to go forward would constitute a real disservice to the congregation. They must also be prepared to clearly explain their reasons for impeding agreement. Finally, they should be asked to again consider the needs of the group as a whole in addition to their own. These five requisites are rigorous, requiring *exceptional conviction* of one's position to maintain independence. While such testing is necessary, no coercion should ever be implied. Recall that Martin Luther was one against many.

Diligent thoughtful pursuit of consensus is successful in most instances and is considered by many to be the preferred method of problem resolution for Christian congregations. Having affirmed this premise, there are difficulties and risks involved. First recognize that consensus is strictly necessary only in those rare instances when support and commitment to that decision is needed from *every* member of the deliberating body, seldom a necessity. Yet we struggle on, often at a high cost. Reaching consensus may so modify or dilute the proposal that no real substance remains. "We kept haggling over details seeking complete agreement until the project was watered down to nothing." Reaching consensus places a tremendous burden on the moderator, to see that all ideas are entertained and included to the satisfaction of their source and that all participants generally, if not in detail, accept the final proposal. Also, those who repeatedly compromise their position to reach agreement may harbor some resentment. Finally, consensus is simply not likely to work where there are diverse and conflicting interests, and may, in fact, antagonize the majority as well as holdouts as repeated efforts are made for everyone to "adjust" to every concern.

Alternatives to Consensus

"....follow the yellow brick road to the wonderful land of 'consensus.' In place of honest argument among consenting adults the politicians substitute a lullaby for frightened children; the pretense that conflict doesn't really exist, that we have achieved the blessed state in which...we no longer need real politics." –Lewis H. Lapham, American essayist and editor.

"Meetings are a great trap. Soon you find yourself trying to get agreement and then the people who disagree come to think they have a right to be persuaded...However, they are indispensable when you don't want to do anything." –John Kenneth Galbraith, American economist.

Consensus, paraphrasing Winston Churchill, "...may be spelt paralysis."

Consensus is a wonderful concept, it is however not a panacea. Recurring unanimous votes may indicate that the problems simply haven't been sufficiently difficult or complex to disagree upon. Settling controversial or intractable issues by consensus, on the other hand, particularly within a diverse group is likely to be an extended uphill battle rather than natural progression. Those adamant in its use may argue a "spiritual" sanction ...*agree, all of you, in what you say, so that there will be no divisions among you.* (1 Corinthians 1:10) And "agreement" is, in fact, always to be sought. To *agree*, however, means "coming into accord or accepted understanding," a substantially less rigorous requirement than the "*full* concurrence by *all* parties" typically expected of *consensus*.

We recommend that congregations seek "agreement" defined as a meeting of minds that seeks, but is not bound, by consensus. While conditions favoring consensus often occur and each person's position deserves respect, there is no reason to believe that a divided group acting on some form of majority rule is automatically less willing or able to build an optimal proposal and effectively carry it out. Recall that the delegates from New York abstained from signing the Declaration of Independence in 1776, yet the document turned out to be quite important after all.

If consensus cannot be reached in a reasonable time or the proposal becomes too watered down, four follow-on decision procedures are recommended and should be in place:

(a) **Step-a-side.** The chair/moderator asks the dissenting individuals if they are willing to have the decision go forward while recognizing their disagreement and excluding them from any responsibility for the decision and its implementation. Step-a-side works only if the dissenting subjects are willing to give up their voting privilege on the issue.

(b) **Consensus-minus-one.** A rule of requiring more than one negative vote to block passage recognizes the very real possibility of at least one dissenting individual in almost any group, and discounts the consequences of such a natural occurrence. The practice can serve as a safety valve against a stubborn resistor and repeated failure at compromise.

(c) **Referendum.** Voting is a democratic and effective means of settling issues that cannot be resolved by consensus. Approval should be based on a two-thirds majority conducted in confidence. Certain matters of broad impact may, of course, require approval by the entire congregation.

(d) **Referral.** Unresolved issues may be directed to a special study group for further investigation, redrafting, and development of feasible alternatives. If such a group is required, consideration should be given to ensuring a fresh outlook by appointment of new players.

(8) Conclude. The council president, having begun the meeting, should conclude it. A properly structured agenda, rigorously conducted, is likely to be completed on time. Trained moderators know how this is accomplished and usually succeed, especially when the participants get use to the control involved. Before concluding, the presiding officer should identify any remaining unresolved issues, areas of further study, task assignments, etc.

(9) End with thanks and prayer. The council chairperson should thank everyone for their participation, collectively and, to the degree possible, individually. The moderator's role should be acknowledged. A concluding prayer, giving thanks to our heavenly Father for his guidance, comforts, unifies, and strengthens all.

Post-Meeting Follow-On

(1) Immediately critique the meeting (council president, moderator, recording secretary, selected others). Identify what actions were adopted that require immediate response. What went right, what went wrong? Are there lessons learned that should be added to the meeting instructions?

(2) Respond promptly. Make appropriate assignments. Ensure all responsible parties receive and understand the decisions reached and response expected.

(3) Prepare and post minutes. The congregation should be kept informed of the activities and actions of the church council and various committees by published minutes that include not only the eventual decisions reached, but also the nature of the preceding deliberations. Always attempt to explain the "why" of decisions, the most unanswered silent congregational question.

Role of Moderator

The moderator/facilitator is an individual trained and skilled in interpersonal group dynamics, collaborative problem solving, consensus building, and conflict resolution. The principal task of the moderator is that of assisting colleagues to work together effectively, utilizing their full potential to help the organization express and achieve its vision and goals. The moderator is always a *neutral* third party, refraining from contributing ideas, opinions, or evaluating others, thereby enabled to advocate open, fair, and impartial hearings.

Role of Moderator at Structured Meetings[6]

The role of the moderator/facilitator is to secure effective group thinking about a particular topic. This is accomplished by encouraging full participation, promoting mutual understanding, and cultivating shared responsibility. In restricted circumstances with a fixed agenda, such as church council meetings as opposed to open discussions, additional subject and time restraints, as well as reaching a workable conclusion, must be imposed. Of assistance in defining and training group moderators are these six principal responsibilities and the underlying philosophy of meeting deliberations.

Chapter 12. How to Conduct Meetings and Reach Decisions

Moderator Duties
- Clearly define the moderator/facilitator's role.
- Clarify the exact nature of the issue(s) to be addressed (provided earlier via handouts)
- State previously prepared findings, alternative responses, and recommendations (earlier handouts).
- Manage the deliberations maintaining focus on the subject at hand.
- Work toward agreement through adjustment, compromise, and creativity.
- Manage conflict to arrive at a constructive understanding (see Chapter 8, pages 88-92).
- Foster inclusive solutions that allow consensus or lesser levels of agreement.
- Succinctly summarize and thank participants.

The Philosophy of Christian Deliberations
- We gather in Christ's name and in his presence, depending always on prayer.
- We seek guidance from the written Word.
- We address change as an opportunity. Faith demands that we be elastic in our behavior, able and willing to respond to God's will wherever it leads. In the midst of the complexities of this modern age, we struggle, too often caught up in our own secularism and denial to quietly listen. God's message remains the same; it is we who must reinterpret it anew each day in a changing world.
- We recognize that church management is a common, shared congregational responsibility. We strive to nurture individual contributions by creating an inspirational, supportive background. However, control time by limiting audience participation (assuming opportunity for advance written commentary has been provided). Curtail tangential and distracting commentary.
- We ensure hearings are fair.
- We search for and listen to the knowledgeable among us. *Do not stifle inspiration or despise prophetic utterance, but test them all; keep hold of what is good and avoid all forms of evil.* (1 Thessalonians 5:19-22)
- We strive for consensus, but are satisfied with partial and gradual acceptance. The best solutions are often those most inclusive, integrating various perspectives and means. Yet half a loaf is better than none. Be generous, acquiesce in small matters, accommodate minority opinion when possible. *....bringing every thought into captivity to the obedience of Christ.* (2 Corinthians 10:5)

[1] The reason why so many councils devote so much time to lower echelon matters is their failure to delegate responsibility, leading to endless need to supervise. And the circumstances behind this failure are that such action would leave only big issues often difficult or awkward to face.

[2] Probably the worst time to hold a church council meeting is Sunday afternoon during the national league football season after a long worship service and prepared lunch. Anytime on weekends during the summer also risks absentees.

[3] "Mirth is like a flash of lightning, that breaks through a gloom of clouds, and glitters for a moment; cheerfulness keeps up a kind of daylight in the mind, and fills it with a steady and perpetual serenity." – Joseph Addison (1672-1719) English essayist.

[4] Deliberations in problem solving are variously labeled "participatory decision making" (PDM) or "Interaction Method." However titled, the involvement of all in a unified resolution is the common core.

[5] One is reminded that "group think" is not always superior to that of individuals by President John F. Kennedy's quip at a 1962 dinner for 49 Nobel laureates, "the most extraordinary collection of talent, of human knowledge, that has ever gathered at the White House, with the possible exception of when Thomas Jefferson dined alone."

[6] For detailed guidance on the moderator's role see Sam Kaner, *et. al.*, *Facilitator's Guide to Participatory Decision-Making* (Philadelphia: New Society Publishers, 1996), 255 pp.

Functional Responsibilities

Part V.
Worship

Chapter 13
The Worship Service

I was glad when they said unto me, "Let us go into the house of the Lord!" (Psalm 122:1)

"Called from the world, we come together, deliberately seeking to approach reality at its deepest level by encountering God in and through Jesus Christ and by responding to this awareness." –Common liturgical introduction.

"To worship is to quicken the conscience by the holiness of God, to feed the mind with the truth of God, to purge the imagination by the beauty of God, to open the heart to the love of God, to devote the will to the purpose of God."

–Graham Kendrick, *Learning to Worship as a Way of Life.*

A recent account describes the unique spiritual experience of attending a church service of unparalleled emotion and appeal.

Frederick Buechner describes the church he discovered during his stint teaching one sabbatical year at Wheaton College in Illinois. Such was the lure of that congregation that Buechner did not so much go there on his own volition as he was transported there by a magnetic power beyond himself. His interest in Saint Barnabas' was piqued, first of all, out of "pure curiosity." But he kept returning there because the congregation, like the words that were uttered in its midst, possessed "music and magic and power"–the power to proclaim the Gospel so that it could be heard, as he puts it, "in a new way." That power, he says, "kept taking me back Sunday after Sunday." *He*, he states, did not go to Saint Barnabas'. Rather, he *found himself* going there. "And I remember, too," he writes, "that the last time I attended a service there, there were real tears running down my cheeks at the realization that the chances were I would probably never find myself there again. When I got home, I thought I could not rest until I found a church like that."[1]

Oh, that our worship experiences everywhere elicited this response, to experience God's true presence. Through our heavenly Father this, and much more, is possible among all churches seeking his will. We build upon a foundation of church traditions, many inspired by the Spirit and thus pleasing to our heavenly Father. To this we need only add what God tells us to do.

This chapter on planning the worship service helps us in this discernment. It is organized in three parts: "The Nature of Worship," "Design Topics and Procedure," and "Elements of Worship." Contemporary worship requires a separate chapter. "New Needs–New Responses," Chapter 14, describes the new alternatives employed, all designed to guide the faith journey of often young and questioning spiritual seekers.

The Nature of Worship

It is misleading to describe Christian worship exclusively in human terms for it most importantly involves the divine sanctification and intercession of the Holy Spirit. The Spirit brings us into the very presence of Christ our savior, whose death and resurrection establishes a transforming relationship with our heavenly Father. Thus blessed and enabled, we respond through conscious commitment of our mind, body, and soul through praise and thanksgiving, allowing our heavenly Father to enter into and guide our lives.

We gain initial understanding of the nature of worship from the New Testament, however brief its description. Jesus said, *"God is Spirit, and those who worship him must worship in spirit and in truth."* (John 4:24) Paul, in his most important letter sent to the Christian congregations in Rome, writes, *Offer yourselves as a living sacrifice to God, dedicated to his service and pleasing to him. This is the true worship that you should offer.* (Romans 12:1). Hebrews, more sermon than letter, describes the first covenant rules for worship and its man-made place, and then replaces them with Christ himself as the holy tent, his sacrificial gift replacing the blood of goats and calves. (Hebrews 9:6-14) From this brief scripture we know that the essence of Christian worship is inner *commitment* to our heavenly Father, *truth in belief*, and *dedication through Christ,* our lord and savior. To this we add *celebration and thanks* for Christ's gift of forgiveness and life. Thus, worship ascribes commitment and accountability for oneself, establishing a right relationship with God, and celebrating the risen Lord.

These responses are fostered and made holy by coming into God's presence and hearing his Word. Worship, literally "ascribing worth" to God, is our encounter with him in response to his promised presence in Jesus Christ. Worship is fervent love and devotion to God expressed through ceremony, prayer, and meditation. It is a holy celebration, sanctioned by Christ. His "Lord's day." No human enterprise this, for worship is a community of saints! It is coming together with the living God in his presence, in the pages of Scripture, in the sacrament of the Eucharist, and in Christian brotherhood and fellowship, all unified by the Holy Spirit. Indeed, we are glad and rejoice when asked to go into the house of the Lord!

Worship must always be recognized as *participatory* in nature, between God and man, demanding true personal involvement. We do not attend worship; we join with others in conscious shared communion with God. The essence of Christian worship is God's presence in our hearts and minds.

In addition to its sacred nature, worship can also be described in certain practical terms, most notably its changing themes structuring the church calendar. The chronology is organized into a spiritual pilgrimage through the Gospel events of Christ's birth, life, death, resurrection, and empowerment. The story of our salvation and God's transforming power is celebrated through seven seasons outlined below.[2]

Season	*Gospel Story*	*Congregation's focus*
Advent	Anticipation of the coming of the Messiah.	Time preparing for God to enter into our lives with transforming power.
Christmas	The birth of Christ.	Celebration, allowing Christ to be born within.
Epiphany	The manifestation of the divine nature of Christ as portrayed by the coming of the Magi.	Let Christ shine in and through me that I may witness to others.
Lent	The preaching and teachings of Jesus.	Self-examination, repentance, and identification with Christ.
Holy Week	Entrance into Jerusalem, institution of communion betrayal and crucifixion.	A time to feel the suffering and death of our Lord, a time of vigil.
Easter	The resurrection.	A time to emphasize what it means to be born anew.
Pentecost	The coming of the Holy Spirit.	The gift of the Spirit as comforter and counsel.

Finally, the meaning of Christian worship can be further understood from various related descriptive terms:

Apostolic...remembering and practicing the traditions of the twelve Apostles.

Catholic...faith that is universal.

Celebrate...observances of respect and praise, festivities and rejoicing.

Christ centered...the Messiah, the "anointed one," Son of God who reveals God to us and saves us by his crucifixion.

Epiphany...the gifted revealing of God omnipotent and the divine nature of Jesus Christ to those who believe. God's actions and grace become manifest in the service, an indwelling spirit. Christ's true presence.

Evangelical...in accordance with the Christian Gospel, the "Good News" of Christ and his saving grace.

Sacraments...the visible forms of God's grace in the rites of baptism and the Holy Eucharist, the sacramental meal which commemorates our redemption by Jesus, the Christ.

Sanctify...to make holy and pure.

Trinity...three in one, God omnipotent and creator, God incarnate through Jesus, the Christ, and God the Holy Spirit, comforter and sustainer.

Role of Traditions

Man responds to God's omnipresence with our whole being, each sense played and interwoven to indicate his abiding presence–processions with banners and cross, sacred music, recited liturgy, candles, incense, colorful and historic vestments, sign of the cross, kneeling, and folded hands. These rites have been handed down through generations as part of the living and holy culture and fabric of worship. They are preserved in church *liturgy*, the fixed forms or rituals of our Christian ceremonies. In a society committed to progress and accustomed to constant change, such traditions provide a unique continuity and welcome refuge.

Rituals serve to preserve, express, and embolden belief among practitioners. They are outward signs of spirituality and unity, establishing our identity. Observing the Sabbath by not working creates an oasis in time that focuses attention on God rather than on worldly routine. The practice of praying five times daily reminds Muslims of things eternal. In describing these practices in a *Washington Post* article, Christopher Ringwald (journalist and author) cites the great teaching value of action and repetition. At its least, not eating meat on Friday jogged people's memories that their faith asked something of them. At its most, it recalls the day of the week on which Jesus is believed to have died and a response of self-denial and identification with one another in faith. "Before we dismiss familiar practices, we should consider what we put in jeopardy."[3]

Visible signs and symbols also identify and witness our belief. They appeal to the senses and imagination–beautiful stained glass windows, the cross, vestments, icons, and incense. Even movement has its place–kneeling as a sign of respect, for example, humbling oneself before the Almighty. Processionals even have their distinctions. Fifty years later, the author still recalls the vivid impression made in his youth by the Saint John's Lutheran Church (Minneapolis) choir as they proceeded down the sanctuary aisle, swaying first left then right as they slowly walked in unison. God often works in mysterious ways, seek them out.

Attributes for an Effective (God-Focused, People-Oriented) Service[4]

"She say, Celie, tell the truth, have you ever found God in Church? I never did. I just found a bunch of folks hoping for him to show. Any God I ever felt in church I brought in with me. And I think all the other folks did too. They come to church to *share* God, not find God."
—Alice Walker, *The Color Purple*, 1983.

Few changes in the church are likely to create more controversy yet hold greater promise for membership growth than changes in the style of worship. The divisiveness is usually over the fashion of worship rather than doctrine or theology. Quite frankly, many observers suggest that if a congregation still worships through long liturgies, impersonal sermons, and stately hymns, the odds are membership is declining. The substitution recommended is a revitalized audience-oriented service speaking directly to and intimately involving each member in a spiritual adventure. Such services evoke joy, rededication, tears, commitment, understanding, and thankfulness, all components of spiritual growth.

A people-oriented worship service is one that recognizes and adapts itself to the needs of the congregation and community to attract participation and ensure wholehearted enthusiastic learning and spiritual uplifting. It is not as difficult to achieve as the goal might suggest. The idea is simply to create a spiritual and educational environment in which the Holy Spirit works the miracle of God's grace on all attending. To this end, the style and format must be comfortable and appealing, and here the possible need for more than one type of service becomes apparent.

It is hard to be all things to all people, even though all are faithful believers. Congregations should endeavor to find out what they do best and discover their calling, then focus on these things. Sometimes this will resolve into development of what is now being called a "contemporary service." This important development receives special attention in the next chapter.

Regardless of the outward manifestations of the worship service, traditional or contemporary, the worship character in Christ remains the same. We are bold here to list eight essentials of responsible worship services, independent of outward design:

• **Spiritual** *God is Spirit, and those who worship him must worship in spirit and in truth.* (John 4:24) *Jesus answered him, "I am the way, the truth, and the life; no one goes to the Father except by me."* (John 14:6)

Christian worship is reverent love and devotion for our heavenly Father in spirit and truth with the whole mind and heart and soul, without reservation or restraints, and in all honesty and integrity. Worship recognizes the true presence of God and the resulting holy veneration required. *"For where two or three come together in my name, I am there with them."* (Matthew 18:20) In spiritual worship, prayer and the sacraments receive the sanctity deserved for God's holy involvement.

Spiritual also means *Christ-centered*, worship that is about and for God as known through Jesus Christ.

- **Inviting/unifying** Worship invites and welcomes all into Christian fellowship in love and trust in Christ and for each other. In worship we become one, united in our common discipleship.[5] Worship is a gathered community, connected parts working together as the "body" of Christ.

- **Participatory** Worship services succeed only to the degree to which the congregation actively participates. For the majority, this engagement is evident in deliberate and earnest response to the liturgy and music, recitation, prayer, and attentive listening to the spoken Word. Such attention can only be achieved through making God's presence real. And, of course, this is the central element of worship, coming into God's presence with thanksgiving and joy.

- **Inspirational** Worship should be uplifting, resolving all in a continuing endeavor to lead godly lives. More pastors need to recognize that their congregations need to be stirred up, to be invigorated and enlivened to serve the Lord with enthusiasm and energy. The ambience of the service should be one of profound, immediate, vital importance, evident in the enthusiasm and dedication of all involved.

- **Instructive** The worship service should lead us to the crucified and risen Lord, instructing us in living the Christian life and in obeying and serving God according to his intentions. We come as his accepted, loved children. In this humbleness we acknowledge our ignorance and need to be taught. The spoken word presents the Good News responding to the problems of mankind with substantive answers and adequate explanation. The requirements of good preaching and the means for its accomplishment are the subject of Chapter 15, "The Spoken Word and Prayer."

- **Joyful** *May you always be joyful in your life in the Lord. I say it again: rejoice!* (Philippians 4:4) "Joy is the ineffable sign of the presence of God." Our obedience and joy reflects our love of God and response to his reaching out to us. Worship is then a joyful *celebration* of God's rule and our salvation. Should not our response to God's blessings be one of exuberance, enthusiasm, and unrestrained joy?[6]

- **Aesthetic** The worship service provides opportunity to heighten our awareness of the beauty of God's creation and mankind's response. We marvel at and are awed by the architecture and splendor of the world's great cathedrals. Edgar Jackson goes so far as to attribute to architectural creation an "atmosphere of inspiration."[7] Yet even the most austere designs are made beautiful by God's presence. So we honor him by all visible means, however modest–banners, vestments, candles, and for the more affluent, stained glass, works of art, and tapestries. God is pleased by all, but perhaps no more than for the oiled colored paper designs of children.

Music is the heart of the congregation's vocal participation, the major vehicle for personal celebration and communication. Edgar Jackson views music as church architecture, in the most magnanimous terms, "...a cementing force...which at once creates unity and intimacy, even in the most heterogeneous congregation." With this great potential and the seemingly endless possibilities of score and instrumentation, the need for informed and careful planning is obvious. This challenge is discussed in the "Music" section of the service elements, page 191 of this chapter.

• **Eclectic/renewing** The worship service must be like Saint Paul in becoming...*all things to all men, that I may save some of them by any means possible.* (1 Corinthians 9:22) This means we include and adapt all manner and cultures of worship into a composite superior whole, brimming over with the best discernable parts, always being refreshed with new elements. This amalgamation is labeled by some a "blended" worship. To accomplish such integration one must be a student of Christianity, familiar with and appreciating the old as well as the new, one denomination as well as another, for much good resides in each.

I am about to do a new thing; now it springs forth, do you not perceive it? I will make a way in the wilderness and rivers in the desert. (Isaiah 43:19) We are called to respond anew to God's challenge, replacing the old with new as we are called. Should not this mandate be clear? The Good News must be placed in "new wineskins," in new means of delivery, responsive and attractive to an ever-changing society (see Chapter 14, "New Needs, New Responses")

Design Topics and Procedures

Designing the worship service is the joint responsibility of the pastors, music director, and Worship and Music Committee representing the congregation. (See Appendix B for the committee's job description.) Often a subdivision of the committee, the pulpit advisory group, also has a special role (see "Pulpit guidance," page 184). The common task is that of developing a worship service of reverent love and devotion to God through ceremonies, prayers, and spoken word. The approach is *eclectic*, one that uses favored elements from a variety of sources in various combinations over time. And in no endeavor is prayer more essential.

The principal tasks of the above participants regarding the design of the worship service are as follows:

(1) Service structure. Recognize foremost that the worship service is the celebration of the living, dying, and risen Christ, and that through the Spirit, Word, and Sacraments we learn to live holy lives and receive everlasting life. Within this Christocentric focus, we are guided in day-by-day service design by the construct imposed by the church calendar as previously described. The first half of the Church Year, called the Liturgical Seasons, consists of Advent, Christmas, Epiphany, Lent, and

Easter. During the second half, Ordinary Time, we are taught how to carry out the ministry to which we are called, using Jesus' teachings as a guide. The weekly scripture lessons and collects, the basis of the Sunday theme, are organized by the Eucharistic Lectionary over a triennial cycle.

The service responds to the church calendar through the scriptural readings, musical selections, spoken word, vestments, symbols, and colors. The intent is to follow and reinforce the central theme. There remains, however, considerable latitude in implementing the calendar. Creativity here requires informed architects who are willing to listen to where God is leading the congregation. The tools available are the ability to change and improve the mechanics of sound, and visibility and motion, that transmit understanding and emotion. To this end, members of the Worship and Music Committee must be students of worship, reading guidance works and visiting other churches. At the same time, they must be sensitive to the traditions and membership of the parish, and, of course, the calendar restraints. Yet, ultimately, the committee should be continuously dissatisfied as it seeks God's perfection in his worship.

Of special value in service appraisal are member and visitor commentary. Secured by survey (see Chapter 11, page 161) or informal discussion, such assessment, particularly those of anonymous respondents, are often especially observant and forthright.

(2) Laity participation. Cultivating lay ministry is a sign of strength and confidence in the congregation. It marks our shared discipleship. Worship provides four involvement opportunities: choir membership, lay ministry, ushering, and service support. The congregational choir often represents, at once, the largest degree of participation and the strongest evidence of talent and calling. Recruitment should be continuous, according all opportunity. Lay ministers assist the presiding pastor in the conduct of worship by offering prayers, reading the scripture lessons, leading responsive psalms, serving the Holy Eucharist, and other designated duties. Youth serve in bearing the processional cross, lighting the altar candles, and assisting in communion. They may, on occasion, conduct the entire service. Ushers traditionally "guide, protect, and honor," and it is well to think their role is the same today with the added duty of extending a cordial welcome. Service support includes altar preparation, sanctuary decoration, communion preparation, and similar assignments. All these things down to the least one are favorable in God's sight.

(3) Pulpit guidance. In the belief that none of us as individuals, including our pastors, can discern God's voice for humanity with complete clarity and wisdom, we recommend broadening the identifying base as an ongoing task of the whole congregation. To this end a small "pulpit advisory group" should be established to assist the pastor(s) in planning sermons and occasionally offering constructive critiques. The advisory group responsibilities include:

1. Conduct an annual planning session with pastors to propose sermon themes relative to the church calendar.
2. Receive topic recommendations from congregation and transmit to pastors.
3. Hold periodic congregational seminars on homiletics, transmitting findings to pastors.
4. Periodically critique sermon subject matter and delivery with pastors.
5. Build and maintain a library of transcribed sermons and/or recordings for use by shut-ins, absentees, etc.
6. Encourage periodic study of sermon topics by volunteering Sunday school classes.
7. Assist in selecting and scheduling visiting pastors.

(4) Administrative duties. Administrative duties pertain to service scheduling, announcements, name tags, and other sundry responsibilities. Multiple services are commonly scheduled at 8:30 a.m. and 11:00 a.m. with time between for Sunday school. Three services may be scheduled 8:00, 9:30, and 11:00 with church school at 9:30 and 11:00. By shortening the first two services to 45 minutes, it is possible to schedule services at 8:30, 9:45, and 11:00, and still maintain 30 minute "intermission" periods for coffee and fellowship.

Summer months require alertness to the early service needs of worshipers intent on "early starts" for their Sunday excursions. Single common services uniting the congregation in a festive spiritual bonding are also summer events.

Considering the preparation required, the most neglected announcement is likely that of church school offerings. Both invitation and subject matter need affirmation in the Sunday bulletin and church newsletter.

Wearing name tags has both its advocates and opponents ("tacky"). If we desire God to know our name, why not also be so known among his disciples, our fellow parishioners? Those in the military clearly recognize the value of being able to address by name those of all ranks, fellow comrades in arms. Are we not an even closer brotherhood? *Lift up your eyes on high and see: Who created these? He who brings out their host and numbers them, calling them all by name."* (Isaiah 40:26) *Then Jacob asked him, "Please tell me your name." But he said, "Why is it that you ask my name?" And there he blessed him.* (Genesis 32:29) Allow us then to seek God's blessings on each one by name.

Elements of Worship

This division outlines the setting and components of the worship service for purposes of study and development.

The Setting

The worship context and environment consists of three elements planned and arranged well in advance of conducting the service itself: the Sunday service bulletin; symbols, color, and ministerial dress; and sanctuary design–lighting, sound, and seating.

Service Bulletin

The Sunday worship bulletin guides worshipers in following the service. Understandably, it is one of the most important church documents employed. Its purpose is to list the service's order of events; present content for responsive readings, hymns, and prayers; and provide guidance on content sources and service procedures. The bulletin, despite its mundane name, is a spiritual missive in structuring and guiding worship.

Secondarily, the bulletin provides service-related information on such matters as attendance registration, contacts for learning about and joining the congregation, child care, assisted listening devices, transportation assistance, invitation to refreshments, etc. Other topics such as prayer requests, ministry opportunities, special events, calendar of activities, Sunday school offerings (when detailed), and the like are generally reported in separate inserts/flyers.

Appropriate content for the Sunday service bulletin includes:

- Attractive cover with art and scripture or other quotation.
- Welcome message of joy and gladness to all present.
- Instructions regarding the entrance period of meditation and reflection, "Passing of the Peace," Holy Communion, signing the attendance register, and related participation guidance.
- Meditation prayer generally related to the church calendar's message.
- Service order, preferably organized around major themes, e.g., "We Gather in Reflection and Meditation," "We Unite in Praise and Confession," "We Proclaim God's Word," "We Respond to God's Word," and "We Go Forth to Serve." Service bulletins are increasingly being expanded to include a majority if not all congregational responses (generally printed in bold italics). This coverage is a great aid to visitors and parishioners, encouraging participation.
- Listing of service participants. These credit lines acknowledge lay participants such as scripture readers, soloists, ushers, etc. Occasionally church officers should also be cited.
- Special descriptions and artistic designs. The multiple elements of the service warrant occasional description. In addition, the church calendar offers many opportunities for informative commentary and introduction of related art, liturgical colors, and symbols.
- Sunday school offerings. The church school's curriculum and instructors should be periodically reported. Christian education is a vital supplement to Sunday worship and should receive all appropriate

publicity and encouragement. *Train up a child in the way he should go; and when he is old, he will not depart from it.* (Proverbs 22:6)

Renewal **handout.** It is appropriate here, in association with the church bulletin, to encourage use of the *Renewal* handout illustrated in Appendix D. The single sheet *Renewal*, distributed with the bulletin, presents scripture, sermonette, art, music, poetry, and other offerings related to a given Sunday in the church calendar. Its content represents the best of mankind's literary and artistic response to God. *Renewal* will eventually be freely available on-line, able to be downloaded and printed by congregations so disposed. Space on the cover will be available for inserting the using church's name. Development of *Renewal* is a work in progress and contributions and recommendations are encouraged. Please write or contact the author.

Symbols, Art, Color, and Ministerial Dress

Symbols, art, color, and ministerial dress are an exceptional means of communication, allowing us to *see* in addition to hearing and reading the Bible's message. These and all visual means are, in a sense, enhancements of the spiritual message. Indeed, the visible spectrum provides remarkable opportunities for interpretation and creativity. And such signs are also one of the more readily prepared and altered elements of worship. Be sure to observe copyrights.

The number of Christian **symbols**, counting numerals, easily extends to well over fifty. Symbols, in which "...the Infinite is made to blend itself with the Finite,"[8] convey the essence of a greater, unseen reality. We need not individually identify this wealth of material, although the temptation to do so is great for each stirs up much meaning. For example, the presence of a single live dove[9] may make a more lasting impression of the Holy Spirit's descent at Christ's baptism than any verbal or written description. This is especially true among young people. Let us see the nails of the cross, the crown of thorns, a money bag for the 30 pieces of silver, the lilies of Easter, the scepter or royal staff, as well as the more commonly displayed cross, chalice, and bread. God works through such symbols to strengthen faith and understanding.

The Sunday worship service should provide attendees some opportunity, however limited, to see the world's great **Christian art**, its paintings, icons, and frescoes, so that all may be awed by mankind's own interpretive response to our creator. In such surroundings we are indeed in the heavenly company of saints. Young impressionable minds especially are often more responsive to what they see than hear. It is saddening to realize that most worshipers pass their entire lives without ever seeing such inspirational treasures, especially when all can be photo reproduced, screen projected, or otherwise made available, even distributed with the Sunday service bulletin. (See *Renewal* cited above, Appendix D.) We are often remarkably provincial in this regard, evidently complacent with our immediate surroundings, however modest and mundane.

The **liturgical colors** are commonly blue, suggesting purity and hope–Advent; white, representing purity–Easter and Christmas; green, signifying spiritual growth–Epiphany and Trinity; purple, suggesting royalty–Lent; red of fire and blood–Pentecost; black of mourning–Good Friday; and less frequently gray, the color of ashes–Ash Wednesday. These colors are traditionally displayed on ecclesiastical stoles, and altar and pulpit paraments. They may be shown in other ways such as on banners, flower colors, and selected printings, so long as their sacred meaning is honored. Banners especially can be strikingly beautiful, dramatically depicting in symbols and words the Bible messages. Possibly even more dramatic is the use of color in stained glass windows. Where such works are beyond budget, window inserts of designed oiled colored paper of surprisingly high quality can be inexpensively substituted.

Ministerial dress[10] appropriately distinguishes and sets apart the clergy, acolytes, choir members, and others assisting in the service. It is refreshing here to see the addition of monastery robes and brightly colored stoles to the clothing attire of many clergy. Choir gowns are less frequently varied because of cost.

Sanctuary Design–Lighting, Sound, and Seating

Karen Lebacqz in her book, *Word, Worship, World, and Wonder* (Nashville: Abingdon Press, 1997) tells the wonderful story of a little girl living next door who was invited to attend the wedding of the author's friend.

> This child was about four years old, and she had never been taken to church before. When we walked in the door, she beheld for the first time in her life the stained-glass windows, the rich, dark wood of the pews, the white flowers decorating the altar, the gold cross, the red carpet, the high beamed ceiling, the sheer size and beauty of it all. She stopped dead in her tracks, her little mouth formed a perfect circle, and she whispered, "Wow."

Lebacqz goes on to say that this "wow" reaction is what churches need today, awe and wonder in response to the presence and mystery of God.

The sanctuary, God's sacred place, is seemingly the most stable element of worship. Yet some remarkable opportunities for modifications and accents are possible, extraordinary because of their exceptional transforming power. Just as incense pervades an entire enclosure, so also does light and sound. These media thus have great power, often seemingly exceeding their source. The darkened shroud of Good Friday becomes the brilliant light of Easter. Somber quiet is replaced by jubilant praise! This is the alpha and omega of Christian light and sound.

Light may be dimmed or brightened according to the mood sought. It may be focused to draw attention to the scripture reading and pulpit delivery. When employing such dynamics, care should be exercised to avoid any impression of "theatrics." However, the author has always found a light on the preacher in a dimmed sanctuary a strong means of focusing attention.

Less subject to adjustment are sanctuary **acoustics**. Obviously, speech should be clear and audible. There should be no "back seats" as far as hearing is concerned. Sanctuaries "in-the-round" or in the shape of the symmetrical Greek cross allow the closest audience contact. Long sanctuaries are best served by locating the pulpit in the middle of one side. Barring that, delivering the sermon while striding up and down the aisle can be remarkably effective.

Least understood and appreciated are the acoustical requirements of music. Few realize the necessity and returns of such investment. The interior of many modern day sanctuaries simply ruins transmission and desired reverberation by an excess of carpeting, cushions, acoustical tile, and other sound absorbent materials. A reverberation time approaching two seconds is optimal; however, perfection in this regard escapes rigorous definition, remaining primarily a matter best judged by the ear of the beholder. Longer reverberation times are, in fact, simply impossible in many modern structures. What can be said is that most congregations have little understanding or regard for acoustics other than they be able to hear the pastor. Unfortunately, there is far more to it than that, as experienced by all who have heard the wonders of music in a great cathedral.

Congregations typically sit in long **pews** facing the front. That's usually the end of it. But pews can be unanchored and realigned at a slight inward cant for a more common central focus. Interlocking or regular chairs may be substituted for greater flexibility, even arranged in arching configurations so that attendees are more aware of each other's presence. We know of sanctuaries where the altar has been moved from the front to the center with half the pews turned around! Occasionally, seating may even be arranged in stadium fashion around a central altar. The objective in each instance is to eliminate, in so far as possible, "rear" seats, subject to all the distractions that such separation entails. We should all want to be in the front row in Jesus' presence. Designing the best possible unifying seating arrangement is a legitimate planning responsibility.

The Service

The worship service brings us together in love and devotion and in praise and prayer, seeking our heavenly Father's blessings and message. Today's service contains some very old parts, certain psalms in their original form date from possibly as early as the tenth century BC. And some parts are quite new; for example, *Amazing Grace*, probably the most popular hymn in the English language, was authored by John Newton in 1779 and set to music by James Carrell and David Clayton in 1831. And we are continuing to keep pace today, evident in Dave Brubeck's stunningly beautiful "To Hope! A Celebration" mass composed in 1979 and featured in a 2002 film. This is all by way of saying that the worship service is a living, evolving testimony of collaboration between God and man needing continual development and refinement.

Today's service is a composite of inter-related historical and modern parts, unified by a common allegiance and heritage. From many orderings we identify here 15 elements warranting individual attention by service planners. The task in every instance is to review existing practice in light of God's present guidance. (For discussion of the special nature of contemporary service design, see Chapter 14, "New Needs, New Responses.")

Entering

"Called from the world, we come together." Entrance to the sanctuary is entry into the presence of the Holy Spirit and should be conducted accordingly in reverence. Ushers need only indicate their welcome with a nod and smile as they pass the bulletin and perhaps assist in seating. Previous conversation and greeting should end upon entrance.

In contrast to the sanctuary's quiet solemnity, initial greeting upon entering the church should be one of enthusiasm and joy, including a proffered handshake. Everyone should be greeted by name.[11] (The importance of name tags becomes apparent to everyone serving in this capacity.) Visitors especially should be made to feel welcome and encouraged to remain for "coffee." If possible they should receive a special nametag distinguishing them as a visitor.

Reflection and Meditation

Entering God's house one leaves the outside world behind. The sanctuary invites people to prepare for worship in silence and meditation. One enters into prayer seeking to draw near to God's presence in mind and spirit. A prayer theme printed in the bulletin may well guide this personal quest. Preparation may also be a period for self-examination. *Search me, O God, and know my heart; test me and know my thoughts. See if there is any wicked way in me, and lead me in the way everlasting.* (Psalms 139:23-24)

Prelude and Postlude

The *prelude* voluntary is typically a short piece of solo organ music played as an initial part of the church service, also called an introductory voluntary. The prelude helps the congregation, seated in reflection, to turn their attention from self-examination to the community service.

At the close of the service many congregants remain seated during the organ *postlude* voluntary in appreciation of the music and performing musician, to offer a closing prayer, and to gradually transform from the peace of the sanctuary to the cares of the world.

Words of Welcome

Following the prelude the pastor begins the service with a spiritual greeting, for example, "In the name of the Father, Son and Holy Spirit," followed by opening words of welcome, and possibly a brief description of the present day in the church calendar.

Music and Processionals

"....the art of music, one of the most elevating, innocent and refining of human tastes, whose influence on the habits and morals of a people is of the most beneficial tendency." —James Fenimore Cooper (1789-1851) first major American novelist.

Music is the heart of the congregation's audible sensibilities and participation. It is the major vehicle for listening pleasure and for personal celebration and communication. Its repertoire is endless for those sufficiently skilled and more than adequate in its lesser complexities. We list our favorites in Appendix A.

Some may argue for culturally relevant music, others classical compositions, still others contemporary and modern designs. A variety is perhaps most appreciated, the choice of individual selections more critical than the genre itself. The main advice is to recognize the great range and massive amount of Christian music available, then extensively review and carefully select, striving for quality and representation. The Worship Committee should assist the Music Director in this responsibility for it is understandably an extended task. Selections should, of course, support the scripture lesson when possible.

Voice and instrumentation, as with musical selections, can also be remarkably varied as skill and talent permit. The congregational choir and organ accompaniments are, of course, the mainstay of service music. And, for our listening pleasure, flute, trumpet, violin, and all manner of instruments increasingly grace our worship, including electric guitar and keyboard of this generation. Also, some of the choruses of newer musical compositions can often be effectively blended into traditional settings. What remarkable and inspiring combinations are possible!

We are frequently graced by an abundance of vocal talent. We offer only these caveats. Soloists should be instructed on diction and clarity. Balance should be encouraged although the apparent natural abundance of sopranos suggests a major role. However, attention should be given to cultivating all manner of voice parts and grouping. Some intermediate ground between the dominance of soprano solos and the essential absence of, for example, male quartets should be encouraged. The lesson here is not so much catering to our preferences, but rather building as eclectic voicing as possible. Finally, too little advantage is taken of securing guest performers. Many such choral groups, soloists, and musicians are honored by an invitation. Seek them out.

In conclusion, processions are a time for pomp and pageantry—banners, cross, candles, incense and colorful and historic vestments.

Liturgy

Church liturgy, the "work of the people," is a prescribed set of forms for Christian ceremonies. The more commonly practiced liturgical elements of today's Christian services include: short pieces of music (*Introit* and *Canticle*); petitions and responses (*Kyrie* and *Litany*); spoken praises (*Acclamation*); praises usually sung (*Gloria, Gradual,* and *Doxology*); brief prayers (*Collect*); lessons (*Old Testament, Epistle,* and *Gospel*); recitation of creeds (*Apostle's* and *Nicene*); sermon meditation (*Exhortation)*; and communion (*Holy Eucharist*).

The church liturgy is a living heritage of our relationship to God, a corporate memory, if you will, that maintains and teaches the traditions of people with whom God has covenanted. It allows us at once to both honor and derive strength from God's relationship to his people.

Prayer

Prayer is reaching out to God in love and faith and in his presence receiving his grace and healing power in boundless measure. Prayer "renews a right spirit within us." This redeeming communion with our heavenly Father is best done alone in private as Jesus advises, *"...go to your room and close the door, and pray to your Father, who is unseen. And your Father, who sees what you do in private, will reward you."* (Matthew 6:6) And prayer should be done without distractions. "I throw myself down in my chamber, and I call in, and invite God, and his Angels thither, and when they are there, I neglect God and his Angels, for the noise of a fly, for the rattling of a coach, for the whining of a door." –John Donne, English cleric, preached in 1626. And prayer should be from the soul on bended knee. *Come, let us bow down in worship, let us kneel before the Lord our maker.* (Psalm 95:6) "There are thoughts which are prayers. There are moments when, whatever the posture of the body, the soul is on its knees." –Victor Hugo (1802-1885) French novelist, poet, and dramatist. Silent personal prayer, humbly beseeching our heavenly Father for forgiveness and grace and quietly listening for his response, should be an essential element of all worship.

The need for solitude with God makes public prayer more difficult. Matters are made even worse by long "instructional" prayers, spelling out ostensibly for God but more likely for the participants, more detail than necessary. "Long prayers, superstition, and creeds clip the strong pinions of love, and clothe religion in human forms." –Mary Baker Eddy (1821-1910) founder of Christian Science. "Prayer is not asking. It is a longing of the soul. It is daily admission of one's weakness...It is better in prayer to have a heart without words than words without a heart." –Mohandas K. Gandhi, *Young India* (January 23, 1930).

Public prayer is susceptible to becoming simply fanciful recitation, noble to a degree, but not of oneself, expressive but without reality. To engage in true prayer is exceedingly difficult, easier to illustrate than explain. Only once have I have been totally taken with public prayer. The pastor, an elderly gentleman, mounted the pulpit, leaned forward on the lectern clasping his hands tightly together. And, with eyes tightly closed and upturned face, he prayed aloud as if his very soul was dependent, beseeching God in great earnestness and passion, seeking mercy and forgiveness, straining to reach out with all his faculties to discern God's will. No one present could ever be convinced other than at this moment and in this place, this disciple was talking with our Lord, and through him we also. What does this tell us? That public prayer must be prayed with all earnestness and conviction. That it must be stated boldly and with heart, slowly and with meaning. And prayer must be relatively short for true meditation and intercession is emotional and draining.[12] Public prayer should have the same honesty and sense of privacy as personal prayer, man alone with God. Supporting elements include kneeling with hands clasped together eyes closed, a period of quiet preparation, simple petitions,[13] heartfelt sincerity in his presence, and brief common responses. No other conduct can so bind a congregation together as this simple act of united prayer. Finally, and most importantly, we take responsibility and comfort in the words of Saint Paul.

Rejoice in the Lord always, and again I say Rejoice! Let your gentleness be known to all people. The Lord is at hand. Be anxious for nothing, but in everything by prayer and supplication, with thanksgiving, let your requests be made known to God and the peace of God, which surpasses all understanding, will guard your hearts and minds through Christ Jesus. (Philippians 4:4-7)

Scripture Lesson

"Let us be attentive to God's Word." The lessons of both testaments must be accorded all sanctity and reverence. They must however be studied rigorously so as to fully understanding their meaning. In this way we show our love for the Scriptures. No rote recitation here!

Churches should be cautious about dispensing with two lessons (Epistle and Gospel, or Old Testament and New Testament). The Old Testament is becoming almost completely unknown in too many congregations.

Readers should be advised to consult a Bible commentary or companion volume to ensure understanding of the assigned text. A brief parenthetical word of explanation from the reader may be called for during the actual delivery. New readers should be rehearsed to check volume and clarity.

Meditation

Saint Paul writes, *If I proclaim the gospel, this gives me no ground for boasting, for an obligation is laid on me, and woe to me if I do not proclaim the gospel!* (1 Corinthians 9:16)

The "Spoken Word" invites belief, strengthens faith, and encourages earthly lives of love and service in our Savior's example. It is God's gift through Christ, brought to us through his ordained messengers. How blessed we are to have them! We therefore approach this subject with utmost reverence, knowing we are dealing with God's true disciples. A whole chapter 15, "The Spoken Word and Prayer," is necessary for this task. Here we briefly discuss the mechanical aspects of homiletics as it relates to the entirety of the worship service.

The purpose of the sermon component of worship is to establish in our hearts and minds the true meaning of the Gospel–the saving grace of redemption, the exemplary life of Jesus Christ, and the commission of love for one another and discipleship. So entrusted, God blesses all those preaching this message. We can only provide human instruction, minimal in comparison to that of the Spirit. In this context we are bold to suggest the following guidelines for effectively integrating the sermon into the body of worship:

(1) The sermon topic should be consistent with the Lectionary lesson or otherwise properly distinguished.

(2) Sermon length should be 12 to 15 minutes as a consistent design element of the service.

(3) The sermon text and delivery should observe the principles of sound homiletics relating to substance, interest, clarity, delivery, and brevity (see Chapter 15).

(4) Preaching pastors should be responsive to congregational observations and recommendations as presented by an established pulpit advisory group. See this chapter's "Pulpit guidance," page 184.

Holy Eucharist

Regarding this most sacred rite, we respectfully express only the need to support the very real presence of the risen Christ at his table, and to gladly welcome the participation of all. It is a table of true transformation in which we become one with Jesus, changed through God's grace into new persons with joyful hearts. In the silence of partaking of the bread and wine we take comfort in his forgiving and healing power.

Announcements/Offering Collection

Brief announcements and the offering collection are appropriately conducted immediately after the sermon delivery. Announcements should be for emphasis rather than full delineation. Choir renditions are commonly provided during the collection.

Passing of the Peace

The passing of the Peace has its origins in the New Testament. In several letters, Saint Paul urges the faithful to "greet one another with a brotherly kiss." In the early church this affection took on a specific function in the liturgy, to visibly demonstrate that all present were one in faith and that no sin stood in the way of this unity. Today it verifies again that we are all members of Christ's body. In this meaning, passing the Peace is a sacred symbolism and should be so respected. It is performed graciously and kindly with a handclasp or embrace with the words, "Peace be with you," "God's blessing," or similar spiritual favoring. Passing of the Peace should be no mere secular greeting but a real expression of God's love for one another.

Personal Intercessions and Laying On of Hands

At some juncture, usually in a separate location during communion, individuals may be encouraged to kneel in prayer and supplication to receive brief words of encouragement and the physical touch of the pastor's hand. God works through his disciples this way, through healing contact. *All the people tried to touch him, for power was going out from him and healing them all.* (Luke 6:19) We need such contacts as a personal blessing. Touching strengthens the Holy Spirit's presence in our lives and encourages rededication. We need to both hear and be personally united for this assurance. It reminds us that God is working through his disciples. Many parishioners go their entire church lives without ever receiving personal words of gratitude, encouragement, affection, and love. We all need such support, yet congregations and pastors seem hesitant to bestow such individual affection. Corporate love, however abundant, is no substitute. Oh, that Christ's love for us all would be manifest through our own kindness and love for one another.

Personal Testimony

One of the least employed but most moving worship elements is the public declaration of religious experience. The congregation may be asked to respond to such questions as "What is God saying to this church?" "How is God speaking to you? "What has God done for you?" "How has God made himself known to you?" "How do you wish to thank God?" Individuals may be asked to stand and respond in place. Such sharing strengthens all. The church bulletin generally advises speakers to be succinct.

Benediction and Closure

"Depart in peace in love for God and one another." "Now to him who by the power at work within us, is able to do far more abundantly than all we ask or think; to him be glory in the church and in Christ Jesus to all generations, forever and ever." "Now may our Lord Jesus Christ himself, and God our Father, who loved us and gave us eternal comfort and good hope through grace, comfort your hearts and establish them in every good word and work." These examples typify the numerous benedictions that may close the worship service. All may be found in pastoral texts and on the world-wide web.

For some parishioners the after-service greeting is their only personal contact with the pastor. It should be as warm and friendly as possible, fashioning ties upon which greater involvement can be built. Additional conversation can take place during after-service coffee, although too few pastors take advantage of this informal opportunity.

Post-service coffee is a time for Christian fellowship and bonding. It is a time for coming together, friendship, sharing, and fraternity in Christ. It is a time for welcoming visitors, offering congratulations, extending invitations, and expressing sympathy and gratitude. It is a time to invite members to attend Sunday school. Assigned greeters may also serve in promoting these interactions, being especially attentive to ensure that all are made to feel welcome. Warm greetings should be extended in particular to visitors and those appearing to be neglected. Appointed "hosts" can assure this hospitality.

---

[1] Frederick Buechner, *Telling Secrets* (San Francisco: Harper, San Francisco, 1991), pp. 82-86. Quoted from Charles E. Bennison, Jr., et. al., *In Praise of Congregations, Leadership in the Local Church Today* (Cambridge: Cowley Publication, 1998), p. 1.

[2] Adapted from Robert E. Webber's excellent chapter, "Enacting Christ in the Services of the Christian Year." See Webber, *Blended Worship: Achieving Substance and Relevance in Worship* (Peabody, MA, Hendrickson Publishers, 1996), pp. 118-136.

[3] These examples are cited by Christopher D. Ringwald, *Washington Post*, December 7, 1997, in which he also recounts "...the good old days of discipline and fear, when many Catholics spent more time making sure they did not chew the communion wafer than contemplating God's presence in the Sacrament."

[4] Many of the attributes of people-oriented services described here have previously been identified and encouraged by a number of authors. The content of this section is largely adapted from one of the strongest voices in this regard, William Easum. See William Easum, *Dancing with Dinosaurs: Ministry in a Hostile & Hurting World* (Nashville: Abingdon Press, 1993), 128 pp.

[5] In contrast to this strength in unity, Alexis de Tocqueville noted more than 150 years ago that American individualism not only makes "every man forget his ancestors" but also "hides his descendants and separates his contemporaries from him; it throws him back forever upon himself alone and threatens in the end to confine him entirely within the solitude of his own heart."

[6] The author has always welcomed and enjoyed the outward signs of response and enthusiasm expressed by congregational members, particularly evident in our brethren African American congregations. What comfort and support to hear a fellow member, a brother or sister in Christ, spontaneously speak out as the Spirit encourages, not interruptive but supportive and affirming.

[7] "In his religious architecture, man has always tried to bring inspiration to his spirit through an art form. The temples, the churches, the cathedrals are designed to create a response, emotional and spiritual, that draws up from within the individual some innate need and capacity to reach upward. Who can deny the response of the 'organism as a whole' when he walks into a Gothic cathedral with its lofty arches, its rich color and its mood of ageless and vibrant stillness? There is the atmosphere of inspiration." Edgar Jackson, *A Psychology for Preaching* (Cambridge, Harper and Row, 1961), p. 89.

[8] Thomas Carlyle (1795-1881) Scottish-born British historian and essayist.

[9] As an aside, it is interesting to note the contrast between the abundance of living things throughout the world and in almost every human habitat, with the near total exception of such living evidence of God's creation in his own house. It may take greater resourcefulness than I expect to maintain such living testimony

[10] With regard to ministerial dress, one is reminded of the 1776 episode of Pastor/Pfarrer Henry Melchoir Muhlenberg of New Hampshire. One Sunday morning he concluded his sermon with this unique challenge–"There is a time for all things, a time to preach and a time to pray, but those times have passed away. There is a time to fight, and that time has now come." He then dramatically removed his clerical robe to reveal a soldier's uniform beneath. Muhlenberg led 300 men from his congregation that day to form the "Muhlenberg Brigade" in the War of Independence. He retired from the military in 1783 as a Major General and returned to preaching sans uniform.

[11] The importance of such a gregarious remembering of names is even emphasized in our society, as, for example, "Where everybody knows your name" at the Cheers bar in Boston (NBC TV situation comedy of the same name, 1982-93).

[12] Our Lord's prayer is thirty-eight words (Luke 11:2-4). Saint Thomas Aquinas' all encompassing prayer, "Grant me, O Lord my God, a mind to know you, a heart to seek you, wisdom to find you, conduct pleasing to you, faithful perseverance in waiting for you, and a hope of finally embracing you," is equally short, 37 words. Some great prayers are but a single sentence. "Give us the mind of Christ." "Give us courage to live the gospel without reservation." "Renew a right spirit within us."

[13] Great prayers are always seemingly simply. Here are some favorites.

Have you not known? Have you not heard? The Lord is the everlasting God, the Creator of the ends of the earth. He does not faint or grow weary; his understanding is unsearchable. He gives power to the faint, and strengthens the powerless. Even youths will faint and be weary, and the young will fall exhausted; but those who wait for the Lord shall renew their strength, they shall mount up with wings like eagles, they shall run and not be weary, they shall walk and not faint. (Isaiah 40:28-31)

Search me oh God and know my heart; try me and know my thoughts; see if there is any wicked way in me. Lead me in Thy way everlasting. (Psalm 139:23-24)

"I have no idea where I am going. I do not see the road ahead of me. I cannot know for certain where it will end. Nor do I really know myself, and the fact that I think I am following your will does not mean that I am actually doing so. But I believe that the desire to please you does in fact please you. And I hope that I have that desire in all that I am doing. I hope that I will never do anything apart from that desire. And I know that if I do this, you will lead me by the right road, though I may know nothing about it. Therefore, I will trust you always, though I may seem to be lost and in the shadow of death. I will not fear, for you are ever with me and you will never leave me to face my perils alone." –Father Thomas Merton (1915-1968), American writer and Trappist monk.

"Lord, make me an instrument of thy peace. Where there is hatred, let me sow love; where there is injury, pardon; where there is doubt, faith; where there is despair, hope; where there is darkness, light; where there is sadness, joy. O Divine

Master, grant that I may not so much seek to be consoled, as to console; to be understood, as to understand; to be loved, as to love. For it is in giving that we receive; it is in pardoning that we are pardoned; and it is in dying that we are born to eternal life." –Saint Francis of Assisi (1182-1226), founder of the Franciscans.

"Teach us, good Lord, to serve thee as thou deservest; to give and not to count the cost." –Ignatius Loyola (1491-1556), Jesuits founder.

Chapter 14
New Needs, New Responses[1]

"We live in a time of religious plurality. We live in a time of cultural diversity. We also live in a time when the Christian reaction is too often strident, when doctrine and dogma and orthodoxy become more important than people–where little Kosovos happen in kindergarten. But I believe as the song says, 'What the world needs now is love, sweet love.'"

–The Very Reverend Nathan D. Baxter, Dean, National Cathedral, Washington, D.C.

Jesus said, *"Neither is new wine put into old wineskins; otherwise, the skins burst, and the wine is spilled, and the skins are destroyed, but new wine is put into fresh wineskins, and so both are preserved."* (Matthew 9:17)

I am about to do a new thing...do you not perceive it? (Isaiah 43:19)

A large segment of the American population is non-church going. Estimates indicate 30% of all adults attend less than twice a year. Only two-of-five participate with some regularity, and an even smaller one-in-three of those age 18 to 29. Yet despite this modest involvement, 87 percent of those polled express a belief in "a God." Why the dichotomy? There are many reasons, the dominant being the pervasive conviction held by most that "it's what's in my heart that counts," not church attendance. Others simply claim they "don't have the time," Sundays being reserved for rest, relaxation, and family. Simple laziness is also an apparent factor. But the most damning evidence is that for most adults, church attendance simply isn't that attractive. Services are perceived as old-fashioned, irrelevant, boring, guilt-laden, and money-grubbing. Fair or not, this is an indictment to which we can and must respond. And many leaders have. Over 800 modern-day Protestant churches in the United States now average 2,000 or more parishioners in weekly attendance. At least seven have an astounding 18,000 people in weekly worship, including the famous trend-setting Willow Creek Community Church near Chicago. Thus there are plenty of believers out there who are just not sure that church is the best place for finding God. But as mega-churches have demonstrated, we have the capability to meet the challenge as each is called.

What Are People Looking For?

We begin with four general observations. First, recognize that basically **all people seek a connection with the sacred**, a sense of the purpose of life, inner peace, and a feeling of belonging to something larger than themselves. In essence, they are looking for God. The church community and worship can fulfill these needs more than any other institution.

Second, let it be clear **that there is no harm and a great deal of good in worshiping God in a variety of ways** that are attractive to different people. This is our evangelistic responsibility. *And the one who was seated on the throne said, "See I am making all things new."* (Revelation 21:5) A more inclusive worship service draws a larger community into Christian brotherhood as part of God's universal church. At the same time we should make every effort to maintain unity and understanding among current congregational members, tempering boundaries that may tend to separate or fragment. Differences, per se, are not successful unless they grab and focus attention; modern is not better unless it is easier to relate to and improves understanding.

Third, **preference for one style of worship over another should be understood as primarily a matter of taste, upbringing, and spiritual needs or maturity**, not liturgical correctness. One design is not inherently better than another, just different. And all designs have strategic value in bringing people to God.

Fourth, because of their number and often searching status, **young adults and families** (comprising almost three-fourths the total national population), **are the principal target audience** of most new worship designs. Strategies are thus primarily directed to the under 55-year-old age group. Within this large segment there are a number of specific target groups—current young members seeking greater participation and reality, young adults apathetic towards organized religion, youth and college-age skeptics, parents with children seeking reality, and non-attendees who profess belief, but are "turned-off" by organized religion.

Within these parameters, what, in fact, are the expressed worship preferences of non-affiliated people, especially the younger, seeking generation? In broad terms, all seem to be looking for an informal but intense experience, an upbeat responsive atmosphere, friendly associates, simplicity and straightforwardness, a feeling of safety and honesty where one can simply be oneself, and lastly, allowance if not encouragement, of casual wear.

From this evidence, new forms of worship must respond to four paramount needs:

(1) The seeking generation **wants to focus on God, not man.** They "...long to experience a transcendent God during a worship gathering rather than to simply learn about him. They want fluidity and freedom rather than a neatly flowing set program. They want to see the arts and a

sense of mystery brought into the worship service, rather than focusing on professionalism and excellence. This will shape how a worship gathering is designed."[2] And worship focused on God *celebrates* God with praise, thanksgiving and rejoicing!

(2) A major reason for empty seats in churches is that today's public seeks greater engagement in their activities and pursuits. Passive listening hardly fits the degree of physical, emotional, and intellectual participation people have grown accustomed to expect. In order to be so responsive, **religion must be more interactive, demanding real involvement of all present**. Such passionate involvement, as it has been called, is evident in "deep personal engagement, which becomes apparent both in speech and in body language."[3] This ardent love and enthusiasm grows out of the spiritual lives of pastor and people.

(3) The real issue, in most instances, is not what one might expect; i.e. the unattractiveness of the rituals or liturgy, but rather it is the **style of music** used in traditional worship. Younger Americans want to hear their kind of today's music, culturally relevant, with a beat and modern instrumentation, not music that reflects the times and places of 16th and 17th century Europe. Surprising to many is the fact that today music is an integral part of the lives of young people, the major vehicle for celebration and communication, and the principal means by which they expect to worship. Music, as William Easum expresses, is "the ritual of our time," replacing written liturgy as a new vehicle for conveying the Christian message.

(4) Young people seek **a caring church community** to provide love and comfort as well as guidance and direction; a community sensitive to their needs, a listening community, one that helps them to discover who they are and uncovers their gifts. As much as anything, they are looking for the opportunity to belong to a small group and thereby be nurtured and supported. We need to be, in effect, good "parents" to young people, shepherding them in all discernment and care. Such caring invariably stems from an attitude of goodwill existing throughout the congregation, where all feel as family members. It is not surprising to find that some of the oldest members are often most open and supportive of new worship plans, for they want their children and grandchildren to be attracted and attend.

In alternate form, the above directives may be expressed as challenges as Dan Kimball advises. "Did people encounter God here? Was Jesus lifted up in honor? What have we trained people to think when they leave? Do they say...'That was a good message,' or are they thinking, 'I encountered God today.'" When we take our faith seriously, when we seek God's presence in our worship, when we understand the nature of "gathering" as opposed to "attending," then the true nature of worship emerges.

Our Response

Christian worship is an evolving entity as God speaks to us in new ways. Even the most traditional of services is different from its predecessors, each a growing entity, a unique composite of old and new suitable for the present time and location. Within this growth and variation, however, two poles may be distinguished—"traditional" and "contemporary"—with a broad, shared interface. Both strive to be transcending, lifting one into the presence of God, both seek to praise, both seek to instruct. The difference is in the means involved.

"Traditional" worship forms are essentially present day versions of a long evolutionary line of worship services dating back to the early Christians. At their core, the traditional service is sustaining and harmonious, characterized by selective retention of the best of the past. One speaks to God in prayer and learns about him through scripture and the preached message. The tone is somewhat restrained, thoughtful, reverent.

"Contemporary" worship on the other hand is regenerative, interactive, and multi-sensory, where one seeks transcending experience with God. It relies on a common scriptural theme woven throughout the service, intimately involving everyone in multiple worship sensations and experiences. Contemporary worship has a casual feel to it, relaxed, somewhat spontaneous in nature. The music has a familiar sound and beat.

The predominant goal of contemporary worship is to provide opportunities for people who seek spiritual meaning in their lives. To a degree this is evangelistic in purpose as opposed to pure worship among believers. Willow Creek Community Church, for example, forthrightly acknowledges that their Sunday morning services are designed for evangelism. Their midweek evening services are intended for believers. Because spirituality means different things to different people, a variety of worship experiences is thus often required. Today's churches are challenged to provide selected alternative conduits for the faith journeys of specific target audiences insofar as resources allow.

"Blended" worship. Many churches add a contemporary service for their younger members, continuing a traditional style for the older generation. Such division, although not without difficulties, typically minimizes conflicts and hardship. But it also sharpens focus on taste, fostering a consumerism orientation to worship. It also hampers genuine community by separating younger and older worshipers, depriving traditionalists of new expression of faith and robbing enthusiasts for the new of the wisdom of Christian tradition.

Such drawbacks highlight the considerable merits of a "blended" alternative. Blended services attempt to combine the best of both traditional and contemporary styles in a composite enriched whole. It will surely frustrate to some degree the advocates of each, but if designed in a constructive, balanced manner the result can have broad appeal. Continuity is essential. The best combination is likely to evolve through trial-and-error, with everyone alert to the need for compromise and balance. Planning can begin by ordering the basic elements of each service, then seeing how the most critical components can be retained in a unified whole. Similar elements may require only slight modification to emerge as acceptable entries. More extreme elements may have to be excluded initially with the understanding they will be periodically reviewed to see how they may eventually "fit in."

The joy and enlightenment of gaining such common ground as opposed to "splitting" the congregation with two distinct services, is one of the great rewards of this effort. For details on this subject see Martin Thielen, *Ancient-Modern Worship: A Practical Guide to Blending Worship Styles* (Nashville, Abingdon Press, 2000).

Derived Benefits of Attractive New Service Configurations

An attractive service has a powerful retention affect on the lifelong spiritual journey of youth. Studies indicate that young people who regularly attended church services are much more likely to continue their attendance into adulthood than, for example, youth who only participated in church youth group activities. Habits formed early often are very durable.

Donald Brandt points out that "New services remove barriers that discourage and frustrate visitors with little or no church background. This results in a service with a heightened evangelistic dimension, a service that could well become a congregation's single most effective outreach effort."[4] Brandt further suggests that congregation members are far more likely to invite their friends to a new contemporary service than an existing traditional version. Members know that the new service is specifically designed to welcome and involve first-time visitors, and consequently they feel far more confident in inviting their friends. Thus contemporary services are themselves a means of recruitment and also build confidence among those engaged in evangelistic efforts.

Cautions in Implementation

"I believe I am not mistaken in saying that Christianity is a demanding and serious religion. When it is delivered as easy and amusing, it is *another kind of religion altogether*." –Douglas John Hall, Professor of Christian Theology in the Faculty of Religious Studies, McGill University, Montreal, Canada.

The sanctity of worship must always be preserved for we are in God's holy presence. Care must be exercised to never be superficial or too entertainment-oriented. The message of salvation through Christ should be made relevant to today's society and culture but never in a pandering manner. Remember the emphasis is not on *selling* but rather on *proclaiming* the Gospel message of God's redeeming grace. People hungry for faith can distinguish the true message, one that is *in* the world, but not *of* the world.

However, crossing the line between proclamation and entertainment is seldom an issue. Far more likely is the failure to heighten involvement by the absence of stimulating music and drama that reaches out rather than requiring deliberate attention. Inspirational music and drama generally reach the emotions better than the spoken word.

Note, as previously advised, nothing must be allowed to disrupt unity within the church. The rationale for introducing new types of worship must be sound, the introduction accommodating, and the eventual conduct supportive of the overall church mission. Traditionalists must not be deprived of new expressions of faith, nor enthusiasts for the new be denied the wisdom of Christian tradition. We are foremost a *community* of saints. We must always treasure this common bond in all ventures.

Implementation

How God leads us to new understanding about how we are to be good and faithful followers requires a willingness on our part to change according to his will. To a degree this involves balancing the old with the new, inserting and discarding, substituting something better for what already is good. We must always remain a meeting ground where old and new are combined, where different viewpoints can co-exist, and where discovery and growth are continuously sought. Polarization except singularly in Christ has no place in the Christian community. *Welcome those who are weak in faith, but not for the purpose of quarreling over opinions.* (Romans 14:1)

What we seek is God's hand in the design of his service. Thus all "design" teams must get down on their knees and pray for guidance. Dan Kimball advises "Lord, may we never rely on human engineering or creative artistry as a substitute for what only your Spirit can do." Creating new worship services therefore requires pastors and church officers to spend as much time praying, pondering, studying, consulting, designing, and experimenting in the creation of worship opportunities as in their actual implementation.

The Common Ground

The shared common purpose of all service designs is that of reaching people for Christ. All seek to establish the reality of God, to point to Jesus as our teacher and savior, and through the Spirit of God transform lives. So configured, all service formats are good in God's sight. However, there is a fine line between remaining true to such intent and making the service meaningful and palatable to spiritual seekers. The service must always reflect genuine and authentic belief; it is not a performance and not a show. Maintaining this honesty is occasionally a challenge, for there is a temptation to sell out to marketability and expansion. Thus it is important to be ever mindful of the core elements of Christian worship common to all services, thereby ensuring their retention and enhancement.

The common elements of Christian worship shared by all service designs are organized here under four topics–spiritual, hospitality, gathering place, and worship construct. Elements, largely distinct to contemporary services, are detailed in the next section ("Contemporary Innovations," p. 207).

Fundamentals

Faith seekers of all ages, young and old, really want to find Christ in their lives and seek it where Christ can best be experienced. They seek a real encounter with God, not entertainment, not a slight trip but a real venture into God's presence. This quest must be taken seriously in defining why and how we gather, with all necessary reverence and commitment.

- The fundamentals of Christian faith never change–allegiance and obedience to God, worship, fellowship, discipleship, ministry, and evangelism. Human traditions, on the other hand, are subject to all kinds of error and mischief. *See to it, then, that no one makes a captive of you with the worthless deceit of human wisdom...and not from Christ.* (Colossians 2:8)

- True worship is from God. Exceeding personal thought and effort, we seek through prayer and scripture the ways and means of worship that are acceptable in God's sight. Let the Holy Spirit enter and guide us in our designs. *"God is Spirit, and those who worship him must worship in spirit and in truth."* (John 4:24)

- All worship is Christ centered. *For the full content of divine nature lives in Christ, in his humanity...* (Colossians 2:9)

- There is no single *best* worship design, all have their individual merits. One proceeds through selection and combination to reach out to the intended audience in the best Spirit-guided manner.

- Excellence is to be sought in all worship designs and conduct.

- Differences in style must not be allowed to tear the church asunder.

Hospitality

The most warm, sincere greeting must be extended to all, especially visitors. *Hospitality* in New Testament Greek means "care of the stranger." Newcomers should be introduced to others, invited and accompanied to coffee after the service, and genuinely queried about themselves in an inviting supportive manner. *Do not neglect to show hospitality to strangers, for by doing that some have entertained angels without knowing it.* (Hebrews 13:2) Is it not exciting to think that God makes his presence felt to us through strangers in our midst? Follow-on personal or telephone contacts with visitor registrants should be initiated as soon after the service as possible. Upon becoming a church member, all newcomers are to be treated with the same courtesy and respect accorded those of longstanding.

The Worship Place

The aesthetics and environment for worship should lead to inner reflection and outward spiritual seeking. It may be as simple as a quiet place and lighted candle, or as impressive as a great cathedral. However modest or splendid the surroundings, whenever we gather in his name we are subject to the awe and wonder of God's presence. Each place becomes a holy *sanctuary*, a sacred refuge that engenders respect, focuses attention, and creates inner tranquility. It is in our *gathering* together in belief that we behold his presence. *"For where two or three come together in my name, I am there with them."* (Matthew 18:20)

- The worship space must foremost show respect for God. Christ may be introduced to people in the most unlikely of places, wherever invitees feel comfortable and not threatened. The church basement,[5] local theater, or even classroom may well serve as such "neutral" initial gathering places. However utilitarian such places may be, when put to sacred use they must be accorded appropriate respect and honor. A simple wooden cross may be all that is necessary, a lighted candle, even a display of children's artwork telling the Bible story.

- The sanctuary should be a place of silence for God speaks to us out of stillness. Recall how God came to Elijah (recorded in 1 Kings, Chapter 19), not in a great wind or earthquake or fire, but in "a sound of sheer silence." Silence is respectful, reflective, and attentive. The great mystic Meister Eckhart[6] is said to have observed that "nothing in all creation is so like God as stillness."

- Service designers should be alert and responsive to the multi-sensory dimensions of worship supported by Scripture and practice. God is in all things, so through all things we can experience his glory–*listening* to word and song, *seeing* in imagery and color, *touching* in the laying-on of hands, *tasting* the bread and wine, and *smelling* the fragrance of pine boughs or Easter lilies and the inclusive incense as one with the ever present Holy Spirit. These symbols and sacred acts have a transcending power that helps us discern the reality of God.

- Our focal point should always be the empty cross, to be ever mindful that we are here to praise God and worship the crucified and risen Christ. Hallelujah!

- When possible the speaker should be as close as possible to the audience, but always visible. There is no more effective preaching than that performed amongst, in the midst of the multitude, as did our Lord. Surrounded, slightly above is next best; then, from an elevated pulpit, preferably at the side, but more commonly in front. We seek *oneness* of mind and purpose, most possible through closeness. *...and (they) begged him that they might touch even the fringe of his cloak.* (Matthew 14:36)

Worship Construct
- All designs must seek to maintain the fundamental character of worship—the expression of reverent love and devotion for all that God has done for us in Jesus Christ. We show our love for God through praise, adoration, and thanksgiving. In this setting the ever-present Holy Spirit works in our hearts and minds, uplifting and empowering.
- Allow time for God to enter all present, spontaneously, unimpaired by human intrusion.
- Obtaining real participation is critical. Christianity is not a commodity dispensed during church service, but rather a participatory event where parishioners seek to experience God, not just be told about him.
- Our experience with God is manifest in joyful uplifting music. *Let us come before him with thanksgiving and extol him with music and song.* (Psalm 95:2)
- Readings and prayer should be conducted with all integrity and sincerity.
- Preaching must be meaningful and authentic.
- Aim for whatever form of worship speaks to people's hearts and understanding. Just as this precludes incomprehensible language and thought, be careful also of "dumbing-down," where everything is simplified for the sake of audience appeal and perception to the point of shallowness and superficiality.
- Avoid doing anything that seems to be a performance. Worship is neither entertainment nor theater. It is communion, spiritual fellowship with God. Be cautioned that some may place soloists in the performance category when lyrics are unintelligible.
- Avoid self-serving worship preference. "Worship is for God...It is surely a tragedy when the pleasure we receive, and the satisfaction of our own tastes and preference, become the whole object of the exercise."

–Graham Kendrick, *Learning to Worship as a Way of Life*, 1984.

Contemporary Innovations

Enlarge the site of your tent, and let the curtains of your habitations be stretched out; do not hold back; lengthen your cords and strengthen your stakes. For you will spread out to the right and to the left, and your descendants will possess the nations and will settle the desolate towns. (Isaiah 54:2-3).

In *The Emerging Church: Vintage Christianity for New Generations*, Dan Kimbel advises, that as Christian missionaries we must adopt a "seeker-sensitive" approach to worship design which means an alert and responsive understanding of the lifestyle and mind-set of all those seeking faith. The task is to develop an entry-level non-threatening environment to which seekers can relate and then be transformed by the message of Jesus.

There are a lot of differences among the people we hope to bring to Christ. Services must consequently be sensitive and responsive to each group's singularity. It may be necessary to repeatedly survey attendees to insure we understand their particular needs and preferences. If the service is not that much different, we may find we are attracting the same types of people already in the congregation. Real newness requires a distinctly different style, occasionally buttressed by scheduling at a unique time and place. Design teams must consequently be bold in this regard, identifying and honestly responding to the needs of the *target* group. Evangelistic efforts in particular must know their subject, individuals typically seeking a holistic experience but often unable to see themselves as one with the church.

In general, new contemporary services are designed to meet the needs of younger rather than older adults, be comfortably accessible, involve modern music, have an upbeat atmosphere, engage the eyes as well as the ears, and move at a fairly rapid pace.[7] However, these descriptions represent only the central thrust, allowing wide variation in practice and preference by various audiences. Thus trial-and-error testing becomes an almost automatic part of every introduction of new worship strategies.

Cautions. A religious service is not theater, not a spectator event; there are no performers or spectators, only worshipers seeking God. We have spiritual leaders not production managers, worshipers not an audience, musicians not entertainers. Care must therefore be exercised to ensure that in trying to make Christianity appealing, the sanctity of God's presence is preserved and the substance of Christ's message is not lost.

Designers must avoid unintentional over-focus on any single service component, be it the worship leader, singers, band, or audio-visual augmentation. The flashier forms of presentation must not distract people from the voice of God which speaks most clearly in the inner stirrings of the heart. Remember, we are not in the business of entertainment, rather that of encountering God. Technology also can easily turn worship into a "spectator" event, whereas a quieter, simpler approach is often more likely to engender a spiritual involvement. The focus should always be on the congregation together with God, not on those on stage.

Mission

• Contemporary services, however central, are part of a series of opportunities for spiritual formation that depend more on self-initiative than passive dependency. Other means that encourage spiritual seekers to feed themselves include community formation, group bible study, and personal education.

Remarkably, the very newness of contemporary worship is itself an attraction to new seekers. Donald Brandt (*Worship and Outreach: New Services for New People*) and others have noted that "...new people more readily join a new group than they do an existing group," which is exactly the opportunity afforded by contemporary services. People will attend because they feel more comfortable as part of a group of other newcomers sharing the same possible discomfort they feel. And they may also feel some sense of authorship in "starting something new." So newness, by itself, has an evangelistic substance and value.

- If the intended audience is primarily seekers, then the service should be designed to attract and inform, leading attendees to Christ through instruction, prayers, and sharing interaction. Newcomers attend church looking for answers to questions that the world cannot provide.

- If the intended audience is primarily young adults, the service should emphasize the fundamentals of Christian faith, hope, and love. But again, as with most academic guidance, survey information is congregation specific, timely, and ultimately more reliable.

Ambiance

- Contemporary worship services strive to be supportive, comfortable, and non-threatening. The environment is typically more relaxed and informal than traditional counterparts. This casual atmosphere creates connecting points for people so they can better relate to others attending, and through this sharing and community see that the church is relevant to their lives.

- Contemporary services often have a greater feeling of belonging, togetherness, and shared love for one another, i.e., "belonging" as opposed to "membership." The gatherings are more interactive, encouraging personal relationships. This intimacy is in response to the strong sense of and need for belonging among young worshipers. It is encouraged by smallness in numbers, reaching out to all in friendship, and emphasizing fellowship groups.

- Although not in full agreement, many seekers prefer the quiet somberness and focusing power of a darker environment. It seems that emerging generations feel a spiritual kinship and oneness in this shared, slightly somber atmosphere. It has the strange ability of bringing together those so enclosed. Darkness evokes tranquility and inner reflection; at best, nearness to God. Candles can be used in such conditions to symbolize the light of Christ, simply and effectively.

- The degree to which seeking, questioning, young people find stained glass consistent with their search is also mixed. Most find the beauty and story depiction inspiring evidences of man's adoration of our creator. But collectively, all the adornments of the sanctuary may overwhelm some, even intimidate the uninitiated. Simplicity, comfort, and near neutral surroundings are often the safest initial environment.

Inclusiveness

- Contemporary worship congregations are typically exceptionally visitor friendly, always extending a warm welcome and encouraging supportive, interested conversation and interaction. This outgoing behavior is due in large part to the fact that most church members attending contemporary services are themselves fairly new and hence sensitive to the discomfort and needs of visitors. Long-time congregants in contrast are frequently engrossed with their own group of friends.

- The hallmark of contemporary worship is greater involvement of members in singing, responsive reading, preaching, and instrumental accompaniment.
- We reach out with *open* arms to gather in whomever God so directs to us. Contemporary services are intended for *all*, everyone is welcome and valued. Part of this openness includes no attempt to assimilate or impose our hegemony on newcomers other than the cross of Jesus. We relinquish all personal authority and privilege in discipleship and brotherhood. The church is after all the embodiment of the reign of God and hence all are *followers*. This great equalization is founded in the knowledge expressed by Saint Peter, *I now realize that it is true that God treats all men on the same basis.* (Acts 1:34)
- Children are welcome and encouraged to attend worship together as a family. There should always be a children's message for those present.

Bulletin

- As much of the service content as possible should be printed in the service bulletin, including song lyrics except those projected on screen. Visitors may have little familiarity with worship and should not be burdened with complicated references.

Service Style

As Graham Kendrick advises, previously quoted on page 207, "Worship is for God...It is surely a tragedy when the pleasure we receive, and the satisfaction of our own tastes and preferences, become the whole object of the exercise." Worship is not a performance, not a show, not a spectator gathering. Rather, it is in the truest sense our mutual praise, adoration, and thanksgiving for what God has done for us in Jesus Christ.

- Contemporary worship can accommodate a great range of designs, allowing for modest beginnings and extended opportunity for growth. Service designers should not be intimidated by any need to put on a performance. The purpose is, after all, to praise God, not demonstrate our abilities.
- A theme should be maintained throughout the service based in some instances on interpretation of immediate needs as opposed to lectionary lesson. Yet the gospel lesson is just as alive as it ever was and is always relevant to today's life style.
- The service should convey the spirit of God, creating an atmosphere of joy resulting in a positive experience for all.
- Art is an important element in contemporary worship. The vast resources of the Internet and libraries combined with modern reproductive technology allow creation of visuals depicting the original work of the great artists of the world. The scenes of biblical events tell the stories of

Christ's life, death, and resurrection in powerful reality. These graphics plus the creative work of congregational members can produce a vast array of artistic expression that extends understanding and belief. Experiment yes, but always guard against the incursion of material content into our sacred homage to God.

• Contemporary worship allows time for sharing and personal testimony when people can talk about their lives, their faith, and experiences with God. Faith-sharing lets people know they are not alone in their spiritual concerns, and reaches out to them in common hope and understanding. What God has done in a person's life is a powerful witness to his transforming power and healing spirit.

• As part of its newness, contemporary worship may often replace centuries-old rituals with appropriate elements of popular culture, most commonly in music.

Music

• Music is a major integrating element in contemporary worship. The greater range and use becomes the thread that weaves and holds together the various service elements, providing continuity and transitions. Music may make up to one-third, even half the service, most components involving all present. The music director is consequently an intimate, vital part of the service planning team.

Selection of participatory music must be done with care, beginning with a "top forty" list representing the best from a variety of hymnals and songbooks. Volunteers may assist the director in this selection. The songs should be relevant to the scripture text and sermon whenever possible. The number of stanzas sung should be limited to two or three.

• Select modern upbeat music that is familiar to, better understood by, and more applicable to young people. The opportunities here are extensive including soft rock, rhythm and blues, jazz, country, and Broadway, to name a few. Don't, as too many starters do, limit yourself to folk music, fine as it is. A variety is always preferable. Music selection is critical, so be sure to have a knowledgeable crew involved.

• Contemporary worship is characterized by exuberant singing. *Clap your hands, all you peoples; shout to God with loud songs of joy.* (Psalm 47:12) Should we not clap and shout for joy in God's presence? Here a song leader is most effective in developing wholehearted participation and energy. The leader should always be up front making eye contact. A musical team of vocalists with a designated song leader is also effective as a leading element.

• Modern services are distinguished by extended instrumentation. In order of popular combination, instruments commonly employed include piano or keyboard, guitar, bass guitar, and drums. More than perhaps any other characteristic, modern music is distinguished by its rhythmic tempo or beat, primarily provided by drums. Music without drums is positively foreign to modern ears. But note that the appearance and sound of this instrument in particular is often jarring to some traditionalists.

Choose musicians who really appreciate contemporary music. You will be surprised how choice of modern music will soon attract quality musicians. It is well also to note that good music, of any type, naturally requires good instruments that cost money but are worth it. Contemporary listeners have quite discerning tastes in musical quality.

- Young people prefer small vocal groups rather than traditional choirs.
- Recorded music is a reasonable possibility, particularly when finances are limited. There is absolutely nothing wrong and a great deal right with playing recorded Christian music on quality fidelity sound systems. Consider it may possibly be the only time in many people's lives that they will have the opportunity to hear most of your selections. And you will be presenting some of the great composers, musicians, orchestras, opera stars, and singers of the world.

Liturgy and Holy Communion
Liturgy, "the work of the people."
- Contemporary worship services strongly encourage attendees to fully participate in the liturgical rituals through scriptural reading, responsive readings, creeds, confessions, testimonials, and prayers.
- Modern services are sensitive to visitors who may not fully understand Holy Communion. The invitation explains the participation requirements of faith that our Lord is truly present in the bread and wine and the forgiveness of sins through Christ's suffering and death. All who so believe are then invited to come forward to partake.

Spoken Word
The intent of the spoken word is to preach the Gospel and build discipleship; and to love and know Christ with such confidence and trust that one is enabled to steadfastly practice his presence and live according to his teachings. Becoming apprentices of Jesus, living as the Spirit tells us, is what Christianity is all about, a transforming journey. Dependent on the Holy Spirit, we must then strive above all else to lead people to discipleship, through the Gospel message proclaimed. That is the pulpit message.

The spoken Word in contemporary worship remains the heart of the service. Good preaching requires considerable talent and lots of practice. We devote the whole of Chapter 15 to the subject. Here, in the context of contemporary worship, eight elements of guidance are especially applicable.

- Young people and spiritual seekers need instruction on what it truly means to be a Christian. The emphasis should be on teaching with a strong scriptural focus and relevancy to today's world. Practical applications of biblical teachings in daily life are common contemporary sermon themes.

- A primary distinction of some contemporary preaching is that the sermon topics have moved away from the lectionary. Rather than citing scripture, explaining what it means, and then how it applies to our lives, some contemporary practices begin with personal needs and how scripture then responds. Considerable attention is given to helping people gain perspective on their lives, lifting them out of their difficulties and relocating them in God's care.

Other practitioners emphasize just the opposite. Today's generation wants greater attention on what the Bible says and less on the personality and interpretation of the preacher. Here the role is to draw people to the Scriptures, to encourage them to depend on Scripture with less need for pastoral interpretation.

- The spoken Word in contemporary worship is generally reinforced through video clips, drama, and other supporting medium to enhance the message. Contemporary preaching uses visual imagery to illustrate and dramatize sermon topics, places, and objects. All manner of subject matter may be shown including photographs, maps, art, and diagrams. The altogether endless possibilities, enhance, clarify, and reinforce the accompanying spoken Word. And such illustrations are more apt to capture some of the wandering minds too often encountered in passive listening.
- In reaching out to young people and seekers, it is important for the preacher to make it abundantly clear that he or she is primarily a shepherd and fellow journeyman, that *together* in Christ we seek God's word and grace.
- Seeker congregations require a culture that encourages thinking and questions, one that provides opportunities for individuals to discover the truth of Christ for themselves. After-service forums can accomplish this by engaging members in deeper dialogue about the sermon message. Questions may be raised, doubts expressed, challenges proffered, creating a dialog that in general leads to greater understanding.
- Readings from the world's great sermons provides not only exceptional messages, but also a wonderful opportunity for lay "preaching."
- On occasion, the worship message should be delivered in as close proximity to the congregation as possible, standing and walking in the center aisle, at or near eye level. This closeness minimizes any distinction between "stage and audience."
- Perhaps more than for traditional worship, the pastor of contemporary services needs to have a clear conduit to the congregation's instructional needs. A pulpit advisory team is a must.

Multi-Media

- Drama may be effectively used to act out or illustrate scriptural lessons. Short skits introduce a degree of reality to the lesson or sermon quite beyond the spoken message.

- New visual media can be used to dramatically illustrate, teach, and make the Gospel come alive. Projection technology allows Christian art to be vividly displayed. Projecting lyrics allows people to look up rather than sing down into a hymnal. Even sermons may be visually augmented.
- High tech audio systems are a must for contemporary music. Hi-fidelity "surround" sound is exciting and energizing, even expected among today's generation.

Facilities
- Contemporary worship sanctuaries bring the Gospel to life through the visual arts. Pictures can evoke powerful emotions and strengthen our understanding. Admittedly, far too little attention is given the great amount of magnificent Christian art that tells biblical stories as no other media can. Words can be quickly forgotten, images may be remembered a lifetime.[8]
- Seating may be rearranged in a fan shape to improve sight and acoustics, and even intimacy.

Guidelines for Introducing and Developing Contemporary Worship

Among the weak in faith I become weak like one of them, in order to win them. So I become all things to all men, that I may save some of them by any means possible. (1 Corinthian 9:16-23)

I can do all things through Christ who strengthens me. (Philippians 4:13)

As Saint Paul admonishes, we must adopt all means possible to save our brethren for Christ. At its worst, introducing new service designs can be traumatic, divisive, and fragmenting, the opposite of the adaptability and acceptance sought. At its best, new worship is a great shared awakening that further engages and bonds a congregation in mutual ministry and love for one another. The key is introduction with propriety, care, and understanding. This guidance applies:

(1) **Start with a dedicated, knowledgeable team.** "I propose that the missing ingredient in developing multiple worship services is not the lack of new people, but the lack of compelling drive to reach an enlarged harvest, the lack of vision in how to raise enough lay talent to staff the additional services, and the lack of effective leadership that can do the political maneuvering necessary to rally the church in support of such new outreach." –Carl George in *How to Break Growth Barriers.* In addition to drive, vision, and leadership, planning teams must be capable of obtaining and analyzing all the information that will be required for the informed decisions that will be necessary. Planning new services is generally no picnic. Remember also, the planning team will need the full support and participation of the church's pastor.

(2) **Ensure the presence of a solid worship foundation before proceeding.** Investigating new approaches to worship should be

undertaken only when the congregation is confident in their present sense of community and form of worship. Otherwise it is best to direct energy toward repairing and strengthening the existing format. The necessary starting point exists when a majority of congregation members are satisfied with the current service design; service attendees experience the living God; cell group opportunities for community discipleship, service, and fellowship exist; and the gifts of everyone are called forth for mutual ministry. Success of any new endeavor is largely dependent on such current strengths.

(3) **Encourage as many parishioners as possible to participate in the development phase.** By its amorphous nature, contemporary worship is highly dependent on member volunteers and their diverse creativity and talents. Extended involvement, however fashioned, engenders broad support. On the other hand, don't encourage people to participate who are not really into it. They only dampen our spirit. Various means of recruiting are discussed in Chapter 19, "Our Call to Stewardship."

Keep in mind that non-participating congregational members are likely to be called upon to attend the new services to show support until the program gets off the ground. So in one way or another all can be productively involved.

(4) **Test the ground, then get the word out early and fully.** Be reasonably confident of the target audience(s) before starting. Don't even begin if you feel the new endeavor will in any way threaten the energy and vitality of existing services, particularly any operating near the margin. The new offering is likely to drain away attendees that can be ill afforded. Remember, the current traditional service represents the church's stable, intractable base. Only when assured all is sound should one begin. Then inform everyone of what is to be undertaken, the opportunities possible, and difficulties likely to be encountered. All this should be worked out with council pre-approval and sensitivity to those disposed towards traditional offerings.

(5) **Determine what you believe will be your principal target audience.** Determining the principal target audience is an extremely important early decision. Perhaps as much a hope on first try as reality. But the initial service design will be based on this choice so it must be made as deliberately as possible. The planning team may well begin by canvassing the surrounding area to determine local spiritual needs and interests. It is far easier, however, to simply start by noting what other local churches are doing and who they serve. Copying success can then later be modified to better suit one's own situation.

Not surprisingly the most important target clientele is often close at hand, within the congregation itself, in fact. It is evident whenever members express dissatisfaction with current offerings or inquire whether something more attuned to their needs and preferences might be provided.

This is a group to which most congregations enthusiastically respond, to help better serve their very own.

Target groups are principally defined by age and marital-parenthood status. Any one of the four common divisions can be a reasonable target group. The divisions are: (1) youth, ages 13-18; (2) young adults, single or married without children, ages 21-35; (3) parents of school-age children, ages 23-55, i.e., the "nesting stage"; and (4) seniors, age 60 and older. The central core of each category represents a distinct generation status with its own special interests and needs, hence best served by responding tailored worship. Obviously, there is considerable diversity and overlap involved as is evident from a cross section of any congregation taken as a whole. Race, ethnicity, and socio-economic status generally should not be used as target criterion since such distinctions may divide rather than integrate the church consitutency.

If new targets or unexpected attendees emerge, the service may be redesigned accordingly. Audience and presentation must be compatible for effective interaction. Sometimes a new worship service will attract a whole new unexpected group of respondents, often because of their preference for the music. Be prepared for this evangelistic effect.

(6) **Consider the target audience in selecting your gathering place.** Recognize that many non-church goers are intimidated by church surroundings and feel out-of-place. They can be more readily attracted to a neutral environment such as an auditorium or church basement effectively arranged. Young members of the church, however, will feel right at home in the sanctuary during a service designed for them. Whether their guests will feel the same is a matter of speculation.

(7) **Prepare a mission statement.** A rigorous, well-defined mission statement underlies and explains the entirety of any new service undertaking. It states *who* we are attempting to serve, *what* is to be provided, *how* the service is generally to be performed, and *why* such an undertaking is necessary and/or desirable. All statements are tentative at this early date, especially the additional *when*, and *where* aspects which can be developed later. Further description, especially for new undertakings, should include explanation of various alternatives considered and justification of selections. Developing this content requires planners to really think through all aspects of what they hope to accomplish and to seriously consider alternatives. A well prepared mission statement also keeps the congregation fully informed, a real plus in new undertakings. Many revisions and updates of such a paper are likely as work progresses.

(8) **Design the service to meet the needs of the target audience.** This implementation phase should be conducted working closely with the church pastor. The team must be multi-talented, resourceful, and creative, and vigorously led. This is not a "do-it-yourself" project. Don't let

individual personal tastes dictate the design; rather, there should be wholehearted common agreement after due consideration of alternatives.

Selected references should be consulted, with careful notes taken on key ideas and recommendations. In addition, much can be learned by visiting other modern church services and consulting their development teams. This homework will greatly pay off in immediate quality surpassing anything any single team might accomplish alone, plus saving time and energy.

The initial structure of the new service should be written out in some detail to include a brief listing of alternatives considered and defense of the choices made. The planning team does, after all, represent the congregation and is thus responsible for fully reporting its deliberations and conclusions. A good record provides historical perspective for later decisions and documents the process, of considerable value to all interested parties within the congregation.

The role of the homiletic message in contemporary worship requires careful deliberation between pastor and design team. The distinctions between traditional versus contemporary sermon content and delivery should be understood and agreed upon. Then the qualifications and interest of the current staff in delivering such sermons must be addressed. These can be sensitive issues so care should be exercised to ensure a positive support outcome.

Finally, note that some experimentation in service design should be anticipated. Ultimately, the quality and suitability achieved will depend on how well the service is modified and updated to meet changing needs and preferences (see guideline #13).

(9) **Introduce new worship opportunities with propriety and secured approval**, attempting always to be supportive and compatible with current offerings rather than disruptive. Flexibility and accommodation ensures the broadest acceptance and success. Keep in mind that traditional worship is the liturgical anchor for most congregations. Tradition runs deep! Therefore, it is important that contemporary worship be always *added* to the roster of services. It should never or seldom be a substitute for an existing service with the exception during an initial brief familiarization period. Familiarization can also be accomplished by temporarily adding a short 15-minute contemporary supplement immediately following regular worship. People will stay around to see what it's all about. *Do your best to preserve the unity which the Spirit gives, by the peace that binds you together.* (Ephesians 4:3)

Once the new service is in place, it obviously must receive equal billing and importance to that of traditional offerings. This status requires the whole congregation's support, at least through sanctioned approval if not preference. On the other hand, remember that existing services are the lifeblood of the congregation. Take no unnecessary risks with their well-being.

And one final cautionary note, never attempt to mix the two service formats. Keep each–traditional and contemporary–separate and distinct for they have their own advocates and followers. This rule necessitates two, if not more, separate and distinct service presentations.

(10) **Schedule the new service** based on a sound understanding of the target audience's preference times. This knowledge may require a survey of attendees and subsequent revision over time. Nesting-stage parents (ages 23-55) frequently prefer to attend an adult class while their children are in Sunday school or nursery care. This opportunity is most conveniently arranged between worship services held, for example, at 8:00, 9:30, and 11:00 a.m. Some traditional service regulars will also be more likely to attend a following new service as opposed to one held later in the day. Supplementary church school classes can also be easily scheduled Sunday morning. Other service times include evenings and late Sunday and Saturday afternoon. The greatest difficulty encountered here is getting enough initial attendance to appear attractive to those involved and also worth the effort. Plus at these isolated times there can be little or no interaction with worshipers at other services. Yet busy young families may find a late Sunday afternoon service the best fit for their schedule.

(11) **Begin modestly, but vigorously**, attempting to adequately cover the broad spectrum of requirements imposed by a new service. Newness typically requires adapting to a limited budget, marginal staffing, and possibly secondary facilities. No obstacles, however, are too great. Demonstrate excitement, rigor for the Lord in this new thing!

Invest wisely in priority items–necessary video and audio equipment, an electronic keyboard, and possibly drums–while relying heavily on volunteer involvement for music and liturgical delivery. Insure that all in-house talent is reasonably employed before hiring new staff. Then start with a part-time choral group leader. Music, as a central element of contemporary worship, must be selected and led by an extremely knowledgeable and talented person. A printed bulletin detailing all congregational responses and music lyrics is desirable. Childcare is a must. Direct mail advertising, addressing the needs of the intended audience, is another priority. Finally, follow-on contacts need to be made. Fortunately, volunteers can perform much of this work, and, in a surprisingly large number of instances, new worship services bring in more than enough revenues to cover necessary expenditures. The aim, of course, is self-sufficiency, but this is not a dictate.

(12) **Regular practice and rehearsal** ensures a smooth, relaxed, seemingly spontaneous, service. Making all the pieces come together in an apparently seamless, effortless effect takes a great deal of commitment, planning, and work. Take refuge in the strong possibility of slow initial growth with experience being a tough, but invariably correct, teacher.

(13) **Evaluate, study and develop extensively and continuously.** Is the new service meeting its goals? If not, why not? Maintain records of

attendance and non-returns. Query participants about their likes and dislikes. Call visitors not returning and ask why. Such information is necessary to correct and improve. At the same time, the staff should be reading all it can about contemporary worship, talking with other practitioners, and visiting other churches to ensure every design feature is known and considered. Guidance through prayer remains, as always, the foundation on which all else is dependent.

(14) **Develop an assimilation strategy** that effectively introduces and integrates new service worshipers into the congregational community with love and respect. Ensure that inter-congregational events are handled in an even-handed way such that both contemporary and traditional elements receive balanced attention.

Lest we forget amongst all these recommendations and instructions, it is God we seek in worship. And his presence is there without thought to the surroundings. *"For where two or three come together in my name, I am there with them."* (Matthew 18:20) It is the Spirit we seek. So we design all manner of worship humbly, searching for truth in renewed ways.

"(Worship)...is kindled within us only when the Spirit of God touches our human spirit...We can use all the right techniques and methods, we can have the best possible liturgy, but we have not worshiped the Lord until Spirit touches spirit...Singing, praying and praising all may lead to worship, but worship is more than any of them."

–Richard Foster, *Celebration of Discipline.*

---

[1] Of many works reviewed for this chapter, the author is most indebted to Dan Kimball, *The Emerging Church: Vintage Christianity for New Generations* (Grand Rapids, MI, Zondervan, 2003). Many of his observations, more rigorously expressed in the original, have been introduced here in abbreviated form. Readers are encouraged to pursue the original.

[2] *Ibid.*, p. 121.

[3] Ronald P. Byars, *The Future of Protestant Worship: Beyond the Worship Wars,* (Louisville, Westminster John Knox Press, 2002), p. 53.

[4] Donald M. Brandt, *Worship and Outreach, New Services for New People* (Minneapolis, Augsburg Fortress, 1994), p. 43.

[5] The author recalls his congregation being relocated to the church basement while the sanctuary was being refurbished. The small number of attendees during the early morning service were seated together in a circle around a temporary altar as opposed to previously being scattered about in the relatively cavernous sanctuary. Everything was now intimate, creating a climate of togetherness never before experienced. Many of us felt somewhat bewildered and isolated when we retreated back to the sanctuary. Despite its new beauty, we missed the comfort and closeness of our more humble basement.

⁶ Eckhart von Hochheim, 14th century Parisian Professor of Theology, "...expounds the eternal mysteries in a style that is fresh and original in the best sense. The depth and universality of von Hochheim's teaching has drawn seekers of truth, Christian and non-Christian alike. His radical and penetrating insight makes him a natural point of reference for a genuinely ecumenical understanding." Source: The Eckhart Society.

⁷ Byars, *The Future of Protestant Worship*, p. 54.

⁸ Pastor Henry G. Brinton tells this story of the lasting retention of visual imagery. "'Show, don't tell' is an old writing rule that we religious leaders need to keep in mind as our culture becomes increasingly image-oriented. I was reminded of this on a recent Sunday, when I discovered that I was preaching on the very same Scripture text I had used three years earlier, during my first sermon at the church. I asked the congregation if they remembered that Scripture, and they laughed–no one did, of course. But then I reminded them that I had brought some stones with me that day, and had built a dry stone wall during worship to illustrate the kind of church we needed to be: One that was made up of 'living stones' that could stand together and also shift together.

They remembered the stones, but not the particular Scripture of the day, or even my specific preaching points. The image remained, long after the words were forgotten." Article in the *Washington Post*, December 14, 2003, "Don't Miss the Big Picture on Sunday!" page B4.

Chapter 15
The Spoken Word and Prayer[1]

And he said to them, "Go to the whole world and preach the gospel to all mankind." (Mark 16:15)

"Through the activity of preaching, God himself speaks. Every sermon should lead the listener to the presence of God."
  –Karl Barth (1886-1968), Swiss-German professor and pastor.

All we need ever know about preaching the Good News is exemplified in the life and teachings of the master, Jesus Christ. His message is still our message; his concern for people our concern. The task of preaching is thus "making Jesus live again in sharp relief"[2] in the hearts and souls of all who hear. We need to look first to Christ and how we might possibly follow his example. What was the nature of his words and delivery that may guide us today?[3]

• Foremost, **Jesus spoke with authority** as only the Son of God can do. He "spoke personally of himself and of his heavenly Father establishing his authority and revealing his true nature." Through Christ, the living presence of God is made known. Through grace, we are entrusted with the authority inherent in discipleship and ministerial commission.

• He was **not afraid to be personal and declarative**, to make himself a part of his message and thus alive and vibrant. He always spoke from his own heart, personally, with conviction.

• The master's approach **never violated a sense of reality**. He did not demand the impossible or create unreal situations. He did not minimize suffering or ignore sin.

• He **used poetic structure of beauty and parables** to illustrate and clarify. *"Consider the lilies of the field, how they grow; they neither toil nor spin, yet I tell you, even Solomon in all his glory was not clothed like one of these."* (Matthew 6:28-29)

• **His preaching was straightforward and understandable**, even simple without adornment or complexity. His stories were related to the experience of his hearers. Each had one main point that stood out too clearly to be misunderstood. No one from child to scholar could be confused by what he said. The same simple messages can be taught today in the same manner.

• **Christ taught with true love for all**. With God's help, even this encompassing love is within our grasp.

Through Christ's example, the Holy Word, and the power of prayer, we are mightily equipped to be perfect in all we do including preaching the

Good News. Our hearts yearn for the good news that sets us free and strengthens us for service. Pastors are entrusted to deliver this message so that all may hear and believe. It is a sacred commission, to convey the Gospel in all truth and honesty as simple messengers without embellishments, personal authority, or pride. Preaching is thus the essential element of being a church pastor, the first and foremost of all responsibilities on which everything else depends. We thus begin with confidence in the commission and Word, and reverence for all preaching emissaries.

The Nature of Preaching

I command you to preach the message, to insist upon telling it, whether the time is right or not; to convince, reproach, and encourage, teaching with all patience. (2 Timothy 4:1-2)

In truth, the Word becomes flesh and a living presence among us through the Gospel preaching. Preaching has no existence apart from the thing preached. It is the "King's message" that is the vital element, the announcement of the word of God. Preaching more than all other human endeavors sets life-changing forces in motion.

Definition

"God comes to us in many ways, making His immediate ineffable presence known to us through the preaching event." –Edward W. Bauman

The primacy of worship is listening and responding to God's Word. The means by which the Good News is delivered is through the act of preaching, instruction and advocacy of the Gospel. Preaching keeps before us the example of Christ, our savior and teacher. It is the *spoken* Word, the Bible scripture expressed orally and thus directly, personally and expressively as God so directs. As Paul admonishes the Corinthians in citing his weaknesses in preaching, *Your faith then, does not rest on man's wisdom, but on God's power.* (1 Corinthians 2:5) So it is God working through his preaching servants, not human effort, that brings about faith. This absolute dependency must always be kept foremost in the minds of pastors and congregants.

Preaching has often been called "persuasive rhetoric," similar to teaching and public speaking in the sense of convincing communication. And **teaching** the Gospel for all to understand is a basic component of preaching.   But there are great differences.   Pastors preach with commissioned and Christ **sanctioned authority** imparted by God to those elected and trained as his ministers. Preaching is the blessed **proclamation** of the Word of God. Through God's amazing grace–his divine love and protection bestowed freely on all the faithful–we announce and proclaim God's Holy Word, the Good News, for all the world. Through preaching God's immediate loving **presence**, Christ's dwelling within us,[4] is manifest. (Ephesians 3:17)   Preaching emphasizes **persuasion**, advocating and inspiring all who hear to follow Jesus. Lastly, preaching is an **enabling** power through which we experience the wholeness of life beyond all expectations. Saint Paul writes, *I can do all things through Christ who strengthens me.* (Philippians 4:13).

The spoken Word may be further described in ecclesiastical terms. Preaching is **sacramental**, a liturgical event of gathering, teaching God's Word, and prayer. It is a *transcended* event, a wonderful inward and spiritual form of God's grace lying beyond the ordinary range of perception. God uses *our* preaching to make *his* presence known. Preaching is **Pentecostal**, filled with the Holy Spirit of God. And, preaching is **incarnational**, living out in the real world the Good News of what God has done through Jesus Christ.

Comparison with other forms. Preaching is not a speech or oration, lecture, conversation or discussion. It is not intended to be liked or disliked. Rather, sermons are designed to instruct and inspire, revealing God through his Holy Word. They differ from all other forms of communication by involving the listener intellectually, emotionally, and spiritually in God's presence with the aid of the Holy Spirit. Where other forms typically focus on a subject, sermons have an object, the intent of making a practical spiritual difference in the lives of listeners. A single descriptive word for preaching might be *exhortation*–a stirring argument, admonition, advice, and appeal. *Revealing* and *proclaiming* also come to mind. The intended *effect* or product sought–knowing God's abiding love for all–is always created in the hearts and minds of the hearer. "Preaching then is not just the imparting of ideas or information, but the affable presence of God speaking to us through our pastors."[5]

Importance of Preaching

"The essential task of the minister is that of mediating God's power and love and mercy through a capacity for soul-communion that manifests itself through both preaching and pastoral care." –Edgar Jackson

Preaching is the central role of ordained pastors. Christ comes to us in the Sacrament and spoken Word. "In one sense the whole life of a preacher is an act of preparation for that moment when he stands in the pulpit. All of what he sees, all of what he hears, all of what he does, and all of what he is, work together to produce the healing, stimulating, guiding word he utters."[6] Effective preaching changes lives in many wondrous ways. It provides insight and understanding of God's desire for mankind, it prompts rededication and renews enthusiasm, it brings us to our knees seeking forgiveness, it provides a sense of comfort and peace, it provides solutions to life's problems.

How important is preaching from a congregation's standpoint? Outside of generally unalterable conditions such as denomination and location, the quality of preaching is the number one factor governing people's selection of a church, followed closely by the friendliness of members and expectations of being truly wanted (see Chapter 20 on the inreaching responsibility). Through prayer and effort all three—preaching, friendliness, and sense of being needed—can, fortunately, be improved over time.

The Preaching Domain

The ingredients, constituent parts, perhaps even ethos in the sense of character and fundamental values, of the preaching domain, establishing its spirituality and mission, consist of five essentials:

(1) **Interactive love between pastor and congregation.** The pastor loves the congregation as seekers and followers. The congregation in turn loves the pastor as its mentor and shepherd. Such love is all embracing, including respect, encouragement, and listening on both sides.

(2) **People gathered in God's name in a holy sanctuary to worship and hear his word.** The congregation is prepared, intent on listening, learning, and realigning their lives. And, being together as a group is itself a supportive healing element engendering special emotional strength, well-being, and a sense of common welfare.

(3) **The presence of the Holy Spirit and the Word.** *"For where two or three come together in my name, I am there with them."* (Matthew 18:20) The presence of Christ, the comfort and counsel of the Holy Spirit, and the guidance of Scripture are the foundation of all spiritual strength.

(4) **The sanctuary ambience** provides a supportive background of design, light, and sound that focuses our attention on spiritual matters. At no time does the sanctuary take on greater significance than upon initial entry in silent meditative prayer. We enter God's house filled with his presence.

(5) **The prepared messenger of God's word.** The message must be Bible oriented and substantive, designed to establish the reality of God and his saving grace in the hearts and minds of listeners. From a technical standpoint, the message should be well organized with a definite focal point and delivered in clear and understandable language. Sermons should be interesting, challenging, and occasionally even memorable.

The Interactive Elements

In studying the spoken Word, we focus on the three human elements of the preaching domain cited above—the interactive love between pastor and congregation, the gathering together of people in God's name, and the pastoral spokesperson of the Word

The Pastor-Congregation Bond

"The minister who walks close with his people during the week, who identifies his life with their daily interests, has no difficulty on Sunday in speaking so that the listener in the pew knows what he means."

–Edgar Jackson

"This endeavor to help people to solve their spiritual problems is a sermon's only justifiable aim." —Harry Emerson Fosdick

Preaching is a ministry of love, love of the pastor for the congregation, love of the congregation for its pastor. Love is the foundation upon which preaching is built. There is no substitute. It is built on the pastoral ministry of kindness, understanding, and support. It is manifestly evident in the congregation's trust and sense of well-being.

Few observers more aptly describe the pastor-congregation relationship than Edgar Jackson. He explains it this way.[7] "The capacity for sensitivity, the ability to feel with and for his people, is a pastor's supreme art." The essence of the relationship is that of sensitivity to the individuality, value, and needs of each member. This understanding and love "...is a discipline of life, to live in the beyond-self, in the life and thought of the people served." Thus in preaching the pastor must attempt to literally "see" the congregation as they really are, thereby making himself at one with their needs, hopes, and fears. "They are not empty vessels into which he pours his wisdom. They are living, struggling souls who come seeking a light." The congregation is brought together in oneness with Christ and in confidence and love for he who brings the Scriptural message.

The varying makeup of the congregation means that each member will receive and identify with the sermon message in a slightly different manner and context. However, hearing the Word together is, to a degree, a bonding experience, often integrating the lonely or depressed person into the group through shared emotions and response to the delivered message. As the disciples said to each other, *Were not our hearts burning within us...* (Luke 24:32), as they listened *together* to Jesus. Togetherness, in and of itself, has a tremendous unifying, healing affect. The sharing of feeling and emotion in the presence of the Holy Spirit brings about a common identity, a binding together beyond human capacity.

The Preaching-Listening Synergy

"The kind of preaching that sees people, that makes them feel that they are loved because they are understood, invites an active personal response on the part of the listener." –Edgar Jackson

Psychological studies suggest that in order of effectiveness, purposeful personal experience is the most dependable form of instruction, followed by contrived or devised personal experience, then involvement in dramatic play acting, participation in demonstrations and field trips, then viewing exhibits, motion pictures, still pictures, and visual symbols, and lastly, verbal communication. Passive listening is thus the nadir of real communications. To gain and hold a congregation's attention, members must be brought into direct personal involvement with the speaker. Preaching must consequently be person-centered, not self- or idea-centered. And the content must be of keen interest. "What can God do for you?" "What is the reward of Christian living?" "It is not easy to tell right from wrong." Stating a problem in as simple and personal terms as possible makes listeners feel it is their problem also, and with the pastor they enter into seeking its solution.

The great difficulty of preaching, as with all public addresses, is that *listening* is the principal, near exclusive means of reception, as opposed to reading and seeing for example.[8] Any personal response or interaction is thus essentially non-existent. The listener has only one chance to understand any particular thing that may be said at the instant it is said. Ten seconds later it is gone with no chance for retrieval. What is not grasped immediately is lost for good. And while attempting to hear and understand, the listener must rely on memory to put the successive pieces together into a cogent whole. With such difficulties, it is little wonder that speakers are continuously advised to develop a manner of orderly speaking that comes through clearly the first and only time listeners will hear it. The object is to create wholeness and reality in the listener's mind.

Effective preachers always hold the listening congregation dear to their hearts and minds. This personal concern is immediately evident in eye contact, seeing members of the congregation individually, one-by-one, as the sermon is delivered. This interface must be continually renewed or revitalized for listeners are prone to serious lapses of attention. The expert communicator jerks attention back by telling a story, more energetic delivery, asking a series of questions, or something else unusual to renew and focus attention.

Audiences, large or small, are essentially a collection of individuals whose response is most affected by what engages them personally. The audience then must never be taken for granted. It must be "engaged," "plugged in" to the business at hand. This "turning on" is initially performed by the very presence of the pastor, his or her known loving, kind disposition, recognized immediately from an engaging smile or nod to all. It is evident in the pastor's unashamed love for God and the congregation in the opening prayer and by the conviction and sincerity of the opening remarks. And the engagement is furthered by the pastor identifying him or herself with the congregation as one of them earnestly seeking God. "We know he loves us, for he speaks from his heart to ours."

Partners in Proclamation

"The capacity for sensitivity, the ability to feel with and for his people, is the pastor's supreme art." –Edgar Jackson

The sermon is actually created in the minds and hearts of the listeners. The preacher starts and prompts the process. Hearers process the input, defining, interpreting, shaping, integrating, and accepting or rejecting the bits and pieces. Pastors must know and understand this process in a very literal and realistic sense by talking with their parishioners about the sermon. This interactive feedback and dialogue provides insight into the listener's side of the equation, allowing the pastor to construct his delivery so as to optimize the transmission-reception process.

Unfortunately, most churches do little to prepare hearers for an active role in preaching or to encourage preachers to create such a synergy of joint involvement. Preaching that begins with a full understanding and appreciation of the hearer's position and needs is not so likely to be abstract or generic, more likely to be in the listener's terms, images, and language. This bonding comes about when the preacher knows his parishioners as an active, faith-filled people, fervently seeking to better know God.

The responsibilities of the congregation in receiving the Word are far more stringent then commonly believed or practiced. First there is the matter of attentiveness during the message; second, the following engagement response; and third, the role of advisement. Preaching is not a *delivery*, but rather a *sharing* of the Good News. Thus congregation and pastors together are a single entity, voicing and experiencing the Word as common disciples.

Attentiveness

Gaining and maintaining the congregation's attention is an essential component of delivering an "effective" sermon. One must begin by securing the congregation's thoughtful consideration of the preparatory Gospel lesson. Reading from the center aisle, among parishioners, invariably secures such attention. Then there is a short invocation prayer for the pastor and the congregation recognizing God's presence and inviting his blessing. Sermon content and delivery are, of course, the essential elements in gaining and maintaining contact, and we address these rudiments later in the chapter. Even under the best of circumstances, however, it may be necessary to periodically remind the congregation that God's word is being spoken and that attention to the message is a personal responsibility of utmost importance.

Therefore we must pay greater attention to what we have heard, so that we do not drift away from it. (Hebrews 2:1)

Response

The Gospel message is a stimulant, prompting reflection and inviting response. Shaking hands with the pastor after the service, however, is often the only opportunity congregants have for any interaction, and then, at most, a word or two of appreciation or brief comment is possible. Real interchange requires more time, preferably as an informal class gathering immediately following the service. This conduit provides an exceptional opportunity for the congregation to speak together on the meaning of the sermon. And, hopefully, the pastor will attend at least briefly to field questions and gain the listener's perspective.

Advisement

Formation of an appointed "pulpit" team of laity advisors regarding the preaching role is recommended. The mission of this team is that of periodic involvement in delivery discussion and topic planning. Laity are in a unique position to provide fresh perspective and broad insight into needed topics. Pastors may be initially hesitant to encourage formation of such a group as a perceived negative inference. However, over time, such sharing is a great confidence builder in perfecting the preaching responsibilities. Confidentiality is essential and counsel must always be constructive, never openly critical.[9] Such support does not involve a shift of pastoral responsibilities, the process being exclusively that of advisement.

Pastoral Preparedness

"...the true preacher can be known by this, that he deals out to the people his life–life passed through the fire of thought."
 –Ralph Waldo Emerson, 1838 Divinity School address.
I can do all things through him who strengthens me.
 –Saint Paul (Philippians 4:13)
"...moved by compassion and filled with insight, he uses the medium of the pulpit to reveal and communicate with others."
 –Edgar N. Jackson

Prepared, mentally and physically ready for service, and armed through prayer, the pastor with Scripture and Holy Spirit is God's instrument in proclaiming the Word.

Posture and Approach

"He is a believer in spiritual power, and because he believes, he lives his belief. And because he lives his belief people feel the genuineness of his ministry." –Edgar N. Jackson

The collective character or personality of the pastor is a vital part of the preaching ministry. One cannot divorce what is spoken from the qualities of the speaker, rather they are mutually reinforcing. Thus the preacher must live as he speaks. The strength and goodness of Jesus gives a perfect model for us to strive towards–mild of heart, warmth and concern for everyone, indefatigable love.

Martin Luther cited 10 qualifications required of the effective preacher of the gospel:[10]

1. Ability to teach (the essential element for Christian growth).
2. A good mind (dedicated, addicted to learning).
3. Eloquence (speech that is "memorable, descriptive, and persuasive").
4. A good voice (well modulated with clarity foremost).
5. A good memory (speaking from the heart always maintaining eye contact assuring listener attention).
6. Power to leave off (brevity works to strengthen quality).
7. Diligence ("perseverance and painstaking effort" promote success)

8. Whole-soul devotion to his calling ("The importance of saving souls has no rival; it is second to none.").
9. Willingness to be bothered by everyone (accessible and willingness to give of one's time to all without resentment).
10. Patience to bear all things (courage and character to wait with fortitude).

A person of God. Underlying all preaching is great faith in God and our Lord Jesus Christ. Faith empowers and strengthens beyond all understanding. The immediate presence of God must be real to the preacher. James Braga writes "...the most important factor in the preparation of sermons is the preparation of the preacher's own heart. No amount of knowledge or of learning or of natural endowments can take the place of a fervent, humble, devoted heart which longs for more and more of Christ. Only the man who walks with God and who lives a holy life can inspire others to grow in the grace and knowledge of Christ. Such a man will spend much time in secret with Jesus, holding daily, uninterrupted, unhurried communion with Him in His Word." Regular daily prayer results in sermons that "...will not be the product of mere intellectual effort but will be heaven-sent messages."[11]

Being a person of God also means a person of God's book, a student of Scripture living a life according to Scripture. "Throughout his life he must spend hours every week in diligent study of the Bible. He must saturate himself with it until it grips his heart and soul."[12]

A person of integrity. The ethical soundness of the pastor's life is an essential part of preaching. There must be a willingness to tackle tough subjects and experiment, to preach the truth no matter how hard it is. This honesty is best accomplished by letting the Gospel address controversial issues rather than from a perspective within the congregation.

A person of varying strengths and weaknesses. What the pastor preaches is an extension of himself as well as that of holy witnessing. The quality of the message as well as the manner of delivery reflect our human nature, both its goodness and faults. "So the aggressive pastor may use the pulpit to flay his people, while the empathetic pastor moves into their thoughts and feelings with a desire to bring peace and comfort as well as helpful insight"[13] Thus it is important that each individual recognize their strengths, weakness, and dispositions, using this perspective to adjust and modify any natural proclivities into their most constructive and balanced form.

A person of humility. For Christians, humility goes beyond personal modesty. It requires subordination of our personal will to that of God, a giving of oneself totally to him and his cause. "Humility is the energy of faith, the backbone of hope, the essence of true love."[14] Humility gives deference to others, respects all viewpoints, lets others take credit, allows insult to pass. Edgar Jackson advises pastors to cultivate an attitude of empathy and understanding reflecting the great love of God for all mankind. The sermon deliverer is after all only a messenger. The message is always the same as sought by Jesus, "...to release the power of God's kingdom within his hearers."[15]

Love of congregation and understanding of human nature. To reach people a pastor must be familiar with and have a sympathetic understanding of their "spiritual and emotional problems and personal cares."[16] Paul says to the Christians at Philippi, *I have you in my heart.* (Philippians 1:7) Such intimacy can only be gained through a sincere interest in the congregation, ministering to them in personal ways at every opportunity.

Sustained, quality preaching requires extended time for prayer, Bible study, and preparation. "The foundation of preaching is our own experiences in the presence of God, simply allowing God to use us." Edward Bauman then describes the "excitement" of "waiting to see what God will bring out of the passage" as he works with Scripture in sermon preparation.[17]

Seek to minimize the cult of "personality. "The personality of the worship leader favors Jesus Christ above all else. Personal idiosyncrasies should be hidden, exhibitionism guarded against.

Rarely are pulpit deficiencies attributable directly to faulty pastoral *intent.* Raymond W. McLauglin defines them as "ethical violations."[18] Problems cited of this type include: (1) Reading into biblical texts the pastor's own personal interpretation or giving only one interpretation. (2) Distortion of the truth such as softening the reality, exaggerating, stacking evidence, or over-generalizing. (3) Inadequate personal preparation involving failure to do one's best and use of others' material without proper citation. (4) Unethical personal practices such as preaching for personal power or prestige and failure to practice what is preached. (5) Adapting to the audience by avoiding unpleasant subjects and not listening to advice. (6) Submitting to psychological and crowd pressures by offering over-simplified solutions to complex problems.

Delivery Style and Skills

Christ did not send me to baptize, but to proclaim the gospel; and to do it without recourse to the skills of rhetoric, lest the cross of Christ be robbed of its effect. (Saint Paul in 1 Corinthians 1:17)

Set your hearts on spiritual gifts, especially the gift of speaking God's message. (1 Corinthians 14:1)

"Unless we are filled with the Holy Spirit and the power of the Holy Spirit, then no amount of method can be effective in preaching."
   –Edward W. Bauman

"Substantive and interesting content delivered with clarity and conviction pretty well sums up effective public speaking."

Nothing is more important in preaching than the fact that it is God's Word that is being taught, bringing about his very presence in the Holy

Spirit. The preacher is truly effective only to the extent that listeners experience this reality, occasionally even the awesomeness of God's calling. We recognize of course the difficulty pastors have in being truly spiritually involved in delivering the sermon while engaged in the required mechanics. To be free to be God's messenger in spirit as well as mind requires exceptionally thorough preparation and prayerful petition.

From the human perspective, preaching is essentially an art form where ideas are the medium and are formed into artful expression dependent on the personality and skills of the preacher architect. The skill, creativity, and personality of the pastor are thus integral to the preaching task, inseparably bound up with what is communicated.

The nature of oral delivery. "And [in speaking the genuine gospel] you hear done in the most clear, plain, simple, unaffected language, yet with an earnestness becoming the importance of the subject and with the demonstration of the Spirit." —John Wesley (1703-1791), English theologian, evangelist, and founder of Methodism.

Foremost in any oral delivery is content, then mechanics, then style. First, above all, there must be a *substantive* message, in preaching Scripture. Without this base and focus, preaching becomes little more than a lecture, without spiritual meaning. Second, the *mechanics* of verbal expression must be observed; namely, voice clarity, volume, and pace. Third, and subject to great latitude and personal choice, is delivery *style*. Substance will be treated in "Content Design" beginning on page 233; mechanics in "Ten Guides to Effective Delivery," page 232. We skip now briefly to personal style, the greatest variant in many instances.

Personal style. "We are not won by arguments that we can analyze but by tone and temper, by the manner which is the man himself." —Samuel Butler (1835-1902), English author.

The manner in which a sermon is delivered can elevate the presentation from commonplace to acceptable, occasionally even memorable. The various nuances involved, when mastered, can establish a certain *poetry* of speech most pleasing to the ear and mind. We are speaking here of such distinctive features as sound and meter (tone, inflection, and cadence); artistic imagery (description that creates a mental vision); and emotional sweep (conviction, dedication, and enthusiasm). Even a pause can be effective, letting an idea or thought sink in and be interpreted. A chuckle can aid in sharing a humorous moment. More important than mannerism however, is the conveyance of burning conviction. A strong certain belief is contagious, firing the spirit of listeners.

Style, of course, is partly natural and inherent in the individual. Preaching, especially, depends largely on the personality of the preacher.[19] Characteristics such as outgoing friendliness versus a more reserved countenance, sense of humor, and an analytical approach as opposed to creative artistry may be more inborn than acquired traits. The careful preacher will respond to these natural tendencies by cultivating the positive and limiting the negative, the idea being to be your best possible self. This is all God asks anyone.

Let your convictions show. It is not enough to simply know and practice the rudiments of preaching; it must come from the heart and soul through Jesus. Heartfelt, true expression and conviction are the absolute underlying essentials of effective preaching. The rest, fluency, grace, and the like, are merely elected window dressing, decorative but basically ornamental. The preacher who exhibits his emotional attachment to the Gospel, who shows the congregation he really understands and cares, gathers them together in shared involvement and commitment. People long for genuine sensitivity and passion. They want to be caught up emotionally in the Good News.

Ten Guides for Effective Delivery:

1. **Speak directly** and unreservedly to the congregation, addressing the listeners as individuals in a personal forthright manner. Look directly at the audience, first one person then another, then a third–really look at them. Eye contact signals warmth and sincerity, making a sermon highly personal.

2. **Project an intimate association with the congregation**, one of friendship, personal concern, and love for all present. Speak as if you're talking one-on-one to each individual member, honestly, sincerely, conversationally. Think of preaching as animated conversation, simply and directly. As Edgar Jackson observes, "The fact that he (Jesus) sat down to speak indicates a practice of informality that invited people to come closer." Nothing is superior to being taught person-to-person as exemplified by Jesus.

3. **Observe sound speech mechanics.** Speak in an audible, clear voice. Enunciate clearly. Don't run words together. Don't let your voice fall at the end of a sentence. Use voice modulation (pitch, intensity, and tone) to change the mood, rising inflection in expressing a question, for example. A sepulchral tone has a ring of insincerity.

Speak at a reasonable pace for understanding and with sufficient deliberation to indicate the importance of God's Word...better a little slow than too fast. Pause between divisions to indicate a transition or emphasize a point. Speech rate may speed up slightly for secondary or transitional material.

4. **Speak from the heart, from first-hand experience, and hence with authority.** Conviction and sincerity are absolutely essential to effective sermon delivery. When you believe in what you have to say and are passionate and honest about your subject, people will listen.[20]

5. **Speak with vitality, life, energy, and enthusiasm**, occasionally with passion, even burning conviction. People need to first experience the speaker's energy in order to hear what is being said. Pastors must be filled

with the Holy Spirit to preach a living present God. This intensity of faith is often as important as the message itself.

6. **Look pleasant, smile occasionally**. Humor should be used as an incidental "discovery" as one proceeds.

7. **Limit gestures** to what is natural to the delivery. Avoid distracting mannerisms

8. **Get as close to the listening congregation as possible**, even speaking from the aisle. Proximity ensures attentiveness.

9. **Use notes as inconspicuously as possible**. Looking directly at the congregation while concurrently determining what to say is a powerful means of personal communication. We use this thought-speech process everyday in our personal conversations and come to expect its directness and intimacy. Public speaking, on the other hand, presents far more difficulties in this regard, more so for some than others. Peter Marshall,[21] for example, wrote out his sermons in detail and read them word-for-word in order to secure the exact verbiage and nuances intended. Thus no hard and fast rule is prescribed. The object is to *appear* independent of script. Thus repeated reading of a sermon will eventually so well fix the content in mind that only an occasional glance may be required.

10. **Listen to recordings of your delivery.** Self-examination is valuable in identifying minor detracting mannerism and faulty syntax, repetition, etc. More important, listening "can give the preacher a clearer idea of the movement of his sermons. He can sense the development of ideas and the effectiveness of his logic and the strength of his points. It is a chastening experience to sit down with a tape recorder, week after week and listen to a whole service."[22]

In closing, pastors are advised to take advantage of all opportunities for continued theological training. Fortunate indeed are those attending such prestigious post graduate courses in preaching as offered by the Cathedral College of Washington National Cathedral in Washington, D.C. At the local level, homiletic training is offered throughout the country by many denominations, e.g., the yearly "Finch Lectures on Preaching" sponsored by the Western North Carolina Conference and the Finch-Hunt Institute for Homiletical Studies, Charlotte, N.C.

Content Design

"The preaching of the word of God *is* the word of God"

–John Calvin (1509-1564), French theologian and reformer.

For it is not ourselves that we preach; we preach Jesus Christ as Lord, and ourselves as your servants for Jesus' sake. (2 Corinthians 4:5)

"The ability to get attention, and put the message across is of critical significance for effective preaching. To get attention sermons must relate to the interests of the people in a fresh way and concern genuine areas of life experience." –Edgar Jackson

Poor preparation and poor content is never truly productive no matter how eloquently delivered. In contrast, real substance can rivet attention however modestly proclaimed. This content-design division is organized in four parts: "Types of Sermons," "Principal Messages," "Content Sources," and "The Planning/Writing Process." All are interactive elements in sermon preparation. And rules for content design, however insightful, are, of course, subservient to prayer and guidance of the Holy Spirit.

Types of Sermons

Sermons and their settings are most commonly characterized as either formal or informal. An example of the stately extreme is the formal, pulpit-delivered, expositional, and cogent delivery practiced by the formidable Harry Emerson Fosdick (Pastor, Park Avenue Baptist Church, later renamed Riverside Church, 1929-1946). The informal style, in contrast, was typically employed by Norman Vincent Peale[23] who simply stood up and talked, usually beginning with a problem and observation, continuing in a conversational tone with stories and anecdotes. The choice between these two extremes is typically a matter of degree rather than absolutes, depending primarily on the calendar theme and the personality of the speaker.

Sermons are also classified by "type," e.g., topical, textual, and expository, based primarily by the breadth of textual source material involved.[24] However, classification in this manner by genesis, is as much an academic exercise as a view of reality. In truth, few sermons are prepared with any real thought given to observing source boundaries. Also, audiences, if they recognize any form of sermon classification, are most likely to note perceived differences in personal impact or response. Thus sermons are viewed by listeners as "instructional" or "inspirational."

A synthesis of the "type" nomenclature can be evolved as a precursory guide, the purpose being simply to indicate the breadth and opportunities involved, and possibly alert pastors and congregations of the need for more comprehensive overall coverage as well as caution in certain areas. Bear in mind that sermons are seldom directed to a single effect which moderates the distinctions listed. With these caveats in mind, the following five element audience response taxonomy[25] is advanced:

Repressive/inspirational. Defined by Jackson as "...a deliberate effort to repress the unpleasant and irritating in life and substitute emphasis on the good and wholesome."[26] Such a positive approach, employed with success by Alcoholics Anonymous, emphasizes the inner resources of individuals and strength through commitment and resolve. For Christians, the message is one of inspiration and hope through Christ. Congregations are generally relaxed and comfortable during these types of sermons, ready and willing to respond. Attendance may even increase.

Exposition/analytical. This approach openly examines life experiences together with the means available for individuals and families to deal openly and realistically with their problems. Hard to understand events may be targeted. In the religious context, self-examination, spiritual growth, inner resources, and family support are sought. Yet the burden for improvement is placed strictly upon man. Congregational response to analytical type sermons is often restrained and contemplative. Requests for pastoral counseling may increase significantly.

Proclamation/exhortation. These types of sermons are noted for their vim and vigor in announcing the word of God and inciting enthusiastic response. Pastors filled with ebullient vitality and energy cannot help but stir the souls with strong appeals, encouragement, and admonition. Earnestness is the hallmark of all proclamations and exhortations. Every once in a while congregations need to be jolted out of their complacency by this type of sermon, made to sit up straight and praise God with every ounce of their energy.

Therapeutic. Restorative preaching has the specific intent to affect some improvement in the hearer, to change his or her state or condition (mental, emotional, or religious). The aim is to cure and restore to health. Reconciliation to God's care is an underlying goal.

Instructional. Instructional sermons are primarily for the purpose of imparting knowledge and understanding. They are explanatory in nature, typically dealing with academic or difficult topics such as church history, Christian tenets, politics, and contemporary issues. Catechetical instruction also falls in this category. Simple direct teaching of Christian basics should be the common core of all preaching. Associated precautions include limiting subject matter to what can be absorbed, insuring clarity, and adding sufficient embellishments or analysis to encourage attention.

Principal Messages

"Preach the Bible! Begin, live, and work with biblical text. Allow the text to dictate the flow and main points. First, it is the Word of God and thus the ultimate and primary source. Second, people are hungry for the Bible, to feel the richness of the Scriptures, the power and love of God. Don't try to please the congregation, teach the Bible."

–Edward W. Bauman

Announce to the world the Good News that the essential being of God is *for us*. We are enabled through his grace to experience God's immediate "infilling" presence. We need only give ourselves permission to let our heavenly Father love us.

Generally, most Sunday sermons are based on Scripture according to the church calendar.[27] And this is perhaps all that needs to be said about content, for proclaiming the Good News of Christ's teachings and resurrection is the essential goal of all preaching. Other considerations are, of course, the life situation of the congregation and social and national issues at hand. Surveys of congregational preferences for sermon content typically give highest priority to personal problems growing out of immaturity, conflict, loneliness, immorality, and suffering. Family problems of parenthood and child rearing are a second major concern. People come to church hurting, seeking God's grace and healing power.

Pastors must look beneath the exteriors of people to "see what's inside," where the need is greatest and where the healing spirit of God can provide refuge. The pastor who walks with his people during the week experiencing their condition and feeling their feelings, has no difficulty on Sunday speaking so that listeners know what he means.

What Are The Principal Bible Messages?

No definitive list of major sermon topics exists. The closest approach is the theme listings found at the front of many Bibles. The following heading list from *The Holy Bible, New Revised Standard Version*, contains approximately 87 sub-component themes:

God: Creator and Redeemer
  This Good World
  The Human Creature: Special and Spoiled
  God's Concern for Humanity: Covenant
  God of Goodness and Mercy
  God is Love
  The Triune God

The Person and Work of Christ
  Incarnation
  Atonement
  Resurrection
  The Healing of Humanity: Amazing Grace
  Justification by Faith
  Faith and Works

The Holy Spirit and the Church
  The Spirit of Power, Truth, Love
  The Community of the Spirit
  The Sacraments
  The People of God

Dimensions of Hope
  The Kingdom of God
  The Coming Kingdom
  Our Father's House

A sense of topic priorities can also be gained from the frequency of referenced Scripture. From the table, page 237, we see that the Gospel of Saint Matthew, Chapter 5, was most frequently cited in submitted sermons. Matthew, Chapters 6 and 7, were also principal sources. The topics of these three chapters suggest messages which in practice receive high sermon priority. The verses involved include: The Beatitudes, The Law and the Prophets, Concerning Anger, Concerning Adultery, Love for Enemies, Concerning Almsgiving, Concerning Prayer, Concerning Treasures, Serving Two Masters, Do Not Worry, Judging Others, The Golden Rule, The Narrow Gate, and Hearers and Doers.

A second source of sermon topics can be confidently based on the wondrous elements of Christian faith—Faith, Hope, Inspiration, Obedience, Love, Trust, Grace, and Forgiveness. Too often these fundamentals are neglected in the press of responding to contemporary needs.

Most popular Bible chapters cited as sermon texts
Over half (54%) of 4,388 sermons listed are based on 9 percent (105) of the Bible's 1,189 chapters.

Book	Chap	Number of related sermons	Book	Chap	Number of related sermons	Book	Chap	Number of related sermons
Matthew	5	116	Ephesians	1	21	Luke	8	14
Romans	8	93	James	4	21	Acts	3	14
Matthew	6	63	John	5	20	Acts	6	14
Philippians	1	55	Romans	2	20	Genesis OT	12	14
Romans	1	54	James	5	20	Psalms OT	23	14
Ephesians	4	54	Malachi OT	3	20	1 Corinthians	11	14
James	1	48	John	8	19	1 Corinthians	15	14
Matthew	7	44	John	12	19	Galatians	4	14
John	1	44	Luke	1	19	Exodus OT	20	14
Philippians	2	40	Acts	8	19	Matthew	1	13
Romans	3	37	Acts	9	19	Matthew	10	13
Acts	2	36	John	19	18	Matthew	28	13
Philippians	3	36	Luke	23	18	John	16	13
John	14	33	Genesis OT	1	18	Luke	4	13
John	15	33	Genesis OT	3	18	Luke	12	13
Romans	5	33	Hebrews	11	18	Acts	17	13
Ephesians	6	32	John	20	17	James	3	13
Luke	2	31	Romans	4	17	Exodus OT	3	13
John	6	29	Romans	9	17	Isaiah OT	9	13
Galatians	3	29	Luke	15	17	1 Peter	1	13
John	17	28	Acts	1	17	Matthew	22	12
Ephesians	5	28	Galatians	1	17	Luke	17	12
John	10	27	Matthew	11	16	Luke	19	12
Mark	1	27	Matthew	26	16	Acts	20	12
Galatians	5	26	Philippians	4	16	Genesis OT	2	12
Romans	6	24	James	2	16	Genesis OT	4	12
Romans	7	24	Revelation	1	16	Galatians	6	12
Galatians	2	24	Jonah OT	1	16	Revelation	3	12
John	3	23	Matthew	27	15	Mark	10	12
John	4	22	John	7	15	1 Peter	2	12
John	11	22	Romans	11	15	1 Peter	5	12
Ephesians	2	22	Acts	4	15	Colossians	1	12
1 Corinthians	1	22	Hebrews	12	15	1 John	2	12
Revelation	2	22	Hebrews	13	15	Jude	1	12
Joshua OT	1	22	Matthew	12	14	Ruth OT	1	12
						TOTAL	105	2,361

OT = Old Testament
Source: Derived from data reported in Sermon Links.com

Every pastor asks, "What does God want to say to this congregation through me?" The answer is always to seek to preach like Jesus, teaching the Good News about God in a way that makes it possible for those who hear to encounter the living God for themselves. The answer is never a matter of personal choice, but rather one between the pastor and God in prayer and Scripture reading. One that is gained through contemplation and study. One understood by working with associates, listening and learning. One secured through knowing the congregation and their needs. Expect the preaching mission to make God's presence known, to actually bring God into each and every heart.

One would hope to conclude this section on sermon topics with a widely accepted scholarly list of essential subject matter. None exists, as earlier noted. In its absence, the responsibility remains with individual pastors and their congregations. And preparation of such a list is invaluable in insuring properly focused attention and comprehensive coverage, two paramount objects of any sermon calendar. As a start, consider this modest syllabus:

- To known God's grace and abiding love for mankind, freely bestowed.
- To know the significance of the risen Lord our Savior.
- To know the meaning of faith as a gift of God to all believers.
- To know the meaning of forgiveness through confession and repentance..
- To put God first in our lives as followers and disciples of Jesus Christ.
- To see the face of Christ in others and live accordingly.
- To lead spiritual lives of prayer and study of God's Holy Word.
- To strengthen faith. *To have faith is to be sure of the things we hope for, to be certain of the things we cannot see.* (Hebrews 11:1)
- To encourage Christian behavior–worship, service, study, and generous sharing of our gifts.
- To follow the constant call of Jesus to conversion and to action.
- To share with others the Good News of the risen Lord.
- To know through Christ's teachings how to respond to God's love and commandments. *In the past God spoke to our ancestors many times and in many ways through the prophets, but in these last days he has spoken to us through his Son.* (Hebrews 1:1-2)
- To create a sense of the purpose of life and its encompassing empowerment and joy.
- To address evils and societal ills of this world as one who lives in grace.
- To help persons preoccupied with self to see beyond themselves in fulfillment through reaching out to others, sharing, and generosity.
- To ease the burdens of life by living with encouragement and hope.

Content Sources

Simon Peter answered him, "Lord, to whom would we go? You have the words that give eternal life." (John 6:68)

Preaching is "...an art form which can be enriched by insights from many sources but always preserves for itself those qualities that owe more

to the mysteries of inspiration than to the disciplines of technical mastery."
–Edgar N. Jackson

"Listen to hear what God has to say for us today." Preparation always begins with prayer and scriptural study, the ultimate sources of all wisdom. The creative effort is also derived from one's lifetime of seeing, hearing, and doing. Pastors are well advised to preach what the congregation is living.

Available Resources

"The preacher who has developed the habit of looking to new and fresh material will begin to see it cropping up here and there." –Edgar Jackson

It is a wise pastor that appreciates and utilizes the extended array of resources available as homiletic aids. Their use should be recognized as a multiplying enriching factor, creative and supplemental rather than elemental. A personal or church library may easily assemble the best of published homiletic assistance works. The most noteworthy likely number less than a dozen. Some dealing with homiletic preparation are cited in this chapter. Keep in mind that however important such written materials are, they are simply complements to general reading and life experiences.

A good Biblical *dictionary* is a very useful basic tool, defining words particular to the Bible plus commonly providing an atlas, references, etc. *Concordances* list the multiple locations of given words allowing repeated impressions to be garnered. *Commentaries* and Bible *handbooks* provide insight into Scriptural text by the authors, often in great scholarly detail. They are concisely available on compact disks.

A vast array of self-help sources exist to aid pastors in sermon preparation. Hardcopy texts include T. T. Crabtree's *The Zondervan Pastor's Annual* which offers a week-by-week guide to the Lectionary together with sermon outlines, illustrative stories and appropriate hymns. Many anthologies are available such as James W. Cox's *Best Sermons* (annual), the *Abingdon Women's Preaching Annual*, and Christopher Howse's *Best Sermons Ever*. Commentaries abound, some with verse-by-verse text-positional explanations and interpretation.[28]

The World Wide Web is a new colossus of homiletic material ranging from brief outlines to completely prepared sermons available for downloading and word-for-word delivery. Judicious review of such material is likely to help any searching pastor with a good running start.

Lastly, we encourage use of the most immediate yet least often employed source of pulpit guidance, the informal critique. Such assistance related to both content and delivery is provided in strictest confidence and always constructively focused. Congregational members elected to this role must have exceptional qualifying credentials in language skills and Bible content. And, it goes without saying; it takes a mightily self-confident pastor to accommodate such an inroad into an otherwise personal jurisdiction.

Creativity and Citation

Creative effort is critical to designing a sermon message responsive to immediate local needs and consistent with the speaker's persona. It establishes and communicates the integrity of the speaker-message relationship. Fortunately, creativity exists in many forms—originality, expressiveness, imagination, and yes, even resourcefulness. Only the Gospel is totally creative, all else is essentially responsive. Thus selective use of materials including that of others is entirely legitimate, often desirable, and even necessary in achieving excellence.[29] Pastors are, after all, disciples working *together* in teaching the same Good News message.

While all may be preaching the shared Word of God, no unique standard for use of another's material is implicit. Most pastors properly feel a personal responsibility to do their very best. This obligation, however, is too often accompanied by an overriding ego, an inflated sense of self reliance that blocks any effort to include the work of others. The typical rationale is professional and ministerial ethics. But there is no universal agreement. Keith D. Miller writes that assumptions about words as property are fundamentally different within the preaching tradition than they are within the written culture of publishing. Some clergy operate on the basis that "words are shared assets, not personal belongings,"[30] the premise being that congregations are entitled and the preacher responsible for delivering the very best which by definition includes much of others. Whatever the latitude assumed, according credit is absolutely essential, not only in being truthful but also by enriching a presentation with the distinctiveness of others by name. And such attribution should be painless, reflecting as much if not more scholarship in searching out the elegant and profound, as opposed to exclusive use of only one's own possibly limited and flawed material.

We urge preachers to disavow the narrowness and self-centered curtailment to preach only what is their own, and expand their repertoire to include a sampling of the best of others. Just as we unquestioningly cite Scripture, may we not equally enlist the inspired work of Christ's modern day disciples? As Paul Greenberg, editorial page editor of the *Arkansas Democrat-Gazette*, has written, "After all, when either Cervantes or Shakespeare has said almost anything better, why say it worse?" Congregations deserve the very best possible. For those pastors who have difficulty in producing compelling sermons, judicious borrowing should be considered a duty; for the rest an elective element. Remember, repeating the best is still *the best.*[31]

Search and Maintain

One must continually look for new and fresh material, even different combinations of older material. Repeatedly rereading Scripture often brings such new insights.

At the same time one is continually seeking new content, systematically stored for future use. A filing system is essential to maintain in some organized fashion the bits and pieces of content and ideas as they are gathered and generated. Organizing by subject matter is perhaps the most logical system, although others may be equally practical. Edgar Jackson writes of a minister acquaintance who maintained a three-part system. The "incubator," contained various seeds of ideas and scripture texts. When a central theme appeared feasible, it was distinguished in a "starter sheet" to which various subsequent ideas were clipped as content came to mind including transfers from the incubator. When enough material was gathered to establish a true core, it was moved to the "brooder" which served as a topic depository ready for final construction. "Such a program encourages the slow, sure development of worthwhile ideas, and at the same time discourages the frustrating search for material at the last minute..."

The Planning/Writing Process

Let your speech always be gracious, seasoned with salt, so that you may know how you should answer everyone. (Colossians 4:6)

What does God want to say to this congregation through me? The task of preaching is to teach the Good News as Jesus taught, in a way that makes it possible for those who hear to encounter the living God for themselves. Expect to make God's presence known, to actually *bring* God into each and every heart, not to distance oneself by talking *about* God.

The planning/writing process is described here in four divisions–The Enabling Retreat, The Topic Agenda, Supporting Mechanics, and Guidelines for Content Preparation. We begin with the most important component, the pastor alone with his helpmate.

The Enabling Retreat

"Though each man's work habits are different, there are certain essentials in the process. There must be time for quiet and thought. There must be an alertness to ideas and materials that can be used. There must be a creative moment when the thought and the materials begin to take a form that can make them usable." –Edgar Jackson

Pastors must have a reserved time for solitude, contemplation, and communing with self and with God. This is when God's love and message are made manifest above and beyond all that the individual is capable of alone. Sermons are thus best formed in the mind enjoined with meditation, prayer, and Bible reading. God speaks to pastors everywhere as they prepare, breathing new insight into the spiritual message. However derived, content will be changed and invigorated by prayer and contemplation, responding with new life and vitality, quite apart from its original nature and source. New ownership is created so that the message can be preached "with integrity and passion because then it is our message."

"The preacher must pre-eminently be a man of prayer. His heart must graduate in the school of prayer. In the school of prayer only can the

heart learn to preach. No learning can make up for failure to pray. No earnestness, no diligence, no study, no gifts will supply its lack."
–E. M. Bounds (1835-1913), Methodist minister and devotional writer.

The enabling retreat is also deeply rooted in Scripture reading. In working with the text it is possible for the sermon to literally grow out of the reading. "Because of its special nature, God is able to use the occasion of our reading of the Bible to reveal his immediate presence in life-giving and life-transforming ways." –Edward Bauman

The Topic Agenda

Planning sermon topics months in advance assists in providing balance and coverage to the overall scheme. It also creates time for sermon development, to grow in the subconscious, to mature with additional insight that might not otherwise occur if rushed into being. A commonly practiced plan of preparation is to use the summer vacation to map out a tentative outline of sermon topics for the coming year. This overall structure provides perspective and can be designed to give balanced emphasis and a possible progressive movement. Edgar Jackson suggests that a preset sermon agenda provides the opportunity for "unconscious growth of the mind" to occur as "...the mind is alerted for any fresh or new material that can be used in the sermons scheduled. There is time to mull over ideas and accumulate a variety of material that one would not be able to find if the subject were approached with only a week's notice."

Supporting Mechanics

Preparatory and process mechanics required in sermon preparation are briefly described here.

Preparation time. Pastors must set aside sufficient time to adequately prepare. No role is more important than preaching. Delegate and curtail as necessary, but attend to the principal pulpit responsibility. Some suggest an hour preparation time is required for each minute of presentation. But recall that the overall process from concept, through gathering material, to reflection and final write-up should be spread out over many months.

Engage in research. In this instance, *research* is that investigative study of a sermon topic necessary to secure true and comprehensive insight. It is the search for fundamental understanding which must be achieved if the delivery is to be of real value. Research replaces the shallow and obvious with depth and underlying meaning. It can be accomplish only by extended study of multiple source materials. As such, the generally slight rewards garnered versus the extended energy required must be a consideration. However, the relative rarity of such scholarship makes it a most welcome and appreciated element by alert congregants.

Write and rewrite until the content is perfected and solid in your mind. According to historians, Lincoln wrote and rewrote the "Gettysburg Address" over and over again, draft after draft. If you've written it enough, then you gain the added bonus of being sufficiently familiar with the content to be able to speak with a minimal number of notes. Forget about the exact wording. It's a mistake to concentrate on such details because it puts too heavy a retention burden on you.

Either an outline or full script is acceptable. Most speakers require at least an outline of key points. Each statement should be as concise as possible and written on a separate line, appropriately indented and/or numbered, for quick systematic referral. Consider the lucky few who, after repeated reading, can deliver a full sermon with only an occasional look at abbreviated notes. Others, however, including the eminent preachers Peter Marshall and John Henry Jowett, to name but two, relied on a full text to insure the exact wordage, cadence, etc. sought.

Over an extended period, seek appropriate comprehensive biblical coverage of the liturgical calendar. Careful, judicious selection[32] of topics is required. Topics should also respond to the congregation's situation in life and current issues of society, but never in overriding fashion. See discussion of sermon topics, pages 236-238.

Guidelines for Content Preparation

With regard to the immediate task of preparing a specific sermon, we offer these 12 guides abstracted from a variety of sources:

1. Always expect and plan for God's joyful presence and help in the "preaching event."

"All during the week I look forward to the worship service in order to see what God will do in our midst with the preaching event" —Edward Bauman

In *The Theory of Sacramental Preaching*, Bauman discusses the wonderful graciousness of God who comes to us through Jesus Christ using the occasion of preaching to make his immediate presence known. Bauman rejoices in the presence of God working in the congregation–healing, challenging, equipping–lifting a terrible burden off the shoulders of preachers. Know that God works only for good in all who love him.

2. Seek personal listener involvement.

Come to grips with real problems for real people that immediately engage the listener. Seek to secure the congregation's participation and response by forming questions in their minds about the topic or even themselves, or by an open challenge, possibly even a threat. "Are we our brother's keeper?" "Woe to the rich man!"

3. Keep the essentials of content design foremost.

There are four essentials of sermon content–substance, focus, clarity, and brevity. The two elements of *substance*, cited by Dee Bowman, are content that is informative, instructive in the Gospel, and content that is challenging, tasking people to follow Christ. *Focused* sermons direct and maintain attention on a particular theme or lesson without distracting diversions. *Clarity* is a matter of content being readily and completely understandable. *Brevity* is concise, elemental expression, to the point. In this latter instance, it is not that the congregation cannot be retained longer, it is more commonly the inability of the speaker to maintain the necessary fervor. As Thomas Babington Macaulay (1800-1859, English historian and author) remarked in referring to Francis Bacon, "He had a wonderful talent for packing thought close, and rendering it portable."

4. Start with a specific aim or objective.

Once the purpose of the sermon is established it serves as a central overarching theme, guiding design of the entire contents. Selecting a given topic will invariably address a need within the congregation. It should always be based on biblical Scripture. A sermon is, after all, the Word of God.

Sermons should emphasize the power and centrality of the Gospel message...the life and work of Jesus Christ, his saving grace and love for mankind, and his death and resurrection. Contemporary issues, in contrast, are focused on mankind rather than God. Thus it is important to link the daily experiences and challenges of people to biblical text, putting the Gospel into action.

5. Seek unity, a single consistent focus or purpose.

All parts must contribute to the central whole. "When a sermon is the embodiment of one vigorous idea, when the whole of it becomes simply the elaboration and extension of that idea, then it produces in the listener that concentration of effect which is called unity." –H. Grady Davis, *Design for Preaching*, 2003. "No sermon is ready for preaching, nor ready for writing out, until we can express its theme in a short, pregnant sentence as clear as crystal." –John Henry Jowett (1864-1923), gifted and dedicated preacher in both England and the United States.

Every sermon must attempt to transmit at least one message that each listener is likely to take with him or her and apply to their lives, something of real personal value. What have I learned from this sermon that will help me be a better person? What do I now understand? The whole thrust of a sermon must be to drive home, in the minds and hearts of the congregation, at least one point, be it instructional, motivational, or inspirational.

6. Organize and order content into a logical related congruent whole.

Always start and build upon an outline. The outline organizes the various parts and lists key points. It establishes order and sets boundaries. It has been aptly described by Dee Bowman as "comparable to a blue print." It is the framework of broad topic areas and key points upon which the later sermon details will be built. A good outline ensures unity, that the content stays on course, and that topics are covered in proper order, agreement, and detail. Since it consists of only a number system and short topical sentences, a lot of shifting can be easily performed to insure the above objectives are accomplished. For some, a well fleshed-out outline will be all that is necessary to guide the actual delivery.

In terms of organization, a sermon "...must have a theme, a center of concentration and a point of focus." (Edgar Jackson) This is a matter of maintaining continuity to establish a coherent whole. Brevity helps in this regard, no rambling or divergence. Extraneous and unimportant material is discarded.

Contrary to some advice, it is psychologically sound to make your strongest point first. When the opening material is strong, listeners will be attentive and seek further information; if it is weak, the listener is immediately lost, making it difficult to win back their interest. And, all key points should be made with clarity and emphasis.

Sermon components generally include a title, introduction, discussion, and conclusion.

Title the sermon to express the main substantive element in a short attention-generating phrase. The title need not be clever, but should exhibit some imagination. Most importantly, the title should convey real meaning, a "sermon in miniature" when possible.

The **introduction** "prepares the minds and secures the interests" of the hearers. (James Braga) It explains the purpose or intent of the sermon, where it will lead the audience, and what might be expected of them. A good introduction, forcefully delivered, will immediately establish contact with the audience, creating interest, and inciting a need to hear more.[33] Such a positive beginning calms both speaker and audience, easing any possible initial "jitters." The introduction should conclude with a **proposition or thesis** statement, i.e., a succinct declaration of the subject or sermon topic.[34] It takes time to evolve a good thesis statement, but once prepared it serves to evaluate the relevancy of all subsequent content. "This morning I will speak of the importance of daily meditation as a vital element of Christian living." The proposition not only clarifies the intent of the sermon for the congregation, it may also hint at the direction in which the sermon will proceed. No wandering is expected after an announced subject. Developing a right proposition insures an accurate understanding of the central truth of the subject Scripture lesson. The proposition may be immediately followed by a few statements regarding the nature of the central issues involved, to be presented in the following discussion.

The **discussion**, or central element of the sermon, is typically organized in divisions which distinguish and arrange in orderly fashion the various substantive components involved. Each division should focus on a main point related to the common theme. Each point should be relatively, if not entirely, distinct. The divisions should progress systematically in order of importance, time sequence, analytical arrangement, or other appropriate pattern. James Braga and others recommend as few divisions as possible, three to four normally sufficient to cover most distinct ideas involved.

Within the sermon's discussion, each spiritual truth or lesson typically engenders some sort of responsive requirement on the hearer. The responsible preacher not only defines the obligation imposed but persuasively encourages a proper response. "Preaching that does not finally persuade the hearer to apply the information to his own life is not actually preaching, it's teaching. Preaching persuades or it isn't preaching."[35] Such "**applications**" can be made real and practical if they relate to common human problems and needs and encourage action with sufficient motivational impetus. Occasionally the congregation may require admonishment to make straight the Lord's path. There should be no fear here ever for preaching God's truth.

The **conclusion** is the last portion of the sermon in which all that has been previously stated is summed up in a final encompassing, forceful impression. James Braga calls it a "burning and powerful focus" that produces a "vigorous impact" upon the congregation. Conclusions will hopefully be remembered. They should tie together, summarize, and respond to the sermon content in a manner that ultimately strengthens the listener. They may take the form of a judgment, decision, or recommendation, even an exhortation to "do so likewise," or simply encouragement.

Conclusions are generally brief and straightforward. The importance of securing a lasting impression means that the exact wording should be carefully chosen. The conclusion can take the form of a recapitulation of the central theme, a dramatic illustration, or a direct appeal to the congregation. In every instance, however, the sermon "thesis" (central subject) should be restated together with a final "application" plea or call to action. "Today we have learned of the critical importance of steadfast prayer in our daily lives. We thus renew again, together, that odyssey that carries us into the waiting arms of our Heavenly Father."

7. Be substantive and straightforward.

Sermons should be prepared with substance and interest foremost, clarity an accompanying obligation. Work to isolate and define the central Bible message chosen, then explain it as simply and directly as possible. Use the sermon title to establish the theme and create interest. Never "water-down" the message. And note that rhetorical excellence is not a goal.

Make the sermon as personal as possible, seeking a response from each individual. The aim is for every listener to make a personal application of the sermon to their own lives and behavior.

In terms of what is substantive, Martin Luther suggested that time be given to good catechetical instruction to teach the principles and meaning of selected biblical content. We too often neglect establishing a rock-solid Christian base within the congregation. More often than not, the harder the text, the more interesting and compelling it is to the listener when preached forthrightly.

8. Be clear and direct in language.

Every sentence must be readily understandable. Use words effectively in terms of their necessity, interaction, strength, familiarity, etc.[36] Speak in a manner everyone can relate to and comprehend, not above or beneath the congregation.

An adjunct to word choice is adherence to correct grammar and use of an appropriate vocabulary. The right word is frequently essential in accurately conveying meaning, expressing subtleties of emotion, and enlivening a presentation. Word enhancement should be viewed as a useful preaching tool.

9. Use stories, anecdotes, quotations, and similar means to illustrate and make content real and vivid.

Jesus used parables, word pictures, to illustrate and dramatize his teachings. Today we use the contemporary equivalent, a simple story. Brief narratives dramatize problems, helping people to more readily visualize and understand what is being said. Illustrations not only clarify the message, they arouse attention and enliven interest. They may demonstrate the reality of what is being said in a true-to-life example.

An apt quotation or verse of poetry may also be used effectively to emphasize or clarify a point with a different touch. It helps to know that someone else, perhaps some famous person, expressed the same thoughts or feelings in an eloquent manner. All such devices should be employed in the natural order of things—a ready inclusion, something almost in passing, relevant, light, supportive.

10. Use humor sparingly.

It is most important for the preaching pastor to exhibit a sense of pleasure and joy in the preaching event. And this pleasure will occasionally, naturally, lead to humorous situations for all to enjoy. Humor should be relevant, seemingly spontaneous. An infectious, knowing smile is often subtle humor at its very best. Dean Charles R. Brown of Yale University remarked, regarding humor, "Let him use, if he will, those lighter statements which bring a sense of surprise. ....just in passing, with a touch and go, never waiting for a laugh..."

11. Limit personal references.

Pastors are well enough known by the congregation to preclude any need for further divulgence from the pulpit. Speak of oneself with caution. However, sharing a personal story can often be exceptionally effective because it shows that the pastor is comfortable being with the congregational audience, that he or she likes and trusts them as friends. Preachers must show their human side, their frailties, and the sharing of the common struggle to gain listener's ears.

12. Limit length, conclude while the listeners are still intensely interested.

It is best to conclude smartly when you have made a telling summary point that can be well remembered. A high level termination keeps interest and thoughts about the content high and lasting in the minds of listeners. Brevity combined with informative and interesting content always insures attention. Close promptly. Shorter sermons, in excluding marginal content, are typically more focused.

Regarding sermon length, preachers "...should make it a practice to err on the side of brevity rather than on the side of the listener forbearance" as Edgar Jackson recommends. The time to quit, as stated, is shortly after the final telling point while listeners are still interested, not when their attention is waning. Duration should seldom be greater than 20 minutes, preferably 15. (Note, some congregations are accustomed to and have grown to prefer fairly long Sunday services with lengthy sermons actively engaging the audience.)

Leading Prayer[37]

"Ask, and you will receive; seek, and you will find; knock, and the door will be opened to you. For everyone who asks will receive, and he who seeks will find, and the door will be opened to him who knocks. ... And bad as you are, you know how to give good things to your children. How much more, then, your Father in heaven will give good things to those who ask him!" (Matthew 7:7, 11)

"Jesus, stand among us. Amen" (very short prayer)

Communion with God is the essential element of worship, a fervent and reverent expression of love and devotion. We begin our Christian services with prayer, bringing people into God's presence and focusing our attention on right things. We also pray briefly before the sermon asking God's guidance in speaking and hearing. And we commonly petition God at some length following the homily. The task in these instances is always to open our minds and hearts for God to enter.

Prayer is the most direct way to experience the presence of God. We are held in God's embrace in prayer. Therefore, in this loving manner we are called to pray in all places and at all times. The Sunday service is the most public of these instances and thus has special opportunities and obligations. Corporate prayer is unique in being led by an officiating pastor, spoken aloud, shared among all, and typically prepared in advance.

If any "guides" for corporate prayer are possible, they would possibly speak to the following aims:

Heartfelt. Seek God earnestly, directing our hearts and minds to him, expecting him, waiting for his response, listening to him.

Humble. Seek God's forgiveness and saving grace. A humanizing touch is for the pastor to come down to the altar rail and kneel in reciting prayer.

Openness, total listening and abandonment to God. *For we do not know how we ought to pray; the Spirit himself pleads with God for us..."* (Romans 8:26) The essence of prayer, as described by Edward Bauman, is "total listening and abandonment to God."[38] He then explains that we initially begin our prayer life asking God for his help and mercy. As we spiritually mature and devote more time in prayer, we spend less time talking and more listening, seeking to learn his will for our troubled souls. Would it thus not be well for congregations everywhere to reserve more quiet time each Sunday to *listening* to what God is saying to them?

For others. Prayer betrays its true responsibility when it is too immediate and locally focused to the exclusion of the total human condition.

Concise. "Long prayers, superstition, and creeds clip the strong opinions of love, and clothe religion in human forms." –Mary Baker Eddy (1821-1910), U.S. founder of the Christian Science movement.

Reinhold Niebuhr (1892-1971), a stalwart critic of American Protestant life, observes that the pastoral prayer is often both too long and too formless. A series of short prayers, each devoted to a particular concern is more likely to fully involve the congregation. A bidding announcing the prayer subject is also helpful.

Niebuhr also notes that the language of prayers should aim for purity of expression in both Biblical material and Biblical phraseology. Banality and commonness, sentimentality, and extravagant expression are to be avoided

In closing, consider this beautiful paraphrase of the Lord's prayer.

Father,

I abandon myself into your hands;
Do with me what you will.
Whatever you may do, I thank you:
I am ready for all, I accept all.
Let only your will be done in me,
And in all your creatures –
I wish no more than this, O Lord.

Into your hands, I commend my soul;
I offer it to you with all the love of my heart,
For I love you Lord,
And so need to give myself,
To surrender myself into your hands,
Without reserve,
And with boundless confidence,

For you are my Father.

–Charles de Foucauld, (1858-1916), hermit, servant of the poor.

[1] This chapter on homiletics written by a lay person is necessarily heavily indebted to the professionals, pastors everywhere and in particular teachers of the art. In this instance, the work of Edgar N. Jackson, *A Psychology for Preaching* (Cambridge, Harper and Row, 1961) has proven especially valuable and is frequently cited.

Equally important, we extensively cite homiletic guidance authored by Edward W. Bauman. Of special value was his lecture series entitled "Sacramental Preaching" delivered by Dr. Bauman at the Institute for Homiletical Studies, Charlotte, N.C., 1980.

Two other authors are also frequently cited: Dee Bowman, *Common Sense Preaching*, (Temple Terrace, FL, Florida College Press, 1999), and James Braga, *How to Prepare Bible Messages,* (Portland, Multnomah Press, 1981). Thanks to these two fine scholars for their exceptional work in the homiletic field.

In addition to this indebtedness, any entry into the field of homiletics by laity must necessarily defer to the professionalism of all pastors. We advise as recipients, not experts, asking all those who preach to pardon our errors and omissions.

[2] Jackson, *A Psychology for Preaching*, p. 162.

[3] These observations are largely adopted from Jackson, *A Psychology for Preaching*, pp. 162-163.

Bowman, *Common Sense Preaching*, pp. 55-58, describes Christ's preaching style in this manner:

(1) His preaching was informative.
(2) His preaching was indicting.
(3) His preaching was explosive.
(4) His preaching was urgent.
(5) His preaching was relevant.

[4] Edward Bauman recalls this exceptional example of becoming aware of Christ's living presence within us, dwelling in our hearts. "There is a wonderful story of a college town, where they were having a union worship service in the college chapel but the parishes of the community had joined in. The college chaplain who had a Ph.D., a highly educated man, was conducting the service, and they had agreed that during the service they would have a brief testimony time, and that anyone in the congregation who had something to be very joyful for or thankful for or had a deep concern could just share it for a few moments. Well one of the black churches had joined in this union service and there was a 60 year old black women from that church who was so moved by the service and all that was going on, that she got up to speak. They found out later the beautiful person that she was. She hadn't learned to read until she was in her fifties, and she had learned to read primarily because she wanted to read the bible for herself. A very simple and beautiful spirit. Well when she got up in front of this crowd of people, many whom were faculty members of the college and the rest, she became so embarrassed she froze and she could not speak. And everyone was so embarrassed for her because she was obviously embarrassed. And finally after what seemed like an eternal silence she was able to blurt out the words, 'I know that my Redeemer lives, for he lives in my soul. Glory hallelujah,' and then she sat down. Well there was this profound silence then

because everyone realized that something very beautiful had happened. But then they wondered what would the chaplain say to break the silence and get the service moving again. He said, 'What our sister has just said is the highest word that can be spoken. The highest word of the human spirit. I rejoice that she is in the fellowship of Christ's people tonight. I rejoice that I can be in her fellowship. And all I can do is repeat her words for myself, I know that my Redeemer lives, for he lives in my soul. Glory hallelujah.'"

Edward W. Bauman, "Christ in You the Hope of Glory," An example of Sacramental Preaching, January, 1980.

[5] Bauman, "Sacramental Preaching."

[6] Jackson, *A Psychology for Preaching*, pp. 36-37.

[7] *Ibid.*, pp. 64 and 67.

[8] Video casting selected content on a large screen is now employed in many large churches to assist parishioners in mentally fixing key sermon content.

[9] Typical of the more serious observations and criticism of sermon content and delivery that a pulpit group may expect to hear include these reactions: (1) too complex or archaic language, (2) boring, dull, uninteresting content, (3) irrelevant content, without concern for the needs of the audience, (4) failure to encourage and strengthen, (5) lack of clarity in the central message, (6) failure to lead to change, improvement in the hearer.

Source: Clyde Reid, *The Empty Pulpit: A Study in Preaching as Communication,* cited in Bowman, *Common Sense Preaching,* pp. 197-200.

[10] Cited and described in detail in Bowman, *Common Sense Preaching,* pp. 15-22.

[11] Braga, *How to Prepare Bible Messages,* p. 12.

[12] *Ibid.* p. 12

[13] Jackson, *A Psychology for Preaching,* p. 62.

[14] Bowman, *Common Sense Preaching,* p. 24.

[15] Jackson, *A Psychology of Preaching,* p. 171.

[16] Braga, *How to Prepare Bible Messages,* p. 209

[17] Bauman, *Sacramental Preaching.*

[18] Raymond W. McLaughlin, *The Ethics of Persuasive Preaching* (Grand Rapids, MI, Baker, 1979), cited in Bowman, *Common Sense Preaching,* p. 206.

[19] Saint Francis of Assisi was most known for his preaching. Of his style we can say that it was altogether unstudied. He never prepared anything but, depending upon the inspiration of the moment, addressing himself with burning intensity to those before him. His whole body seemed to preach, and his gestures were vivacious and, perhaps, violent. Had it not been for his crystalline sincerity he might have struck people as absurd. Probably, too,...his feet danced while he spoke. His great dark eyes, full of fire and tenderness, seemed to look each person present through and through. He had a voice so resonant that it was startling, coming from so frail a man. It was fortunate that he had that asset of the orator, for his physical presence was not at all impressive, and what slight advantages he might have had in

this respect were thrown away because of his appearing in a coarse habit patched with material still coarser, sack-cloth that did not even match in color. Adopted, with slight modification, from a free essay on *Saint Francis of Assisi* available from 123Student.com web site.

[20] Henry C. Gregory tells the story of a young seminary student who returned to his home church and asked permission to recite the Twenty-third Psalm. Permission was granted, and the student stood proudly and recited the entire psalm without a flaw, to applause. Then an old woman stood up in the congregation and hobbled to the front of the church. She also recited the Twenty-third Psalm, but in a weak voice, with poor diction. Yet when she finished, "mothers clasped their children, and fathers who had long been strangers to tears found new fountains." Why the difference? Gregory asks. "The student knew the psalm, but the saint knew the shepherd." The old woman spoke a word of truth because she had lived all the pain and it was reflected in her hunched shoulders and bent back. The student's diction was flawless, but articulation of the word requires more than flawless diction. It requires the ability to speak a truth that comes from the pain of living and that reaches our passion and evokes our tears. Henry C. Gregory, pastor, Shiloh Baptist Church of Washington, D.C., 1972-1990, quoted in Karen Lebacqz, *Word, Worship, World, and Wonder* (Nashville, Abingdon Press, 1997), p. 48.

[21] Peter Marshall (1903-1949), Scottish immigrant preacher and Chaplain of the U.S. Senate.

[22] Jackson, *A Psychology of Preaching*, p. 42

[23] Norman Vincent Peale (1898-1993), pastor, New York City's (Manhattan) Marble Collegiate Church for 52 years; author, *The Power of Positive Thinking* (20 million copies); started *Guideposts* magazine; conducted weekly radio program, "The Art of Living," for 54 years.

[24] *Topical* sermons deal with a general subject unfettered by any textual restraints. *Textual* sermons are based on a short passage or perhaps a paragraph of Biblical text. *Expository* sermons interpret more or less extended portions of Scripture, in some cases even a whole book. All three types share attention to a single theme. Both Dee Bowman and James Braga, identified in footnote 1, as well as others, extensively treat the distinctions of sermon preparation based on these three divisions warranting no further attention here.

[25] Based primarily on Jackson, *A Psychology for Preaching,* pp. 49-57.

[26] Jackson, *A Psychology for Preaching,* p. 49.

[27] The church calendar selects and organizes scripture into a comprehensive systematic whole. In *Preaching the Calendar,* J. Ellsworth Kalas (professor of preaching and worship, Asbury Theological Seminary) describes the calendar's beginning as likely emanating from God's instructions to Moses and Aaron in Exodus 12:2. "This month shall mark for you the beginning of months; it shall be the first month of the year for you." From this decree the Jews established a collection of holy *faith* days "...linked to their walk with God and generally celebrating some instance of God's care for them as people." Christians have added the anticipation, birth, preaching and teachings, and death and resurrection of Christ

in Advent, Christmas, Lent, Holy Week and Easter, and the coming of the Holy Spirit in Pentecost.

[28] Illustrative of current and historical guides to sermon preparation and sermon compilations are the following:

James W. Cox (editor), *Best Sermons 1* and *2* (San Francisco: Harper & Row, annual).

James W. Cox (editor), *The Minister's Manual* (San Francisco: Jossey-Bass, annual).

J. Ellsworth Kalas, *Preaching the Calendar: Celebrating Holidays and Holy Days* (Louisville: Westminster John Knox Press, 2004), 144 pp.

Clarence Edward Macartney, *Great Sermons of the World*, (Boston: The Stratford Company, 1926), 586 pp.

Michael Warner, editor, *American Sermons: the Pilgrims to Martin Luther King, Jr.*, (New York, The Library of America, 1999), 939 pp.

[29] Pastors might learn from architects. "Very few sane architects commence an edifice by planting and rearing the oaks which are to compose its beams and stanchions. You take over all such supplies ready hewn, and choose by preference time-seasoned timber. Since Homer's prime, a host of other great creative writers have recognized this axiom when they too began to build: and 'originality' has [become], like chess and democracy, a Mecca for little minds." –James Branch Cabell, Richmond author, 1879-1958.

[30] Keith D. Miller, "Composing Martin Luther King, Jr," *Publisher's Modern Language Associate,* #105, January 1990, pp. 70-82.

[31] Russell H. Conwell, pastor and founder and president of Temple University, delivered "Acres of Diamonds" more than 6,000 times in towns and cities throughout the country, but never in the same way, always slightly tailored to respond and relate to the conditions and problems of the audience. The story, by the way, is of a man who sold his property in order to search for diamonds only to find that his old farm had within its land the largest diamond deposit in the world, the moral of course being that opportunity abounds at our doorstep.

[32] Harry Emerson Fosdick (1878-1969), professor of practical theology, Union Theological Seminary, once said that in all his years in pastoring, he had "...yet to see anybody come to church on Sunday passionately concerned about what happened to the Jebucites."

[33] The introduction should quickly identify the sermon topic with obvious relevance to the congregation. Harry Emerson Fosdick was a master at this. Consider these opening sentences cited by Jackson, "Our thought starts this morning with the plain fact that it is not always easy to tell the difference between right and wrong." "There is a picture that haunts the imagination these days concerning which I wish to speak seriously with you...."

There is no doubt here to whom the pastor is speaking and the importance and relevance of the message to follow. Such introductions take the congregation immediately into the confidence of the pastor which makes them feel important and the real object of the message. Other intriguing opening sentences cited by Jackson include those of Dr. Harold Cooke Phillips. "It is a fair question which we put to ourselves in our times–'What is the reward of Christian living?'" "We shall speak today of the wisdom of Jesus as it bears on what is considered the greatest social problem of our age–the problem of war."

[34] Ideas introduced as propositions, wrestled with from all sides, invariably secure audience attention, honoring them with the "academics" involved before eventual resolution. This approach is especially effective in presenting controversial issues to those who appreciate honest, intellectual debate. A proposition followed by emphasis on the wrong side creates a silent rebuttal among listeners.

[35] Bowman, *Common Sense Preaching*, p. 142

[36] H. Grady Davis in *Design for Preaching* (Minneapolis, Augsburg Fortress, 1958) has these recommendations regarding how to use words effectively for the ear in public speaking:

(1) Express yourself in as few words as possible. Unneeded words are in the way.

(2) Use words that sound well together.

(3) Cultivate a preference for short, strong, clear, familiar words.

(4) Cultivate a preference for concrete rather than abstract, and specific rather than general words. Words that appeal to the senses suggest pictures that the mind can see, sounds it can hear, things it can touch, taste, and smell.

(5) Rely on strong nouns and verbs to carry the weight of thought. Davis's illustrations include: "We are born into time whose hands are full of promise; we come to our last hour with the clutch of time about our throats." –Joseph A. Sittler, Lutheran School of Theology at Chicago. "Of what use to us is a golden key if it is unable to open what we desire?" –Saint Augustine.

(6) Structure sentences to effectively use the two positions of strength– the beginning and the end. Consider these alternative positions of a six-part sentence:

> I will gladly do this for you, my dearest friend.
> I will do this for you gladly, my dearest friend.
> For you, my dearest friend, I will do this gladly.
> This will I gladly do, my dearest friend, for you.
> Gladly for you, my dearest friend, will I do this.

[37] See also section on prayer, Chapter 13, p. 192-193.

[38] Edward W. Bauman, *God's Presence in My Life* (Nashville, Abingdon Press, 1981), p. 128.

Part VI.
Discipleship

Chapter 16
Parish Life

You are the people of God; he loved you and chose you for his own. So then, you must put on compassion, kindness, humility, gentleness, and patience. Be helpful to one another, and forgive one another... And to all these add love, which binds all things together in perfect unity. (Colossians 3:12-14)

Jesus said, *"You must be perfect just as your Father in heaven is perfect"* (Matthew 5:48)

The focus of this chapter, cultivating the congregational experience together in Christian love for one another and in spiritual growth and fellowship, is the heart of our living and serving together as disciples. The responsible church committee, commonly titled "Parish Life" but variously labeled, underlies and supports all congregational activities, for it builds and maintains the inherent operating element, members themselves.

Nature of the Christian Community

"Christianity means community through Jesus Christ. We belong to one another only through and in Jesus Christ. Christians need others because of Jesus Christ. Christians come to others only through Jesus Christ. In Jesus Christ we have been chosen from eternity, accepted in time, and united for eternity." —Dietrich Bonhoeffer (1906-1945), German theologian and Protestant resistance leader.

"Wherever the covenant of reconciliation, wholeness, caring, and justice takes place there one discovers community. People are not searching for a merry-go-round of business activities and committee meetings; they are searching for people with whom they can live out life together." —Kennon L. Callahan, church management consultant.

What is the nature of the Christian church community we seek? We know it is identified as the body of Christ, the communion of saints, and the people of God. This means that through God's grace we are called to share our lives in community together with him. "By searching together for closeness with God, we position ourselves to experience the reality of his presence and the fullness of his love."[1] Thus the soul of the church is its community of believers. The institutional forms involved—physical structure, organization, and budget—are necessary and important primarily as supporting elements. It is our spiritual lives that are central, experiencing God's presence in the community of Christ.

And the members of this "body" of Christ are so closely joined together that, as Paul describes, "If one part of the body suffers, all the other parts suffer with it; if one part is praised, all the other parts share its happiness." (1 Corinthians 12:26) Thus this *koinonia* fellowship of brotherhood and love brings about life-transforming rejuvenation and great joy.

Edward W. Bauman, who speaks forcefully of the underlying and central importance of the Christian community, defines the church in much the same manner. He cites three major church functions[2] the third of which is community:

(1) Provide ways for people to be with God, to experience the real presence of God. A place of such spiritual reality that those in prayer are often "afraid to put out their hand, lest they touch God." Luke describes such intensity this way "...the place in which they were gathered together was shaken; and they were all filled with the Holy Spirit." (Acts 4:31)

(2) To serve our mission of sharing God's power and love with the world. To share the Good News and live for others

(3) To be an "extended family" in our life in Christ, bringing healing and hope to all.

The challenge then, for all churches, is to encourage and enable all the members to truly love each other and to be a genuine community in caring for one another and in worship. God's transforming power is best experienced in this manner, together as brothers and sisters in Christ.

The Meaning of Membership

And he said to all, "If anyone wants to come with me, he must forget himself, take up his cross every day, and follow me." (Luke 9:23)

No other organization asks so much yet demands so little as modern day Christian churches—more in the sense of seeking total commitment and sacrifice, less in terms of actual expectations. "I belong but that's about it. They have never really asked me to do anything." The servant-led church rigorously seeks the opposite, requiring everyone to become active disciples of Christ's encompassing obligations.

We recommend a "covenant" of member obligations, an agreement and commitment of service for a period of time to be renewed upon completion and rededication. A formalized call to discipleship of this nature typically includes an affirmation of faith together with an acceptance of responsibilities. In addition, a code of ethics and means of grace enabling the duties to be carried out may also be included. To illustrate, consider the following model covenant.[3]

Affirmation of Faith

The Affirmation of Faith is a declaration of fundamental Christian beliefs, essentially those found in the Apostles' Creed and Nicene Creed.

Chapter 16. Parish Life

Means of Grace
The Means of Grace are the ways ordained by God whereby he conveys to mankind his sanctifying grace of redemption and salvation. The chief means are prayer; reading, hearing and meditating upon the Scriptures; and receiving the Lord's Supper. Through these means, empowered by the Holy Spirit, and in the consciences and counsel of our common Christian discipleship, all things are possible. A covenant reaffirms the individual's belief in these relationships.

Code of Ethics
The content here relates to various standards of human conduct chiefly related to obligations as citizens to society, fairness, specific virtues, and human rights. The moral choices involved often relate to difficult and complicated situations. Positions or points of view may be based on religious conviction, patterns of nature, personal bias, and occasionally even sound reasoning. Typical issues involved include war and violence, sexuality, feminism, divorce and remarriage, bioethics and medicine, capital punishment, the environment, and poverty and welfare. The wording of ethic clauses should be carefully thought out and perhaps somewhat general if a majority are to accept the code.

Accepted Member Responsibilities
Specific personal commitments cover a wide range of options and degree and should, in most instances, be tailored to the individual and re-defined yearly. All such resolutions are assumed with the need for God's help and the support of the congregation. Examples of personal obligations and opportunities as people of God are listed below and detailed throughout this Part VI. "Discipleship" division. Note that these member responsibilities obligate the church to provide the associated involvement opportunities.

- Live an ordered joyful and thankful life with daily Bible study, prayer, and meditation.
- Faithfully participate in the worship life of the congregation, partaking in communion.
- Participate in Sunday school and other Christian education opportunities.
- Seek to love and serve others within the church community and mankind everywhere.
- Discuss one's Christian faith with other congregational members as a means of community bonding in Christ.
- Actively engage in church functions, faithfully exercise any assigned ministry.
- Participate in a least one service project.
- Regularly share one's income.
- Proclaim the Good News and witness outwardly for Christ.
- Live sacrificially including periodic fasting.

The Embracing Mission of Caring and Involvement

"When we are born again as individuals we are born into a new family, a new fellowship of sharing, a new community of love, and the more we allow ourselves to be drawn into this family, the more we discover the joy of God's presence. Here we find a place where rebellion is accepted and forgiven, where selfishness is conquered by love, where hidden guilt is brought into the light and healed, and where anxiety is examined and overcome. All this is possible because God makes his presence known in powerful and life-transforming ways in the faith community. The deeper we enter into this fellowship of life-sharing, the more opportunities we have to respond to him."
—Edward W. Bauman, *God's Presence in My Life*.

Perhaps the best case for meeting the needs and cultivating the involvement of the congregation itself is made by Norman Shawchuck. His description of a congregation that really cares deserves reporting.

> There is an ambiance about a responsive congregation that is quite unmistakable. These congregations have managed to imbue their paid and volunteer workers with a spirit of service to members and strangers alike. Ushers, custodians, and secretaries go out of their way to answer questions, smile, and be helpful. The ministry team and lay boards continuously ask persons what they think of the worship services, church school, music, outside signs, indoor signs, bulletins, attitude of custodians, office staff, and so on. Based on the responses, the leaders constantly work to improve the overall experience that members and strangers have when coming into contact with the congregation and its buildings, staff, and ministries.[4]

The logic of such outgoing, receptive attitude is incontrovertible yet too often restrained in practice. The unresponsive congregation is described by Shawchuck as overruled by bureaucracy that replaces personal judgment with impersonal polices, and failing to respond to needs and opportunities outside the existing framework. In contrast, the responsive congregation views all its members and visitors as the essential *raison d'état* for its work. Leaders are continuously alert to discovering the unmet needs and preferences of members and to discover ways to improve supporting services. This alertness and receptivity is central to all the endeavors of the Parish Life Committee.

The encompassing mission of the Parish Life Committee is to work with pastors and members to develop and sustain a true Christian community within the church, one of love and care for each member as manifest in our Lord Jesus Christ. To this end, the committee should be attentive to establishing and maintaining a Christian community as described below. When these conditions are fulfilled, it is likely that congregation members will be highly involved, enthusiastic, and satisfied.

The Essential Elements of the Christian Community

"Congregations are called to offer care and acceptance to all people because that's the essence of the gospel's invitation and proclamation. God the Spirit calls, gathers, enlightens and makes holy each congregation as well as the whole Christian church."[5]

The Christian community enjoys special blessings accorded by the saving grace of Jesus Christ. These rewards are cited here as guiding rules for our behavior toward one another.

- **To welcome all, especially visitors.**

Welcome one another, therefore, just as Christ has welcomed you, for the glory of God. (Romans 15:7)

Be not forgetful to entertain strangers for thereby some have entertained angels unawares. (Hebrews 13:2).

God's house welcomes all with joy and hospitality as of a waiting father. Visitors should be identified at the entrance door and sought out for further invitation and conversation after the service. Follow-up actions may appropriately include telephone contact, personal visit, and a small remembrance gift. Visitors should always be recognized as a special opportunity for establishing friendship.

Ushers and greeters should be instructed to be as friendly and personal as possible, warmly welcoming each and every person upon entering. These duties continue during post-service coffee time when they should seek out visitors and those seemingly neglected.

For newcomers electing membership, the "welcome" continues through initial orientation training including receipt of a church "handbook," introduction to the congregation, and in being assigned a "shepherd" care provider during the first year. Memberships are made or broken by the bonds forged this first year.

- **To enrich members' lives with the joy of Christian love and fellowship.**

"A new commandment I give you: love one another." (John 13:34)

As with our Lord should we not "abound in steadfast love" for one another? Each person is a child of God, to be truly known, loved, and cherished. All must be treated equally with honor, respect, and reverence; every little kindness extended. This is a spiritual undertaking, a transforming experience, in which we truly love, value, and serve one another. And the most effective means of securing this intimacy is through small group membership of every individual (see Chapter 17, Small Group Ministries).

- **To be responsive to the needs and wants of every individual, with knowledge of the distinct needs of special groups such as youth, singles, aged, those that live alone, and the impoverished.**

Contribute to the needs of the saints. (Romans 12:13)

"A responsive congregation is one that makes every effort to sense, serve, and satisfy the needs and wants of its members and the groups it has targeted to serve..." —Norman Shawchuck, *Marketing for Congregations.*

Needs and hardships must be promptly identified and addressed with personal comfort and support. Pastoral visits are especially important, often long remembered and treasured.

- **To establish for each member a place and sense of belonging in the congregation community bonded together as one.**

In him the whole structure is joined together and grows into a holy temple in the Lord; in whom you also are built together spiritually into a dwelling place for God. (Ephesians 2:21-22)

"There is hardly anything that can make one happier than to feel that one counts for something with other people. What matters here is not numbers, but intensity. In the long run, human relationships are the most important thing in life." —Dietrich Bonhoeffer

We reaffirm the inclusive nature of the Christian community based on the understanding of the importance of each individual. There are no dividing walls. Everyone should feel that they "belong" to some if not all the elements of the church organization. All must be welcome at every meeting. No one should ever feel anonymous or an "outsider." This means, in the final analysis, according everyone, as brothers and sisters in Christ, deep respect.[6]

Colbert I. King, in a *Washington Post* editorial (Sept. 2, 2000) recalls the nature of respect accorded within black congregations in the early 1950s, precisely that sought by today's churches in a different context.

Prayer and praise were only part of their reason for being. Church was where people went to get the respect that was denied them during the workday.

It was a place where elderly black women and men—accustomed to being called by their first names on the job by white kids—were awarded the respectful title "Sister" or "Brother" and treated with admiration and deference. Church was where everybody had a title.

It was a place where a maid became transformed on Sunday into an influential deaconess, where chauffeurs occupied seats on the exalted trustees' board, where children looked upon ditch-diggers and hod-carriers not as unskilled laborers but as ushers and deacons and pillars of the congregation and community.

Part of respect is knowing someone's name. Name tags solve many problems in this regard, yet often are reluctantly supported. We strongly encourage their use as a sign of Christian brotherhood. Another aid is the periodic publication of member photos, generally as part of the church telephone directory. This possibility can usually be arranged inexpensively with a commercial photographer.

- **To nurture spiritual growth.**

Faith is shared by talking to others about their beliefs, inviting people to worship and Sunday school, and spreading the Good News everywhere. Every member has untapped potential, which only needs our recognition and cultivation. God has the highest intentions for each of us down to the very least one. We must be equally attentive to his callings, personally encouraging and guiding members in their participation.

You have made them a kingdom of priests to serve our God and they shall rule on earth. (Revelation 5:10)

- **To encourage and welcome full involvement of all members.**

The participation of *every* member must be rigorously sought and treasured. We recognize, listen to, and pay attention to each other. Gordon Cosby calls it being "enablers of each other." What an inspiring word! To *enable* means to supply with the means or opportunity and encouragement. In this way everyone is built-up in Christ through their calling response. (See Chapter 19 "Our Call to Stewardship"). From a practical standpoint, focus on the individual means that *everyone must be known, appreciated, and sought out.* And this intimacy and support can best be started through personal interviews and recording (page 262), and maintained through small group membership, Chapter 17.

- **To celebrate the contributions of every member.**

We must take every opportunity to identify and acknowledge the services of our fellow members. In gratitude we recognize good deeds as evidence of God working through his disciples, models for all to follow.

- **To ensure that all are treated with fairness, justice, and a concern for all interests.**

You must not distort justice; you must not show partiality." (Deuteronomy 16:19) Fairness extends to treating all the same; all are favored sons and daughters. And fairness means providing a suitable array of leadership and service opportunities and cultivating through personal contact the involvement of every member without exception.

- **To exercise every opportunity to determine the will of the congregation and respond to their wishes and needs.**

There must be no "we-they" mentality, rather an attitude of encouragement and acceptance. A democratic society is characterized by voting rights, open nominations, open petitioning, and unrestricted debate. These ends must be rigorously protected and pursued or they will be gradually eroded by overzealous leaders and disinterested parishioners. Popular participation is encouraged and supported by rigorous announcements of elections and issues, attentive and responsive officers, the presence of an ombudsman and suggestion system, and periodic congregation surveys.

- **To ensure that the pastors and all lay leaders are accessible and responsive to the congregation.**
Council and committee officers should be readily accessible and receptive. Distinctive name tags and a posted church organizational chart with officer photos assists in identification. Most important, church officers should make every effort to be accessible and converse with parishioners regarding their topical area. As previously mentioned, a pastoral home visit is, for most congregants, a treasured occasion.

Means for Accomplishment

A number of instruments are available to the Parish Life Committee in promoting the above code of Christian behavior. Also, consult the means employed by the evangelism committee in their sustaining inreach responsibility, Chapter 20, beginning on page 327.

- **Member handbook.** Handbook topics generally include denominational beliefs; church and member responsibilities; participation encouragement, church mission statement, history, and organizational structure; calendar of events; Christian education program; opportunities for service; and similar orientation content.
- **Introductory training for new members and assignment of sponsors.** Orientation training introduces new members to the beliefs and structure of the church and, as important, provides a fortuitous welcoming opportunity. New members may be subsequently assigned a "sponsor" during their first year to provide assistance and encouragement.
- **Member information system.** Detailed member information is essential if all congregants are to be known and effectively involved. Entry data, based on a distributed questionnaire, is preferably recorded directly by members in a computer-based information system. Personal counsel and assistance in making entries should be an integral part of the data gathering system. Entry information may include name and address (temporary address for college attendees or military service), birth date, marital status, children, education, interests and skills, employment, income bracket, etc. In addition, both the worship and involvement habits of members may be tracked to assist in ascertaining spiritual health. Churches are negligent when they fail to note absentees or sporadic attendance. Members quickly note when they're not missed. They also grow increasingly apart from a congregation that makes little note of their contribution. "It seems of little importance whether I give a lot or nothing." Most members need personal guidance and recognition in giving.

The employed computer program should allow retrieval of individual factors and multiple combinations, e.g., all male members 18-to-35 years-old with home repair interests or skills. Such a system is invaluable in initially identifying high potential contacts. All information is, of course, confidential.

- **Coffee-time.** The time immediately after the service should be used for friendship and encouragement, no member left ungreeted, no visitor unattended. For many members this will be the only opportunity they have to talk with the pastor.
- **Nametags.** Strong pastoral and laity support is necessary to secure this simple practice of great value in getting everyone to know each other. Nametags are, in effect, a friendly greeting, more often than not prompting a response. We are inclined to speak to those we can address by name. Visitors can be given a temporary adhesive paper tag if they so elect.
- **Small group ministries.** This important means of involving everyone in the church community is presented in the next chapter (17). No vehicle is more effective in developing a sense of belonging than small group membership.
- **Council meetings.** Hold some council meetings between regular services or immediately after a single abbreviated service. This proximity greatly encourages attendance; otherwise the council will work in splendid isolation.
- **Visitor follow-up.** Visitors are always most welcome in God's house. They should be accorded special attention and courtesy. All should be contacted shortly thereafter with an appreciative message recognizing their attendance, asking if they have special needs, and encouraging their continued attendance and possible membership. More than one contact shows continuing real interest which most visitors find complimentary.
- **Membership requirements.** Congregations who are really attentive to each congregant's spiritual growth allow no wishy-washy membership. "We seek every member to emulate Christ." Such involvement can only be obtained when extended opportunities are in place together with a rigorous program of guidance and admonition through small group ministries (Chapter 17) and a yearly commitment renewal (See "Use Pledges," Chapter 19, page 296). Leadership terms should be two years and vacancies announced.
- **Home visits by pastor and church laity and open luncheons.** There is no substitute for face-to-face informal conversation in cementing the bonds of Christian fellowship. A single home visit is likely to build a lifetime friendship. Do you not remember every pastor's visit? Open luncheons with the church staff and morning prayer sessions also build the caring brotherhood so essential for congregational community and well-being.
- **Surveys.** Surveys indicate to respondents the value placed on their judgment. Plus, leaders too often simply do not know the majority's will and direction. Surveys therefore should not be neglected although they entail considerable work. Structuring is critical. Questions should be designed to secure the exact type of information sought. Topics should also be mutually supporting, i.e., complement each other in developing a

complete picture. Lastly, the questionnaire should be thorough to extract all the information sought, not just a partial record. Survey design is discussed in the "Long-Range Planning and Self-Study" section of Chapter 11, page 161.

---

[1] Edward W. Bauman, *God's Presence in My Life* (Nashville, Abingdon Press, 1981), p. 47.

[2] Bauman, *God's Presence in My Life,* pp. 53-54.

[3] Derived from Harold E. Bauman, *Congregations and Their Servant Leaders,* Chapter 16 "Parish Life and Membership Obligations," (Scottdale, PA, Mennonite Publishing House, 1982).

[4] Norman Shawchuck, *Marketing for Congregations* (Nashville, Abingdon Press, 1992), p. 68.

[5] Nathan Frambach, "A Larger Vision," *The Lutheran,* April, 2001, p. 34

[6] The importance of respect and value of the individual is unforgettably expressed by the storied soliloquy in Arthur Miller's "Death of a Salesman" from Willy Loman's wife, Linda: "I don't say he's a great man. Willy Loman never made a lot of money. His name was never in the paper. He's not the finest character that ever lived. But he's a human being, and a terrible thing is happening to him. So attention must be paid. He's not to be allowed to fall in his grave like an old dog. Attention, attention finally must be paid to such a person."

Chapter 17
Small Group Ministries[1]

Two are better than one, because they have a good reward for their toil. For if they fall, one will lift up the other, but woe to one who is alone and falls and does not have another to help. (Ecclesiastes 4:9-10)

"In small groups we can create the climate and nurture the trust in which a deep giving of ourselves can happen."
—Elizabeth O'Connor, *Servant Leaders, Servant Structures.*

Christianity is a *relational* religion, not individualistic. The most effective means of establishing loving Christian relationships within congregations is through small group ministries guided by a trained mentor. The mutually reinforcing interaction of the group together with the supportive guidance and leadership of the mentor make a highly productive combination. And the returns are not only in Christian growth but in member retention. Two of the major reasons why people are inactive church members or leave altogether are their inability to assimilate and feelings of rejection, both mightily countered by small group ministries.

Development of successful small groups is highly dependent on the time pastors spend teaching and equipping the laity for this self ministry. And a substantial commitment it may be indeed. But the returns are great, for the multiplying effect of this instruction extends the leadership and skills of the pastorate to the resultant lay leaders and through them to the vast majority of the congregation. The congregation eventually takes major responsibility for their own self nurturing as well as outward evangelism. Pastors can have no more pivotal and central role than initiating and supporting such cells as the fundamental church unit.[2]

Definitions

Some definitions are in immediate order. By **small group** we mean 7 to 15 individuals gathered, in this instance, specifically and exclusively to interact and support each other in spiritual growth and love for one another. They have no other competition, no assigned mission other than to share their collective wisdom and ministry experiences. This freedom gained in centered personal focus is distinct; in complete opposition to the numerous service responsibilities assigned to essentially all other church organizations which are *not* included in the small group entity defined here.

As a Christian **ministry**, the group is presided over and served, in this instance, by an appointed **mentor** entrusted to care for and counsel group members, individually and collectively, as children of God. "Christian mentoring is a dynamic, intentional relationship of trust in which one person enables another to maximize the grace of God in their life and service." (John Mallison) Mallison continues, "Good mentoring involves bonding, connectedness, rapport, mateship, affinity, things in common and genuine concern." We can see from these descriptions the inclusiveness and demanding nature of mentoring. But when shared within a group the process is both reinforced as well as divided, making individual responsibilities acceptable and counterbalanced by accrued personal returns.

While mentoring is important, it is not the essence here. The keystone is the group itself, providing incredible care and nurturing of each member, allowing individuals to become family. In his seminal work *Dancing with Dinosaurs*, William Easum, another strong advocate of small groups, describes their purpose this way.

> Small-group ministries...build people, not churches. Their internal-care networks take incredibly good care of people. Newcomers are invited into small groups composed of people of similar background, need, or mission. The people become "bonded" to one another, instead of merely joining the church. Helping people discover a relationship with Christ and one another is the mission of these communities. Instead of focusing on programming and structural matters, leaders equip laity to become servants in caring networks.[3]

Only in this Christ-centered intimacy can people establish deep, honest relationships and lasting commitments toward one another. And extending over all is the strengthening power and guidance of the Holy Spirit.

Role of Small Groups

In summary, **the central purpose of small group ministries** is to assist each individual in developing their relationship to God, and to provide Christian fellowship and support through a shared ministry of empathy, love, and response. Small groups provide:

- **a means of listening to God and responding to his will.** This first vertical dimension means that the group gathers in the name of Jesus, centering its attention on prayer, biblical reflection, and Christian fellowship.
- **a place where people are welcomed, cared for, and nurtured by one another** through God's saving grace and thereby renewed for ministry. People are the agenda; joining together and sharing are the means; spiritual growth and Christian friendship are the goals. Newcomers and strangers are always welcome without qualification. (Leaving one chair empty serves as a poignant reminder of the evangelism mission.)
- **a forum for healing.** Bringing into a right spirit is fostered by trust and bonding.
- **an alternative opportunity for involvement** through personal interaction as distinct from more traditional worship and service means.

Small groups provide a unique personal vehicle for discovering individual spiritual gifts. They must, however, always remain integral parts of the church community as a whole, never acting in isolation or in competition.

- **a safe setting** where no one is judged and confidentiality is expected.
- **a trained guiding mentor** to focus group interaction and counsel individuals. The presence of a number of mentors relieves pastors of this duty allowing them to focus on mentor training. Numerous texts on small group ministry are available as suitable training guides.[4]

The mentoring task itself may be structured in various degrees and dimensions. Group affiliations are generally most effective, but one-on-one is preferred by many and is particularly suitable to small congregations. The common shared experiences within the group create bonds, shared goals, and reinforcement, often more powerful than possible between two individuals. And there is the multiplying effectiveness of administering to a group rather than a single person. From a content standpoint, most mentors favor a fairly structured, systematic approach rather than casual informality.

Small Group Formation

The formation of the congregation into small groups can be a very large undertaking indeed. A congregation of 500 organized in 12-member groups, for example, would require 40 or more leaders! To obtain such a commitment requires strong pastoral support, deliberate leader selection, and mentor training. The whole endeavor can be facilitated by observing these fundamentals:

- Small group ministry is based on the premise that *every* **congregation member will benefit by such an alliance**, thus *all* must be invited and their personal involvement strongly encouraged. Reluctant participants may have to be repeatedly contacted. But first one must learn why an individual is hesitant and relieve these concerns before issuing additional invitations, and then in the most kindly, supportive, manner, without judgment. Special attention must also be given new congregation members, for if they don't soon make friends their attendance is in jeopardy. The church should never let anyone fall through the cracks; let people know they are missed and cared about. Love is unconditional.
- **Small group ministries are always sensitive to established church structures and programs.** Formation of the distinct small groups advocated here are as additions, not subtractions, from existing program arrangements. However, small groups can and often become the fundamental church unit, the central focus of the staff in leading and training its leaders.
- We recommend a **heterogeneous mix of members** within each group to provide the breadth and depth of experience from which all will benefit. Plus it's very democratic. In few other instances is such

membership latitude possible for most church alignments are for specific purposes attracting similarly oriented individuals.

While favoring newly arranged groupings, we recognize the likelihood that some individuals will prefer to enter into mentored fellowship within their existing alignments, e.g., choir or Sunday school class. In other instances, shared interests, age, family status, home location, or other distinct identification or uniting focus may naturally draw people together. Members can, in fact, be polled regarding their grouping preferences.[5]

While the church should be flexible in such structuring, customized grouping is not the objective here; building new unfettered relationships is. The mission responsibilities of most existing organizations invariably overrule any attempted small group focus, and there is always the risk of inherited friction and cliquishness within long-standing arrangements. It is better to start with a clean slate.

- Group **membership must be dynamic rather than static**, i.e., continually reconstituted by exchanging members, perhaps every two years, on a first-in, first-out basis. This refreshment renews and stimulates the group in exciting fashion.

Small Group Dynamics

Let us be concerned with one another, to help one another to show love and do good. Let us not give up the habit of meeting together, as some are doing. Instead, let us encourage one another, all the more since you see that the Day of the Lord is coming near. (Hebrews 10:24:25)

Two are better than one, because they have a good reward for their toil. For if they fall, one will lift up the other, but woe to one who is alone and falls and does not have another to help. (Ecclesiastes 4:9-10)

We have three entries here—group members, God's Holy Spirit, and leader-mentor. A group has its own dynamics, each individual feeding from and at the same time serving others in a mutual exchange of expressed needs and supportive response. No one should feel alone, rather surrounded instead by the *koinonia* of Christian brotherhood. And, as with any such gathering, the most important of all ingredients, God's Holy Spirit, is always present to guide and encourage. Lastly, the group activities are organized and overseen by a trained lay mentor, selected from the congregation.

Group Ambiance

Small groups, especially those bonded in Christian fellowship, have great potential for gaining a number of distinct virtues that make such an assembly especially advantageous. The ambiance sought is characterized by a sense of:

- **unity, accord, and harmony** that invariably establishes a close, caring relationship among members unobtainable by any other organizational unit. In

large measure, public worship is a corporate activity. Small groups, in contrast, are personal, intimate in nature, a fertile environment for personal bonding.
- **trust, followed by openness, honesty, and sharing.** Listening and showing genuine compassion leads to trust and then closeness. The emotional tone should be one of mutual respect, without fear of rejection, a totally non-threatening environment. Only under these supportive conditions will members be willing to express their doubts, fears, and failures.
- **joy, warmth, and well-being.** The joy of Christian fellowship is unmatched and perfected in small groups. "To associate with other like-minded people in small, purposeful groups is for the great majority of men and women a source of profound psychological satisfaction." —Aldous Huxley (1894-1963), British author.
- **a relaxed pace.** Groups are inherently unhurried, an advantage for those seeking refuge and refreshment. Slowing down allows God to work, refocusing our attention away from the shallow and temporal. We must be still to listen to what God has to say.
- **permanency and commitment.** A church group, however loosely structured and volatile, should be considered a permanent church entity. This reliability is the foundation on which all the lasting benefits depend.

Required Leadership

Iron sharpens iron, and one person sharpens the wits of another.
(Proverbs 27:17)

"Jesus Christ is the real and decisive agent in Christian mentoring. Jesus' mentoring prototype is not merely a static blueprint of days past; it is operational as a formative power through the Holy Spirit today."[6]

For small groups to work, the congregation must be willing to accept leadership and pastoral care from among their own. Lay mentoring should be viewed as a sacred responsibility of great value to others as they grow in Christ, and as a rich reward in seeing this maturing process.

In selecting mentors, one must first choose individuals who live Christ-centered lives, loving Jesus with all their heart, striving to continuously perfect themselves through his grace. *"...apart from me you can do nothing."* (John 15:4) Then prospective mentors must possess that gift that underlies all Christian relationships, unconditional love. All else is subordinated and derived from these treasured possessions.

So we choose first as mentors good disciples who attentively care for others. Then the other personal qualities sought—friendliness, joyfulness, resourcefulness, experience—are either already in place or can be developed. In summary, the essential qualities sought in all mentors are:
- Christ-centered (to love and search for Jesus Christ).
- Friendly (to enjoy being with others and putting them at ease).
- Caring and constructive attitude (to appreciate the value in everyone and desire to listen and help).
- Experience and depth (to relate to and understand the conditions of others).

- Integrity (to be open, honest, and trustworthy).
- Energetic (to have the inner drive and resourcefulness to see the mission through).

Mentor Training

To the exceptional attributes above, we add the additional element of *training* to create the final qualified mentor product. At least a day or so of initial instruction is generally required, with periodic updates, often of even greater value, as members share their experiences. (See footnote 4 for suitable training texts). The success of small groups will also greatly depend on the clergy being willing to devote themselves to this training plus seeking outside expertise.

Responsibilities and Means of Mentoring

...let us consider how we may spur one another on toward love and good deeds. Let us not give up meeting together, as some are in the habit of doing, but let us encourage one another... (Hebrews 10:24, 25)

The above scripture admonishing us to "spur one another on" sums up the responsibilities and means of group mentoring. It implies, as John Mallison notes, "...calling forth, summoning, inviting, prodding, urging, earnestly appealing to, inspiring to act."

Mentoring Duties

The mentor's basic responsibility is that of assisting all to build each other up in Christ by means of group interactions. Mallison defines the collective effort as "...a supportive team spirit whereby members can encourage and learn from one another from their collective wisdom and ministry experiences."

To this end the basic mentor duties include those listed below. (The closely related *means* whereby certain of these responsibilities are performed are reported in the succeeding "Tools of Effective Mentoring.")

- **Initiate and maintain contact with group members** and their families between meetings and throughout the year, always being supportive and encouraging them as individuals and members of the group. Be especially attentive to inactive members by personal caring contacts with emphasis on listening and encouraging, never lecturing. Discover how the church can better meet their needs. Never give up on any member.

- With counsel from group members, **determine when, where, and how often to meet.** Meeting times and locations must be convenient; for example, immediately after the Sunday church service may be the opportune time for most.

- **Guide group meetings.** See following "Tools of Effective Mentoring."

- **Evaluate meeting dynamics** and seek improvement.

- **Respond to special needs** by being available to group members for private discourse and counsel. Be accessible, but encourage advance

scheduling. Often a simple phone call is sufficient to maintain the necessary contact.
- **Keep informed and abreast of available resources** such as printed material and other media, seminars, and personal contacts that may assist members in their spiritual development.
- **Identify and nurture talents and emerging leaders** within the group. The intent here is to help individuals discover how they may do the work of ministry that best fits his or her gifts. These interests are then cultivated and employed in the most suitable manner whether within or outside existing programs. Note, in particular, that interest shown in evangelism should be especially nurtured as laity are often the most effective emissaries in the mission field.
- **Respond to possible exclusivity within groups**, patterns of isolation, and self-proclaimed "group think." Group members should never become comfortable with their theology, rather always challenged to do God's bidding. The mentor must help members navigate around these pitfalls and also recognize when member rotation is in order.
- **Facilitate learning** by asking good questions, encouraging self-examination, exploring options, working through issues, and setting goals. Mentor training should include familiarization with relevant Scripture and identification of references.
- **Model what is taught**, showing others by example, albeit imperfect. As described by Mallison, "We significantly enrich the learning process by who we are (our attitudes, values, and behavior), by what we say (our conviction and commitment) and what we do (a living demonstration of the gospel)."

The above responsibilities most often extend beyond the capabilities of any single mentor. Thus the overall care, supervision, and evaluation of small group operations requires a team of leaders consisting of the individual group mentors, overall small group director, church pastors, and assigned congregational leaders. This team is responsible for overseeing the small group program, continuous review of group dynamics, and implementation of improvements. "Are the groups working?" "What lessons have been learned that should be introduced in future training?" Running a congregation of small groups is a major undertaking, perhaps the most encompassing activity of all church operations.

Personal Temperament and Style

The group mentor is the embodiment of versatility, being at once spiritual guide, coach, counselor, teacher, sponsor, and model. A caring response is interwoven in all, blurring the distinctions and moderating the specific expertise required. The insightful mentor will intuitively recognize which approach to adopt in a given situation. More often than not, simple encouragement—an arm around the shoulder, a word of hope or praise—is the most valued response that can be provided.

Mentoring "style" is the distinctive features which characterize an individual's mentoring behavior. Here we basically seek sensitivity, gentleness, and a reassuring nature not unlike a loving parent. Yet the style must always treat everyone as equals, all group members being children of God, beneficiaries of his grace. Thus the most important element of the mentor's "style" is that of conveying the equal importance of all.

Tools of Effective Mentoring

The mentor's task is to seek openness and honesty among all, a willingness to share our doubts, fears and failures, as well as our joys and successes, and to do this through interactive constructive discourse in Christ's blessed presence. Believing in this mission, we strive to see each other through the eyes of Jesus.

The specific means whereby the mentor seeks to cultivate this community include:

1. **Engaging God's guidance and strength through prayer, Bible study, and quiet reflection together.** We know that all good comes from God so begin in petitioning prayer and end in thanksgiving prayer. Mentors must also pray privately beforehand for wisdom and grace. With regard to Scripture, a number of sources can be of great assistance in identifying subject-related passages based on a few key topic words. See, for example, the ncccusa.org website.

2. **Focusing on specific topics to get at real issues and needs and obtain some depth.** Choose important, interesting, and productive topics to gain and then hold attention.[7] However, the group's initial conversation may naturally lead to a substantive focus without leader intervention. Once comfortable, members will often initiate topics, seeking answers to their own problems, even if concealed by apparent personal disassociation. The mentor's task in all such instances is simply to encourage as constructive a dialog as possible.

3. **Listening attentively to truly understand.** Mentors must seek first to discern and understand what group members are really trying to say. This requires undivided attention and concentrated, nonjudgmental reception. Empathetic listening is the most important instrument in the mentor's toolbox. It requires concentrated nonjudgmental focus on the other person, an orientation few possess naturally. Thus mentors must be taught the selfless means of true listening through dedicated attention, feedback to confirm reception, encouragement, requested clarification, occasional questions, and responsive eye contact and body language.

4. **Encouraging participants to secure a positive, constructive outcome.** "Encouragement is love expressed." (John Mallison) Encourage all to be open and honest with each other, to share their faith, and to apply Scripture to their lives. Motivate by honest interest and questions. *Therefore encourage one another and build up each other, as indeed you are doing.* (1 Thessalonians 5:11)

5. **Seeking to build durable, friendly supportive associations.** Be relative easygoing in your relationships to one another, no harsh words or criticism.

6. **Observing certain precautionary rules and boundaries such as keeping confidences, avoiding favoritism and excess intimacy, and respecting individual rights.**

7. **Providing teaching and counsel.** The mentor assists in developing disciples through sound instruction based on God's word. Guidance within the group and among members is also involved. The messages are well known—God is the source of all true love; God is merciful, full of grace; God is faithful and ever-present; God is all-knowing and all-powerful. It would be well for pastors to assist in preparing mentors by providing a brief catechism of instruction on the nature of God and his saving grace, the ever-present and healing power of the Holy Spirit, the responsibilities of being a Christian, and other elements of belief and precepts.

Special Needs Response

In this last section we illustrate how the church directs attention to the special needs of various groups. Three examples are addressed—youth and young adults, singles, and individuals facing life crises.

Youth and Young Adults

In an increasingly secular society where the traditional two-parent family and social pressure for religious affiliation are declining, it is becoming increasingly more difficult for churches to retain their young people. Teenagers have so many opportunities and are often so busy that churches need special programs to attract and keep them. Once off to college there are no guarantees they will ever return.

But other factors are positive. People turn to God in time of momentous changes and adolescents are no different. Religion is becoming important in many teenagers' lives and the accrued returns are significant in terms of both their mental and physical well-being.[8] Congregations are thus obligated to enlarge their traditional family perspective to include young people as the new, great crusade.[9]

It is most important for churches to establish a real sense of *community* for their young members, one of nurturing fellowship and productive involvement. The isolation and misunderstandings between generations must be surmounted by a concerted effort to build companionship and trust. In addition, the natural divisions among young people themselves—high school youth, college-age (generally 19-24), and older young adults—require distinct identification and response.

Secondly, youth want to be where the action is, doing, not just sitting and listening. They are searching for meaning in life through spiritual experiences rather than through doctrine, instruction, or a particular denomination. Thus real life ventures are the underlying catalyst. Fortunately, a host of vehicles are available ranging from traditional youth choir to rock band, from classroom to mission trips,[10] and from self-assessment to community service.

It is best to approach these activities in terms of the contemporary values and images appreciated by youth, i.e., through the mechanisms of personalized agendas, personal friendships, informal conversation, altruistic response, and popular music and movies. We must speak the language of youth.

Singles

The aim of the church in ministering to single men and women (usually of post-college age) is essentially that of providing a safe friendly meeting ground, encouraging friendships and possibly matchmaking leading to fulfilled lives. It is the very nature of being single that warrants special attention, the possible loneliness, fear, lack of self-confidence, and poor self-esteem, which must be overcome by counsel and programs. Also, fate has little to do with securing friends or finding someone to marry. The church can respond to the dynamics involved as with all human needs with great effectiveness. There is no more attractive place for singles than the Christian church. But a special ministry and concerted effort must be established, one that genuinely helps people to meet, enjoy each others' company, and possibly to eventually marry.[11]

One of the problems, of course, is the usual age differences typically involved, ranging from college youth to mature adults, so many separate groups may be required. And the congregation's traditional "family first" mentality must be overcome.

Those in Need of Special Care

The "Stephen Ministry" and similar entities provide one-to-one Christian care to individuals facing life challenges and difficulties. This care and encouragement allows God to work within the afflicted bringing comfort and rest.

Stephen lay "ministers" are trained in nonjudgmental listening, understanding personal feelings, praying for and with care receivers, and working through their crisis or difficult period. Attention is frequently directed to ministering to the divorced, hospitalized, bereaved, and aging. It is understood that the focus is on loving care rather than advice or counsel. One of the difficulties involved is that of overcoming the reluctance of many to ask for help. Outward expressions of the love and care available and the assurance of confidentiality is always a necessary part of the ministry.

¹ This chapter on group mentoring is largely dependent on John Mallison, *Mentoring to Develop Disciples and Leaders* (Lidcombe, NSW, Australia, Scripture Union, 1998), 206 pp. Mallison's focus is primarily on one-on-one mentoring adapted here to a group application. Readers are strongly encouraged to read his excellent and comprehensive treatise on this important means of Christian caring for one another.

² Pastors and laity who are more concerned with control and power than helping people help themselves will likely find the small group model threatening. Great care and sensitivity should be part of any transitional movement.

³ William Easum, *Dancing with Dinosaurs: Ministry in a Hostile & Hurting World* (Nashville, Abingdon Press, 1993), p. 60. See especially Chapter 5, "The Demise of the Program-Based Church" which details Easum's rigorous emphasis on replacing program orientation with small group emphasis, and realigning pastoral responsibilities from personal caring and recruiting to equipping the laity to do so.

⁴ Numerous resources are available to assist in the formation and conduct of small groups. See, for example: George S. Johnson, David Mayer, and Nancy Vogel, *Starting Small Groups—and Keeping Them Going* (Minneapolis, Augsburg Fortress, 1995), 144 pp.; Jeffrey Arnold, *The Big Book on Small Groups* (Downers Grove, IL, InterVarsity, 1992), 264 pp.; Robert Wuthnow, *Sharing the Journey, Support Groups and America's Quest for Community* (New York, Free Press, 1994), 450 pp.; and Neal F. McBride, *How to Lead Small Groups* (Colorado Springs, Navpress, 1990), 118 pp.

⁵ The range of various types of church groups is extensive. Groupings are typically based on intent, e.g., task responsibility, support and recovery, issue study, spiritual growth, prayer, individual nurturing, and fellowship. In addition to these functional or mission focuses, congregational groups may also be organized by such secular factors as geography, age, special interests (music, social issues, book review, gardening, etc.), parents of young children, and similar centering affinities.

⁶ John Mallison, *Mentoring,* p. 39.

⁷ Engaging subject matter for group discussion includes: how to pray, systematic Bible reading, church attendance, personal time management, attitude toward money, family harmony, coping with stress, resolving conflicts, how to be a friend, building self-confidence, setting personal priorities.

⁸ Nathan Frambach, "A Larger Vision," *The Lutheran,* April, 2001, p. 34.

⁹ A commission convened by Dartmouth Medical School studied years of research on children and concluded that young people who are religious are better off in significant ways from their peers. They are less likely than nonbelievers to smoke and drink and more likely to eat well; less likely to commit crime and more likely to wear seat belts; less likely to be depressed and more likely to be satisfied with their families and school.

¹⁰ Henry Brinton, pastor of Calvary Presbyterian Church in Alexandria, Virginia, reports the widespread popularity of summer youth mission projects across the country. "Teenagers spend a week in the summer building houses in Mexico,

working with children in West Virginia or cleaning up flood damage in North Carolina—focusing more on Christian action than on Christian doctrine."

[11] See Ellen Varughese, *The Freedom to Marry—Seven Dynamic Steps to Marriage Readiness* (Joy Press).

Chapter 18
Christian Education

The Lord God has given me the tongue of a teacher, that I may know how to sustain the way with a word. (Isaiah 50:4)

"First and foremost we have the duty to teach the Word of God."
—Martin Luther (1483-1546) German monk, father of the Reformation, Bible translator.

"To honor both Christ and children necessitates that we immerse our youth in the traditions of the faith and in Jesus' way of life, that we cultivate in them both the community's *beliefs* and its *practices*."
—Marva Dawn, New Testament scholar.

The mission of church education programs is spiritual nurturing, forming Christ in the minds of our children and ourselves through attention to God's Word, sharing the faith journey, and Christian fellowship. This encompassing task is pervasive in strengthening through its participants the entire congregation. Thus, no other church ministry has such expansion potential for growth in faith. As commonly expressed, "As the Sunday school goes, so goes the church."

The Role of Christian Education

The church possesses unique power through the work of the Holy Spirit to change lives. Nowhere is this truer than through Christian education where even one hour of participation a week can have a strong influence. Should not everyone then attend Sunday school? The answer is, of course, a resounding "yes," and recognizing this central role is pivotal in understanding the emphasis and support required to conduct effective church school programs as a major and integral part of congregational life.

To know God and Jesus better, to know how his word is proclaimed through the church, art, and music, to understand the Bible, are all missions of Christian education. Before continuing, however, these exceptional claims for church education should in no way be interpreted as a substitute for family responsibility. The primary setting for all spiritual growth is the family. The parent-child relationship can be closer to that of God's love for mankind than any other human experience. Thus the family has certain God-given responsibilities which it cannot surrender even if it so chooses. It is the Christian climate of the household, the unplanned events and indirect teaching that establish the vast bulk of the child's early learning, planting the seeds of spiritual growth.

The church school serves a greater number of people at any given time and over a longer period of time than any other laity-led component. In addition to the regular school year, the education calendar may be extended to vacation Bible school and church camp. So we're talking about year-round emersion, as the immediate target, at least for younger members.

The Special Opportunity of Adult Education

Most adults have a sketchy piece-meal understanding of Christianity and Christian living based, at best, on early catechetical and Sunday school instruction followed by sporadic church attendance. The early education years are crucial in planting the seed of faith. Yet the elementary level involved and the immaturity of the participants generally reduce the substantive content retained into adulthood. At the same time, adults must continually fend off values imposed by society and the need for survival. Consequently, the Christian life of adults may often be tenuously dependent on residual beliefs of little real conviction.

After completing church school, most adults spend the remainder of their lives seeking to know God through the spoken word. And there is no diminishing this indispensable role in nurturing our Christian spirit. However central, sermons can never provide the breadth and depth required in all the many areas necessary for full Christian literacy. Adult Sunday school, on the other hand, has this potential, if for no other reason, because of its duration of 50 or so minutes each week, year after year. The curriculum also can be structured to be comprehensive and rigorous. Perhaps most important of all, the classroom provides opportunity for student and teacher *interaction*, intimate involvement essential in developing personal belief and real understanding.

Of all the areas of congregational life normally practiced, none is likely to be more effective in changing people's lives than an effective church education program. It is a magnificent vibrant showering of God's favor on our lives. Education increases our knowledge and understanding of the Bible and ourselves as disciples. It causes us to grow in wisdom and faith, to renew our ministry, and to communicate our faith to others. What a wonderful and encompassing role and response, one that must receive the church's highest priority.

In thankfulness, we extol the virtues of Christian education as the best means of:
- providing detailed instruction, answering questions, and engaging in interactive discussion and debate.
- initiating and maintaining ties to children and adolescents.
- developing personal growth in faith maturity and loyalty to one's congregation.
- directly addressing individuals, their problems and needs.

- engaging in in-depth discussions of controversial issues.
- sharing Christian growth and fellowship.
- providing opportunity for lay leadership at the highest level, teaching the Word of God.

To obtain these great rewards, Christian education programs must be carefully structured, taught, and promoted. It is a welcome challenge shared by church staff, lay leaders, and congregants. But, interestingly enough, as in only certain other church missions, the principal leadership elements, teachers, are primarily laity. We are indeed blessed with this sanctioned responsibility.

Promoting Christian Education

Worship, education, community service, and fellowship are the cornerstones of church affiliation. Accordingly, every child should be strongly encourage to regularly attend Sunday school, and every adult summoned to participate yearly in at least one elective course as an inherent component of membership. In the latter instance, such "low dosage exposure" invariably generates continuing expanded interest. It has been repeatedly demonstrated that "of all the areas of congregational life, involvement in an effective Christian education program has the strongest tie to a person's growth in faith and loyalty to one's congregation."[1]

The beginning of each school year provides an excellent opportunity to promote enrollment. The entire curriculum with detailed course descriptions should be broadcast to every congregational member and visitor via a mailed flyer. "Every member" personal contact is an effective follow-on, showing we really care. Promotion should continue throughout the year with weekly entries in the Sunday service bulletin and regular listings in the church newsletter. Inserts are advisable in announcing and describing new courses.

The most effective form of publicity is personal testimony and recruitment by teachers and participating students. "Telling a friend" combines first-hand knowledge and a personal invitation. A pulpit message extolling the virtues of attendance is also persuasive testimony. Pastors may also conduct short "starter" courses to initiate attendance. Finally, to ensure blanket coverage, membership records should be canvassed with in-person follow-on invitations directed to all non-participants. All other recruiting efforts pale in comparison to that which encourages church school attendance.

Managing the Church School

The education committee is responsible for planning and conducting the church's learning ministry. The church school superintendent focuses on guiding day-to-day operations and is a principal committee advisor. The job description of the church education committee typically includes responsibilities for curriculum development, staffing (recruitment and training), support (facilities and equipment), publicity, and financing/budgeting. See Appendix B for a job description example.

In selected detail, the education-specific duties of the committee consist of six responsibilities. The first two—development of a comprehensive rigorous curriculum, and selection and training of teachers—are by far the most important:

• **Curriculum design and evaluation** with intent to develop a comprehensive two to three-year program responsive to the education needs of a majority of the congregation. Such design, including recommendations on specific course content, should be based on comprehensive review of the extensive body of literature available in the religious education field. See following "Curriculum Design" section.

• **Teacher recruitment, instruction, and encouragement.** *In the church, then, God has put all in place: in the first place, apostles, in the second place, prophets, and in the third place, teachers.* (1 Corinthians 12:28) Potential teachers should be sought out and encouraged at every opportunity. Short courses offer excellent opportunities to introduce and "try-out" new instructors. Some hidden pearls can be discovered in this manner.

We recommend a two to three-hour "refresher" course be given all teachers each fall at the beginning of the school year. The experience of the group should be extensively utilized in discussion sessions and "lessons learned."

• **Assessment of class dynamics: subject matter, class composition, and quality of instruction and learning level.** Periodic evaluation builds quality. Assessment can be based on class visits and confidential student interviews. Visits should be infrequent and unobtrusive. Findings should always be disassociated from the immediate source and broadcast generically to all teachers collectively as general guidance.

Selection of church school subject matter is discussed in some detail in the following "Curriculum Design" section.

Class composition can take many reasonable turns. A heterogeneous membership benefits from the various experiences and backgrounds present. A diverse outlook and perspective greatly contributes to discussion and debate. Eventually individuals gain confidence and comfort in such a group. On the other hand, immediate camaraderie generally prevails among members of similar age and background. Also, we are often most influenced by our peers, particularly youth and young adults. The recommendation here is to encourage volunteer shifting or trading of class members among similarly composed groups. Let us share our fellowship with all.

The "skills" part of instruction receives the necessary extended treatment in the "Learning and Teaching Skills" section beginning on page 284.

- **Define the duties of the church school superintendent.** The superintendent is primarily concerned with managing school operations. The responsibilities typically include teacher recruitment, selection, training, and administrative support; chairing teacher meetings; overseeing budget expenditures; and arranging substitute teachers. It is understood that the superintendent is the education committee's principal contact with instructors, source of operating information, and central advisor in planning and budgeting.
- **Promote church education programs** through extensive and repeated announcements, advertisement, and individual testimony and invitations. See this chapter's "Promoting Christian Education," page 279.
- **Prepare and promote the church school's yearly budget.** All budget submissions should include a summary of key revenues, expenditures, changing conditions and their financial consequence, future plans, etc. See Chapter 23, "Administration Ministry."

Curriculum Design

God instructs us on discipleship through his church school and disciple teachers. Christian schooling is a high calling requiring proper design of subject matter and effective delivery. Fortunately, the breadth and depth of the Bible and all derived content is partially counterbalanced by the duration available for study, from childhood through adulthood. However, despite this latitude, content must always be carefully screened and progressively arranged to align with student-age group and prerequisite completion. This is the task of curriculum design to which may be added the initial critical selection of source materials and preparation of lesson plans, both performed in conjunction with the teaching staff.

The intent of curriculum design for youth is to provide a grade-level sequence of study that progressively builds the Christian mind and spirit. For adults, a limited core of "required" courses is desirable, underlying a majority of electives. In both instances, the intent is to build upon a solid base, making up early shortcomings with later "refresher" courses. To this end, member education records should be maintained for all students and individuals advised regarding possible deficiencies.

Some introductory rules regarding curriculum design are the following:
- **Begin by observing the mechanics of curriculum design.**

(1) Strive for comprehensive subject matter coverage over time by careful study and integrated use of all available church school curriculums.

(2) Be critically selective in the sense of identifying and concentrating on the best available resources and alertness to new material. Subscribe to publisher announcements. Consider all media delivery systems.

(3) Distinguish between mandatory or highly recommended and elective content.

(4) Organize content in cohesive, digestible size units. Condense and abstract as necessary.

(5) Present course work in sequence, i.e., build on pre-requisite or related content. Strive for continuity.

- **Always build on a "Bible-based" core.** Most Sunday school curriculums are designed to completely cover the Bible during the course of a year or more time period. The treatment must typically be selective, focusing on central messages, key events, and personages. Helpful reference materials include Bible handbooks,[2] dictionaries and companions, commentaries, concordances, bibliographies, and atlases.

The church school curriculum is altogether dependent on the Bible. Accordingly, the power of God's Word must necessarily underlie and constitute an integral part of all instruction. Such reliance strengthens and provides perspective and guidance beyond human capabilities. Teachers are therefore rigorously advised to continuously keep the Bible at hand to assist and supplement whenever possible.[3]

- **From toddlers through senior high school, lesson content must be age-specific**, i.e., structured to match the maturity and learning skill levels of the participants.

- **Evaluate course content yearly** based on teacher and student assessment. Upgrade whenever possible.

- **Use surveys** to determine the education needs of upper-level students and adults. The curriculum should have enough breadth and variety throughout the year to attract almost all parishioners to at least one course. Adults seeking involvement should be briefly interviewed and steered to appropriate classes responsive to their needs.

- **Use short courses (e.g., 6 weeks) to get people started** without extensive commitment. Short courses are also a good means to test new content with minimal risk.

- **Use the Sunday sermon as a subject source** for a specialized course so focused.

Curriculum Design Procedures

The intent of curriculum design is to develop a systematic, complete, and attractive course of study for attendees of all ages. Can a specific church school curriculum be recommended? Not in detail for it must be tailored to the educational needs and instruction resources of the individual congregation. However, a simple taxonomy, shown on the following page, illustrates the content.

The designing task is not as difficult as it may initially appear. The two essentials are a meaningful division of labor and trained content reviewers. Consider these three steps:

(1) Using the example curriculum, or one of your own choosing, assign a resource "expert" in each principal topic area. The representative taxonomy would require perhaps as many as 14 such assigned specialists.

(2) Task each expert to periodically monitor and evaluate potential content material in their assigned area and make associated recommendations. Most investigations will begin with denominational sources followed by library and internet searches. Note the exceptional amount and quality of free Christian education material on the World Wide Web. In addition, there are numerous ecumenical resource centers throughout the country with exceptional collections.

(3) Teachers, together with their resource expert, review recommendations taking into account previously presented related class content. Make final selections.

Curriculum Taxonomy

A composite type church school curriculum drawn from a number of sources may be outlined as follows:

Youth — Pre-school, kindergarten, primary, middle, pre-teen, young teen, and high school (this program involves at least these seven divisions).

Bible study — Study may be conducted book-by-book, by themes, by key events, or by individual personages.[4]
Old Testament Pentateuch (1st five books), historical (Joshua through Esther), wisdom books (Job through Song of Solomon), and the prophets (Isaiah through Malachi).
New Testament—life of Jesus (four Gospels), the beginning of Christianity (Acts), the letters (Romans through Jude), and The Apocalypse (Revelation).

Catechism — Church doctrine (creeds, Ten Commandments, Lord's Prayer).

Religious thought, history, and art — Bible parameters (placing the Bible in historical, cultural, and geographic context). The history and presence of the faithful community. Includes the lives of living and past saints and religious leaders as models for the Christian way of life. Comparative religions, church history, religious art and music, church architecture and symbolism.

The spiritual life — Knowledge of the grace of God, source of our life, faith, hope, love, truth, and wisdom. Understanding the place of personal and corporate worship, Bible study, and prayer in daily life. Discovery of serving God through Christian commitment and service to mankind.

The church today — Role of the church in society, homiletics, missionary program, lay leadership, management issues, evangelism.

Modern society — Developing and maintaining the Christian character and virtues. Family values, morality and social values, peace and justice, creation and evolution, contemporary issues (e.g., AIDS, population explosion, welfare).

Learning and Teaching Skills

"Ask the Lord of the harvest...to send out workers into his harvest field" (Luke 10:2)

Christianity is concerned with establishing a dynamic, living relationship between God and man. Faith itself, however, is a gift bestowed by the Holy Spirit on those who earnestly seek. We, in turn, as living parts of this relationship, can, and are in fact so commissioned to serve as instruments or channels for the Holy Spirit, helping others to understand their dependency and seek God's grace.

The essentials of learning—student motivation, interest in subject matter, and knowledge of goals and progress; organization and clarity of content, enthusiasm and repetition of delivery; and peer reinforcement, and reward—are generally well known but should be reviewed in a teacher's meeting at the beginning of each school year. What we know beyond doubt is that students primarily learn through a process of involvement in content that has real meaning to them. Thus attractive, informative subject matter is essential, coupled with rigorous group discussion, followed at some distance by manner of presentation.

All the rules of learning can be boiled down to one simple underlying principle; *the student must be involved*, in active listening, observing, or discussion. And then, in matters of personal conduct and emotions, change occurs only when the individual also discovers *meaning* in the message. And the forces involved may lie deep within oneself, not easily touched by a few words of good advice. The teaching method must then rely on the Holy Spirit to call forth a response from the student. Without such involvement of both Spirit and individual no instruction is ever successful. The saddest spectacle of all is that of the eloquent lecturer who believes that by simply saying the right thing the learning process is energized. In opposite fashion, the church school teacher can be no better prepared than by seeking God's presence and active student involvement.

Creating Effective Learning Conditions

Without a teacher, learning, if evident at all, is typically accidental, random, inefficient, and often of little real purpose. In contrast, effective teachers create optimal learning conditions, albeit still dependent on the student's willing involvement. Within the classroom, these climate design and procedural responsibilities include:

(1) Limit **class size** to no more than 20. This restriction establishes the intimacy and importance of the individual plus facilitating group interaction. Mechanical size limitation permits members to sit around a large table or face each other in a circle promoting eye contact and a feeling of joint deliberations.

(2) Package **subject matter** in 6 month or less increments. Studying any one topic for longer periods risks flagging attention and possible overkill.

(3) Provide each student a printed **syllabus**, however brief, outlining the course purposes, content to be covered, and student responsibilities. Subsequent handouts a week before each class may assign reading, highlight critical content, and indicate likely discussion topics. Preparing students in advance in this manner greatly facilitates content coverage and learning. Discussion, elaboration, clarification, profitably replace straight lecture.

(4) Maintain an **attendance roster** to flag absentees to contact. Every member should be made to realize their individual importance. Noting absences with a supporting phone call demonstrates this appreciation as few other outward acts can.

(5) Emphasize **group discussion** as opposed to lecturing. Lecturing is suitable for rapid, controlled dissemination of information. Developing attitudes and beliefs, on the other hand, can best be accomplished through involvement and discussion. People are inclined to change when they personally arrive at a decision as to what is desirable, supported by group agreement. Always remember that establishing belief and creating a right spirit is something the pupil receives from the Holy Spirit. We are only conduits at best.

Teachers should view themselves as facilitators and instructors, willing to encourage and listen as much as to teach. Remember, new thinking on the part of pupils requires responsive cultivation, not one-sided delivery. While there is a delicate balance required between involving students and the ends toward which the subject matter is directed, the latter can always slide to another day.

(6) Seek the **expertise of the class**. Students collectively have a great deal to contribute. Sharing the teaching load acknowledges and responds to their unique talents and experience. In light of such class credentials, it is not surprising that differences of opinion will arise. In such instances, avoid degeneration into arguments, attempting to affirm the legitimacy of differences whenever possible.

Reframing Confirmation

"Let everybody know that it is their chief duty, on pain of losing divine grace, to bring up their children in the fear and knowledge of God, and if they are gifted to give them opportunity to learn and study so that they may be of service wherever they are needed." —Martin Luther

Confirmation, the great rite of passage into adult church membership, will be briefly treated here exclusively in terms of recent innovative changes in the required preparation and the expressed justification. Pastors and parents will always jointly and independently bear responsibility for devising and updating the confirmation program. In the broadest sense, this obligation extends to familiarity with current options and their claimed merits.

Few changes in recent church history have had greater affect on young members than those related to confirmation training. Consider here as illustrative the following new innovative approaches being advocated:[5]

- Rather than initiate training at a fixed age, encourage selective entrance based on maturity and readiness. Further, confirmation may be extended, beginning earlier more modestly, extending later to more gradually assimilate youth into the congregation. Some churches in fact begin "confirmation" as early as the third grade, getting to know the child as an individual and gain parental support. After confirmation, contacts are maintained through senior high school to respond as a caring community and youth ministry. Confirmation is, after all, a life-time commitment.

- Enlist parents to more fully participate in the confirmation experience by reminding them of the promises they made at their child's baptism, by urging them to help their children in confirmation homework, and, most importantly, by encouraging their setting an example by leading an exemplary life. Home and family should be viewed as a central thread holding the confirmation ministry together.

- When feasible, dedicate a special "home room" for confirmands to call their own, a safe place to congregate, study, and associate as a special group. The idea is to build a sense of trust and community.

- Address confirmands in a more holistic way through small group interactions and experimental learning led by adult lay leaders sensitive to youth subcultures. Other supplemental approaches include individual mentoring, confirmation camp, retreats, service projects, interviewing congregants, and leading Sunday worship. There are many avenues leading to understanding and faith.

- During the first year, seek to experience the living God based on the reality of where the confirmands are with respect to this transcendental event. All means possible are likely required—prayer, discussion, testimony, stories, reading, homework, music, visuals. Only after young people begin to discover God in their own way is gradual assimilation of the Bible feasible. Let God spring forth in living reality by whatever means—no examinations, no pressure, only the goal of increasing awareness.

- The second year is one of structured doctrinal study to create the mind and spirit of discipleship. Martin Luther's five parts of the catechism—the Ten Commandments, Creed, Lord's Prayer, Baptism, and Lord's Supper—can serve as a prescribed pattern. This is a studious endeavor involving homework, memory, responsorial sessions, and testing. Memory of selected Bible passages, knowledge of church history, symbols, key figures are additional component parts.

- In contrast to a standard curriculum, providing confirmands some choice among a limited number of electives allows some tailoring to individual needs and interests. Choices may also extend to workshop topics and field trips.

- Public examination, the initiation ritual provides public expression of the preparatory work. The testing includes not only memorized responses but interpretations in the confirmand's own words. The latter can be quite rigorous and time consuming to ensure real understanding. Nothing less should be expected least of all by the confirmands themselves after their long and arduous preparation.

---

[1] Search Institute, "Effective Christian Education," 3½ year study of Christian education programs in 561 congregations in six Protestant denominations (1990).

[2] One of the foremost Bible handbooks worth everyone's attention is by John Bowker, *The Complete Bible Handbook: An Illustrated Companion* (1998, DK Publishing, New York), 544 pp.

[3] Inputting a short subject phrase, the ncccusa.org web site will locate all Bible passages with the exact same wording. For example, inputting "love one another" identifies this phrase initially in John 13:34 followed by 13 additional matches through 2 John 1:5.

[4] References are available, interestingly enough, for all three approaches. See, for example, Allan B. Stringfellow, *Through the Bible in One Year, Great Characters of the Bible,* and *Great Truths of the Bible,* Hensley Publishing, Tulsa, OK.

[5] Largely adopted from Walter Wangerin, Jr., "Costly confirmation," *The Lutheran,* May 1999, Vol. 12, No. 5, p. 6.

Chapter 19
Our Call to Stewardship

"Do not be afraid, little flock; because your Father is pleased to give you the Kingdom. Sell all your belongings and give the money to the poor. Provide for yourselves purses that don't wear out, and save your riches in heaven, where they will never decrease, because no thief can get to them, no moth can destroy them. For your heart will always be where your riches are." (Luke 12:32-34)

Each one, as a good manager of God's different gifts, must use for the good of others the special gift he has received from God. (1 Peter 4:10)

"I am not entitled to own anything that everyone cannot own." —Mahatma Gandhi (1869-1948), Indian nationalist leader, advocate of passive resistance.

"For it is in giving that we receive." —Saint Francis of Assisi (1181-1226), founder of the Franciscan Order.

The dictionary defines *stewardship* as "the management of another's property, finances, or other affairs." The meaning is thus remarkably unique in its custodial nature, guarding and caring for that which is not truly our own. For Christians the acknowledged owner of all is our heavenly father. So indebted, God imposes yet an additional requirement, that of sharing our gifts with a loving and caring spirit. In combination a new more challenging definition emerges—to manage and generously share with all, in loving kindness, the gifts that God has so graciously bestowed upon us his servants in Christ Jesus. Such interpretation is, however, necessarily of secondary value to that of our primary source. In his letter to Jewish and Gentile Christians scattered throughout Asia Minor, Peter writes of stewardship, *Each one, as a good manager of God's different gifts, must use for the good of others the special gift he has received from God.* (1 Peter 4:10)

The Nature of Managing God's Gifts with Charity

"Let us more and more insist on raising funds of love, of kindness, of understanding, of peace. Money will come if we seek first the kingdom of God—the rest will be given." —Mother Teresa (1910-1997), Roman Catholic missionary to India's poor.

"Our use of all that God gives us goes to the very heart of our 'Spirituality.'" —Theodore Schneider, Bishop of the Metropolitan DC Synod of the Evangelical Lutheran Church in America.

To get immediately to the essentials of Christian stewardship, we list nine interwoven, mutually reinforcing elements of our spiritually blessed stewardship to our heavenly Father:

• **All we have is a gift from God,** including life itself and the most precious gift of all, faith. No one is left out in receiving God's gifts.

- **We are therefore caretakers, not owners,** stewards entrusted by God with responsibility for the good employment of all our blessings. God has given us independent authority and dominion over all, to act freely on his behalf, to wisely use all to accomplish his purposes.
- **Such gifts are bestowed in abundance**, encompassing *everything* we require. *"Watch out, and guard yourselves from all kinds of greed; because a man's true life is not made up of the things he owns, no matter how rich he may be."* (Luke 12:15)

Consider our true riches in order. First the most precious gift of all, our Lord Jesus Christ, our redeemer and teacher, together with the Holy Spirit, our sanctified guide and comforter. Then the Holy Gospel which we are entrusted to obey and proclaim. This is followed by life itself, all that we are in God's image; then our personal gifts of family, time, talents, property, health, and friendships. Lastly, we are entrusted to protect God's beautiful creation by using the earth's resources carefully, preserving without waste. So encompassing is this entrustment that quite rightly *all* things may be called concerns of God.

- **God calls everyone to use their time, talent, and tithe to further the work of the Lord throughout the world.** The pursuit of possessions is not the mandate of our lives. We receive the gift of abundance so that we may be rich in God's service, to nourish our souls rather than our appetites. We must think of ourselves as in our last days, with the opportunity to store up for ourselves treasures in heaven. This we must do gladly and sacrificially, buttressed by prayer and self-examination. And in our giving, we broadcast God's loving concern for all. Together, for we do not do this alone, we become ambassadors of Christ.
- **Underlying all giving, especially financial offerings, is trust in God and satisfaction with what remains.** "Giving is an act of faith as well as a response to needs."[1] God earnestly desires our faith and service. He will always provide us more than we need (2 Corinthians 9:8). Therefore we must not fear, for life is more important than food and clothing (Luke 12:22-31).

The obligation to share acknowledges God's blessings bestowed upon us. It reflects our trust in his promise of all things through Christ Jesus. What gives life true meaning then is letting God take over, placing our complete trust in him. And one of the first evidences of this trust is the relinquishing of control over ourselves and our fortunes. We can equate faith, trust, and stewardship. In sequence, they become one and the same. *"Your Father knows that you need these things. Instead, be concerned with his Kingdom, and he will provide you with these things."* (Luke 12:30-31)

There is much to be said for traveling light in this world. We need liberty from our possessions to be free to pursue God's purposes for us. Unencumbered allows us to focus on that which is important without distractions. Consider Christ's guidance to the disciples. *"Carry no purse, no bag, no sandals; and greet no one on the road."* (Luke 10: 4)

• **Sharing should always be done as an act of discipleship, in true love for others, gladly, unselfishly, with gratitude and thanksgiving.** *Each one should give, then, as he has decided, not with regret or out of a sense of duty; for God loves the one who gives gladly.* (2 Corinthians 9:7)

The intent of all stewardship is to encourage people to give "out of a deep-felt response to what God has done, and is doing, with them in Jesus Christ."[2] Open our hearts! Rejoice in your riches in heaven where rust and moths do not enter. Nothing is more satisfying and rewarding than giving of oneself for others. Let us therefore leap with joy to what the Lord has called us to do.

What we must all seek in our giving is a charitable spirit, the virtue defined as love directed first toward God, but also toward oneself and one's neighbors. We give out of gratitude and thanksgiving for all that God has given us.

And though I bestow all my goods to feed the poor, and though I give my body to be burned, and have not charity, it profiteth me nothing. Charity suffereth long, and is kind, charity envieth not, charity vaunteth not itself, is not puffed up. (1 Corinthians 13:3-4)

• **Our gifts bear much fruit.** *And God, who supplies seed for the sower and bread to eat, will also supply you with all the seed you need and make it grow, to produce a rich harvest from your generosity.* (2 Corinthians 9:10) We are at our greatest productivity when we serve the Lord. We seldom recognize the great multiplying effect of our gifts. A kind word, an invitation, encouragement, a contribution, whatever the good deed, the benefits, seen and unseen, outweigh the cost in every instance.

• **We are not diminished by our gifts, quite the contrary, we are enriched in mind and spirit and blessings** in greater abundance and duration than anything we have given or deserve. *"Give to others, and God will give to you: you will receive a full measure, a generous helping, poured into your hands—all that you can hold. The measure you use for others is the one God will use for you."* (Luke 6:38)

"While you have a thing it can be taken from you...but when you give it, you have given it. No robber can take it from you. It is yours then forever when you have given it. It will be yours always. That is to give." —James Joyce (1882-1941), Irish author.

In giving we ourselves reap much reward, both in our increased awareness and sensitivity to the needs of others, and also in the happiness and fulfillment gained from serving God in this manner and in seeing others helped. In charity we experience life in all its human vitality, overflowing in richness of quality and depth. And not only do we gain life abundantly, but we also build treasures in heaven *"where moths and rust cannot destroy, and robbers cannot break in and steal. For your heart will always be where your riches are."* (Matthew 6:20-21)

Bring the full tithe into the storehouse, so that there may be food in my house, and thus put me to the test, says the Lord of hosts; see if I will not open the windows of heaven for you and pour down for you an overflowing blessing. (Malachi 3:10)

- **Our entrustment is a responsibility for which we must give an accounting.** "It is normal to give away a little of one's life in order not to lose it all." —Albert Camus (1913-1960), French-Algerian philosopher and author.

Giving is not an option, it is a Christian obligation and he who fails will surely be held accountable. Recall how Jesus spoke of the unproductive servant who failed to invest his property wisely. When the master returned he spoke angrily *"...throw him outside in the darkness; there he will cry and gnash his teeth."* (Matthew 25:30)

Envisioning the above elements and scope of true Christian stewardship, one readily contrasts it with the more common corrupted meaning of simply contributing a modest amount of money. Stewardship is a permanent and continuing obligation, joyfully surrendering all one possesses in prayful obedience to Christ.

The Harsh Reality

Before proceeding with the manner in which nurturing stewardship within a congregation is cultivated, a few harsh admonitions are necessary. Jesus leaves no doubt that much is required and little expected of those with riches. *"How hard it will be for rich people to enter the Kingdom of God! It is much harder for a rich man to enter the Kingdom of God than for a camel to go through the eye of a needle."* (Mark 10:23, 25) Thus, beware that a token gift is essentially nothing. If it is of no consequence to you, it is of no consequence to God. The more we have the more will, in fact, be required. *"The man to whom much is given, of him much is required; the man to whom more is given, of him much more is required."* (Luke 12:48)

Heed the warning. "Today we North American Christians, who can only be defined as rich relative to the global distribution of wealth and power, would do well to reflect at length on this terrifying triplet ('how hard it is to enter the kingdom of God'). For it remains as dissonant to our ears today as it was to the disciples in the story, provoking the same kind of astonishment."[3] Let there be no doubt. Discipleship is costly. No one may become a disciple without divesting oneself of the centrality of possessions (Luke 14:33), seeking first, beyond all else, the kingdom of God. *"But strive first for the kingdom of God and his righteousness, and all these things will be given to you as well."* (Matthew 6:33)

But we fail miserably in our giving, tolerant and commiserative of each other in our self-righteous miserliness. We are compulsively addicted to our wealth, self-convinced we cannot and need not change.

Ched Myers calls it a "culture of meritocracy, materialism, and elitism."[4] And we are unequivocally wrong. It is the church's best kept secret, preserved out of some false sense of entitled privilege and necessary privacy. Since when is this failure less open to debate than any other sin, for that is what it is? We should be shouting to the housetops: "Trust God!" "Serve one master!" "Give of yourself and your wealth!" "Sacrifice for the Lord!"

We must do everything in our power to encourage people to place their trust in God, not self-reliance; to make stewardship a way of life, a perpetual theme, not a special campaign;[5] to make a fierce commitment of self and wealth, not a mere token offering. As for our leaders, they are responsible for vividly portraying the need and broadcasting the value of helping. The reality of the world's suffering must be made known. We adults need tangible and concrete evidence, not like little children to whom all suffering is very real. Instead, we exhort and write checks and wonder why in our abstract detachment we feel no greater compulsion.

Stewardship Committee Duties

"There is a large harvest, but few workers to gather it in." (Luke 10:2)

The function of the church stewardship committee is to secure workers and resources for the Lord. It seeks nothing less than developing Christian lives. The chief responsibility is, of course, securing *everyone's* involvement. The committee specifically, and the church in general, must be more interested in caring for its members and encouraging their Christian growth than in how much money they give. It is entirely too easy for the committee to succumb to outside and even self-imposed financial pressures to the neglect of spiritual growth.

The committee accomplishes its goals through a program of education, guidance, and encouragement extended to every member. These and other responsibilities are outlined in the stewardship committee job description in Appendix B. A committee which understands and takes to heart its full responsibilities will find that its work is never complete, and that securing pledges is definitely a secondary function. The committee operates best with bold members striving to serve as examples and to perfect all in Christian service and sharing. Because of its great responsibilities, the stewardship committee deserves the council's particular attention and support.

Members of the committee should be skilled in public relations, organization, and salesmanship. They should be continuously involved in study of the relevant literature,[6] investigation of successful programs, and preparation and updating of the stewardship agenda. Finally, members should personally witness for stewardship by gifting at least five percent (others might say tithe) of their adjusted gross income to charity.

Because of its embracing, often assertive, involvement in the lives of all congregants, the stewardship committee must keep the church council well informed of its intentions and results. As the leading element, the committee must never be hesitant or retiring in performing its mission. Gaining full participation requires energetic, resourceful, even pervasive action. Where such rigor is required, keeping the council well informed is good politics.

Stewardship is a year-round, focused activity. The committee is continuously engaged in stewardship education, presentation of service opportunities, every-member visitations, and occasional special fund raising events. In attempting to secure meaningful and responsive engagement, the committee inherits a degree of responsibility to see that individuals are truly *gainfully* employed, not merely busy. George Odiorne calls the myriad of typical church pursuits an "activity trap" in which the church "having lost sight of the higher purposes for which it was originated, now attempts to make up for this loss by an increased range of activities."[7]

The committee must also be alert to present and past trends in overall and member service and offerings. Individual records of skills, service, and gifts are essential.[8] Without such intelligence the committee is likely to follow a path of least resistance, identifying position candidates simply from those they know or are readily available rather than canvassing the talent of the entire congregation.

Warning about special campaigns. Special fund-raising campaigns may be necessary to meet *exceptional* needs and we address that situation on page 309, but such efforts should be viewed as an unusual measure. A sound stewardship program may generally be relied upon to provide a steady financial base, adequate for all but the most inordinate demands. If not, something is fundamentally wrong with the program requiring repair, not resorting to special measures.

Means of Gaining Everyone's Involvement

How is the great task of securing loving participating stewardship among all congregants accomplished? First, not a farthing will be gained without seeking God's grace and guidance. Except for evangelism, no other congregational ministry is so absolutely dependent on prayer and earnest petitioning. For we can guide, encourage, and create opportunities; but only the Holy Spirit can change people's hearts.

Our Lord God calls us to work in his vineyard and to leave no one standing idle. Consider then these rules which we are entrusted to follow in properly managing our time, talents, and resources: [9]

Responding to God's Call

• **Stewardship is foremost a heartfelt response to our love of God** for all he has done for us, a deep desire to share the bountiful blessings he has bestowed. Our time, talent, and wealth are inextricably woven together as manifestation of God's blessings. All three are equal in terms of necessary commitment.

Reaching Out to Embrace All

• **To secure involvement, congregations must continuously reach out to every member, for stewardship is a combination of calling and response.** When people feel they are truly loved and needed they are attracted and seek association. To create good stewards then, we must first show persons how important they are and how valued their talents. When each truly believes in their own personal importance in God's kingdom, they will respond abundantly.

Reaching out should be understood as a continuous responsibility to be steadfastly cultivated and nurtured, not exploited on an intermittent or temporal basis. Churches must personally guide and persistently encourage. Families cannot be left entirely on their own to figure out their stewardship. Nor can the message be told just once a year during an annual campaign. Occasional, accidental contact also suggests little real concern. One must not passively rely on volunteers. Asking for volunteers and using sign-up sheets secure only those interested. This means is too impersonal to be effective for most, for a majority of members are likely to respond only to personal attention.

In opposite fashion, real interaction with members throughout the year shows deep strong interest. Every member, young and old, must be convinced that Christ and the church really want and need their faith and involvement. Such engagement requires one-on-one contact to discern the personal interests and abilities of each individual. It also requires some flexibility on the part of the church organization to create places suitable for every type of talent and time available. Let no one be allowed to remain idle.

The initial task always is to encourage members to discover their personal spiritual gifts; then secondarily, to identify the appropriate means whereby these gifts can be effectively employed either within or external to the existing structure. *The key to stewardship is growth of the individual.* Any other focus, such as getting someone to do a particular job or give more money, is doomed to ultimate failure for impersonal involvement builds no lasting strength or commitment.

Guiding and Supporting

• **Findings and responding to our calling is a matter of appealing to God for guidance, personal self-appraisal, and support from our fellow congregants.**

We serve in response to prayer, inner reflection, and the encouragement of others. Every member must be instructed on this path. Privately, or with the aid of a counselor, we must first seek God's wisdom and the guidance of the Holy Spirit in our lives. Then, again preferably with counsel, we inventory our abilities and interests and how they may be most productively employed. How may I best serve, Lord?

Prayer and self-appraisal, in this instance, are best conducted in the warm embrace of Christian fellowship within a small group. Responding to our calling is difficult. The small group provides the loving care and supportive attention necessary for hesitant individuals. Small groups help open wide the door. Once so involved, members seek to respond in kind, and stewardship becomes a reality to them. (See Chapter 17, "Small Group Ministries.")

• **Pastors and congregational leaders have a responsibility to model**, talk, and teach about generosity and sacrificial giving, for it is a very important part of the Gospel. Theodore Schneider, Bishop of the Metropolitan DC Synod of the Evangelical Lutheran Church in America, points out that of Jesus' 36 parables recorded in the New Testament, 26 speak about the meaning and use of money. "Neither pastors nor church councils have any business asking our people to do that they themselves do not do. Those who are unwilling to be good stewards of all that God gives ought not to be leaders in the church, either lay or ordained!"[10]

Pastors and church leaders must set the example in commitment of time, abilities, financial gifts, and in nourishing their own family life. When church pastors and council members commit themselves in clear and measurable ways, others are inspired to respond likewise. And generous leaders are able to ask others to do likewise. They need not apologize for rigorously asking of others what they themselves are doing. To show this leadership, evidence of the involvement and giving of council members might be reported.

Ensuring Opportunities and Effective Employment

• **Create as many leadership opportunities as possible** to allow a maximum number of members to lead as well as follow. This expansion can be accomplished by limiting terms to two years, not allowing dual roles, and discouraging repeated dependence on a few. Leadership positions can also be tripled by simply creating pro-tem and ex officio capacities. Encourage designees to serve as such in preparation, and immediate retirees as advisors. Consider this consequential expansion. Every six years, 30 leadership positions serving three-year terms results in 60 appointments. With ex officio and pro tem positions and two year terms, 270 opportunities are provided over the same period, more than 4 times the previous number! But what a difficult sell. Congregations seem to want to conservatively husband their leadership among a proven few, which recognizably simplifies matters. But it does not garner well for encouraging leadership growth.

A second means of creating opportunities centers on the attention staff give to working themselves out of various responsibilities. An overworked pastor and staff simply fail, in most instances, to adequately train and delegate. They have come to rely on too few for too much. The vineyard, however, need not employ only the best and brightest. Second and third string players under the tutelage of former leaders will likely do well enough, and the reward to those added is more than compensation for any resulting deficiencies.

- **Compare returns among alternative service uses to obtain the most productive employment of resources.** This analysis is especially applicable to elective expenditures, beyond the confines of the basic core budget. We have a Christian duty to optimally employ all our resources. The tool employed is marginal analysis, i.e., seeking to make the last dollars expended in each activity equally productive.[11] This is mostly theory. In practice, decisions are generally based on last year's budget with comparisons limited to new proposals and their relative merits. Other programs are typically allowed to grow naturally, their funding increased as a yearly expected progression. In some instances, committee or program members may appear over-worked or underutilized, prompting staff changes. However conducted, churches should be reasonably confident that no further shift in dollars or personnel would improve their mission accomplishment.

- **Maintain a programmable inventory of member interests, skills, and service.** We strongly recommend a spiritual gifts and service record for every member. Church officers need hard input data to be able to knowledgeably "equip the saints" to do the work of the ministry that fits their talents. Be aware that the resulting wealth of talent exposed is likely to result in "an explosion of new leadership."[12]

A computer-based inventory typically records member birth year, sex, family status, type of employment, income bracket, education level and field, skills, interests, previous church service, monetary contributions, and estimated average hours of contributed service per week. The inventory should be updated yearly, preferably based on a personal interview, possibly within the small groups advocated. A number of software programs are available for maintaining such data bases. Be sure the program has the sorting and other capabilities you need.[13] Records must be strictly confidential, accessible by only a single individual. A roster of code numbers can be substituted for member names as further security.

- **Every member visitation** is required for stewardship contact when small groups are not present. The intent is to not only share the mission and needs of the church, but also the joys, concerns, and needs of each member on a one-on-one basis. Trained counselors are advised; however, again this requirement can be negated and the matter of stewardship better handled in small groups (see Chapter 17). An annual membership canvass is far inferior to such on-going interaction.

Securing Commitment and Providing Recognition

- **Use pledges.** A pledge, in the church context, is often more a sought goal or aiming point than guaranteed result; more a declaration or intended commitment than binding promise. Pledges are what we strive to do with God's help. And they are a wonderful vehicle for encouraging and steering us along strenuous paths.

We make the case for comprehensive, individually tailored pledges that encompass a broad array of commonly accepted responsibilities of which financial giving is but one. Such breadth bonds members to the church and places finances in the proper perspective of giving of one's whole self. Consider this annual member commitment form from which the congregant may choose those he or she seeks to honor.

Seeking an abundant life in Christ Jesus, I pledge with God's help to:
1. Live an ordered life with prayer each day to our heavenly Father, giving thanks for all his blessings, and in regular Bible study.
2. Keep the Sabbath holy by faithful church attendance and commitment to family.
3. Be a welcoming representative of the congregation to all visitors and a friend in Christ to all members. Wear my nametag as a mark of friendliness.
4. Participate in Christian education by attending each year at least one church short course of my own choosing.
5. Be a good steward of God's gifts of talent and time by periodic services as a church lay leader or group member.
6. Be a good steward of God's gifts of fortune by commitment to yearly financial support of ___ percent of my disposable income.
7. Witness outwardly for Christ by discussing my faith with others and proclaiming the Good News.
8. Live sacrificially as best I am able in a temperate life of moderation, self-restraint, and periodic fasting.
9. Be spiritually forgiving of others in both interpersonal and social spheres.
10. Be a member of a small group within the church, sharing and encouraging spiritual growth and friendship.
11. Commit myself to occupational accountability in performing my work in a responsible Christian manner of value to all people.
12. Address issues of local, national, and international social and economic policy from a Christian perspective.
13. Affirm the gift of my body and commit myself to its proper nourishment and physical and mental well-being.

While securing stewardship is a year-round activity, pledges are commonly made once a year, typically on Consecration Sunday. The rules here are to precede pledging with preparatory sermons, announcement letters signed by the congregation president, and handouts. The idea is to encourage extended thoughtful consideration, well before commitment. So prepared, pledge cards are handed out on Consecration Sunday, and, within the encouraging supportive environs of others, prayerfully completed. Cards and stamped return envelopes are mailed to absentees.

- **Recognize service.** *Outdo one another in showing honor.* (Romans 12:10) People need to know that their services and support are being effectively used and appreciated.

Financial Giving

• **Financial giving requires a clear understanding of the need and the returns expected.** Financial stewardship is thus built on a base of understanding and involvement—understanding the joy of giving and the value of our gifts to others, involvement in shared time and talent. Being completely prepared is critical. Dean Hoge found that denominations that *teach* tithing as scripturally commanded have higher levels of giving. His study also found that planned giving results in greater giving.[14]

People give when they are convinced there is a real need and that something truly good will result. Giving should not be viewed as a duty to a budget, rather as an opportunity for generosity. It should not be a hard sell for the needs of this world are of truly epic proportions. People must understand the reality of the world's suffering and know that their help, however modest, will be an alleviating force. Then giving becomes not a duty but a welcome sharing. Similarly, the productive use of talents encourages their contribution.

• **Educating youth** on the role of money in leading Christian lives is likely the most productive long-term approach that may be taken. We must strive to build caring persons, who unselfishly think of others. And children, so dependent on their friendships with others, are very aware of these responsibilities. We need only place their caring in the broader content of Christian sharing.

Forms of Serving

Each one, as a good manager of God's different gifts, must use for the good of others the special gift he has received from God. (1 Peter 4:10)

"I wanted to give the Lord some quality time." —Don Ross, General Electric executive who took early retirement to devote the rest of his life to full-time Salvation Army service.

So let us not grow weary in doing what is right, for we will reap at harvest time, if we do not give up. (Galatians 6:9)

We have been given gifts in abundance so that we may be rich in our service to the Lord. Not only must we be generous, but as good stewards, wise in the use of our talents. "Busyness must not be confused with effectiveness. Nor is a full calendar a mark of our faithfulness."[15]

Service opportunities should be publicized by appropriate means including an annual *Service Opportunities* booklet, flyer announcements, and a yearly "Ministry Fair" where visitors may "sign up."

Twelve service areas may be organized in four ministries as follows:[16]

Outreach

Apostleship Sharing the Word of God through evangelistic programs and field missionaries.

Advocacy Advancing political and social causes with concern for justice, equality, and human dignity.

Community Service Responding to the needs of the community and world through education, service, and support. (Food pantry, blood drive, youth work trips, immigrants, tutoring, hunger and disaster relief, shelter, clothing.)

Nurturing

Education Bringing believers into Christian maturity through prayer, instruction, group support, and personal study. (Preschool through adulthood, newcomers classes, parenting classes, library.)

Counseling/Support Comforting, guiding, and supporting members in time of change or need. (Home and hospital visits, new member sponsorship, transportation, home repair, food preparation and delivery.)

Fellowship Befriending and exploring Christian life together, often as part of small group interaction. (Small groups, youth groups, after service coffee hour, supper club, sport teams, Boy Scouts.)

Liturgical

Worship Service Assisting in the worship service through various liturgical responsibilities including lectors, Eucharist ministers, and acolytes. Greeting, ushering, and altar and space preparation are part of this ministry.

Music Making a joyful noise through choir, instrumentalists, and soloists.

Arts Constructing visible decorations commonly in the form of banners, vestments, stained glass, paintings, and plays.

Prayer group Reverently petitioning our heavenly father, usually conducted informally in small groups.

Management

Leadership Leading others effectively through vision, insight, and direction.

Administration Support Assisting in church administration, finance, and property.

Securing Financial Support[17]

And God is able to give you more than you need, so that you will always have all you need for yourselves and more than enough for every good cause. (2 Corinthians 9:8)

Bring the full tithe into the storehouse, so that there may be food in my house, and thus put me to the test, says the Lord of hosts; see if I will not open the windows of heaven for you and pour down for you an overflowing blessing. (Malachi 3:10)

"No one can be a slave to two masters; he will hate one and love the other; he will be loyal to one and despise the other. You cannot serve both God and money." (Matthew 6:24)

"O divine master grant that I may seek not so much to be consoled as to console; to be understood as to understand; to be loved as to love. For it is in giving that we receive; it is in pardoning that we are pardoned; and it is in dying that we are born into eternal life." —Prayer of Saint Francis

The Reality of Our Wealth and Failure to Share

Most Americans possess more than enough financial resources to adequately fund all the ministry needs of the Gospel. If everyone tithed or gave a growing proportion, we would not only have all we currently need, but would be searching for new and creative ways to spend the bounty. Instead, we have sought out every conceivable manner of extravagant spending, bestowing our excesses on ourselves and immediate family, always with decreasing marginal returns as the last expenditures heaped upon all the others produce less and less satisfaction. How much more productive it would be if we shifted from our least rewarding, self-serving transactions, to richly satisfying gifts to others.

Let's be clear on the financial picture of Americans and their charitable contributions:

- Real sacrificial giving is extremely rare in this country. Even tithing would still leave most of us advantaged by any world standard. Today the wealthiest 20 percent of the world's population receive more than 80 percent of the world's income, while the poorest 20 percent receive less than 2 percent. Most of us are thus in the high risk category of being "the rich man" of Bible verse. The bottom line is that increased giving is a very real economic possibility for essentially all church members. Our low giving is a matter of choice, not necessity.

- In practice we typically achieve only one-fourth the tithing goal. The average three-person American family budget in 2002 was $48,100, including $2,300 spent on entertainment and $1,200 to charities (2.5 percent).[18] And the trend of even this modest contribution is alarmingly downward.

- The church is even losing its market share among its own members. Per-member giving as a percentage of after-tax income has declined over the last 30 years.

- Churches are also losing out to other charitable organizations in receipt of charitable donations. In 1990, religion received 49.1 percent of all private philanthropy. The share declined to 35 percent in 2002.[19] Other charities are obviously offering stronger competition, yet the church has a great advantage with its unique participating membership. The church is its members.

We talk about living simply, but this is difficult in possession-oriented America. The church must serve as a counter balance, introducing love, compassion, and sacrifice into our lives, attitudes beyond commercial value. We clearly need the discipline to order our lives and resources to overcome the habit of economic privilege. "To recognize our public addiction to economic privilege and power means keeping the dysfunctional and deadly disparity of wealth always in view, and daily deciding to 'turn over' our economic lives to the alternative reality of the divine economy of grace."[20]

Recognize that most of us live a life of abundance. So much so that, in the words of Susan Sontag, American essayist, "its material plentitude, its sheer crowdedness conjoin to dull our sensory facilities." Together with this self-shielding detachment, we are further lured into acceptance and complacency by a society which values material wealth, teaches that abundance is produced for personal consumption, and equates wealth with success. The excesses of our culture have so obscured the necessities of life that we have become immune to their importance. Having never experienced hunger, cold, loss, or despair, we have no real sense of the reality of the world's impoverished.

A Permanent Condition of Faith and Self-Discipline

"At the great fund-raising churches in America, stewardship is a perpetual theme, not a special campaign." —George Barna[21]

Stewardship is a permanent condition of faith, leading the Christian life of service and giving as admonished by our Lord. We give of ourselves as a permanent, unwavering opportunity afforded by Christ's example. Complete commitment requires no surcease in our response, only renewal and rededication. Congregations that create a climate of giving associated only with sporadic needs, breed members who will only respond to such distinct appeals. We must strive instead to gain life-time pledges, not singular responses, or we will be tied to a perpetual cycle of fundraising. Yes, special needs often warrant exceptional attention, but only as an add-on, not the core.

Whereas charities explain what they are doing and ask for financial support, the church *transforms* people into disciples who give voluntarily as an act of faith and love for others. So we build the stewardship program on trust and the joy of giving, not church needs or finances. The church that always associates giving with needs, will, instead, create a climate in which people give only when the church asks.

Why People Give

In practice, people express numerous reasons why they give to the church. Joiner lists eight:[22]

- —to express gratitude to God.
- — because it is a biblical mandate, a sense of obligation.
- — they like what they see is happening at church.
- — they are striving to get into heaven, i.e. a good investment.
- — they want to give something to help their children or grandchildren.
- — it is the way they were taught.
- — it might give them status and power within the congregation.
- — because it is a tax deduction.

However, ultimately only one reason should prevail, because we love God and thereby are entrusted to likewise provide, care for, and love our neighbor. All other reasons, while common and often motivating, should be recognized, but are not central. We ask that you focus on the nine elements of spiritually blessed stewardship beginning on page 288.

How to Become Charitable Givers

And though I bestow all my goods to feed the poor, and though I give my body to be burned, and have not charity, it profiteth me nothing. Charity suffereth long, and is kind; charity envieth not, charity vaunteth not itself, is not puffed up. (1 Corinthians 13:3-4)

"The organized charity, scrimped and iced,
In the name of a cautious, statistical Christ."
—John Boyle O'Reilly (1844-1890), Irish author.

For a final time, we caution that stewardship is about building the heart and mind of Christ within oneself, not raising money. Heed Saint Paul's admonishment in 1 Corinthians above.

In light of the above concern, we address financial giving as a faithful spiritual response to all God's blessings. Our attention is limited to the following 10 fundamental actions,[23] listed, to a degree, in order of priority and/or sequence.

1. Preach and teach the centrality of giving from the heart. *"For your heart will always be where your riches are."* (Luke 12:34)

People must be taught to be givers. They want to give, but their upbringing and social climate is unsupportive. They need to be encouraged, taught to understand that they are partners with God in sharing his blessings as good stewards, and that in so doing they build up true, authentic riches in heaven. The message must come from the pulpit augmented by group discussions and instruction in Sunday school.

We seek to move from fundraising to raising Christian philanthropists, loving God and mankind. We seek not money, but discipleship in response to all that God has done for us in Jesus Christ. This "conversion" can best be encouraged by interaction within small groups, possibly in conjunction with related Sunday services.

2. Active involvement in congregational life is the key to all charitable giving. People who come to church seek God in their lives and how to respond to his presence. As they receive these gifts, their spiritual journey leads to an ever increasing need to give of themselves. This involvement is powerful evidence of our response to God's grace. It must be cultivated in every member in every manner and at every level, as a responsibility of our discipleship.

3. Conduct stewardship in depth year-round, as a perpetual theme. Stewardship is an encompassing frame of mind, continuous in its duties and resolve. Annual campaigns, in contrast, are temporal, typically limited in dimensions and commitment. Remember, time is on your side in any financial campaign. Don't be rushed. Work methodically to develop long-term resources.

4. Develop self-discipline. Possessions should not steal from us the joy of generosity and the true meaning and value of life. We must free ourselves from being "financial slaves to our unbridled, unfocused, undirected spending habits and financial pursuits."[24] In a world where "...400 million people are so undernourished they are likely to suffer stunted growth, mental retardation, or death...(North Americans) spend $5 billion a year on special diets to lower their calorie consumption."[25] We, the affluent, clearly need discipline. And no force is better equipped to exert such persuasive control as Christ's church. We must hate the sin of self-indulgence even as we love the sinner. In a caring community, there is no such thing as being too tough in framing the requirements of congregational membership. We must all strive to give generously to the point of awareness, that is until the consequences noticeably "hurt" a little. Only then are we likely to have foregone some things that would otherwise have been purchased. Isn't that the kind of discipline we expect of Christ's servants?

5. Establish the reality of the world's needs and the use and benefits derived from our support. We are so detached from the world's impoverished that they hardly seem real. Churches must correct this remoteness by constantly exposing us to the hunger, poverty, and pestilence that shames this world, not only in terms of presenting its stark reality, but also, and preferably for some, in the positive outcomes possible.

One immediate means of establishing reality is for members to work directly with locally disenfranchised people, not just to help them, but, as importantly, to see them as they really are and transmit that actuality back to the congregation. Such "exposure tours" erase the insulation typically separating the reality of the field from the isolation of the congregation. "The longer we are rooted in such neighborhoods, the more the issues so familiar to the poor become our own. Our work then moves from 'aid' to 'alliance,' from 'sympathy' to 'solidarity'."[26]

6. Secure an appreciation of the role and needs of the church and its mission. This inward appreciation is gained only when the church focuses its attention outward on each individual's faith development and ministry. People who know and love Jesus, love his church and its ministry. That is the order, first Jesus, then the church.

The task of financial stewardship is to convince people that something good is happening as a result of their giving, so that they get excited about the life of the church and want to invest more of themselves and their resources. People commit to the church's financial ministry when they:

— know and wholeheartedly support the church's mission.

— understand how their gifts are being used,[27] and appreciate the need for and value of their personal support. People give to ministries and results, not budgets.

— are encouraged by the possibilities and future, not disheartened by any present shortfall.

— can designate funds for special purposes.

— believe that decisions regarding spending priorities are made on a sound rational basis so that individual allotments are used in the most effective means possible. A corollary here is the obvious requirement of integrity and accountability in the use of church funds.

— are inspired by the special events of the Church calendar year.

7. Church leaders must set the example by leading exemplary lives of attendance, service, sacrifice, and prayer. Leaders should be the first to sign pledges, a majority of which should include tithing.

8. Stewardship should be "negotiated" in every-member-visits, or, preferably, on a continuing basis through "small group" membership. People must understand that they are important as children of God and as members of the congregation. This can only be accomplished by extended personal contacts, preferably within small groups. Loving all in this intimate manner will eventually result in an entire congregation of disciples. Instead of 20 percent of the congregation doing most of the heavy lifting, all will participate. Member neglect is the most serious handicap a congregation can sustain. See Chapter 17 "Small Group Ministries."

9. Recognize and respond to special challenges and opportunities within the membership. People and generations see and hear things differently so we must respond with special invitations and messages. More and more people coming to church, for example, seek an introduction to God, but are not intent on membership or its responsibilities. Younger people are now more often believers but not belongers as in the past—a commitment to their faith, but not necessarily to a congregation.[28] Some members respond to a written message, others require a more personal presentation. Some seek immediate tangible evidence of their generosity, as in the purchase of church hymnals or sanctuary improvements. Others are moved, in contrast, by missions in some far corner of the world. Interviews and group discussions will discover these preferences and encourage related member support.

10. Promote extended and varied commitments. Church members are more fully involved and give more when they make a yearly commitment of time, talent, and resources. Spur-of-the-moment choices are often minimal. Deliberate commitments, on the other hand, invariably are carefully thought out, requiring dedication and perseverance. Real sacrifice is never casual.

We recommend a broad pledge discussed earlier on pages 296-297. Surprisingly enough, as Charles Horton Cooley (1864-1929), American sociologist observes, "When one has come to accept a certain course as duty he has a pleasant sense of relief and of lifted responsibility." The Lord comforts those who commit on his behalf.

Charting

Charts and graphs are able to transmit complicated data clearly. Modern computer software makes their design relatively easy. Yet traditional accounting records remain the dominant, if not the most effective, means of communicating church finances. Here then is an opportunity for the stewardship and finance committees to work together in developing better communication.

The value of graphics is illustrated in the following example which may be used as a guide rather than standard. Consider a congregation of 400 *active* family/individual members, "active" membership being defined by attendance (e.g., at least 12 times a year) and contributions via assigned church envelopes. For each such designated unit, two data elements are required plus a third option: (1) yearly income (adjusted gross income, Federal Form 1040, line 36) or estimate, (2) yearly dollar amount of gifts to church, and (3) average weekly hours of volunteered services. All individual data, are, of course, maintained in strictest confidence.

The income and gift data are arranged by income interval in five groups of an equal number of families. Same-size member groups encourage equal attention. Also, with groups of equal size, the average and total dollar amounts bear the same relative relationship to each other. In the example below, the 400 family congregation is divided into five groups of 80 families each (Table 1, column 1), the first income division occurring at $26,500. The total income of all 80 families in each group is entered in column 2. The total amount of gifts for all 80 families in each group is entered in column 3. The remainder of the table is self-computing.

Table 1. Church Financal and Membership Record

Family/individual income interval	Number of famlies	Total income all families	Total gifts all families	Average income all families (2)/(1)	Average gifts (3)/(1)	Gifts as a % of income (5)/(4)	Gifts by income as % of total
	(1)	(2)	(3)	(4)	(5)	(6)	(7)
Under $26,500	80	$1,825,000	$28,000	$22,813	$350	1.53%	3%
$26,500 to $46,699	80	$2,825,000	$75,000	$35,313	$938	2.65%	9%
$46,700 to $76,399	80	$4,825,000	$110,000	$60,313	$1,375	2.28%	13%
$76,400 to $102,499	80	$6,863,000	$225,000	$85,788	$2,813	3.28%	27%
$102,500 or more	80	$8,958,000	$397,000	$111,975	$4,963	4.43%	48%
TOTAL	400	$25,296,000	$835,000	$63,240	$2,088	3.30%	100%

Chart 1, page 306, reports the distribution of family wealth within the congregation; e.g., the wealthiest 20 percent of the families/individuals earn on average 4.9 times the amount the poorest earn ($111,975/$22,813). Thus church income is highly dependent on its most affluent members.

Chart 2, page 307, presents the average and total gifts per family/individual and gifts as a percent of disposable income. The data show how income positively affects giving and, again, our heavy reliance on the wealthiest families. But note also the great potential involved. If each group doubled its gift percentage so that the church average rose from 3.3% to 6.6% of income, the gift total would, also, of course, double to $1,670,000. This higher giving rate is strictly within the realm of possibility. Each church family should give until there is some "hurt." The congregation will naturally still be primarily dependent on gifts from its most affluent families (Chart 3, page 307), but this is natural and should be expected. We praise God for the gifts from all, large or small.

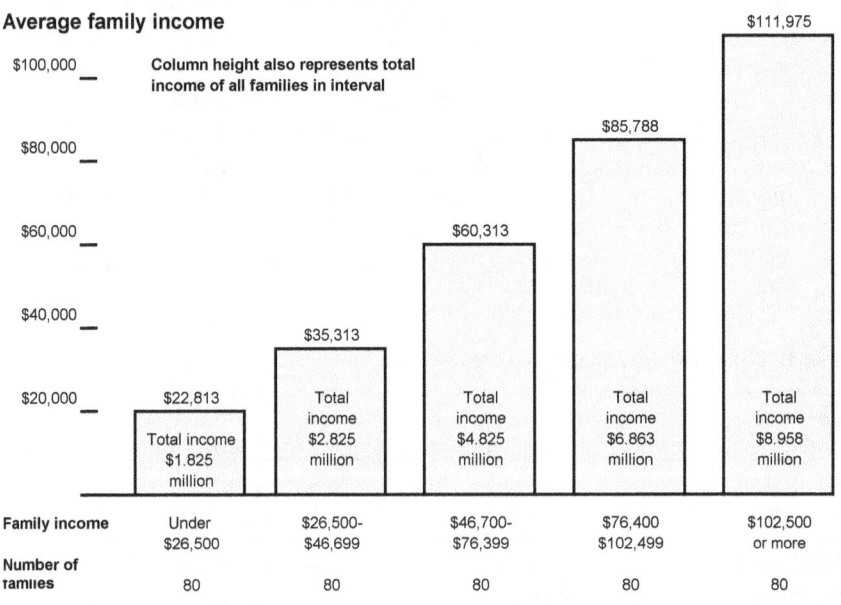

Chart 1. Distribution of family wealth

The church's monthly gift record is reported in Chart 4, page 308. Note the typical late summer decline when families are off on vacation. A wise stewardship committee encourages level giving by emphasizing pledges and routine use of contribution envelopes.

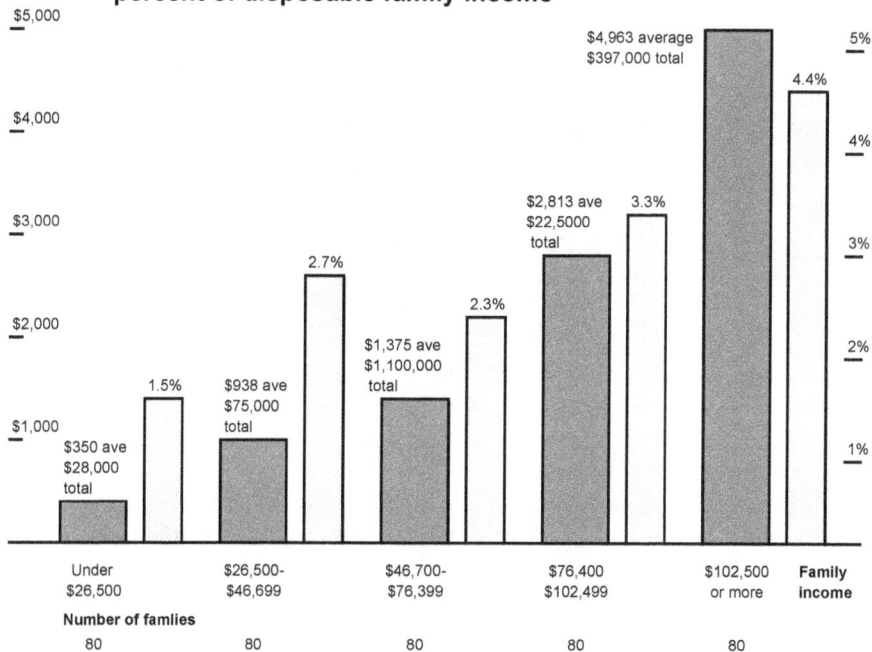

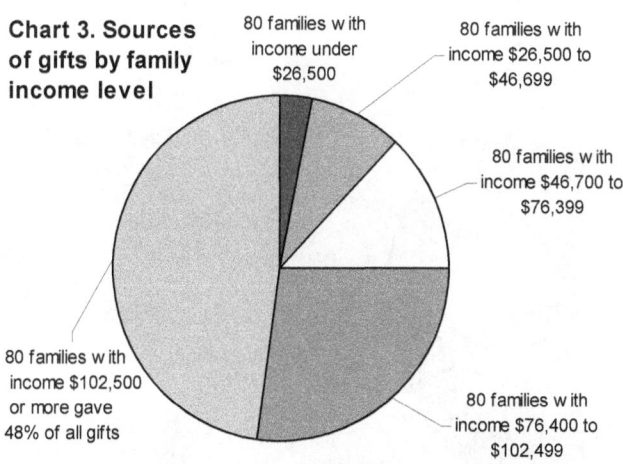

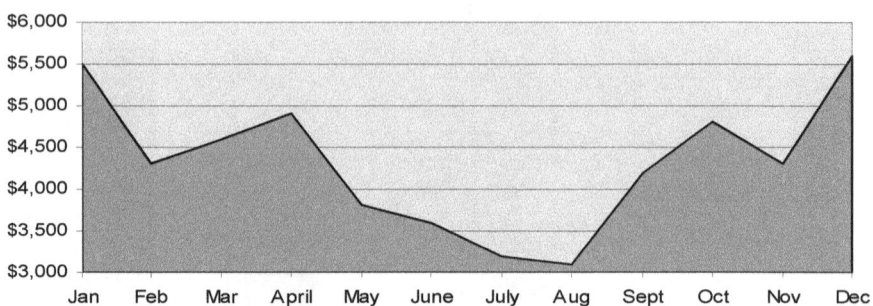

Chart 4. Monthly gift record

Chart 5, below, reports the church's expenditures by function which illustrates the costliness and to an extent relative importance of each undertaking. How the money is being used is generally of foremost importance to discerning donors.

Table 2a, page 309 reports the distribution of church expenditures and contributed services by function. We strongly recommend this detail to present the whole picture of the church's efforts, as well as funding demands and priorities. Major functional categories are listed in the left-hand column. We list eleven, paralleling the committee organizational structure. Paid salaries distributed by function as estimated by the staff are reported in Table 2b, page 309. Contributed congregation services[29]

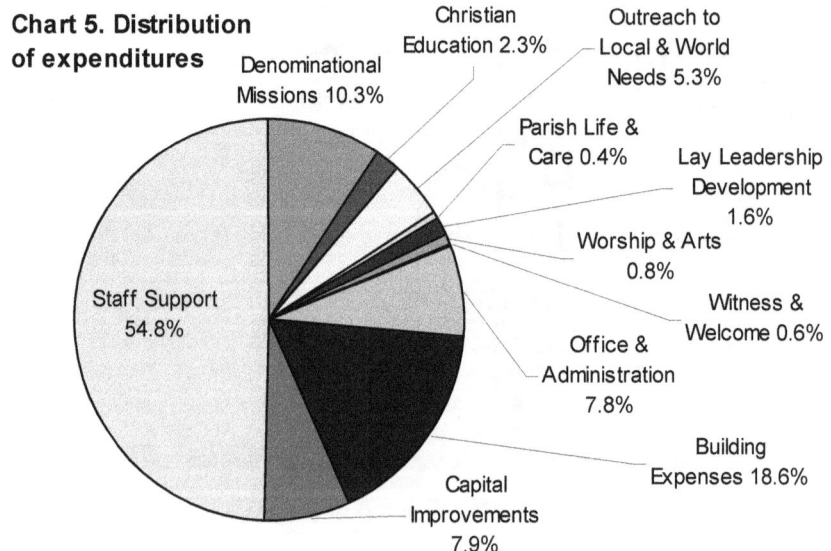

are estimated in hours per week multiplied by a nominal "wage" rate. Reporting such volunteer services provides a "total picture," placing each component in appropriate full perspective. And, this complete scenario is essential in determining and evaluating church priorities. Only if the true total "cost" of each activity is known, can one more rigorously ask if the balance among all investments actually reflects intent or an accident of history.

Table 2a. Distribution of expenditures and contributed services by function

Function	Direct expenditures			Professional staff salaries			Contributed services			Total	
Parish life	$5,000	4%	2%	$14,600	12%	4%	$4,500	6%	1%	$24,100	7%
Worship	$5,000	4%	2%	$44,400	37%	14%	$8,900	12%	3%	$58,300	18%
Education	$7,500	6%	2%	$4,150	4%	1%	$17,200	23%	5%	$28,850	9%
Stewardship	$2,500	2%	1%	$3,550	3%	1%	$2,250	3%	1%	$8,300	3%
Evangelism/missions	$5,000	4%	2%	$1,300	1%	0%	$6,000	8%	2%	$12,300	4%
Youth	$7,500	6%	2%	$2,250	2%	1%	$7,500	10%	2%	$17,250	5%
Community service	$19,000	15%	6%	$2,600	2%	1%	$11,200	15%	3%	$32,800	10%
Council/other meetings	$1,000	1%	0%	$8,150	7%	3%	$5,000	7%	2%	$14,150	4%
Administration	$15,000	12%	5%	$37,600	31%	12%	$9,500	13%	3%	$62,100	19%
Building operations	$45,000	35%	14%	$1,400	1%	0%	$2,250	3%	1%	$48,650	15%
Capital	$17,500	13%	5%				$500	1%	0%	$18,000	6%
Total	$130,000	100%	40%	$120,000	100%	37%	$74,800	100%	23%	$324,800	100%

Professional staff salaries ($120,000) equal 48% of a total $250,000 church budget.

Table 2b. Attributed distribution of professional staff salaries by function

Functional area	Pastor		Organist/Choir		Administrator		Total	
	Amt	%	Amt	%	Amt	%	Amt	%
Parish life, visitations, counseling	$13,200	22%			$1,400	4%	$14,600	12.2%
Worship service & preparation	$19,800	33%	$22,500	90%	$2,100	6%	$44,400	37.0%
Education	$2,400	4%			$1,750	5%	$4,150	3.5%
Stewardship	$1,800	3%			$1,750	5%	$3,550	3.0%
Evangelism/missions	$600	1%			$700	2%	$1,300	1.1%
Youth	$1,200	2%			$1,050	3%	$2,250	1.9%
Community service	$1,200	2%			$1,400	4%	$2,600	2.2%
Council & other meetings	$4,800	8%	$1,250	5%	$2,100	6%	$8,150	6.8%
Administration & staff meetings	$15,000	25%	$1,250	5%	$21,350	61%	$37,600	31.3%
Building operations					$1,400	4%	$1,400	1.2%
Capital								
	$60,000	100%	$25,000	100%	$35,000	100%	$120,000	100.0%

Special Fund-Raising Campaigns

Capital and other large fund-raising campaigns are infrequent exceptional ventures requiring a high degree of visibility and extraordinary effort. They invariably are specially focused, long-term efforts, quite distinct from annual giving. Under these circumstances the following special fund-raising tactics are generally required:

1. Create a special campaign task force of experts and enthusiasts as a largely independent operation. Make sure this effort is distinct and separate from normal contributions. Other special appeals may need to be curtailed, even eliminated.

2. Get everyone involved. The more parishioners employed, the more members feel they are a real part of the effort and contribute accordingly.

3. Deliberate carefully on the need for hiring consultants. See advice in the next section.

4. Think big. Grand schemes are attractive and challenging. They give people a sense of real accomplishment. A campaign for a major project may in fact last a number of years.

5. Ensure that the congregation has a clear concept of the purposes of funding and the financial goals sought. Members need to thoroughly understand and approve any proposal to gain their support. The plan should be explained in a handout to include a project description, justification of costs, and estimated requirements from each family by income level. This information helps members establish the value and reality of the project and consequently the importance of their participation. Updating the most recent construction or other developments keeps members interested and involved, and creates a sense of accomplishment.

6. Every member face-to-face visitations are essential to explain and encourage. These sincere, personal and private, conversations are the genius of fund-raising. Participants need to be comfortable in their surroundings to be conversant and open minded.

7. Members want to hear the pitch from other members, not outsiders. Solicitors should be trained and matched to contacts in terms of age and income to be able to "speak the same language." Contact persons need to be individuals of the highest credibility, integrity, and heartfelt commitment to the church.

8. Expect a majority of the funding to come from a relatively small percent of the congregation. Consequently, it is critical to identify this potential and ensure appropriate encouragement. From those able, we ask much.

9. For large projects with municipal appeal, the community-at-large should be targeted.

10. Encouraging "planned giving" is particularly applicable when capital investments are involved. Congregants like to think their gift will remain in perpetuity. (See following "Special Means" section).

Hiring Fund-Raising Consultants.

Hiring outside consultants and fundraisers should be undertaken only in the most extraordinary circumstances, viz., when the skills of a professional are clearly called for. Consultants provide expert advice, keep you on track, and see the job through. And, despite the many reservations listed below, consultants do know the business and can generally be relied upon to help the congregation realize its fund-raising objectives. Their fee is typically 9 to 10 percent of the funds raised. As an alternative, consultants may be hired for brief advisory stints at a fixed price. Review of plans may particularly warrant such attention.

In addition to the expense, out-sourcing makes the committee dependent rather than self-reliant. The need for consultants suggests a lack of faith and confidence in the skills and capabilities of the committee. And one should recognize there is no "magic formula" involved that isn't already in print somewhere. Fund raising is mostly hard work, and most, if not all, the "heavy lifting" must still be performed by the congregation regardless of the presence of a consultant. A studious dedicated stewardship committee is fully capable of much the same potential, together with permanently strengthening in-house capabilities. Plus members want to hear the pitch from other members, not outsiders. Leadership by members engenders trust, pride, and support within the congregation.

Special Means[30]

Churches that fail to give attention to planned giving from assets or estate are missing a vital and dramatically growing source of income. Gifts from one's accumulated wealth are usually outside the regular offering and designated for purposes other than day-to-day needs of the church. They often result in some tangible permanent improvement for which the donor has a special affinity. Major gifts are intentional acts of faith and trust on the part of the giver. Donors must be confident in the utility, management, and permanency of the use. The church must provide this vision.

Planned giving takes many forms. Gifts may be given during one's lifetime or upon death. Assets simply "sitting around" may be donated and sold at a church rummage sale. Assets, on which the individual is dependent, such as stocks, bonds, real estate, life insurance policies, or personal property, may be recorded with the church as a co-owner, to receive the proceeds only when the person dies. Inclusion of the church invariably requires documentation in the donor's will, living trust, pension plan, or life insurance policy.

Memorial gifts at the time of a person's death, and gifts honoring a living individual are a special response in recognition of the life of a loved one or respected member. It is important for the church to respond with prompt and appropriate recommendations on fund use. Donors always should be informed exactly how the money will be used.

---

[1] Donald W. Joiner, *Creating a Climate for Giving* (Nashville, Disciple Resources, 1989), p. 66.

[2] Ibid. p. 65.

[3] Ched Myers, *The Biblical Vision of Sabbath Economics* (Washington, DC, The Church of the Savior, 2001), p. 32.

⁴ Ibid. p. 53.

⁵ Paraphrase of George Barna's "At the great fund-raising churches in America, stewardship is a perpetual theme, not a special campaign." *How to Increase Giving in Your Church* (Ventura, CA, Regal Books, 1997), p. 107.

⁶ Maintenance of a stewardship library and study by committee members is highly recommended. For starters, consider this sampling of available resources: Barbara DeGrote-Sorenson and David Allen Sorenson, *Six Weeks to a Simpler Lifestyle* and *Tis a Gift to Be Simple: Embracing the Freedom of Living with Less.* Eugene Grimm, *Generous People: How to Encourage Vital Stewardship.* Donald W. Joiner, *Creating a Climate for Giving.* John Reumann, *Stewardship and the Economy of God.*

⁷ George Odiorne, *Management and the Activity Trap.* Cited in Thomas Heyd, *Planning for Stewardship: Developing a Giving Program for Congregations* (Minneapolis, Augsburg Publishing House, 1980), p. 13.

⁸ A member record system, typically based on computer software, is intended to assist in identifying current and past participation activities, interests, skills, and various vital statistics of value in encouraging stewardship and supporting other church programs. The system should be capable of:
  (1) Transferring information between data bases.
  (2) Sorting by text and numbers.
  (3) Creating custom queries and having an unlimited number of queries; the ability to query needs to be fairly sophisticated, i.e., more than three variables.
  (4) Performing math so the recorders can be relieved of some of their duties.
  (5) Creating customized reports.

⁹ Based in part on Dr. Eugene Grimm, *Generous People* (Nashville, Abingdon Press, 1992), and Donald W. Joiner, *Creating a Climate for Giving.*

¹⁰ Theodore Schneider, "Spirituality of money," *The Lutheran,* September, 2002, p. 86.

¹¹ To conduct marginal analysis, each committee is first charged with constructively shifting the least productive funds within its jurisdiction until no further improvement appears possible. Then the "rate of return" of these last expenditures for all programs is compared to see if any further shifts might be beneficial. For example, all the work of the evangelism committee may appear highly productive, warranting greater support, whereas the choir's plan for new robes may be considered extravagant in comparison.

¹² Colonial Hills Church cited in William Easum, *Dancing with Dinosaurs: Ministry in a Hostile & Hurting World* (Nashville, Abingdon Press, 1993), p. 75.

¹³ See footnote 8.

¹⁴ Dean R. Hoge, Charles Zech, Patrick McNamara, and Michael J. Donahue, *Religious Giving in Five Denominations* (Chicago, ELCA Dept. for Research and Evaluation, 1993).

¹⁵ Thomas Heyd, *Planning for Stewardship*, p. 13.

[16] Based in part on Patricia D. Brown, *Spirit Gifts* (Nashville, Abingdon Press, 1996), pp. 37-41.

[17] The reference to which this section is most indebted is Joiner, *Creating a Climate for Giving*. Joiner's book should be must reading for all those leading Christian stewardship programs.

[18] U.S. Census Bureau, *Statistical Abstract of the United States: 2004-2005* (Washington, D.C., U.S. Government Printing Office, 2004), Table 661, p. 440.

[19] Ibid, Table 563, p. 364.

[20] Myers, *The Biblical Vision*, p. 62.

[21] George Barna, *How to Increase Giving in Your Church* (Ventura, CA, Regal Books, 1997), p. 107.

[22] Joiner, *Creating a Climate for Giving,* pp. 46-47.

[23] In compiling this list, we are most indebted to Joiner, *Creating a Climate for Giving,* and Hoge, *Religious Giving in Five Denominations.*

[24] Paraphrase of Dean M. Hunneshagen, Sermon Series "Achieving Financial Freedom," Lord of Life Lutheran Church, Depew, New York, 2000, p. 6.

[25] Alan Durning, *How Much is Enough? The Consumer Society and the Fate of the Earth* (New York, W. W. Norton & Company, 1992).

[26] Myers, *The Biblical Vision*, p. 63.

[27] Illustrate how gifts are used. For example, $17 is spent each week to print the bulletins used by the more than 200 parishioners attending Sunday services. $1,200 is given each week to "Meals on Wheels" to feed the hungry in our area. One day's utility bill averages $50. Salaries account for $5,000 per week. The idea is to establish the reality of how gifts are productively used.

[28] Henry G. Brinton, "Faith and Numbers: In My House and God's House, It's Tough to Talk About Money," *Washington Post,* October 10, 1999.

[29] Hours of contributed services by function may be secured from members, weekly or monthly, on special cards available in the pews and placed in the collection plate.

[30] For details on planned giving and memorial and honor funds see Joiner, *Creating a Climate for Giving,* Chapters 7 and 8.

Chapter 20
Evangelism — Basics and the Inreaching Responsibility [1]

Then Jesus said to Simon, "Do not be afraid; from now on you will be catching people." (Luke 5::10)

"I tell you, there will be more joy in heaven over one sinner who repents than over ninety-nine respectable people who do not need to repent." (Luke 15:7)

"...with God all things are possible." (Matthew 19:26)

The Great Commission is not an option; it is an authoritative imperative at the very heart of Christian discipleship, to reach out and bear witness to all people with the "Good News." It is at once both the most important and difficult of all Christ's responsibilities, to go forth into an often disinterested, even hostile world to teach God's love for all. And the responsibility extends inward, often focusing initially on guiding wayward members back into the fold.

The Christian church has five elemental charges—worship, fellowship, discipleship (teaching), ministry (serving), and evangelism. The last is now also the least. No greater dichotomy exists within Christendom than between this basic requirement and our limited response. The evidence is daunting. For most churches, evangelism is of secondary importance, commonly limited to advertisements and occasional invitations. Even when top to bottom support exists, few members are willing to accept the challenge and rejection expected. Mission training is virtually non-existent. Even pastors typically report evangelism as their least preferred responsibility.

All this can, and of course must, dramatically change. Mission and outreach "...are invariable structures of the church, firmly embedded in the apostolic traditions of our Lord's final summons to his disciples."[2] We must be as concerned for all people "out there" as God is, recognizing their great value to the very least one. Jesus repeatedly emphasized searching for that which is lost—the strayed sheep, missing coin, and wayward son. These parables tell us the importance of the quest and the value and gladness in finding. Where else does the Bible speak of such heavenly joy? Imagine such elation over just one sinner who repents!

Thus nothing should be more exciting and rewarding than befriending and leading others to faith in Christ. When each person on this earth is as precious to us as each is to God, spreading the "Good News" comes naturally and joyfully. And no set prescription is required, no fixed mold for bringing people to Christ, just as no two spiritual seekers are exactly alike. The "magic formula," if one can be so described, is not in ourselves but in the Holy Spirit making all things possible. So strengthened, we embark with joy and confidence in the knowledge of God's continual presence and guidance, knowing that nothing we can ever do is more important than leading others to Christ. This is the great calling.

The Fertile Field

Today's church is plagued with declining membership, changing demographics and economics, and increased public secularism and denial.[3] People are "too busy," their harried, preoccupied lives taking them away from worship. A third of all Americans, in fact, do not belong to a church or a synagogue according to Gallup Polls. Of those who do belong, about 40 percent either seldom or never attend. Together, roughly 60 percent of our population is essentially unchurched, about 125 million adults age 20 and over, a staggering number from any perspective.

As might be expected, most of these so-called secular people are not without religion. They think of spiritual matters. Many typically say they believe in God or some form of higher power and often express a deep interest in or familiarity with religion. They are invariably concerned about lack of religion for their children. They need to answer their child's questions about good and evil, and life and death. Most believe they are good persons, and may even be sympathetic with what Christians are doing. But inevitably they feel that being part of a local church is not necessary. They tend not to accept the tenets of any one faith, giving them a sense of tolerance. And they seldom attend church. Surprising, though encouraging, more than half say they would probably or at least possibly attend a friend's church if asked. Most know, deep in their heart, they are missing something. A feeling of emptiness or need to "go home" exists. They miss a sense of belonging to something greater than themselves. The seed is present, it only needs cultivation.

To be complete, we must also understand that some conditions currently hindering evangelism exist *within* the church. Older members, for example, may speak enviously of the "good old days" when everyone knew each other and there was only a single traditional service. These and other "growing pains" are one of the costs of reaching out to others. Unattended growth risks loss of community, evident in declining connectedness or cohesion among members, less association with the locality, and fragmenting into special interest groups. Love and concern for the needs of others is the necessary accompaniment of all change including growth. Preserving community through the intimacy of small groups frequently provides the means for such personal caring (see Chapter 17, "Small Group Ministries").

But the greatest hindrance to growth lies within ourselves. Churches are invariably more concerned about balancing their budget than in having converts, more interested in the myriad of church activities than in saving souls. Members will demonstrate on a pressing social issue far more readily than they will talk with a stranger about salvation. Outside, a national population that predominately agrees that Christian faith is relevant to the way they live, waits to be drawn into a spiritual family. Yet despite this potential, the church too often fails to extend its hand.

The Commission

". . . your Father in heaven does not want any of these little ones to be lost." (Matthew 18:14)

. . . I give you this charge: Preach the Word; be prepared in season and out of season; correct, rebuke and encourage—with great patience and careful instruction. . . . endure hardship, do the work of an evangelist, discharge all the duties of your ministry. (2 Timothy 4:1-2, 5)

"The 'glad tidings' must be proclaimed to every individual of the human race." —Free Methodist Church, *Book of Discipline*

The greatest blessing a congregation can gain is when every member has a passion for evangelism. Do you know, do you understand, that you represent Jesus Christ our risen Lord? No admonition can be too strong in this regard. Whatever is necessary must be done to wean churches away from introspective self-support as the center of congregational attention. This refocusing is what Christ meant when he cautioned his disciples about pouring new wine into old wineskins. (Matthew 9:17) Today's church must be refashioned as a new wineskin, required to "learn a new language, understand new customs, and find new ways to make the timeless gospel relevant to our culture."[4]

The following ten rules underlie all mission service:

1. **Evangelism is the *primary* mission of the church, the responsibility of *every* believer.** "Evangelism is not the only business of the church, but it is the church's first business and what Jesus Christ made primary, his church dare not make secondary. Evangelism is not an elective. It is a divine imperative... To evangelize is the greatest work in the world." —Jesse M. Bader, *Evangelism in a Changing America*

To reach out to all people with the "Good News," to bear witness, to spread the Word, is tantamount to an absolute command. The key to engendering this spiritual "growth conscience" is a clergy and lay leadership so deeply committed to reaching out to others, that it becomes a way of life for the entire congregation.

Most Christians are content with doing good works, usually within the church confines. And these are honorable duties, but the highest calling is the selfless act of proclamation. We seek to introduce people to God, to transform lives by Jesus Christ. In the light of eternity this is all that counts, both in the church and in our lives. It must become a true vision, relentlessly pursued, energizing the congregation with all involved.

While evangelism is every believer's responsibility, those sufficiently bold should assume the task as a personal calling. They should aspire to gain that generosity of spirit and utter dependence on God manifest only in witnessing. If there is even a single such called individual in the congregation, the church is obligated to provide all necessary encouragement and support.

2. We must never forget that evangelism is a spiritual endeavor. The Holy Spirit will guide and empower each one in everything required; the Bible will be our right hand, prayer our left.

Not by might, nor by power, but by my spirit, says the Lord of hosts. (Zechariah 4:6)

When we set out to act on the Good News, something wonderful happens to us–the Holy Spirit enters and abides in us as it did the apostles, *...like the rush of a violent wind.* (Acts 2:2) The Spirit will enable us to see others not by our human standards but as God sees them. The Spirit will work in us and through us. *"For the Holy Spirit will teach you at that time what you should say."* (Luke 12:12) Without this wondrous gift all our endeavors will be in vain.

The Bible is our tool to tell God's story. It should be carried into the field by all evangelists, much as a pick or shovel is carried by a miner, tools of the trade. Key passages relevant to evangelism should be readily at hand. (See "The Message" section, Chapter 21, beginning on page 344.)

Others cannot come to know God through us until God has spoken to us and built us up through prayer. Prayer re-orients our mind and spirit to witness. We receive our "marching orders," our directions, through prayer. We gain the strength, courage, and determination required to go forward. We must also pray for opportunities to witness and for the people we visit.

3. All evangelism is built on the foundation that Christ and his presence resides in every human soul. All people are important to God and, without exception, worthy of our love and concern. This belief and our caring response underlie all. Heed the insightful guidance of Edward Bauman in this regard, abbreviated here.

> God blesses us all with the spirit of Christ. Deep within the souls of all mankind is a spiritual entity endowed by our Creator. A permanent seed, a living potential for goodness and love derived from our unbreakable bonds to Jesus Christ. Whatever the outward manifestations of our current existence–our race, sex, age, education, beliefs, allegiances, transgressions, no matter who or what we are–God, through his grace in creating us in His image, has given us an inner spirit of Jesus Christ.
>
> This common spirituality, no matter how buried and concealed, no matter how disclaimed, creates an unlimited potential for Christian growth. And this growth may be in other forms, other religious trappings. (Bauman then tells this arresting story.) A Christian in India was talking to an elderly man who was a Hindu and had been all his life. They were sharing their experiences in their various traditions and the Christian took a long time to talk about Jesus the Christ, to

explain what Jesus the Christ meant to him and when he was finished this old man who had been a Hindu all of his life said, "I have known him all my life, and now you have told me his name."

The evangelist knows that the foundation on which all his work must be built is the spirit of Christ within the soul of all mankind. The mission is to free and encourage the growth of this spirit in whatever direction for good God wills. In the extreme some atheists may simply become more tolerant of others. People of every faith and conviction will become better humans through interaction with sensitive Christians, for we know that God works for good in all who love him.[5]

It is well that pastors, lay leadership, and congregations truly agree on this cornerstone, for it is a life-defining truth, requiring great commitment, honored with ever greater rewards.

4. No program of evangelism will be successful unless the great value of a single human being is recognized. *"Aren't five sparrows sold for two pennies? Yet not a single one of them is forgotten by God. Even the hairs of your head have all been numbered. So do not be afraid; you are worth much more than many sparrows!"* (Luke 12:6-7)

We must affirm within ourselves, from the beginning, that God treasures the souls of all mankind, that each and every person is of inestimable value. Then we must convince those outside the circle of faith of this grace. This message, God's abiding universal love, is the central theme of all evangelism. It must be clear and compelling, unequivocal, for we dare not lose a single one because of our own temperate thinking. Special "seeker services" designed specifically to deliver this message should be a part of all church evangelism programs. (See Chapter 21, "A Responsive Congregation and Religious Service," page 350.) Do not be hesitant in this regard.

5. Clergy and church officers, in the "priesthood of all believers," must lead. No individual is more key to successful evangelism than an enthusiastic vigorously involved senior pastor. When the pastor goes ahead, church leaders will follow, and eventually the contagious nature of evangelism will spread to the whole congregation, no one wishing to be left behind in the great adventurous undertaking. "When this happens...*you'd better watch out!* A whole new era of activity and life change is going to explode. If you haven't experienced it before, you're about to feel the exhilaration of being part of a contagious church."[6]

Evangelism must then be at the heart of the pastor's role. In this the pastor must be lifted up by a supporting congregation. Pastors must be allotted enough time for its accomplishment. Attendance at meetings and sundry duties must be curtailed. Training and delegated authority make this possible. Pastors must trust and depend upon the laity if they are to attend to the principal church mission. Furthermore, they must be prepared to attend to their evangelical work at odd hours, on weekends and in the evenings when people are home. All must be designed to spread the "Good News."

Even more important than modeling the role of evangelist, pastors must lead their congregation to passionately care for the salvation of the world. The laity must be motivated and then equipped for the ministry. As with the apostles, they will come to believe that the great commission is their personal responsibility. And as they begin to go out in the name of Christ they gain new strength and vitality that becomes endemic to the whole congregation. We become empowered by the triune God.

6. **Evangelism is not for the faint hearted, but rather for those filled to overflowing with the fervor of the Holy Spirit, confident in God's promises and power.** Acceptance of the evangelism mission requires real leaders who understand what Christ expects of Christians. They are not deterred by challenges of indifference, criticism, or failure. Their task is really two-fold: first, to sell evangelism as the principal church calling, second, to go forth with the message. No job in the congregation is more difficult than developing this focus, yet this is God's wish for us. One way to begin is by creating a task force of church leaders to discuss the subject: "What would Christ want the first business of our church to be?"[7] With some prodding and encouragement they will likely acknowledge that it is to bring people to Christ.

The task is to actively *seek out* people, *proclaim* the "Good News" of the risen Lord, *witness* as personal evidence of belief and joy, and *instruct* in God's ways through his Holy Word. Try this on a street corner to see if courage and dedication are not involved. While most evangelism is not of this nature, no less confidence and resolution is required, especially those engaged in field work. But everyone commissioned in any role must be dedicated.

We conclude with a brief listing of the benefits accruing the evangelist and accompanying costs. Hybels and Mittelberg[8] cite these rewards: adventure and excitement, a new sense of life's purpose, self-fulfillment, spiritual growth, confidence, creating an enduring investment, and honor in being God's agent. The costs include: necessary reading and study, risk of rejection and embarrassment, and adding to life's complications. All-in-all, a far greater balance favors the life of being what the authors call a "contagious" Christian.

7. **The church must accept and prepare for its evangelism mission.**

"What is the congregation's role? It surely is the place where we gather to be nurtured in the faith. But unless it sees itself as a mission outpost, no congregation will—or probably should—survive for long."

—Herbert W. Chilstrom, Bishop of the Evangelical Lutheran Church in America.

Evangelism is the inescapable conclusion to answering who we are, what is our mission, who are our neighbors, what are their needs, and what is God calling us to do? Forthrightly answering these questions begins the evangelism process, the first step. Consistent with this recognition, the evangelism committee must be strengthened with the congregation's ablest committed members, acknowledging this function's central importance.

The second step is that of securing a bona fide commitment to evangelism, initially by the church council, then the congregation as a whole. However modest the authorization, every member should recognize that a seed has been planted that with proper nourishment will grow to be a transforming encompassing mission. Eventually, all will understand that evangelism *adds* to our church programs, not subtracts. No one should feel threatened, for the special programs, even services required, will be designed to complement not compete with existing offerings.

The third step is Bible study and training, typically beginning with the Acts of the Apostles. We must know "why" as well as "how" in order to excel. The instruction must be rigorous, designed and taught by people who know the task and problems of evangelism from first-hand experience. New trainees often then accompany an experienced visitor as part of their final preparation. Note that as many as express interest in such instruction should be encouraged to attend, even though they may eventually forego accepting field work. The aim is to plant the seeds of evangelism in the minds and hearts of *every* congregational member so that outreach becomes an integral part of the total church fabric.

The fourth step identifies various target audiences and the most effective strategies and means of contact.

The last, fifth step, is that of preparing services and the congregation for visitors. Recognize that, for seekers, becoming a Christian is a learning and acclimation process. The church service must consequently emphasize instruction and friendship. The approach must demonstrate that we understand what they are going through, seeking in every instance to ease and support their spiritual journey.

8. Strive to simultaneously employ the three basic means of member-conducted evangelism—personal example, invitation, and going forth.

"By our actions you should know us." Evangelism starts when people see who we are, uplifting examples of the Christian life, loving, ethical, compassionate, and giving. We demonstrate a quality of life that the unchurched seek for their own. And they start asking questions. This effect is what we should all strive for. I'm reminded of the story told by a young Chinese women referring to her conversion to Christianity in Taiwan. She said she witnessed a priest give up his seat on a crowded bus to an old Chinese lady, an unheard of courtesy at that time. She wondered what kind of person would do such a kindness, and that was the beginning. Of such small acts, great transformations grow.

The second stage of evangelism is bound in our compassion for others, our concern for their eternal destinies, which mandates that we share our life-giving faith. We extend invitations to all. "Come with me to church next Sunday."

The third advanced and fundamental element of evangelism is that of going forth, initially indirectly through various media, then, secondly and primarily, through the more important yet difficult personal contacts. We address this outreach mission in the next chapter.

9. Congregations should endeavor to make their church as retentively attractive as possible. Since guests may visit only once,[9] the first impression should be as positive as possible, especially in terms of substantive, compelling preaching; uplifting music; various service and education offerings; faith-affirming activities for children; and enthusiastic, out-reaching members. As important, the highly visible centrality of the pastor makes his persona and inner spirit a major reason why people join a church.

The strongest single force pulling young families back to worship is typically their sense of responsibility for their children. They may want them to be baptized "just in case," or they may by anxious about doing the "right thing." Often they return to pass on the traditions they themselves knew as children. Whatever the reason, young returning parents will keep coming only if they know that the church really cares about them and loves their children.

For themselves, unchurched adults are mostly interested in how they can make their life work, how to be happy and content, not how to be saved. They need to be shown that God really cares about them and that through him they will feel better about themselves and their lives. This is the great comfort and confidence engendered by faith. In the short order of a Sunday visit, this impelling ethos is difficult to initiate. But member convictions, kindness, and availability, are the introduction. More details are presented in the next division, "The Embracing Congregation," beginning on page 323.

10. While attending to all, evangelism efforts should respond to the unique potential and opportunity present in the immediate community and in younger members. A growing church is one that innovatively responds to changing local demographics, appealing to the ethnicity and life styles of the neighborhood. This is especially true for urban churches that must be 're-programmed" to meet the needs of single adults living in apartments around the church. The church must be contemporary in attitude while remaining sound theologically.

A second appropriate focus is on the younger generation as a formative opportunity and our future strength. This means that we must learn everything possible about the target audience and develop appropriate responsive campaigns. Also, parents recognize they are responsible for their children's life and soul. Having children is consequently the strongest single force pulling young parents back to worship. We have the opportunity to raise up a new generation in Christ.

The Evangelism Committee

Of all the church committees, the Evangelism Committee is more a *team* than committee in the sense of personal commitment and involvement. To be successful, the team must be filled with enthusiasm for evangelism and likely already involved in welcoming and inviting people to church. To know the many requirements and subtleties involved, committee members must be on the firing line, in the field with their sleeves rolled up. And when in high gear, the committee serves as the conscience of the congregation, helping to activate the spiritual drive necessary for all to reach out.

A detailed committee job description is provided in Appendix B. A full commitment to evangelism affects every aspect of church life explained in subsequent sections of this and the next chapter. The mission can be divided into two fields of operation—*inreach*, welcoming visitors, and sustaining and strengthening new and marginal members (Chapter 20); and *outreach*, extending the Gospel beyond the church walls (Chapter 21). Both fields are fertile and members are called to each.

Important at this juncture are the distinctive core outreach responsibilities of the committee for they are at the heart of evangelism: (1) identification of candidate evangelists, (2) training, (3) sending forth, and (4) assessment. Select first the boldest possible members of the congregation as candidate evangelists. Discuss with them at length the importance and difficulty of the task. Ask them to attend the training session (4-6 weeks) without further commitment. Graduates should be assigned responsibilities based on their interests and boldness ranging from assisting in flyer design to knocking on doors. Placement must be done carefully to avoid casting anyone in too deep water. Lastly, every effort should be rigorously critiqued for "lessons learned." Remember, the Holy Spirit is heavily involved and will be providing plenty of "instructions."

The inreach evangelism program may well begin by reminding church leaders that, as representatives of the congregation, their constituency extends to visitors who find the church wanting and never return and members who simply stop attending. Inreaching this potential is often one of the most productive yet neglected responsibilities.

Lastly, the evangelism committee needs a good library. Two starter recommendations are listed in footnote 1 of this chapter, with additional volumes cited in the first footnote of Chapter 21. Enough copies should be available for use in recruit training

The Inreach Responsibility

Evangelism begins at home with visitors and wayward members. Before anyone doubts this admonishment, check your church rolls. What percent of visitors actually join? What percent of the membership seldom or infrequently attends worship? Visitors and delinquent members are the evangelism committee's first responsibility, a basic foundation for later outreaching into the world. In the immediate following section, attention is primarily focused on attracting and holding visitors. Then attention is focused on nurturing new members (page 327), and finally on responding to inactive members (page 328).

The Embracing Congregation

Four "commodities" are repeatedly emphasized as essential for attracting and retaining seekers and visitors: attentive religious education for children and support for family life; personal support and reassurance; a sense of community; and inspiration and spiritual guidance. Inherent accompanying components are a powerful personal ministry by the pastor and a congregation living out its faith. The evangelistic outreaching community recognizes and strives to strengthen these assets, the self-centered church is typically content instead with what current members appear to prefer and won't change.

Evangelism must start with a solid congregational base, members involved in worship, attending Sunday school, and sharing in Christian fellowship. On this foundation an outreaching climate can be built in which individuals, one-by-one, become eager to receive others. Such embracing eventually becomes so bold that even the consequential loss of a few disgruntled members is not offsetting. Adaptability becomes the watchword. As Saint Paul admonishes, *So I become all things to all men, that I may save some of them by any means possible.* (1 Corinthians 9:22)

In the following sections we advance numerous inreaching actions. Each is identified by a solid circle symbol (●) All will not be equally suitable for every congregation. However, if even a few members value a recommendation, the possibility should be openly explored.

An Inviting, Responsive Reception

Worship is the primary point of entry for most people, and Sunday morning is the most opportune time. First impressions seem to color a visitor's whole experience, so they are important.

● First off, beginning with the welcome at the door, every effort should be made to identify visitors while avoiding any possible embarrassment to them. When members wear nametags the problem is solved.[10] Otherwise, the initial greeter should ask possible strangers if they are, in fact, visitors and then pass this information on to the pastor and coffee-time hosts.

● The friendliness of greeters, ushers, and worship leaders is vital for it reflects the attitude of the whole congregation. Guests must feel truly welcome and comfortable. At our best, they should feel truly wanted and appreciated. (For a broader discussion of the nature of this Christian community see Chapter 16, "Parish Life.")

- Provide "Visitor's Information" flyers in the pew rack. This take-home pamphlet can present a host of introductory information to visitors and solicit their possible response. Typically included are a brief welcome message, schedule of Sunday worship services, pastors' names and phone numbers, Sunday school class listing, and a tear-off or separate card of requested personal information such as name, address, and phone number, and, of lesser initial importance, age bracket, marital status, spiritual journey status, request for information, etc. Announcement of the "Information Talks" is also appropriate (page 326). Providing much more material to visitors may be intimidating; besides, most first-time guests are likely to prefer more personal attention through conversation with the pastor or members.

- Have "Friendship" cards in each pew rack, or pass a "sign-in" pad, which gives visitors the opportunity, if they wish, to identify themselves (plus address and phone number) and their possible interest in joining or securing additional information. This record must be acted upon promptly.

- Following the service, a personal greeting by the pastor conveying his or her heartfelt joy at the visitor's presence is essential. (The pastor, as a person, always makes a serious impression on visitors.) Guests should then be personally invited and accompanied to the coffee-fellowship gathering. During coffee time, other members should introduce themselves and engage in welcoming conversation. At the same time, discretion should be employed so that visitors are not overly singled out, embarrassed, or feel pressured.

- An excellent nursery in which young parents are confident is absolutely essential.

- Mechanics helpful to visitors include designated parking spaces, room signs, and a church map.

A Compelling Service

Most regular Sunday services can readily be converted to "user-friendly" offerings. Members are as likely to find the changes as attractive as visitors for they have universal appeal. An inspired congregation will find the means necessary. And the adoption need not be precipitous, but allowed to occur over time, as, for example, an "early" service is gradually transformed into one for "seekers."

Recognize, of course, that opening our doors to everyone does not require providing a worship style that appeals to everyone. Hospitality remains grounded in a distinctively Christian tradition that all will not find attractive. Furthermore, while the message of Christ's saving grace may be delivered in different styles, it may not be diluted or altered. After all, it is God's house in which we entertain. Reverence is required; a sense of awe and respect must always be present

Yet, in fact, walking into most churches can be scary for many newcomers—strange symbols, little understood rituals, unfamiliar music, and seemingly distant members. We need to lower the barriers that keep people from coming to church and substitute inspiration and encouragement. This requires creating an intimate environment in which the Holy Spirit's presence becomes known. We must touch people's heart so that they feel connected to God, to know that he is there to help them if they but ask.

In addition to the brief listing below, see Chapter 14, "New Needs, New Responses" for a complete presentation of contemporary service designs.

- The outreaching service exhibits these characteristics:

—Common expressions of love and joy replace the traditional liturgy.

—All congregational responses are completely written in the bulletin to avoid the exasperation and embarrassment for newcomers of trying to find their way through a hymnal.

—Music that lifts the heart. For younger newcomers this means replacing "hymns" with "songs," and use of modern arrangements instead of classical compositions. The newness of such contemporary music often means it is in sheet form, requiring projecting the lyrics on a screen.

- Print as much of the service as possible in the Sunday service bulletin, certainly the public prayers and responses. This courtesy is very comforting to visitors unfamiliar with worship liturgy and procedures.

- An outreaching service generally should be shorter in duration and have a good flow and tempo. Music should be carefully selected, upbeat, and possibly louder and faster paced. Actually some people may initially come just for the music which is okay as long as it gets them in the door.

Dynamic Preaching

The introductory and instructional nature of seeker-services is no more evident than in the spoken word. Willow Creek Community Church even titles its outreach services "Christianity 101." In addition to the listing below, see Chapter 15, "The Spoken Word and Prayer."

- Beyond all matters of style, preaching to people thirsting for life's meaning must focus on Christian fundamentals. "It is our God-given duty to preach regularly and systematically about the basic and perennial themes—the Incarnation and the Atonement, (mankind's) exceeding sinfulness and God's exceeding grace, the life of faith and the life everlasting."[11]

- Address topical issues that help people sort out their lives. But make no mistake, there is no sell-out here. Comfort must not replace challenge. We are called to follow Christ, not use him.

"A good sermon finds people where they live, and helps them to move on to better living, by feeding the mind, warming the heart, stimulating the imagination, kindling high resolutions, strengthening the will, and reassuring the soul."[12]

- Preaching to seekers and the unchurched must be designed to provide an experience in Christ that will *change* the hearts and minds of those attending. It must have a persuasive intent. It must challenge people to get out of their "comfort zone" to a new level where God wants us to be. The pastor must speak from the heart to provide living testimony of God's presence. This is the time for exhortation. Preaching should attempt to "grab people by the ears."

- In matters of style, *earnestness* exceeds all. Purposeful, sincere intent and substantive content is the most persuasive package possible. "We are not won by arguments that we can analyze but by tone and temper, by the manner which is the man himself." —Samuel Butler (1835-1902), English author.

- From a mechanical standpoint the sermon should be relatively short with a clear, sharp focus; the content easily understood by anyone coming to worship for the first time; the style down-to-earth, conversational, not "preaching."

Follow-up Ministry for Visitors

There are many means whereby a congregation can express its appreciation of a visitor's attendance and encourage possible repeat visits. Above all, responses must be sincere and personal, for we are all children of God deserving the utmost respect and love.

- Of greatest importance is the immediate (within three days) personal telephone contact, thanking visitors for sharing in the worship experience and encouraging them in future visits if possible. Always be sincere, repeat the person's name you are speaking to, and listen attentively. In some instances a brief home courtesy call is substituted. A handwritten "thank you for visiting us" letter signed by a member is a very nice additional response.[13] Second time visitors are subsequently contacted by a pastor. For those congregations really into evangelism, the pastor makes many first-time telephone contacts.

However constructed, the important action here is to show visitors they are recognized as such, welcomed, appreciated, and encouraged to return. All such follow-up is, of course, dependent on securing guest names and contact information on the passed register or "Friendship" card (page 324).

- Visitors who show interest should be encouraged to consider attending a series of "Information Talks" by the pastor as a means of introducing them to the fundamentals of the Christian faith. The course series typically covers how a person can come to know God, how to use and understand the Bible, what are the sacraments, church history, and the nature of worship. This is real classroom instruction from which participants will emerged filled with knowledge and the Holy Spirit! E. Dale Click originated the "Information Talks" concept and his subject outline and constructive advice should be sought.[14]

- The church must not restrict its potential membership to people attracted to its existing programs, but rather continually attempt to ascertain why non-returning visitors were not secured and what changes would promote their interest.

The Sustaining Inreach Responsibility

Creating an embracing congregation that provides caring attention to visitors is the underlying building block of all inreaching evangelistic efforts, the necessary foundation. The second and third components are nurturing new members in the faith, and retrieving those long-standing members fallen by the wayside. These subsequent responsibilities are where the going gets rough, where true evangelism begins and most congregations begin to falter.

Nurturing New Members

While evangelism reaches out to people, it must also see that once received, new members become actively involved. They must never be left to fend for themselves. Each must be made to feel as precious in our sight as they are in God's. Building authentic friendships, showing that we really care, is at the heart of the human side of evangelism. New members should feel appreciated as such. Perhaps specially colored name tags would provide them the necessary identification. Obviously, they are not just another long-term member.

- The first ninety days of a new member's church life is critical to long-term involvement and well-being. Assigning sponsors assures provision of the necessary support and guidance required during this assimilation period. And what a rewarding task it is. Sponsors seek to fully integrate new members into the church community by occasionally accompanying them to worship, introducing them to others, possibly escorting them to various Sunday school classes, and, in general, keeping them informed and in contact. This shepherding may last up to a half-year, gradually tapering off.

The task is much like watering and caring for a new seed. This means the sponsor must, to a degree, track the worship and participation habits of those to whom he or she is assigned; cultivating each individual's personal growth in whatever form it becomes manifest.

- Every new member, as with all congregants, must be strongly encouraged, yes expected, to belong to a small group. This is the best possible means to experience and nurture fellowship and support. (See Chapter 17, "Small Group Ministries.") Small or other group membership, such as a Sunday school class, is essential to developing a sense of belonging. They "create the climate and nurture the trust in which a deep giving of ourselves can happen."[15]

- Provide a range of short-term, e.g., six weeks, adult education courses specifically designed to orient new members. The McLean Bible Church of McLean, Virginia, for example, conducts four sequential introductory courses titled: "Knowing God in a Personal Way," "Growing in Your Relationship with Jesus Christ," "Learning How to Share Your Faith," and "Discovering Your Spiritual Gifts."

- New members should be promptly recruited for short-term assignments. Start by making an inventory of their time and talents. This also makes each feel known and needed. And most newcomers expect their membership will, in fact, involve certain participation requirements.

Provide latitude in serving opportunities. Create a "permission-giving" church, one that encourages ministry of any kind to occur anywhere, anytime, by any person. Don't let individual talents and initiative be shackled by organizational structure, restrictive mission statements, or job descriptions. Let the Holy Spirit work in people by a welcoming supportive attitude.

Commitment pledges, previously discussed in Chapter 19, page 296, may be well used in documenting new member participation, however initially modest. The pledge is evidence of the great value the congregation places on their discipleship, as well the fact that Christianity does not come without a price. Think of such pledges as part of getting newcomers "settled" in their new church home.

- Lastly, much can be learned from new members, their first impressions being critical to the success of any evangelism program. To this end they should be surveyed, asking such questions as: What attracted you most to the congregation? What were your immediate concerns? Have you made good church friends? If you didn't join a small group, why not? How effective was the orientation training? What is the church's greatest strength, greatest weakness?

Ministry for Inconsistent and Inactive Members

The major inreach challenge for any congregation is that of tending to its marginal and absent members. Yet once "on the rolls" marginal members are too often simply ignored because, after all, "it's their responsibility now." But when apathy sets in, a real awakening jolt is necessary. The other reasons commonly listed for inactivity[16]—self-sufficiency without church, sense of not belonging, problems with the worship service, change in life style, and, surprisingly, insufficient guidance and expectations—are equally daunting. The recovery task consequently requires mustering exceptional zeal and enthusiasm, every bit as substantial as that necessary in field work. Evangelism always begins at home, striving to retrieve wayward souls.

And let us not succumb in the retrieval process to any air of superiority. Norman Shawchuck (with others) describes what he labels a "fully responsive" congregation as one that overcomes any sense of the "we-they" mentality by "accepting all who it serves as equals with its members."[17] We must always be principally *enablers* of each other.

- Church attendance should be recorded. How else are we to determine with any precision when members start missing Sunday services? When a person or family misses four Sundays in a row or attends on average no more than once a month, a call, particularly from a church friend, is likely warranted. "We've missed you." "How have you been?" "Can we be of any help?" If the subject family or individual is a member of one of the church's small groups, their absence will also be readily noted, prompting contact.

---

[1] This chapter is highly dependent on the works of many others, most notably, E. Dale Click, *Evangelism: The First Business of the Church* (Lima, Ohio, CSS Publishing, 1994), 282 pp.; and Dan Kimball, *The Emerging Church: Vintage Christianity for a New Generation* (Grand Rapids, MI, Zondevan, 2003), 266 pp. These two general treatises are essential to any evangelism library. Many other valuable references are, of course, available and a list of references in the field (for example, Click above, pp. 280-282) should be consulted.

[2] Carl E. Braaten, *The Apostolic Imperative* (Minneapolis, Augsburg, 1985), p. 61.

[3] Among the many survey findings on religious beliefs, these misconceptions stand out: While religion is important to most, "belonging to a local church is not a necessity." "Every person has the power to determine his or her own destiny in life." Christians, Jews, Muslims and Buddhists all "pray to the same God," although called by different names. "There is no such thing as absolute truth." The "purpose of life is enjoyment and personal fulfillment." "When it comes right down to it, your first responsibility is to yourself." George Barna, *What Americans Believe* (Ventura, CA, Regal Books, 1991).

[4] William Easum, *Dancing with Dinosaurs: Ministry in a Hostile and Hurting World* (Nashville, Abingdon Press, 1993), p. 13

[5] Largely adopted from a December 16, 2001 Sunday school lesson by Dr. Edward W. Bauman, Ecumenical Associate, St. Paul's Episcopal Church, Rock Creek Parish, Washington, DC.

[6] Bill Hybels and Mark Mittelberg, *Becoming a Contagious Christian* (Grand Rapids, MI, Zondevan, 1994), p. 205.

[7] From a more extensive discussion of starting evangelism programs by Click, *Evangelism*, pp. 106-110.

[8] Abstracted from Hybels and Mittelberg, *Becoming a Contagious Church*, pp. 26-38.

[9] People tend to "try out" churches, and denomination is often unimportant.

[10] There is much ado about nothing concerning nametags. Many members unnecessarily fret about the inconvenience involved. In reality, they are an indication of hospitality. Show me a church where nametags aren't worn and I'll show you a church whose members don't sufficiently care for newcomers.

[11] Robert J. McCracken, *The Making of the Sermon*, (New York, Harper & Brothers, 1956), p. 17. Quoted in Click, *Evangelism: The First Business of the Church*, p. 66.

[12] Marshall Wingfield, *Central Seminary Bulletin*. Quoted in Click, *Evangelism: The First Business of the Church*, pp. 66-67.

[13] Incidentally, the follow-on letter may be an opportune time to attach a stamped self-addressed envelope asking visitors what they noticed first, liked best, and would improve about the worship service.

[14] Click, *Evangelism: The First Business of the Church*, Chapter 12, "The Information Talks for Visitors," pp. 156-175.

[15] Elizabeth O'Connor, *Servant Leaders, Servant Structures* (Washington, D.C., Potter's House Book Service, 1991), p. 90.

[16] Eric Jorstad, et al., *What Lutherans Can Learn About Outreach: Why People Join and Why They Leave a Congregation* (Minneapolis, Augsburg Publishing House, 1987), 45 pp.

[17] Norman Shawchuck, Phillip Kotler, Bruce Wrenn, and Gustave Ruth, *Marketing for Congregations: Choosing to Serve People More Effectively* (Nashville, Abingdon Press, 1992) p. 76.

Chapter 21
Evangelism — the Outreach Challenge[1]

"Go, then, to all peoples everywhere and make them my disciples; baptize them in the name of the Father, the Son, and the Holy Spirit, and teach them to obey everything I have commanded to you. And remember! I will be with you always, to the end of the age." (Matthew 28:19-20)

"Just so, I tell you, there will be more joy in heaven over one sinner who repents than over ninety-nine righteous persons who need no repentance." (Luke 15:7)

"You have nothing to do but to save souls. Therefore spend and be spent in this work. And go not only to those that need you, but to, those that need you most. It is not your business to preach so many times, and to take care of this or that society; but to save as many souls as you can; to bring as many sinners as you possibly can to repentance." —John Wesley

"We have the means of evangelizing our country; but they are slumbering in the pews of our churches." —John Stott (1921), influential clergyman in the Church of England.

People are so accustomed to "going to church" that they forget they *are* the church. They tend to be more concerned with personal salvation than with any outreaching effort. Such inward focus needs realignment, shifting attention from *programs* to *mission*, from *consumption* to *nourishing*. The imperatives of the Great Commission should be our own—an integral sense of responsibility for others, a pervasive commitment to go forth, and profound durable enthusiasm to deliver the "Good News."

While 81 percent of Americans identify a denomination of preference or affiliation, most simply won't go to church. Some don't have a clear understanding of Christianity and the church's role; others have been previously involved at some level, but have decided not to attend. The mission field, consequently, is immediately at hand, at our doorstep. Dan Kimball, reporting in *The Emerging Church*, talks of Lesslie Newbigin who went to India in 1936 as a missionary, laboring in the impoverished country for over thirty-five years. Upon returning to England at age sixty-five he was quite surprised to discover that the Christian nation he had left behind had now become a mission field itself, one "much harder than anything I met in India. The cold contempt for the Gospel is harder to face than opposition."[2] These conditions now exist here in the United States. To attend to those claiming to have already heard the Gospel and rejecting it, are trying conditions indeed.

Evangelists are not born. Through God's grace, rigorous training, and a certain inner strength and conviction, evangelists, like the disciples, are called and empowered. Fortunate indeed are the few, for theirs is the highest discipleship of all! *In the church then, God has put all in place: in the first place, apostles, in the second place, prophets,* (1 Corinthians 12:28) Apostle messengers must believe deep within themselves that their life is altogether beautiful and complete because of their belief, and that others coming to know God will feel the same. And they must come to believe that spreading the Gospel is his or her indisputable calling, which is the single most important service they can provide.

The Calling

"There is a large harvest, but few workers to gather it in. Pray to the owner of the harvest that he will send out workers to gather in his harvest." (Matthew 9:37-38)

Be ready at all times to answer anyone who asks you to explain the hope you have in you. But do it with gentleness and respect. (1 Peter 3:15-16)

We are compelled by the Holy Spirit to hasten forth with the Good News, to run like Philip to the carriage of the Ethiopian official, to hurry like Mary to tell the disciples of the empty tomb, and to run out like the Father to meet his prodigal son. Evangelism is a mission at full speed, full of enthusiasm and vigor. Our hearts must burn, ablaze with the good news of the gospel!

A Hostile Environment

"Listen! I am sending you just like sheep to a pack of wolves."
(Matthew 10:16)

The first impression of Christianity is good. We are, after all, a professing Christian nation. Eighty-one percent of surveyed[3] Americans describe themselves as Christians, albeit often in the most marginal manner. The underlying problem is not belief; it is the harried distracted life style of most Americans which prevents real commitment. Hostility toward evangelism is thus not so likely to be opposed to the message itself as against the perceived interfering messenger. We are just too busy!

When we turn to the congregation side, we find similar thwarting distractions. The needs and preferences of members always seem more immediate and pressing than those of distant strangers. Congregations are also handicapped by the general reluctance of most members to "interfere" in the lives of others. They will normally talk and demonstrate on pressing political and social issues long before venturing forth to discuss with strangers eternal life. Most are satisfied, even complacent, with doing good works. Congregations must be led to the greater crusade.

Recipient Barriers

When it comes to the target group, those non-professing or non-attending persons, five major obstacles to their retrieval are commonly encountered.

Self-reliance. The first hurdle is their self-orientation and temporal outlook, at the extreme, a view of life as a quick effort to obtain all the personal fulfillment and pleasure possible during a short earthly existence. This ego-oriented self-reliance is in sharp contrast with the biblical vision of serving others and the ultimate purposes of God. And we know that true joy and peace and all good things come to those who love and serve God. The difficulty comes in convincing others of this fundamental truth, the fact that their lives will be more abundant, joyful, fulfilling, and yes, adventuresome as disciples. Our absolute assurance of this is often the first inkling people gain that we speak of something obtainable that is far greater than their present life.

Negative attitude. Many Americans have a negative attitude regarding the church and especially street "salesmen." They may believe that Christians are dogmatic, shallow thinkers, even arrogant in believing that only they have the true answers. Closed-minded and judgmental are common assessments; Christians are always ready to point out how others are wrong and they are right. Overcoming these stereotype images, for they are typically more hearsay than experienced, is best accomplished by opposing, exemplary behavior. The evangelist must live the life of Christ!

Misconceptions. People have so many wrong ideas about God, but the most destructive in turning people away is the false impression that he is detached, cold, and harshly critical, the very opposite of our loving, forgiving heavenly Father. No one can be led to a threatening cynical God. We must know God's love so that we can convey it to others as our deepest strength and comfort.

Fear of the unknown. People are naturally hesitant to talk to strangers, especially those "selling" anything, afraid of getting involved or worse "suckered-into" something. People feel that in most such encounters they are likely to lose more than they will gain. We've got to convince our contacts immediately that we offer only hope and an abundant life, without charge except to love God.

Intellectual roadblocks. So many people *reason* their way out of believing that such response should be expected. Not that they are absolutely convinced, rather that logical counter-arguments are a comfortable, apparently sound excuse for not getting involved. Such opposition must be taken very seriously, making every effort to provide a worthy response. Dispelling counter-arguments are discussed in "The Message" section of this chapter, pages 344-348.

Messenger Barriers

In setting forth, most of us will have to contend with our own personal discomfort and understandably so. We are uneasy with the idea of sharing with others such a deeply personal belief as faith. We risk embarrassment, rejection, and even being seen as foolish or some sort of fanatic. Paul acknowledges our concerns when he writes of our faith as "a stumbling-block to Jews and foolishness to Gentiles." (1 Corinthians

1:23) Even our own clergy and congregations may not be supportive, typically consumed with worship, Bible study, and good works, the latter with its material evidence of success. Congregants consequently seldom suffer any real embarrassment, rejection, isolation, or seeming failure for their faith, all common to the evangelist.

Consequently we go out in faith *and* fear. Yes, fear of the unknown and our own weak hands. But God is with us, our very strength in time of trouble. Among his many admonitions, Dale Click advises us to know and teach that "evangelists cannot lose." "Whenever people go out in the name of Christ and under the influence of the Holy Spirit, something good is bound to happen."[4] How reassuring to know that we are setting God to work, not always immediately evident, but surely in terms of a planted seed! Evangelists must think of themselves as sowers, a comforting analogy.

So relax, messenger of Good News. God will guide you in what to say. *"...do not worry about what you are going to say or how you will say it; when the time comes, you will be given what you will say. For the words you speak will not be yours; they will come from the Spirit of your Father speaking in you."* (Matthew 10:19-20)

Is not this God's most important business? He will not let a single person fall because of what one of us, his disciples, might say or not say.

A Task of Many Demands

Whatever the level of involvement, evangelism is a demanding call. The mechanical aspects alone are daunting commitment of time for training, study, and field work; possibly difficult field conditions including even danger; and involvement with others often in less than cordial circumstances. And we add to this our personal anxieties which are sufficient deterrents for most.

People choose to do those things that give them pleasure and are rewarding. For most churchgoers, evangelism does not meet these criteria. The work is difficult, frequently awkward, unpredictable, and often apparently unproductive. Even pastors feel less positive about evangelizing, listing it near the top of least rewarding activities. So the greatest barrier to a successful evangelism program lies within ourselves. However, God's saving grace intervenes. Our utter dependency on him in this arduous work arms us far better than any self-reliance. *So stand ready: have truth for a belt tight around your waist; put on righteousness for your breastplate, and the readiness to announce the Good News of peace as shoes for your feet. At all times carry faith as a shield... And accept salvation for a helmet, and the word of God as the sword that the Spirit gives you.* (Ephesians 6:14-17)

Ultimately, we are looking for people in whom we can build the strengths required. Church members who invite others to worship, take an unpopular stand, help out in difficult tasks, people of dedication and courage who relish a challenge, all have evangelistic potential. Few of those receiving training are ever likely to possess the fortitude and stamina to actually go into the field, but many more will serve well in moderate supporting roles.

A great variety of personality types can be successful evangelists. There is no single mold. But the following virtues constitute underlying inner strengths that set the evangelist apart.

Authenticity. One must be a truly *authentic* person to be an effective evangelist, conforming in mind and spirit to everything one espouses. Total honesty conveys to others the truth of what we say. It engenders trust. Fabrication to any degree, on the other hand, breeds doubt and rejection, even contempt.

Evangelists, more than any other, must put *"the belt of truth around your waist."* (Ephesians 5:14) Only through total honesty will others see God in us and through us. And the most telling element of this reality is the admission of personal sin, seeking God's forgiveness by forthright confession. Bill Hybels describes this confession as "...a powerful witness to the transforming power of Christ in your life," and consequently in the lives of others[5].

Conviction. *Salvation is to be found through him alone; for there is no one else in all the world, whose name God has given to men, by whom we can be saved.* (Acts 4:12) To bring others to God we must believe in him with our whole heart, soul, and mind. We must believe with certainty that salvation is through Jesus Christ alone. Nothing less is acceptable. Nothing less can produce the compelling drive and fortitude required. Seekers are looking for someone like this, anyone willing to step forward, proclaiming the truth, not timidly or apologetically, but with conviction. Such conviction shows the power and reality of God working in and through us. Remember, Jesus said, *"Whoever remains in me, and I in him, will bear much fruit; for you can do nothing without me."* (John 15:5)

Confidence. Conviction leads to confidence, that inner strength to seek out people wherever and whoever they are without hesitation or fear. Evangelists must have heart-felt assurance that God is with them and they consequently cannot lose. Going out in the name of Christ, supported by the Holy Spirit, always results in something good, perhaps not immediate or tangible, but *always something good.* This faith has to instill confidence.

Sometimes it is best that two go out together, one with more experience, the other to learn. Actually it is *three* who will visit, for Jesus is always our companion on the road traveled. Christ leads the way and is always with you.

At its extreme, confidence nears obsession. The true evangelist has a burning heart, ablaze with the good news of the Gospel; full of zeal, enthusiasm, joy, ready to pump new life into people! We are part of a revolution, to transform the world into disciples.

Compassion. *Be ready at all times to answer anyone who asks you to explain the hope you have in you. But do it with gentleness and respect.* (1 Peter 3:15-16) Kindness cannot be ignored. It leaves an indelible impression that is rarely forgotten. It moves people to wonder why someone would go out of their way to help, to put another's interests before oneself.

Demonstrating Christ's love for all is a powerful magnet drawing people to question the nature and source of such thoughtfulness. The author recalls a story told by Christian missionaries of a young Chinese girl who witnessed a priest give up his seat on a crowded bus for an elderly Chinese lady, then an unheard of courtesy. The girl wondered what kind of man would do this kindness, which led to her seeking and eventually accepting Christ. Of such small incidents, great miracles occur.

Recruiting and Training

"There is a large harvest, but few workers to gather it in. Pray to the owner of the harvest that he will send out workers to gather in his harvest." (Matthew 9:37-38)

Be ready at all times to answer anyone who asks you to explain the hope you have in you. (1 Peter 3:15)

Of all Christian services, none requires more energetic recruitment and training than evangelism. But the commission never should have become either an elective or burden. Evangelism is a "divine imperative, delivered by God for the sake of lost people who matter deeply to Him."[6] We must look first to people with this understanding and appreciation, then those with interest or curiosity, and finally to individuals who like to get things done. Some spark is needed.

Besides personal contacts, candidates may be recruited through advertising. Quite frankly, anyone expressing interest in evangelism should be encouraged to attend training without obligation. All will benefit. Some may only briefly engage in a few personal contacts. A very few may commit to the discipline for life. The course must consequently be repeated over and over to discover who God is calling.

The evangelism curriculum describes the commission and authority involved, the associated importance and required commitment, and the breadth and techniques employed. A number of excellent references are available including, as starters, this chapter plus the texts listed in footnote 1. Bible scripture underlies all, notably these ten from many: Isaiah 52:7-12, Matthew 28:16-20, Luke 8:4-18, Acts 1:7-9, Romans 1:13-15, Romans 10:8-17, 1 Corinthians 9:19-20, 2 Corinthians 4:5-6, Colossians 1:25-29, and 2 Timothy 4:1-5.

Prepared by Prayer and Empowered by the Holy Spirit

"But you will be filled with power when the Holy Spirit comes on you, and you will be witness for me in Jerusalem, in all of Judea and Samaria, and to the ends of the earth." (Acts 1:8)

"We dare not speak to others before we speak to God. Others cannot come to know God through us until God has gone through us. That is what prayer does. It is a fundamental premise of evangelism."
—E. Dale Click[7]

Evangelists must start on their knees. We are obligated to seek God's directions before we attempt to lead others to him, specifically, in every instance, for every contact. Prayer provides the encouragement and inner composure assured by the Holy Spirit's presence and help in telling the Good News. Evangelists, above all other callings, must depend and draw upon Christ's strength for we speak with authority as his ambassadors. One dare not set forth without being armed with prayer.

Witnessing

"If he have faith, the believer cannot be restrained. He betrays himself. He breaks out. He confesses and teaches this gospel to the people at the risk of life itself." —Martin Luther (1483-1546), German leader of the Protestant Reformation.

The harvest is people everywhere, invariably good citizens but living secularized lives apart from the church, but reasonably content if not generally happy. The riches and attractions of this world are the chief enemies of evangelism.

The Available Means

So I become all things to all men, that I may save some of them by any means possible. (1 Corinthians 9:22) Saint Paul is willing, even anxious, to employ "any means possible" to bring Christ's message to "all men." So we also must be innovative, thinking creatively to devise and test different strategies, learning from our mistakes and successes until we come up with means that work for bringing people to the Lord.

The task is to go out into the secular world, to actively seek out and relate to people, and lead them to Christ. Seven courses of action are at our disposal, listed here in typical declining order of use and effectiveness within two divisions. Keep in mind that it is not the process itself that is the end product; it is forming new believers that Christ seeks through us.

Media printed and other means of mass promotions are generally of high quality, easily transmitted, and provide extensive coverage. The major disadvantage is that the public is so inundated with such bulk sales pitches that they often are automatically rejected. Only the very best designs are likely to be read or listened to. *Personal* contacts, in contrast, can be built on enduring friendships. Friends listen to and confide in each other, an open door for the Gospel. The basic disadvantage is the one-on-one "inefficiency" involved requiring many participants for all to be reached. We must be like "salt for all mankind," like "light for the whole world." (Matthew 5:13)

Media

(1) **Flyers** can dramatically present the Gospel message and effectively extend an invitation. They can be inexpensively distributed by mail to large selected target areas and handed out at subway entrances and other highly traveled locations. A single sheet flyer distributed by the author at Arlington, Virginia, Metro stops is illustrated on the following two pages. Announcing "the Good News!" the flyer was held out and taken by passersby at a rate of about 100 per hour.

(2) **Web site.** An inexpensive tool with considerable potential for attracting people looking for a church home. The first page must be specifically designed for welcoming purposes. See, for example, greatchurchwebsites.org for selected outstanding site designs.

(3) **Signs and banners on church property.** May have to be placed and removed each Sunday. Check local ordinances before erecting.

(4) **Radio and TV "spot announcements."** Thirty second "commercials" are prohibitively expensive for most churches.

Personal

(1) **Personal contacts by members** as part of day-to-day living should be the heart of every church's program of evangelism. At the most modest level, this means, when engaging people in conversation, discreetly inquiring about their possible church affiliation. If not attending, an opportunity to extend an invitation exists. Providing a church "calling card" with the location and time of worship will serve as a reminder. If the party seems interested, say you will meet them in the narthex so you can attend together.

Members should try inviting someone once a week. Even so, a very limited number of connections are likely unless an extremely robust effort is initiated and maintained. But the work can be very rewarding, members turning ordinary activities into spiritual ventures, experiencing the joy of being Christ's agents.

(2) **Indirect means.** A whole host of church sponsored yet non-religious activities and events may be held to bring interested members of the local community into fellowship and possible future Christian growth. Activities include sports, socials, music festivals, public service projects, short trips, Boy Scouts, gardening, photography, etc. The idea is for everyone to enjoy themselves leading to companionship and a sense of community and well-being. Then, gradually participants are engaged in conversation exploring and encouraging the Christian life. This mentoring, often by an older person, requires true caring, empathetic listening and sharing of experiences. All build trust. Young people especially want someone to really listen and hear them, to help them discover faith, and encourage them to see their own gifts and how to use them for others.

On Being a Christian

There are two paths to take. One leads eventually to despair and death. The other leads immediately to joy and hope.

"For a small reward, a man will hurry away on a long journey; while for eternal life, many will hardly take a single step." —Thomas a Kempis (1380-1471)

"Now Faith is the substance of things hoped for, the evidence of things not seen." —Hebrews 11:1

"Tell me, how is it with your soul?" —General William Booth to Cecil Rhodes (1898)

If you...
- are one of five who profess belief in God but seldom attend church,
- have just about everything—family, friends, wealth enough, and personal success—but still suspect there may be something missing,
- have a little fear that you might miss the boat if there is eternal life,
- feel broken and lost and need confidence and security,
- have a concern for others but don't really know where or how to begin,

this is the most important message you will ever receive.

God loves you with an abiding encompassing love that transcends all worldly needs, bringing peace and comfort to all who seek His grace.

"Come and see" Jesus' call to his first disciples —John 1:39

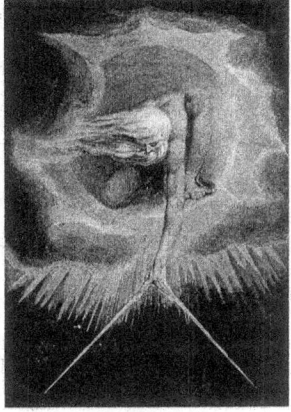

"The Ancient of Days"
—William Blake, 1794

Know from the beginning that God our heavenly father looks down and focuses all His attention on you and me. He has created us in His image, precious and of great value to Him. He loves us with an abiding encompassing love that transcends all worldly needs. He sees what's in our hearts and desires that we grow and flourish in His love. He wants us to know and love him. We need only open are hearts and minds to him seeking faith, and it will be granted. All we have to do is ask. Oh what joy and comfort are ours!

Come and see with us if this is true. You have nothing to lose other than a few minutes time, with the possibility of gaining true happiness and eternal life.

For just a minute, please close your eyes and say this little prayer. **Dear heavenly father I seek your help. Come into my heart so I may believe. Amen** Now admit, don't you feel better. Even if you have just read this without any intent on praying, the Holy Spirit of God has entered your heart bringing a sense of well-being. God is so powerful and desires you so much he cannot be stopped.

What does God promise you?

The Christian life is totally transforming and rewarding. Trusting in God bestows all that we could ever hope for...
+ comfort and peace of mind in the true meaning of life, and ultimately the reward of eternal life.
+ joy and a sense of well being in reaching out to others. There is no greater reward on earth than that derived from serving others.
+ discipline to live a spiritual life.

What will God ask of you? (Living the Christian Life)

The greatest gift of all—eternal life—is free for those who believe. But from that belief will spring true love for God, and then a desire to serve Him. So there is, in fact, a payment involved, but it is in joyous gratitude and service to God for all he has done for you and me.

How are we likely to willingly serve God once we are strengthened and guided by our faith? You may expect to...

+ talk daily with Him through prayer seeking guidance and strength, and help for the world. *"seek and you shall find"* —Matthew 7:7 Prayer also seeks God's forgiveness which is freely given for those who truly repent.

+ keep the Sabbath holy by attending church, scripture reading, and spending quiet time for the Holy Spirit to work within us.

+ be kind and caring to all as shown by Christ's love. And you will find this agape love will become a most rewarding virtue, altering your whole life outlook to one of concern and kindness and sense of well being.
"...give, and it will be given to you. A good measure, pressed down, shaken together, running over, will be put into your lap." —Luke 6:38

God requires that we believe in Him through faith. Thus there is no hard evidence, no proof of His existence. Yet consider these five indications of a divine presence to encourage you to further explore God's presence.

✝ The unimaginable brilliance and complexity of mankind and this world seems unlikely to have happened simply by accident. It would take a deliberate designer to fashion our earth, perfect in size to hold our atmosphere and a nearby moon to light the night.

✝ The belief of 80 million people based on the simple teachings of Jesus 2,000 years ago seems preposterous unless inspired by a supreme presence.

✝ The insight and brilliance of Jesus' teachings seem impossible to attribute to an uneducated and crucified Galilean carpenter without some form of divine nature.

✝ Life cannot arise from non-life, therefore there must be some form of permanent life with no beginning or end which, in essence, defines God.

And, of course, there is the rational position of French thinker Blaise Pascal who held that it is substantially more reasonable to believe than not to. For the rewards are far greater (eternal life) if God exists and the disadvantages far less (some restraints on behavior) if one is mistaken, than the eternal damnation and short pleasures of life for one who doesn't believe and is proven wrong. THINK!!

The Nature of Prayer

Prayer is simply talking with God who is always close at hand, seeking us more than we seek Him. Prayer creates fellowship with God, coming together through our faith and His boundless love for us.

All prayers are "answered," not as we ask but as an all-knowing God deems proper and in full measure, even greater than requested. So we seek God's will in all things with trust and thankfulness.

"Listen! I am standing at the door, knocking; if you hear my voice and open the door, I will come in to you and eat with you, and you with me." —Revelation 3:20

...On the Holy Spirit

The Holy Spirit is often depicted as a descending dove, symbolizing the continuous presence of God dwelling in our hearts, regenerating us into the family of our heavenly Father, and guiding and empowering us in all truth and good works.

The Holy Spirit enlightens our minds to understand the truths of God's Word.

And it is through the power of the Holy Spirit that we are able to go forth as witnesses for Christ, even "...to the ends of the earth." As soon as someone even considers the possibility of becoming a Christian, the Holy Spirit is at work. So we pray as you read this that your mind and heart will be open and searching for the truth.

The Cathedral at Canterbury, England
Photo by Bill Brandt

Here are Bible passages we believe will be most meaningful to you in gaining faith in God through Jesus Christ.

✝ *For the son of man came to seek and save those who are lost.* —Luke 19:10

✝ *There is more joy in heaven over one sinner who repents, than over ninety-nine good people who need no repentance.* —Luke 15:7

✝ *"...for God all things are possible."* —Matthew 19:26

✝ *"Come to me, all you that are weary and are carrying heavy burdens, and I will give you rest."* —Matthew 11:28

✝ *What benefit will it be to you if you gain the whole world but lose your own soul?* —Mark 8:36

When you have finished reading this flyer may we recommend you do four things in this order.

(1) Pray for guidance as encouraged by the Holy Spirit who is now working within you.

(2) Be especially kind to everyone and see how rewarding it is.

(3) Attend any church of your choice and, when God speaks to you, ask for help in belief.

(4) Hand this flyer to a friend, or as a friend to a stranger.

These two nearby supporting churches—Central United Methodist and Mount Olivet United Methodist—and all 10 other congregations in the Ballston area welcome you. Bring this flyer with you and tell them you are a spiritual seeker. *"Ask, and it will be given to you; seek, and you will find; knock, and it will be opened to you."* —Matthew 7:7

An excellent website on Christian faith is christiananswers.net. You may also e-mail us at faith.contact@yahoo.com to talk about your spiritual life. (Your e-mail address will not be shared.)

Now may the peace of God which passes all understanding keep your hearts and minds in Christ Jesus. —Philippians 4:7

(3) **Field contacts by trained evangelists.** "Sidewalk" ministry," going out two-by-two, walking the neighborhood, knocking on doors, engaging people in conversation, handing out flyers, encouraging, inviting, this is evangelism at its fundamental core. There is no experience like it. We devote the remainder of this chapter to setting forth in this manner much as did the first disciples.

The Rudiments of Field Witnessing

The field mission, out in the community at large, is greatly facilitated if the following mechanics are observed:

- **Evangelism requires thorough preparation.** Expect to find opportunities to witness every day. Be prepared with your training, handouts, and sense of mission. Most important, prepare with prayer, asking for opportunity and guidance for we know that all people matter to God.

The Evangelism Committee will have to explore, through trial and error, what forms of presentation seem to work best. Periodically the committee should meet to discuss their visits, identifying and improving on what has worked, discarding what appears unproductive. Let the working evangelists tell their stories so all can profit from their experiences. Talk over the obstacles met and approaches that seem most successful.

- **Discipleship is a shared venture.** Christ sent the disciples out two-by-two, not alone. (Mark 6:7) Working together and sharing in the joy is much more comforting, reinforcing, and rewarding. A companion adds another dimension, lessening the impression of coming in our own stead. Together, we lose a certain degree of personal identity, taking on the mantle of Christ through the shared mission.

- **Initial perception is critical.** The first part of the Christian message is the image we present, living our faith, authentically and boldly. It is how we are *perceived* that is the critical initial contact so essential to success. Our attitude and actions resonate with the recipient as much as what we say. We must behave in such a manner that people are drawn to us by our attitudes and actions of love and concern.[8] They must see Jesus in us by our kindness and love for others. "Being sensitive to the mindset of unbelievers is a biblical attitude (1 Corinthians 14:23) modeled by both Jesus and Paul. It is loving lost people enough to try to relate to them on their level (whatever that is) so Jesus can save them."[9] —Rick Warren, senior pastor, Saddleback Church, Lake Forest, California.

- **Make no effort to force yourself upon anyone.** Always respect the integrity and intelligence of our contacts. Be therefore gentle, kind, and understanding. Evangelism is not high pressure salesmanship, it is not trying to convert people from other faiths, for we typically share goals of ethics, tolerance, and peace. However, we are obliged to go forth, to knock on doors with the intention of telling the Good News. And we do lay claim to the truth and know that believers are saved. Much of this is hard for others to understand or tolerate, so, while we are so commissioned, we must be gentle and understanding in our message.

- **Observe proprieties.** In ringing doorbells, or for that matter in all personal contacts, always practice the everyday rules of etiquette, viz., never invade the privacy of people's lives or homes, wait to be invited in. If asked, the evangelist should always be frank about explaining his or her church affiliation and interest in publicizing its programs and services.

Don't challenge or argue about people's politics or religion, cultivate common ground. We claim the truth, we seek to tell and encourage others, but we recognize and see good in all spiritual persuasions and should make no claim of exclusivity nor reject the beliefs of others. We recognize shared goals and encourage all to be spiritual. Let God intervene in these circumstances.

A final caveat, exclude religious affiliation unless asked. Denomination is unimportant and even a distraction in evangelism. We preach *God's* word, not any special interpretation.

- **Start nearby with friends, then branch out.** Proximity is a major factor in church selection, so start with this advantage, making contacts in the immediate neighborhood, then in the surrounding community. Start also with personal friends, then neighbors and acquaintances, and finally to that great expansion, strangers. We prepare for more difficult conditions with easier earlier experience. Remember, Jesus said to Simon, *"Put out into the deep water and let down your nets for a catch."* (Luke 5:4)

The evangelist must be extremely alert, continually looking for opportunities to talk to people about their beliefs and eventually about Christ in their lives. Any little invite can be a start. Call a friend or acquaintance for example. Their surprise and curiosity may lead to questions about your life or theirs. Watch for such an opportunity. All such contacts can be fruitful, immediately or in the future, if we are prepared in our love and concern for others.

- **Door-to-door and street contacts are likely to be brief.** Time is essential in street evangelism. In your walks through neighborhoods and/or standing on street corners, yours contacts will all likely be brief indeed. You may have only a moment to catch someone's eye, smile, offer a "Hello" greeting, and extend a flyer. There may be something distinctive about the individual—their clothes, age for the young and elderly, apparent disposition, or gait—on which you can positively comment, leading to a possible pause and further talk. Quick, positive, interaction is the ticket. If the contact responds negatively, always excuse your intervention.

- **Begin with friendship and sincerity.** Begin every encounter by extending friendship, showing a kindly interest and goodwill towards the other person. Friendship is proffered by a smile, a handshake, an expression of interest in the other person. Sincere caring is the foundation upon which a bridge of trust and respect can eventually be built. The first impression of the visited must be, "It's okay to talk with this person." The following conversation should always be courteous and respectful. Don't give a speech, talk and listen. Don't be in a hurry, act on a long-term basis.

• **All that is necessary is to plant the seed.** The immediate task of the evangelist then is simply to *introduce* Christ into the thoughts of people, stimulate some sort of spiritual interest. And the key here is that people want to hear *good* things, particularly if it affects them.

Seize every opportunity. A germ of interest is all that is required. Yet those embarking often find it difficult to turn an ordinary conversation into a spiritual venture. The easiest means of making this possible is often simply by asking questions and listening. Don't ever underestimate their latent degree of interest in their own lives and in spiritual matters.

Generally, the conversation must be auspiciously steered, but it can also be spontaneous and even assertive. Some evangelists prefer not to beat around the bush, laying out their beliefs straightforwardly without equivocation. People tend to respect this honesty.

Remember also that you are going to have ready a handout which will greatly augment your introduction and assist in arranging further contact.

Here are some starters for steering discussions toward spiritual topics.[10]

—Ask what difficulties, rewarding experiences, or disappointments, may have been experienced recently.
—Simply ask do they belong to a church.
—Inquiring how things are *really* going often encourages an honest response of concerns and problems for which faith provides comfort.
—Mention some social concern, the value of friendships, coping with illness, or crime, matters of common interest to everyone.
—When asked how you're doing, respond that *spiritually*, wonderfully! This generally solicits a response to elaborate.
—Ask new neighbors if they've found a good church.
—When talking about children, speak of the value you find in their church school attendance.
—Comment on recent announcements of well-known athletes, or other celebrities, espousing the Christian faith.
—When shared problems are identified, confide how you've been helped by Bible scripture and church friends.
—Use the Christmas and Easter holidays to ask if these events seem based on fact or fiction.
—Extend an invitation to a church sponsored event such as a concert, offering a ride.
—For people of a different religious persuasion, ask if they are serious about their faith, if not, would they like to know about the saving grace of Jesus.

- **Use your own life experiences as an example.** Explain how important God is in your own life and the joy and peace that such belief brings.
- **Some compulsion is involved.** It is difficult to interfere with the human soul. You hesitate to engage. Yet we know that Christ and his presence are in every living creature. What comfort and confidence this engenders! The evangelism message of saving grace and discipleship should then be stated with vigor and enthusiasm, no watering down. We are in fact to *compel* them to come. *"Go out into the roads and lanes, and compel people to come in, so that my house may be filled."* (Luke 13:23)
- **Do not be disappointed.** As admonished by Gordon Cosby[11] we must be "...singularly unconcerned with 'success.'" Our heavenly Father knows the trials and tribulations involved and will not task us with anything that we are not capable of with his help. And be bolstered by this scripture: *"In the same way, I tell you, there will be more joy in heaven over one sinner who repents than over ninety-nine respectable people who do not need to repent."* (Luke 15-7)

The Message

Jesus said to his disciples, *"Whoever listens to you, listens to me; whoever rejects you, rejects me; and whoever rejects me, rejects the one who sent me."* (Luke 10:16)

"...do not worry about what you are going to say or how you will say it; when the time comes, you will be given what you will say. For the words you speak will not be yours; they will come from the Spirit of your Father speaking for you." (Matthew 10:19-20)

But how can they call to him, if they have not believed? And how can they believe, if they have not heard the message? And how can they hear, if the message is not proclaimed? And how can the message be proclaimed, if the messengers are not sent out? As the scripture says, *"How wonderful is the coming of those who bring good news!"* (Romans 10:14-15)

The evangelism call or message can be viewed as an awakening process in which the Holy Spirit assists in stirring up imagination and interest. The process is awakening, not training, confrontation, debate, or conversion. *Awake, awake, put on strength, O arm of the Lord!* (Isaiah 51:9)

The principal content of the awakening "message" should be included in a handout flyer and repeated in later conversations with responders. Yet the evangelist must be prepared for occasional unexpectedly long discussions in the field. Whether long or short, the initial contact always seeks to spur interest, hopefully to materialize in later extended discussions at the church or other chosen location. We organize the evangelism message to be presented in two parts, first the pragmatic then the spiritual content.

Pragmatic Content

The evangelist's message is the Good News that Jesus Christ is the Messiah and our savior. However, we would be foolish to start out with this bold proclamation. People are not wandering about asking what must I do to be saved? They are, instead, concerned with how they can make their life work and be happy? Their essential needs are a sense of hope leading to peace of mind, a behavior model, companionship, and a forum for sharing life's joys and tribulations.

We start then with our response to the practical and intellectual needs of people that can be met by the church, typically the first factors considered by contacts in appraising our appeal.[12] They must be listed in the flyer.

Appeal to *pragmatic* reasons why people may seek church attendance:

- to meet a sense of responsibility to our children to provide a Christian education.
- to belong to a loving community in which one feels welcome and cared for. Invite people to enter into our community, not necessarily attend church. People need and seek fellowship, not salvation or events. Friendship and low-key social gatherings are the right beginning.
- to secure comfort amidst personal crises and problems.

Appeal to *philosophical* and *intellectual* reasons for their possible interest:

- to replace a sense of emptiness, angst, possibly even despair in some instances, with the joy of salvation and eternal life. "We saw that our Christian friends were always cheerful and confident, and wondered why?"
- to respond to the intellectual challenge of the existence of God. Start on an exploratory journey toward truth.
- to allay a sense of guilt and fear, substituting peace of mind. God's assurance of salvation by faith alone provides the greatest confidence possible for sinful mankind.

Spiritual Content

We are at once "witnesses," one who furnishes evidence; "ambassadors," a messenger or representative; and "evangelists," a missionary of the gospel.

The lay evangelist is only expected to invite people to "come and see," not to know all the answers nor be a super salesperson or a theologian. And the contact will always be able to read the basic evangelism message in the handout. But to plant even a seed of interest, the lay evangelist must be well versed on the topics below, for any may be the catalyst that initiates interest and further search. And remember that God will provide you eloquence beyond your own abilities. So do not fret over your delivery or the results. Even the people who respond to the message will not be deciding themselves to come forth. It is the Holy Spirit who gives faith and who will be at work through us

The "spiritual content" to be proclaimed is the core of this chapter. The focus is on rebirth in Christ. People need to know how faith makes a difference. They want to see it in our lives, our goodness and joy. Then they can see the possibility in their own.

The following 10 spiritual topics[13] are listed in order of general customary sequence:

- **Does God exist?** God cannot be "proven" to exist, but the evidence of a supreme being is persuasive.[14] For example, isn't it unlikely that in this limitless universe the wondrous earth and all its inhabitants would just accidentally happen? There must have been a first cause somewhere. Consider the many technicalities involved—the earth's tilt, distance to sun, and air composition—all of which if only slightly different would rule out life. Man himself is such a marvel of intelligence and consciousness, as to be beyond any accidental design.[15] It's hard to imagine that we are not part of some great plan.

In the world today, the claims and "miracles" of Jesus, an otherwise seemingly normal person, are preposterous and surreal unless he is, in fact, the son of God. Christ's miracles are either elaborate hoaxes, inaccurate reporting, fables, outright lies, or true. But if untrue how could so many people at the time be fooled? How could they be made to claim that a dead man rose, that the blind saw and the leper cleansed, if it were not actually true? The miracles must have occurred for them to have been so widely accepted and documented in scripture.

Finally, how can an individual's life be totally transformed by an erroneous belief? Wouldn't accepting Christ have long been found of little value if his deity was not true? No, the power of God acting on and in each person is the only explanation for the transformations that take place, altering lives literally and completely beyond all human possibilities.

- **What is God like?** God's love and compassion for us passes all understanding. We are precious in his sight.

He is our "heavenly *Father*," exceeding all the good qualities of our earthly parents. He is perfect, absolutely pure. And this perfection is manifest in his love for each of us and his desire that we be his own.

This holy image extends to God's awesomeness. There is no dimension we can fathom that God does not exceed. He is everywhere all the time, an invisible presence that knows all we think and do. God is *eternal*, with no beginning or end; *independent* of all things; *holy*, utterly without fault; *perfect* in all knowledge; *sovereign* over all; and *omnipotent*, all-powerful. And God will judge all mankind fairly with justice.

No one has seen God but he has revealed himself to us as a trinity of three persons—Father, Son (Jesus Christ), and the Holy Spirit. To know and love Christ is to know and love God.

- **The nature of man and meaning of life.** To think that man is here simply as an accident of nature is a monumental assumption, difficult for even the most pragmatic skeptic to fully embrace. Not only our existence but our superiority and dominion over all earth's creatures, suggests that we are something very special. And indeed we are, created in God's image, ... *a little lower than angels, and crowned ... with glory and honor.* (Psalm 8:5)

But sin separates us from God, requiring his forgiveness which he bountifully gives to all who repent and believe in him, redeeming the faithful to everlasting life. How thankful we should be, how joyfully expectant of the future knowing we are in God's eternal care. The essence of life, exceeding all else, is thus faith in God, belief in his presence.

- **Jesus our Savior.** God sent his only son, Jesus Christ our Lord, into the world to show us how to live by his teachings and perfect life, and who died on the cross for us so that our sins might be forgiven. The central message of the entire Bible is this single passage: *For God so loved the world that he gave his only Son, so that everyone who believes in him may not perish but may have eternal life.* (John 3:16) Christ came into the world to give life, abundantly and forever. He is our savior, our path to redemption. His crucifixion atones for our sins, a "ransom for many."

- **The Holy Spirit.** The Holy Spirit of God comes and resides in our hearts and minds as a gift, to enrich and fulfill our lives, an ever present help and comforter. The Holy Spirit is one of the three forms of God—Father, Son, and Holy Spirit. *It is God himself who has set us apart, who placed his mark of ownership upon us, and who gave the Holy Spirit in our hearts as the guarantee of all that he has for us.* (2 Corinthians 1:21,22) It is this indwelling power that energizes and guides our preaching, teaching, prophesying, and healing, just as the Spirit led the disciples.

The evangelist must believe in and act upon the presence of the Holy Spirit in all men, however seemingly concealed, requiring only an invitation to become manifest.

- **The nature of being a believer.** We believe because God generously grants faith to all who seek it. Faith is gained through prayer by asking our heavenly Father for faith and forgiveness. It is a gift freely bestowed, not earned. Each of us as individuals must personally pursue the gifts of faith and forgiveness. They are not metered out to any group or affiliation. *Everyone who calls on the name of the Lord will be saved.* (Romans 10:13)

Believing and practicing Christianity gives real meaning and perspective to life. We cease to be the center of the universe with all its responsibilities, and, instead, live to peacefully serve God with all its rewards and blessings, knowing eternal life awaits.

- **Repentance.** To be saved one must turn to God in repentance and have faith in our Lord Jesus Christ. Repentance has four dimensions. It first requires honest *admission* of our sinfulness. This acknowledgement must be accompanied by a *contrite* heart, regretting our offenses. Then we must make *amends*; to make right what we have wronged. Finally, we must seek to *improve* ourselves for the future.

- **The Bible, God's Holy Word.** The Bible is the Word of God, inspired by God and therefore sacred, exceeding all veneration or respect we might bestow. The Bible tells us how to live lives devoted to God, serving him, and caring for one another. It shows how God worked through the lives of biblical people. Although subject to interpretation, the Bible text itself is "infallible," incapable of any form of deception. We can place complete trust in its contents. The Bible is also unique in being "inerrant," that is, free of any error. We rejoice that God has provided his message in this forthright manner.
- **How does one pray and are prayers really answered.** Prayer is personal conversation with God, respectful, searching, listening. We are companions, friends with God as we talk together about problems and opportunities. "The most comfortable result of a life of prayer is the security which fellowship with God imparts. His kind and cheering counsel comes darting into the soul like rays of light into a dark room."[16] Through prayer we learn God's mind for us and how to obey his will. Only good things come from prayer, however seemingly unanswered or contrary, for our heavenly Father loves us.
- **Isn't being a good person enough?** Yes, it might possibly be sufficient, for we know that God places great value on each and every one of us, loves goodness, and will judge us fairly. But we also know that Jesus sets the exemplary life we are to lead and faith is its foundation. If any risk is to be taken, why not err on this side? Belief and good works enrich life, not detract from it. Far more is gained in joy and well-being than might possibly be lost through personal sacrifice.

Closing Prayer

Every encounter should end with spoken prayer, however brief, preferably with the contact, or privately in your own heart. Always ask the contact to pray with you whether they believe or not, for God will hear and answer even their most modest petitions. Begin by thanking God for making the meeting possible and for his presence. Pray for him to enter our hearts and minds to show us the way. Pray to grant faith and understanding to all who seek. Gently urge the contact to talk about their spiritual needs or doubts in their own words. Whatever they say or question will be a step in the right direction of opening themselves to God's intervention in their lives. Close by thanking God for all his blessings bestowed.

Explain to the contact that if they do not believe no harm is done and possibly much good. Tell the individual that you will also pray for him or her during the week and should they feel something different it will be the Holy Spirit's renewed presence in their hearts. That should shake anybody up, the possible beginning of awakening!

Follow-on Gatherings

Follow-on gatherings for those newly seeking God's presence can be given any title—"Friendship Time," "Voice Your Own Thoughts," "Give it a Try." The important thing is that they be joyous, informal occasions. God is at work; new pilgrims beginning their journey are present! The likely smallness of the group creates the intimacy and privacy necessary for the Holy Spirit to work in and through all.

Meetings with responding invitees are best held in neutral locations such as in a church classroom or public meeting room. They can even be briefly held in a local coffee shop, park, or even street corner. Wherever all are comfortable. It is best if all are able to sit around a single table. Provide name cards and be sure everyone's name and phone number are recorded.

The nature of the small group meeting provides a number of opportunities not available in neighborhood canvassing. First we hopefully have a number of visitors who will gain insight and comfort from each other's company and commentary. Secondly, we have more time to relax and moderately approach reaching out to God. Third, we can interact in as much depth and as personal as each visitor may desire. Fourth, we can provide some quiet time for inner reflection in which the Holy Spirit can work. Fifth, we can provide additional take-home written materials for later study.

The idea is to make everyone feel comfortable, yet, most importantly and hopefully, part of something very dramatic, bringing God's presence into one's life. Remember also that seekers will be moved by what they hear and see in us. We are, after all, witnesses! All should be able to observe the joy in Christ that we feel.

We can begin by telling our visitors that their decision to attend could change their lives forever, and that we thank our heavenly Father for their presence. Explain that faith is a gift from God to all who seek. The church they see is, of course, not perfect, but God should not be judged by our personal failings. Explain that the way to discover God is simply to talk to him, to pray for help. Then introduce the Bible and give each attendee a written summary of essential Scripture. "Just carry it with you this week and read when you have time. Let God do the rest." Our enthusiasm and confidence will be contagious.

Continue by asking each of the visitors what they would like to talk about. You can expect that most will want to learn about God, starting with his very existence. They are, after all, seeking a sense of hope leading to peace of mind. They may ask about how Christians are supposed to behave and if this life style has any real advantages? They likely will be seeking true friendship and will examine our motives for honesty and integrity. No one should leave the meeting without a feeling that new friendships have been started. Of course, follow-on meetings should be scheduled because, for most, becoming a real Christian takes some time. Typically, an evangelist team member will be assigned each visitor in hope of later accompanying them to their first church service and along their spiritual journey to God's gift of faith. These attending evangelists typically volunteer for this type of service, and are trained accordingly.

Sometime a bite to eat and maybe a song or two with piano accompaniment lightens the load and eases conversation. In some instances, visitors will request and benefit most from private sessions.

Responses to the above content topics should be prepared in written form in advance and learned by all members of the evangelism team. This subject matter, in most instances, is simply elaboration on the brief introductory material of the handout flyer. It is well to have the pastor close at hand or participating in these meetings for his counsel is always invaluable.

Pastoral Role

Laity and clergy work together as evangelists. The laity, in far greater numbers, is the army that goes forth, the vast company of priests bearing the Good News. This greater role defines and sharpens pastoral leadership. Pastors must emphasize that *every* priestly member is a missionary of the Word. They must stir up the fervor required. Most specifically, they must teach members how to be evangelists and demonstrate this practice in their own personal life. Such leadership is critical for this most difficult of all church missions. A spirit of willingness to go forward must be instilled despite seemingly discouraging conditions.

The tools at hand include periodic sermons describing the congregation's evangelistic mission, doctrine, and meaning to every member; outreach enthusiasm to the point of being contagious; setting an example of how the Lord works through his disciples by personal field work; participating in the follow-on meetings with seekers; and lastly and most important, teaching others how to be good evangelists thereby multiplying the congregation into a "cloud of witnesses." Pastors knowing they are obligated to candidates for the faith as well as the churched generally undertake these assignments with enthusiasm.

In training the evangelism corps, the pastor must emphasize the inner spirit and belief required. Those that go forth must understand that "evangelism is not something a disciple does; it is something that a disciple is."[17]

A Responsive Congregation and Religious Service

"A time comes in the life of every group when it loses sight of its goals and must choose them again. Your job will be to sound again the call, to be the bearer of the vision—articulating it in your own life and helping others to see it." —Gordon Cosby, Pastor, founder of the Church of Our Savior and the Servant Leadership School, Washington, D.C.

Chapter 21. Evangelism—The Outreach Challenge 351

A congregation deep into evangelism is a new entity, aware and receptive to the concerns and needs of spiritual seekers. Such congregations are energetic, challenged by the great commission rather than inwardly complacent. They are flexible in developing services and activities that are responsive to the different needs of a variety of non-churched people. They keep asking themselves and outsiders questions, "What shall we do?" They are not consumed by social issues, or structures, or current business.

A "responsive congregation"[18] has these cultivating attributes:

(1) Members welcome visitors and seekers with open arms, are anxious to communicate and bond with newcomers, and welcome and embrace people as they are.

(2) Small group membership is available for all.

(3) Personal invitations are extended to all, particularly visitors and newcomers, to become involved in activities of personal interest.

(4) Special worship services, specifically designed to draw and help new and marginal Christians and doubtful seekers, should take place at least once a month. Such a service is introductory and contemporary in its content, uplifting, simple, and friendly.

(5) A continuous, concerned attempt should be made to identify why seeker invitees are or are not attracted and retained, and what changes might secure their involvement.

The Flyer Message

Printed flyers are likely the most effective means of broad public contact. The message should be dynamic and substantive; the distribution targeted and extensive; the unit cost minimal. In addition to mass mailings, hand delivered flyers door-to-door are also an important and economical means of distribution. A small postcard flyer is illustrated below and on the following page.

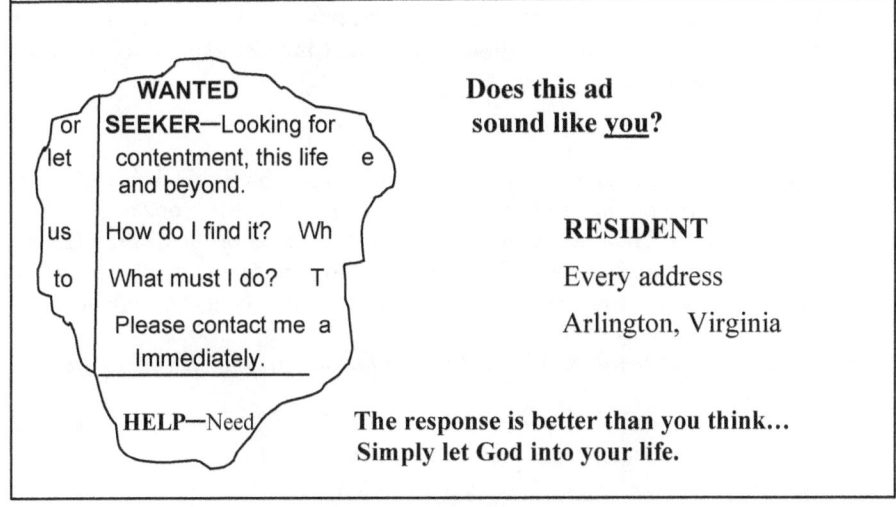

> May we have the pleasure of your company? (**Church Name**) welcomes all with a loving spirit for we are all God's children. For seekers—those searching for life's meaning—we hold monthly open-house meetings in room 5 to get to know one another, enjoy some coffee and cookies, and learn something about the spiritual life simply and informally. Our next meetings are at 7:30 p.m. on January 18th, February 25th, and March 18th. **Come and see!**
>
> Each month, on the third Sunday, we offer a special "seeker service" at 8:30 a.m. designed with visitors in mind, featuring contemporary music and a message for bountiful living in today's world. We look forward to your involvement and friendship. **Please consider!**
>
> Our doors are always open. Should you be so inclined, drop by and talk with one of our pastors or lay volunteers who will be glad for the opportunity. Or telephone (702) 111-1111 if you would like to make contact. Our pastors are— John H. Jones and Mary Smith.
>
> If you have young children, they are welcome to attend our Sunday school program and youth activities. Church school is from 9:30 to 10:30 a.m. with infant care, pre-school, and kindergarten through grade 12 classes. While your children are in school, enjoy one of our many adult classes or a special forum for newcomers.

The flyer should be designed and tailored by the sponsoring church for it must reflect the unique message of the sender and be as personal as possible. Remember, you are attempting to reach individuals who are often uninterested, may be disillusioned, or even outright turned-off by religion. So the message must be dynamic and relevant to their thinking and needs, people at the periphery.

A postcard flyer, bar-coded, pre-sorted, and sent in quantity at standard class prices can be mailed very economically. The front should be attention generating; the back a personal invitation to attend any scheduled special introductory sessions, Sunday worship service, and church school for children and adults. The idea is to start people thinking and then responding.

---

[1] This chapter is highly dependent on the seminal works by Bill Hybels and Mark Mittelberg, *Becoming a Contagious Christian* (Grand Rapids, MI, Zondevan, 1994), 221 pp.; and E. Dale Click, *Evangelism: The First Business of the Church* (Lima, Ohio, CSS Publishing Company, 1994). There are, of course, many other valuable informative works on evangelism. Briefly cited, a starting collection might begin with these popular, largely paperback, entries:

Win Am and Charles Am, *The Master's Plan for Making Disciples* (Baker, 1998), 175 pp.

George Barna, *Turnaround Churches: How to Overcome Barriers to Growth and Bring New Life to an Established Church* (Regal, 1993), 204 pp.

Jerram Barrs, *The Heart of Evangelism* (Crossway, 2005), 288 pp.

Thomas T. Clegg and Warren Bird, *Lost in America: How You and Your Church Can Impact the World Next Door* (Group, 2001), 176 pp. (hardcover)

Robert E. Coleman and Roy J. Fish, *The Master Plan of Evangelism* (Revell, 1994), 144 pp.

Ray Comfort, *Hell's Best Kept Secret* (Whitaker House, 1989), 188 pp.; *How to Win Souls and Influence People* (Bridge-Logos, 1999), 329 pp.

H. Eddie Fox and George Morris, *Faith-Sharing: Dynamic Christian Witnessing by Invitation* (Discipleship Resources, 1996), 160 pp.

George Hunter, *How to Reach Secular People* (Abingdon Press, 1991), 192 pp.

Donald E. Miller, *Reinventing American Protestantism: Christianity in the New Millennium* (University of California, 1999), 262 pp.

Mark Mittelberg, *Building a Contagious Church: Revolutionizing the Way We Do and View Evangelism* (Zondervan, 2002), 416 pp.

Rebecca Pippert, *Out of the Salt Shaker and Into the World* (IVP, 1999), 288 pp.

Thom Rainer, *Surprising Insights from the Unchurched and Proven Ways to Reach Them* (Zondervan, 2001), 288 pp. (hardcover)

Ronald J. Sider, Phil Olson and Heidi Rolland, *Churches That Make a Difference: Reaching Your Community with Good News and Good Works* (Baker, 2002), 334 pp.

Mark Stiles, *Speaking of Jesus* (IVP, 1995), 197 pp.

Roger K. Swanson and Shirley F. Clement, *The Faith-Sharing Congregation* (Discipleship Resources, 1996), 120 pp.

[2] Dan Kimball, *The Emerging Church* (Grand Rapids, Zondervan, 2003), p. 68.

[3] The Graduate Center of the City University of New York, New York, NY, Barry A. Kosmin, Egon Mayer and Ariela Keysar, American Religious Identification Survey, 2001 (copyright). Reported in US Census Bureau, *Statistical Abstract of the United States: 2004-2005,* Table 67, p. 55.

[4] Click, *Evangelism: The First Business of the Church*, p. 141.

[5] Hybels, Becoming a Contagious Christian, p. 62.

[6] Hybels, *Becoming a Contagious Christian,* p. 150.

[7] Click, *Evangelism: The First Business of the Church*, p. 54.

[8] Bill Hybels tells in his book how testimonies are heard at Willow Creek regarding the contagious nature of Christians living out their faith. "I was at work, and I noticed someone in my department who lived a little differently and talked a bit differently and valued some things differently. It caught my interest. I sensed a growing spiritual thirst inside of me that I'd never experienced before." Hybels, *Becoming a Contagious Christian,* p. 42.

[9] Quoted in Kimball, *The Emerging Church*, p. 25.

[10] Largely adopted from Hybels, *Becoming a Contagious Christian*, pp. 135-148.

[11] Gordon Cosby, servant leader and Pastor Church of the Savior. Gordon introduced many hundreds of students, including the author, to servant leadership for which we are all eternally grateful.

[12] Largely adopted from Edward A. Rauff, *Why People Join the Church* (New York, Pilgrim Press, 1979).

[13] Of assistance in developing this content is John Blanchard's helpful booklet *Ultimate Questions* (Darlington, England, Evangelical Press, 1998), 32 pp.

[14] Other "evidence" of God's presence frequently cited include the remarkable accomplishments of the disciples after Christ death, unfathomable unless they believed in the resurrection and were strengthened by the Holy Spirit; the unique design and irrepressible beauty and symbolism of the cross of the crucifixion; and the unusual rainbow phenomenon to remind us of God's presence and promise.

More extended argument is spelled out in a number of testimonial studies. See, for example, D. James Kennedy, *Why I Believe* (Waco, Texas, Word Books, 1980), 164 pp.

[15] This argument, that it would seem that the universe in all its brilliance was somehow *designed* to support and nourish human life, is commonly titled the "Anthropic Principle."

[16] Bishop Charles Henry Brent, quoted in Click, *Evangelism: The First Business of the Church*, p. 54.

[17] Kimball, *The Emerging Church*, p. 218.

[18] Norman Shawchuck, *Marketing for Congregations* (Nashville, Abingdon, 1992), 428 pp.

Chapter 22
Community Ministry

"Let my heart be broken with the things that break the heart of God."
—Bob Pierce, founder, Samaritan's Purse.

"Have no doubt that a committed community can change the world."
—Margaret Mead (1901-1978) world renowned anthropologist.

"This is the first generation in all of recorded history that can do something about the scourge of poverty. We have the means to do it. We can banish hunger from the face of the earth."
—Hubert Humphrey (1911-1978) Senator from Minnesota and Vice President of the United States (statement made in 1965).

"'Down, down,' says Christ, 'you will find me in the poor. You are rising too high if you do not look for me down there.'"
—Martin Luther, 1483-1546, German Reformation leader.

This is how we know what love is: Christ gave his life for us. We too, then, ought to give our lives for our brothers! If a man is rich and sees his brother in need, yet closes his heart against his brother, how can he claim that he has love for God in his heart? My children! Our love should not be just words and talk; it must be true love, which shows itself in action. (1 John 3:16-18)

"Truly I tell you, just as you did it to one of the least of these who are members of my family, you did it to me." (Matthew 25:40)

Helping others enables us to confront God face-to-face. He identifies with the poor so strongly that in caring for them we become as one with him. And as Scripture tells us, whatever we do for the poor we also do for our Lord Jesus Christ. So in all ways we must strive to redirect our energies outward in selfless gifts to others for it is the will of God for us, and we will be guided and protected in all that we do.

I know of no finer contemporary example of caring for others than that of Michael Kirwan, who, as a member of the Catholic Worker community in Washington, DC, for more than two decades, fed, housed, and lived with the poorest of the poor. His September 13, 1999 obituary in *The Washington Post* is touching and inspirational. It reads in part:

> In the winter of 1978, Mr. Kirwan was a graduate student in sociology at George Washington University preparing for a conventional career in business or government. One freezing night he passed a homeless man keeping warm on a heat grate near the State Department. The man asked for food. Mr. Kirwan ignored him and kept walking to his campus dorm room. There, unsettled, he had second thoughts and took back a bowl of hot soup to the man.
>
> So began a life's mission. Mr. Kirwan continued bringing food to homeless people at 21st Street and Virginia Avenue NW.

"One night, as I brought down a large gallon jug of hot split pea soup and set it down on the cement block near the heating vent where they gathered, a rather rough-looking fellow picked up the jar of soup and, in one motion, broke the jar over my head," Mr. Kirwan recalled.

"Instead of running away, I asked the man why he had done that. These were probably the first words I had ever spoken to any of them. He told me that I was doing nothing more than bringing food to the dogs. I was bringing food, setting it down like I was feeding them out of a pet dish and then just walking away. He said, "Talk to us. Visit with us. We don't bite.'"

Mr. Kirwan did begin visiting. "What happened that night," he said, "was that a first barrier had been broken in my perceptions of who homeless people are. I realized that these men and women on the streets had feelings, just like me. They wanted to be loved and respected and listened to. They cared that someone cared about them, but just giving food and a blanket was not enough."

We cannot be a mirror of the world around us, accepting uncritically the prevailing political, economic, and social poverty all about us. *Do not be conformed to this world, but be transformed by the renewing of your minds, so that you may discern what is the will of God—what is good and acceptable and perfect.* (Romans 12:2) We must instead become nonconformists as Mr. Kirwan and countless others, wholly renewed by Christ into commitment to the stranger, the poor, the infirmed, and the outcast. In so doing we will find our true selves in them and not in ourselves alone.

The Community Ministry Committee

Caring for those in need is an integral part of being a Christian. The responsible committee, identified here as "Community Ministry," guides and oversees the outreach mission, often involving more varied activities and hands-on participation than any other church function. Details of committee responsibilities are listed in the community ministry job description, Appendix B.

The Community Ministry Committee is responsible for providing direction in five major areas: (1) assisting pastors in developing a caring outreaching congregation, (2) broadcasting needs, (3) evaluating program suitability and setting priorities, (4) recruiting and training participating personnel, and (5) assisting in related fundraising.

These responsibilities are generally covered in other chapters, notably Chapter 10 "Leadership Roles," Chapter 11 "Communications and Planning," and Chapter 12 "How to Conduct Meetings and Reach Decisions." The task of fundraising is the subject of Chapter 19, "Our Call to Stewardship." The task of evaluating program fit within the congregation, however, is especially critical to this committee and will bear the brunt of our remaining attention.

Setting Community Service Priorities

"The test of our progress is not whether we add to the abundance of those who have much; it is whether we provide enough for those who have too little." —Franklin Delano Roosevelt

There should be little doubt that careful strategy is required to effectively help others in most need. That should be the number one criterion in program selection, providing the greatest help to those in greatest need. But there are other factors that must also be taken into account, most notably matching available personnel and financial resources with appropriate applications. Young, vigorous, adventuresome members may well elect the rigors of inner city service for example. Older individuals might understandably prefer less rigorous, more indirect involvement. While overall priorities count, the capabilities and preference of the congregation must also be taken into account to ensure the most viable responses. Fortunately, there is a multitude of service opportunities from which to choose.

Public service programs across the country number in the thousands in perhaps 50 or more functional areas. The follow taxonomy illustrates the subject range involved:

Economics
  Credit union
  Disaster relief
  Welfare reform
  Tax preparation
  Job preparation and placement

Education/Training
  College and career
  Language instruction
  Literacy and remedial tutoring
  Nursery school

Environmental Protection

Health
  Alleviation of hunger
  Disabled, blind, and visually impaired
  Drug and alcohol abuse
    (Alcoholics Anonymous)
  HIV/AIDS[1]
  Medical and nutrition counsel
  Population planning
  Seriously and terminally ill

Housing
  Shelters for the homeless and aging
  Structure rehabilitation

Human Rights Advocacy
  Native Americans
  Arms, peace & international relations
  Children's rights
  Civil rights[2]
  International justice
  Refugees
  Religious freedom
  Women's rights

Human Services
  Aging, senior services
  Bereavement
  Child sponsorship, foster care,
    and adoption
  Food pantry/kitchen
  Financial management
  Infant and child care/protection
  Referral services

Clothing
Family planning
Legal Aid and Consumer Protection
Safety and Crime
   Animal protection
   Domestic violence counseling
   Gun control

Single parent family
Youth development,[3] Scouting

Prison counseling[4]
Youth counseling

It is not uncommon for a large metropolitan church to have a dozen or more community service projects. Small rural congregations, in contrast, may be limited to one or two local concerns. However varying in scope, most church service efforts evolve in a process of opportunity, response, and adjustment. Eventually the best are retained, projects typically of substance as well as rewarding to the member participants.

Changing conditions and new challenges require community service programs to be periodically reviewed, with the distinct possibility of dropping or curtailing some marginal efforts in favor of more likely productive new startups. Criteria for such evaluation include:

1. How consistent is this program to what we prayerfully interpret as our highest calling?
2. Is the response better directed at the national or local level? Would we be more effective working with an already existing organization[5] rather than starting or maintaining our own effort?
3. Is the local unmet need significant?
4. What are the skill levels required and do we possess these talents? Have new talents and interests emerged?
5. How large an effort is required to make a justifiably acceptable contribution? Do we have these resources?
6. How well are we likely to do in terms of benefits-to-costs versus alternative employment of our resources?

Programs may also be systematically reviewed by checking the appropriate condition levels using the following outline:

I. Project priority
   (1) a continuing and fairly stable need favoring long-term commitment; a substantial number of other organizations involved.
   (2) some time restrictions involved requiring both current and extended response.
   (3) immediate reaction required to unmet critical needs.

II. Management control
   (1) involvement is largely indirect through partnership with an outside group.
   (2) personal participation within a church-managed group.

III. Project costs
   (1) low cost, mostly volunteer service.

(2) moderate operating costs.
(3) some initial capital investment; relatively substantial operating costs.

IV. Operating conditions
Principal work location:
(1) immediately within church confines.
(2) primarily within local neighborhood.
(3) surrounding community.
(4) national and international.

Field working conditions:
(1) no field work.
(2) field work mostly comfortable.
(3) field work occasionally to often disagreeable.
(4) field work can be dangerous.

Repercussions
(1) no appreciable negative effect on congregation or neighborhood.
(2) possible negative reaction should be anticipated and response prepared.[6]

V. Skill level and/or training required:
(1) minimal—simple tasks such as folding and mailing, setting up tables, cleaning, accompanying people.
(2) moderate—short training period required for tasks such as telephoning, letter writing, cooking and serving meals.
(3) considerable—extended training and experience such as might be required in remedial education.
(4) professional—college and/or professional training in such fields as medicine, law, engineering, nutrition, etc.

Community Ministry Management

Leadership, staffing and funding are essential to the success of community service programs. And for church-sponsored effort, our hearts must be of a right spirit, overflowing with genuine love and compassion. We seek God's will and then confidently and joyfully carry out his bidding.

Do not conform outwardly to the standards of this world, but let God transform you inwardly by a complete change of your mind. Then you will be able to know the will of God—what is good, and is pleasing to him, and is perfect. (Romans 12:2)

Amid all the pressures of national and congregational special interests, the Community Ministry Committee must first guard against biased responses. As previously discussed, highest priority projects should receive our first attention. Yet directed funding and limited staffing typically require scaling back to what is feasible. An earmarked endowment must obviously be used for the designated purpose. Youth may often be most effectively involved in limited skill, relatively low priority projects such as house refurbishing and neighborhood cleanup. As a general rule, our efforts are maximized when each individual's qualifications and interests are taken into account, and all are informed of their most productive employments. We must first seek to optimize each person's personal involvement, whatever their qualifications and interests, complemented by engagement in high priority projects whenever possible.

And what are high priority projects? Those that result in the greatest good for the least effort. And here some real study is required for some seemingly beneficial actions fail to get at the root causes. Consider, for example, aiding the impoverished. The usual response is to provide direct immediate aid, typically soup kitchens and emergency shelter. Yet in the long run, education, and for foreign countries capitalism and free trade in addition,[7] are the principal means[8] of lasting improvement. Whenever options of this nature are available, it is imperative that the Community Ministry Committee study the alternatives to ensure close to optimal employment of resources, in the cited instance, inclusion of job training and placement.

Lastly, it is also important for the Committee to ensure participants engage in some personal contact with those aided, lest we lose the reality involved. Antiseptic detached giving is commonly devoid of the enriching qualities of truly involved participation. It is difficult to learn to love our neighbors if they are never seen. It is far better for us to concentrate on seeking this loving experience than to simply demonstrate its possibility by indirect means alone. The Community Ministry Committee thus must make every effort to occasionally get congregation members into the field, to see and involve themselves first hand in God's work. The rewards are great and everlasting.

We close with the inspiring words of Isaiah:

> Is not this the fast that I choose:
>   to loose the bonds of injustice,
>   to undo the thongs of the yoke,
>   to let the oppressed go free,
>   and to break every yoke?
> Is it not to share your bread with the hungry,
>   and bring the homeless poor into your house;
>   when you see the naked, to cover them,
>   and not to hide yourself from your own kin?
> Then your light shall break forth like the dawn,
>   and your healing shall spring up quickly;
>   your vindicator shall go before you,
>   the glory of the Lord shall be your rear guard.
> Then you shall call, and the Lord will answer;
>   you shall cry for help, and he will say,
>   Here I am.
>   (Isaiah 58: 6-9)

[1] To indicate the magnitude of the opportunity here, in 2002 more than half a million babies in the developing world contracted from their mothers the virus that causes AIDS, despite the fact that drugs and therapies exist that could virtually eliminate mother-to-child transmission of the killer disease. Jesse Helms, "We Cannot Turn Away," editorial, *The Washington Post,* March 24, 2002.

[2] Many observers have cited segregation as the greatest barrier to social and economic equity in the United States. "If one puts all of the poorest people together in one area, moves the jobs, decimates the social organization, and so forth, generational poverty is simple inevitable." Take the family out of the inner city ghetto, and the children will do well. David Hilfiker, *Poverty in Urban America: Its causes and cures,"* (Washington, DC, Potter's House Bookservice, 2000), p. 55.

[3] "It doesn't take as much as some people think," says Tyrone Parker, founding president of the Alliance of Concerned Men. "I mean some kids out there you can't really talk to, they're not ready yet. But an awful lot of them are tired of living the street life and just don't know how to turn it around. That's what the alliance is in business to do." William Raspberry, "Society's Last Line of Defense," *The Washington Post,* January 6, 1997.

[4] "Most of the men in here have problems with substance abuse or compulsive behavior, and we hope something will get their attention. It might not happen the first or second time they're in here, it might mean they become a model prisoner for 20 years. But this is about changing one life at a time." Rev. Glen Dale describing his hope for bringing God's grace to men in prison.

"Most of the young men in jail today are confused, belligerent, skeptical of religion, resentful of authority and ready to blame the world for their problems. Still, an enormous number of them ask for Bibles and spiritual counseling." Pamela Constable, "The Soft Cell," *The Washington Post,* February 16, 1997.

[5] See charityguide.org website for charity ratings and guidebooks.

[6] Regarding local community reaction, consider the following "letters to the editor" quote from the *The Washington Post* reacting to planned expansion of a local church's program to feed the homeless. "Again, at issue is *not* the _____ Church's mission to feed the homeless but rather its *insistence to do so in our neighborhood,* which is already crowded with homeless people everywhere you look.

What are my/our rights as residents and taxpayers vs. those of individuals from all over the city who are being brought into our community? What happens to those people after the church closes its doors in the morning?"

[7] Charles Krauthammer, "An Ideal Goes Starving," editorial, *The Washington Post,* April 11, 2004.

[8] Other primary causes of poverty include segregation, lack of jobs to support a family, and inadequate access to health care.

Chapter 23
Administration Ministry

Keep watch over yourselves and over all the flock which the Holy Spirit has placed in your care. Be shepherds of the church of God, which he made his own through the death of his own Son. (Acts 20:28)

Church administration includes personnel, finance, and property. These specialized duties often require professional expertise possessed, at best, by only a few individuals within congregations so fortunate. The functions are therefore typically assigned to committees, distinct from routine office management and administration performed by employed staff augmented by member volunteers.

In small churches all three functions may be conducted within a single administration committee as subcomponent divisions. This umbrella arrangement encourages sharing of expertise and facilitates coordination. However organized, the committee or committees necessarily work closely with the church office manager who maintains all financial, personnel, and property records and frequently serves as a key committee adviser.

Although the tasks assigned appear mechanical, it is the Lord's bidding we seek, and administration is no exception. Those involved therefore, as part of God's plan, have special responsibilities above and beyond the basic technologies involved. These responsibilities include the requirement of absolute honesty, clarity, and timeliness in reporting, and fairness in presenting all sides. In essence, *truth* must be the foundation stone of all church administration. *A false balance is an abomination to the Lord, but an accurate weight is his delight.* (Proverbs 11-1)

Personnel Administration

The purposes of personnel administration are seemingly simple enough: hiring capable people, utilizing them effectively, and maintaining their willingness to work toward the organization's goals. Specifically, five functions are involved:
    (1) Formulation and communication of personnel policies.
    (2) Determination of manpower requirements.
    (3) Recruitment, selection, and training of personnel.
    (4) Maintenance of motivation through adequate compensation, benefits and services, and working conditions.
    (5) Maintenance of records and research.

In all of these activities, personnel committee members must work closely with the professional staff. Routine supervision of the church staff is generally the responsibility of the senior pastor as is their service review and counseling. The senior pastor will also, of course, be integrally involved in all staff hirings.

In light of the above senior pastor involvement and limited number of supporting staff at most churches, the personnel tasks of the committee appear restricted indeed. And so they are, except for the periodic hiring of a new pastor at which time the work of recruitment and selection assumes exceptional importance. Also, the committee's advice regarding salaries is an important function discussed in the salary schedule subsection of this chapter, pages 364-365.

In more routine matters, however, the personnel skills of the committee can well be brought to bear on laity staffing, assisting the stewardship committee in securing member leadership, and in training policy. In fact, whenever and wherever workforce action is involved, the talents of the personnel committee should be considered as a skilled augmenting opportunity.

Finance Administration

Church finance deals with funding, managing, and dispersing the church's monetary assets. A number of key responsibilities are involved. The finance committee generally establishes the annual church budget, forecasts financial needs, oversees allocations, arranges for an annual audit, and guides the work of the church treasurer and financial secretary. Note that fund raising per se is primarily a stewardship task; determining how much is required is a budget projection.

The church treasurer carries out a majority of the financial decisions of the Finance Committee together with normally assigned duties of handling funds and keeping accurate records. The financial secretary receives, records, and deposits all funds.

What follows is mostly finance technology, but financial officers must never forget that as servants of the Lord their chief responsibility is to encourage financial priorities that reflect God's will for the congregation. Money is neutral until we allocate it at which time it makes a powerful statement about our trust and commitment. Areas often receiving insufficient attention include pastoral staff salaries, ministries within the neighborhood community, and evangelism. Prayer and thoughtful discussion should be the mainstay of budget preparation. A congregation should always be able to defend its priorities with confidence.

Funding and Budget Comparisons

Every church has special expenditure opportunities and obligations as well as varied revenue sources. However, same denomination congregations of similar size and physical facilities, operating in similar neighborhoods, may well be considered *peers* for comparison purposes. Average Sunday school attendance may also be used in refining the selection. The resulting peer group should number at least a dozen or more congregations to ensure confidence in the true central tendency of median values.

The financial capabilities and effort of a community of people such as a church congregation are best reported in terms of average values supplemented, if desired, by central tendency medians.[1] Recommended financial measurements typically include average pledge level, numbered envelope contributions per average Sunday service attendee, budget composition, and salary and benefit levels. Supporting records and charting are described in some detail in Chapter 19, "Our Call to Stewardship," beginning on page 305.

In general, contributions per attending member bear little relationship to either family income[2] or congregation size. Gifts are essentially a matter of the heart. Contributions and budget composition are consequently largely matters of congregational spiritual growth, strongly influenced by church encouragement. With such controlling factors, the finances of any given congregation may deviate substantially in some regards from the median or central tendency of a comparison group. While this variance should be expected, every departure should be investigated to ensure its validity under existing circumstances. Surprises are sometimes in store, warranting corrective action. Trends over time similarly should be reviewed principally to ensure they are not consequences of accidental drift.

When making inter-church expenditure comparisons, stick to the basic functions: parish life, worship, education, youth, evangelism, community ministry, administration, and building operations. Salaries are generally compared as a separate line-item. Commitment to missions, major repairs, and debt service vary greatly. Compare these expenditures independently with caution.

Salary Schedule

A number of rules should be followed regarding establishing an equitable church salary schedule:

(1) benefits (housing, health benefits, sick leave, pension, social security allowance, disability, parental leave, vacation time, travel compensation, professional expenses, and continuing education) should be consistent with need and equitable among the various church positions.

(2) salary differentials based on job content, difficulty, and years of experience should be carefully established and reasonably maintained as a "wage structure" over time.

(3) other "special factors" such as family size and adverse working conditions may warrant special compensation.

(4) the wage structure should be adjusted yearly for inflation.

The wage structure can be established by a formula which isolates for individual adjustment each factor and ensures uniformity in application. Consider the following "formula" adopted from a number of synod recommendations:[3]

1. Set pastoral starting yearly *base* salary (excluding separate provision for housing and such benefits as education, travel, medical, etc.) dependent on congregational resources and survey of local and national market conditions for new pastoral entrants: $35,000*

2. Adjust base salary by involved position:

Senior pastor	100%
Associate pastor	+90%
Director of music	+85%
Custodian	+65%

3. Multiply by years of incumbent's total lifetime professional/occupational work experience: +3.0%/yr for first 20 years
   +1.5%/yr after 20 years

1 yr	x1.030
5 yr	x1.159
10 yr	x1.344
20 yr	x1.806
35 yr	x2.258

4. Add qualifications/duties compensation:
   —For 450 hours of continuing education
      beyond the Master of Divinity degree   +7%
   —For additional responsibilities associated
      with a large congregation averaging
      over 225 attendees at Sunday worship.   +7%
   —Merit increase for demonstrating particular
      excellence in one or more major
      responsibilities.   +5%

* Base salary used here represents typical entry level salary offered to master's degree candidates in the humanities in 2005.

Under the above schedule, a senior pastor with 10 years total experience, serving a congregation averaging 250 worship attendees, would annually earn a base salary exclusive of fringe benefits of $50,333 ($35,000 x 100% x 1.344 x 1.07).

Budget Presentation

The underlying rule for all budget presentations is accuracy, clarity, and sufficient detail over time to convey real understanding. Current operating revenues and expenditures should be sharply distinguished and separated from all capital funding. Revenues by source should be reported in both dollar amounts and percentage distribution; expenditures reported similarly by function (See Charts 3 and 5, Chapter 19, pages 307and 308). Typical revenue categories include: pledged donations, plate collections, special gifts, sales and special projects, foundation/trust allotments, property rental, and interest/dividends. Yearly pledged donations by gift size may be reported to indicate relative reliance on large versus small donors. Major changes in revenues or expenditures over time should always be noted. All windfall revenues and exceptional expenditures must always be separately reported to avoid year-to-year distortion. Lastly, account for inflation over all extended reporting periods.

Expenditure divisions generally reflect the various committee activities: parish life, worship, education, youth, evangelism, and community ministry. Additional expenditure groupings may include missions, staff salaries, administrative expenses, building operations, capital debt retirement, and synod/district payments. The budget share for salaries is commonly reported.

Salary Prorating

Shares of the salaries of individual staff members should be prorated to each functional activity to reflect the actual total investments involved. This allocation need not be too detailed, only sufficient to provide a general idea of the total funding emphasis given each function.

A typical pastor's activity schedule, based on full church staffing, training, and delegation of authority, for example, might involve a 50-hour work week schedule as follows:

- 25% Personal study (principally sermon preparation)
- 6% Personal administration (phone calls, letters, etc.)
- 19% Staff administration (staff meetings, instruction, assignments)
- 10% Counseling, weddings, funerals
- 10% Visitations
- 20% Council and committee meetings
- 3% Teaching/Bible study
- 7% Worship service conduct

This schedule might be converted on an estimated basis to the involved functional areas for allocation purposes as follows:

- 22% Parish life (includes all pastoral visitations and counseling)
- 33% Worship (includes personal study and service conduct)
- 4% Education
- 3% Stewardship
- 2% Youth
- 1% Evangelism
- 2% Community Ministry
- 8% Council planning and meetings
- 25% Administration (personnel and staff)

Using these rates multiplied by the pastor's salary and benefits equal the rough dollar value employed for each function. To these amounts are added the salary allocations of other employed staff, together with the direct expenditures involved and values of contributed services, to equal a resultant total "investment" in each function. This aggregation has previously been introduced in Chapter 19, Table 2a, page 309, in explaining to parishioners how their funding is spent. Only such a combination of direct expenditures, allocated staff salaries, and contributed services, reveals true comparative inputs, and hence relative importance of the church's various undertakings.

Investment Strategy

Churches fortunate enough to have inviolate funds from which derived income and appreciation only are available, are responsible for informed, rigorous oversight. Investment policy generally centers on establishing an appropriate balance between a diversified stock portfolio and government bonds. Long-term investment, often five years or more, generally favors stocks and their growth potential; shorter-duration investment provides the security of fixed-income bonds. Comparisons for various time periods provide the essential input information. Consider, for example, the average annual total return rates for three periods ending June 30, 2000: S&P 500 Index -7.3% (1 year), +23.8% (5 years), +17.7% (10 years); Long-Term Treasury Bonds +6.3% (1 year), +7.0% (5 years), +9.1% (10 years). Note that even over relatively long periods, stock are not always the superior investment. From 1960 through 1979, for example, the Standard & Poor's 500 Index returned an average of 5.8% per year, trailing the 6.4% return for U.S. Treasury bills, and the 7.4% average annual inflation rate (*Source:* The Vanguard Group). For most churches holding long-term funds, a stock-heavy mix of indexed funds is generally advisable. Keep in mind that too conservative an investment policy is as great a disservice to the congregation as too aggressive.

Property Administration

The property division provides for the purchase, upkeep, and improvement of the church building, grounds, parsonage, and equipment, including related appearance and safety considerations. Secondary duties include assignment of space and equipment, inventory control, housekeeping, security, compliance with local and federal codes, fire alarms and extinguishers, and facility safety. All of these duties are typically assigned to an employed property manager or management firm, aided by member volunteers and overseen by the committee.

With the heavy load generally performed by assigned staff, the property group may well direct its attention to various church environmental concerns often of major impact on member comfort and involvement. Consider the following check list[4]:

- *Signs* Are entrances clearly marked? Are interior signs appropriately located throughout the building to identify and provide directions? Can outside signs be read by passing cars?
- *Information* Is there a manned information table and bulletin board display?
- *Greeters* Are greeters stationed at the church entrances and trained in welcoming all?

• *Building and grounds* Is the exterior and interior of the building in good repair? Is the landscaping attractive? Are the restrooms clean and fully stocked?

• *Parking* Are there "visitor" parking spaces.

• *Worship service* Is appropriate music being played as people enter the sanctuary in preparation for worship? Is the service bulletin user-friendly? Are church information brochures in the pew racks? Is the sound system clear and audible? Is a clean safe nursery provided?

• *Hospitality* Is everyone made to feel at home following the service? Do members display genuine, outgoing friendliness toward each other and visitors?

• *Interior* Is the sanctuary aesthetically pleasing with comfortable seating. Are all interior spaces clean and well lighted? Is the temperature comfortable?

---

[1] To illustrate differences in average versus median values in reporting funding capacity and effort, consider the following example:

Number of active members	Income level	Average gift	Gifts as % of income
10	$30,000	$900	3%
20	$40,000	$1,600	4%
30	$50,000	$2,000	4%
20	$65,000	$3,250	5%
10	$85,000	$4,250	5%
10	$110,000	$6,600	6%
TOTAL 100	$5,850,000	$274,500	4.7%
AVERAGE	$58,500	$2,745	
MEDIAN	$50,000	$2,000	

In the above illustration, the few wealthy members greatly increase the congregation's overall funding capacity and achievement. Sixty percent of the members earn $50,000 or less annual income and contribute $2,000 or less yearly. Yet the average gift of $2,745 is much higher because of the high income ($110,000) and generosity ($6,600) of the congregation's wealthiest members.

[2] State and county statistics are readily available at quickfacts.census.gov.

[3] Adopted from Rocky Mountain Synod, Evangelical Lutheran Church in America, compensation guidelines. See rmselca.org. Compensation survey resources include James F. Cobble, Jr. and Richard R. Hammer, *The Annual Compensation Handbook for Church Staff* (Christian Ministry Resources); *National Church Staff Compensation Survey* (National Association of Church Business Administration); and *Christian Ministries Compensation Handbook* (Christian Management Association).

[4] Adapted, in part, from "Igniting Ministry" Comfort Checklist, United Methodist Communications.

Appendix A
Christian Music

O give thanks to the Lord, for he is good; his steadfast love endures forever!
—Psalm 118, verse 1. The 150 Psalms were composed and chanted over a long period of time, from the tenth century to the third century BC.

O splendor of God's glory bright, O thou that bringest light from light.
—*O Splendor of God's Glory Bright*, words by Aurelius Ambrose, Bishop of Milan, 4th century.

Joyful, joyful, we adore thee, God of glory, Lord of love;
Hearts unfold like flowers before thee, opening to the sun above.
—*Ode to Joy* from the 9th Symphony, 4th movement, Ludwig Van Beethoven, 1824

Let us break bread togededer on our knees,
  Let us break bread togedder on our knees,
When I fall on my knees wid my face to de risin' sun,
  Oh, Lord, hab mercy on me.
—African American spiritual, early 1800s

All my hope is in you, O Lord, you are my rock and my strength.
—*To Hope! A Celebration*, a mass in the Revised Roman Ritual, Dave Brubeck, 1979

"Hymns are the jewels which the Church has worn…"
—Henry Ward Beecher

Music stirs our souls, leading us into the presence of God through the singing of angels. It nourishes our spirit, engages and focuses the mind, and remains refreshingly available in mental renewal. By whatever metaphors described, Christian music has the capacity of lifting us to new levels of personal rapture and spiritual transport. Thus we follow with joy Paul's advice to the Ephesians. *Sing and make music in your heart to the Lord.* (Ephesians 5:19)

Christian music is characterized by many features, not the least being its exceptional quality, breadth of style and orchestration, and extended history. We focus here on only one dimension, *melody quality*, further confined, in this instance, to the limited perspective and investigation of the author. The intent is simply to *illustrate* the selection/refinement process, thereby hopefully encouraging greater employment of melody quality as a key dimension in Christian music selection. Attentive musicians recognize this appreciation of melody and are encouraged to make their program and orchestration selections accordingly.

Selection Process *Melody quality* is defined here simply as lastingly pleasing to the typical listener's ear, i.e., providing memorable tonal and rhythmic pleasure. Of course, what is pleasing to one ear may not be recognized as such by others. However, this first cut in such a vast field as Christian music, is more likely to be successful than later culling when remaining differences are likely to be less distinct and readily observed.

We present here an initial selection of 139 titles. An extended effort would likely produce 10 times this number.[1] However, the intent is again simply to illustrate the undertaking and encourage self-devised listings.

Excluded from the list are most popular hymns. They are so well known and loved as to constitute an integral part of modern day worship without need for further recognition here.[2] However, a number of lesser known hymns deemed especially melodic are included. And some other selected music also appears in hymn form.

Organization Music is typically organized by genre, that is by style such as classical, rhythm and blues, gospel, soul, rock, and country. Christian music may be similarly ordered, for religion has been a subject of essentially every form of musical interpretation.

Another grouping is by performing artist. Here the Christian list is extensive, for no one, from individual performer[3] to national symphony, appears unaware of the challenge and rewards of such focus.

Christian music may further be organized by the nature of employment, for example as a voluntary, hymn, anthem, offertory, or musical offering.[4] No hard and fast rules are involved, for many compositions may be varied in style, tempo, duration, and instrumentation to fit a number of applications. There are exceptions. Hymns, for example, typically remain in this domain, however alternatively interpreted. And many short works have gravitated through practice to specific uses such as acts of praise, canticles, and doxologies.

Yet generally across the spectrum of Christian music, the breadth of today's multiple interpretations suggest the inherent error of any forced classification. Thus we resort here to simply listing the selections of this appendix alphabetically by title which, at least, facilities title searches. Entry titles are followed by name of musical composer and date of composition in parentheses; arranger; and source (by page number in the instance of the *United Methodist Hymnal (UMH)*, 1989, *Presbyterian Hymnal (PH), 1990,* or *The Faith We Sing (FWS)*, 2000, supplement.[5] Notations are not always complete.

References We bring to your attention two attractive references of particular value in music selection. First, Patrick Kavanaugh's *The Music of Angels: A Listener's Guide to Sacred Music from Chant to Christian Rock* (Chicago, Loyola Press, 1999, 333 pp.). Dr. Kavanaugh guides us through 14 periods of sacred music beginning with the origins of sacred music (1-400 AD) through the chant, medieval, Renaissance, Baroque, Classical, and Romantic periods, concluding with twentieth century modern classic, gospel, contemporary, country, folk, and jazz music. For each period the genre is described, major artists introduced, and recordings recommended. The bibliography includes over 400 references listed by chapter. The index is equally detailed.

The subtitle of *The Story of Christian Music: From Gregorian Chant to Black Gospel, an Authoritative Illustrated Guide to All the Major Traditions of Music for Worship* (Minneapolis, Fortress Press, 1992), 256 pp., suggests the comprehensive treatment provided. The 47 chapters of Andrew Wilson-Dickson's work are organized in eight parts: "The Birth of Christian Music," "Renaissance and Reformation," "The Flowering of Christian Music," "The Path Divides," "Eastern Traditions," "The American Genius," "Music in North America," and "Music in Twentieth-Century Europe." The substantive content is attractively written and supplemented with many color plates and score illustrations.

Selected Christian Music

A Mighty Fortress Is Our God (Martin Luther, ca. 1529) Organ Fantasia arr. by Diane Bish, *UMH* #110.
A Symphony of Spirituals (African-American spirituals) arr. for two pianos by Joel Raney.
All Hail the Power of Jesus' Name (Oliver Holden, 1792) piano solo arr. by Gregor Ralston, *UMH* #154.
Alleluia, Alleluia! Give Thanks (Donald Fishel, 1973) *UMH* #162.
Amazing Grace (19th cent. USA melody) arr. by Robert G. Swift, jazz piano arr. by John Coates, Jr., *UMH* #378.
Aria (Craig Phillips).
"Arnstadt" Fugue in C Minor (Johann Sebastian Bach) BWV^6 #549.
Be Not Afraid (Craig Courtney, 1992).
Be Still and Know (Stephen Curtis Chapman) cello and violin arr. by Alexis Joyce.
Be Still, My Soul (Jean Sibelius, 1899) arr. by Mack Wilberg, *UMH* #534.
Because of Who You Are (Bob Farrell and Bill Smiley).
Bind Us Together (Bob Gillman) *FWS* #2226.
Bless the Lord, O My Soul (Robert G. Swift, 1994).
Born to Die (Glenn Burleigh) cantata for chorus, soloists and orchestra.
Born To Set Me Free (Steve Wood).
Canon of Praise (Johann Pachelbel, 1653-1706) arr. by Hal Hopson.
Change My Heart, O God (Eddie Espinosa).
Christ Has No Body Now But Yours (David Ogden, 2002).
Come Sunday (att. Duke Ellington).
Concerto in G after Walther, Allegro (Johann Sebastian Bach).
Creator Spirit, Heavenly Dove (Robert Powell).
Day by Day (Donald Busarow).
Elegy for pipe organ (George Thalben-Ball).
Eternal Father, Strong to Save, the "Navy Hymn" (John B. Dykes) arr. by John Innes, *FWS* #2191.

Fanfare for the Common Man (Aaron Copland) orchestra and choir.
Fantasie in G Minor (Johann Sebastian Bach).
Fantasy on 'Slane' (Libby Larsen).
Finale from Symphony No. 1 (Louis Vierne, 1898-99).
Foundation, Organ Variations on the hymn tune (early USA melody) arr. by Diane Bish, *UMH* #529.
For the First Time (Twelve Impressions in a Child's Day), Part I. Church Bells (Howard Hanson, 1896-1981).
From Everlasting to Everlasting, Thou Art God (John Ness Beck).
Fugue from *The Double Clavier Concerto in C Major*, (Johann Sebastian Bach) for two pianos, *BWV* #1061.
Give Thanks (Henry Smith, 1978) *TFWS* #2036.
Glorious Things of Thee Are Spoken (Croatian folk song) arr. by Franz Joseph Haydn, 1797, *UMH* #731.
Go Down, Moses (African-American Spiritual) arr. for two pianos by Joel Raney.
Go Ye Now in Peace (Joyce Elaine Eilers) SATB.[7]
God of Grace and God of Glory (John Hughes, 1907) arr. by Paul Manz, *UMH* #577.
Who Stretched the Spangled Heavens (William Moore, 1825) *UMH* #150.
He Touched Me (William J. Gaither, 1963) piano variations arr. by Fred Bock, *UMH* #367.
Here I am Lord. Is it I, Lord? (Daniel L. Schutte, 1981) adapt. by Carlton R. Young, 1988, *UMH* #593.
Here, O My Lord, I See Thee (Edward Dearle, 1874) *UMH* #623.
How Can I Keep From Singing? (Robert G. Swift, 2005).
I Can Hear My Savior Calling (John Samuel Norris, 1844-1907).
I Know My Redeemer Lives (att.to John Hatton, 1793).
I Lift Up Mine Eyes to the Hills! (Robert G. Swift, 1997).
I Want Jesus to Walk with Me (African-American Spiritual) arr. for two pianos by Joel Raney.
If We Are the Body (Casting Crowns).
I'll Fly Away (Albert E. Brumley) *FWS* #2282.
Improvisation on "Ye Servants of God" (attr. to William Croft, 1708) arr. by Roland Diggle, *UMH* #181.
Inscription of Hope (Z. Randall Stroope, 1953).
In the Garden (C. Austin Miles, 1912) arr. by Mark Hayes.
In the Presence of Jehovah (Geron and Becky Davis).
In This Very Room (Ron and Carol Harris, 2004).
Irlandaise (Claude Bolling).
It Is Well With My Soul (Philip P. Bliss, 1876) piano solo arr. by Frank Voltz, *UMH* #377.
It's Okay To Be Different (Gene Grier, Lowell Everson, and Natalie Sleeth) piano solo.

Joshua Fit the Battle of Jericho (American spiritual) piano solo arr. by Frank Voltz.
Joyful, Joyful, We Adore Thee (Ludwig van Beethoven, 1824) arr. for two pianos by Mark Hayes, *UMH* #89.
Kyrie, #2 from *'Requiem'* (Bradley Ellingbow, 2002).
Laudate Dominum from *Vesperate Solennes de Confessore*, K339 (Wolfgang Amadeus Mozart).
Leaning on the Everlasting Arms (Anthony J. Showalter, 1887) arr. by Bruce Greer, *UMH* #133.
Let There Be Praise! (Sandy Patti).
Let Us Break Bread Together (African-American Spiritual) arr. for two pianos by Joel Raney.
Like a River Glorious (James Mountain, 1876) arr. for piano by Bob Walters.
Lord, Here Am I (John Ness Beck).
Lord, I Want to be a Christian (Afro-American spiritual) arr. Jewell Taylor Thompson.
Lord Jesus Christ, Be Present Now (Eugene Butler).
Lord, Listen to Your Children (Ken Medema).
Lord of the Dance (19th cent. Shaker tune) arr. by Joel Raney, *UMH* #261.
Lord, Who Throughout These Forty Days (USA folk melody) arr. by Annabel Morris Buchanan, 1938, *UMH* #269.
Loving Spirit (V. Earle Copes) *FWS* #2123.
Make Me a Captive, Lord (George J. Elvey, 1868) *UMH* #421.
Maker, in Whom We Live (George J. Elvey, 1868) *UMH* #88.
Meditation (Georgeann Weaver).
More of You Lord (Ralph Merrifield).
Morning Has Broken (Gaelic melody) harm. by Carlton R. Young, 1988, arr. by Diane Bish, *UMH* #145.
My Faith Looks Up to Thee (Lowell Mason, 1831) arr. by Robert Elmore, *UMH* #452.
My Help Cometh From the Lord (Jackie Gouche Farris).
My Shepherd Will Supply My Need (William Walker, 1835).
My Tribute (Andrae Crouch, 1971) *UMH* #99.
Myn Lyking/Angel Gabriel (R. R. Terry).
Now Let Us from This Table Rise (*Grenoble Antiphoner*, 1753) harm. by Ralph Vaughan Williams, 1906, *UMH* #634.
O Day of Rest and Gladness.
Ode to Joy, Improvisations on (Mark Hayes).
Oh I Couldn't Hear Nobody Pray (Black spiritual) arr. by Edward Boatner, 1927.
On Eagle's Wings (Mary Donnelly and George L. O. Strid) arr. by Charles Callahan.
On the Jericho Road (J. Ritter Werner).
Open Our Eyes (Bob Cull, 1976) *TFWS* #2086.

Praise to the Lord, the Almighty (Craig Phillips).
Prayer of St. Francis (Helen Litz).
Precious Lord Take My Hand ("Maitland" by George N. Allen) adapt. by Thomas Dorsey.
Prelude in C Major, BWV 846 (Johann Sebastian Bach, 1772).
Redeemer (Claire Cloninger and David Williamson).
Rejoice, the Lord Is King (John Darwall, 1770) *UMH* #715.
Rise and Shine (Andrew Peterson).
Rondeau (Jean Joseph Mouret).
Search Me, O God, and Know My Heart Today (Maori melody).
Sent Forth by God's Blessing (Welsh folk tune) harm. by Leland Sateren, 1972, *UMH* #664.
Sing with All the Saints in Glory (Ludwig van Beethoven, 1824) arr. by Donald Busarow, UMH #702.
Sonata for Flute and Piano, 1st movement (Francis Poulenc, 1956).
Soon and Very Soon (Andrae Crouch, 1978) *UMH* #706.
Spirit of God (Steve Garnaas-Holmes,1987) TFWS # 2117.
Spirit of the Living God (Daniel Iverson, 1926) *UMH* #393.
Spirit Song (John Wimber, 1979) *UMH* #347.
Still, Still, Still (Austrian Christmas Carol, 1819).
Surely, It Is God Who Saves Me (Jack Noble White).
Surely the Presence of the Lord (Lanny Wolfe, 1977) *UMH* #328.
Swing Low, Sweet Chariot (African-American Spiritual) arr. for two pianos by Joel Raney.
Take My Life, and Let It Be (Louis J. F. Herold, 1839) arr. in Calypso style by David H. Williams, *UMH* #399.
Tango on Down Ampney (Mark Sedio).
That Easter Day with Joy Was Bright (Latin hymn, 5th C.) *PH* # 121.
The Best of Rooms (Donald Busarow).
The Dream Isaiah Saw (Glenn L. Rudolf, 2001) arr. by Thomas H. Troeger and Glenn L. Rudolph.
The Gift of Love (traditional English melody) adapt. by Hal Hopson, 1972, *UMH* #408.
The God of All Eternity (John Bell, 1989).
The Lord Bless You and Keep You! (Robert G. Swift, 2005).
The Prayer (Carole Bayer Sager and David Foster, 2005).
There is a Happy Land (George Shearing).
There's a Song of Love in My Heart (Handt Hanson) *FWS* #2141.
This Is My Song (Jean Sibelius, 1899) *UMH* #437.
Thou Art Holy (Craig Courtney).
Thou Who Wast Rich Beyond All Splendour (traditional French carol) arr. by Rick Parrell.
Toccata and Fugue in D Minor, BWV 565 (Johann Sebastian Bach, 1707).
Toccata from *Organ Symphonie #5* (Charles-Marie Widor, 1905).
Toccata from *Suite Gothique,* Opus 25 (Leon Boellmann).

Toccata from Symphony No. 5, Op. 42 for organ, No. 5 (Charles-Marie Widor, 1844-1937).
Trust and Obey (Daniel B. Towner, 1887) *UMH* #467.
Variations on "America" (Charles Ives, 1891-92, 1902).
Variaions on the tune "Assurance" (Michael Faircloth) piano solo.
Variations on the tune "Showalter" (Bruce Greer) piano solo.
We Are Singing (20th cent. South Africa) accom. by Hal H. Hopson, *FWS* #2235-a.
We Thank Thee, Dear God (Johann Sebastian Bach).
We Walk by Faith (attr. to Hugh Wilson) *FWS* #2196.
What Does the Lord Require of You? (Jim Strathdee) *FWS* #2174.
When I Am Lifted Up (Robert G. Swift, 2003), for two pianos.
When I Need Him/Precious Lord (Sandi Patti) arr. by Sandi Patti and Clyde Haas.
When I Return (Homeward Bound) (Marta Keen).
Who Is Thy Neighbor (*"Dalehurst"* by Arthur Cottman, 1874) piano solo arr. by M. Cox.
You Raise Me Up (Brendan Graham and Rolf Lovland, 2002) arr. by Roger Emerson-Steven Shaner.

> O come, let us sing to the Lord;
> Let us make a joyful noise to the rock of our salvation!
> Let us come into God's presence with thanksgiving;
> Let us make a joyful noise with songs of praise!
> —Psalm 95

---

[1] The *Encyclopedia of Christian Music* lists over 1,900 performing artists from the '60s on, with of course many times that number of recordings involved. See Mark Allan Powell, *Encyclopedia of Christian Music* (Richmond, VA, Hendrickson Publishers, 2002) 1,088 pp.

[2] An excellent anthology of such works is Robert J. Morgan's *Then Sings My Soul*, Nashville, Thomas Nelson Publishers, 2003, 308 pp.

[3] Among the many contemporary artists contributing to the wealth of today's Christian music are the following popular entertainers, musicians, and composers: Roy Acuff, Leonard Bernstein, Pat Boone, Oak Ridge Boys, Dave Brubeck, Johnny Cash, Roy Clark, Judy Collins, Aaron Copland, Tommy Dorsey, Bob Dylan, Duke Ellington, Aretha Franklin, Amy Grant, Mahalia Jackson, Barbara Mandrell, Wynton Marsalis, The Platters, Elvis Presley, Ricky Skaggs, Randy Travis, and Hank Williams.

[4] A voluntary is a relatively short composition, usually for solo organ, played before (**prelude**), during (**voluntary**), or after (**postlude**) a religious service. **Toccatas**, often used as postludes, are compositions, usually for organ or keyboard, in free style with full chords and elaborate runs.

Sacred songs (**hymns**) have undoubtedly been the foremost musical element in the Christian church since its beginning. Built on a foundation of Hebrew singing of the psalms, new Christian responsive songs and chants, drawn upon New Testament writings, were sung in the churches of Asia Minor in the latter part of the first century. From the listings in various hymnals, it is easy to infer that well over a thousand hymns gleaned from the ages are in use today. And more are added yearly. The *Faith We Sing* supplement to the *United Methodist Hymnal,* for example, lists 284 new hymn additions for the intervening 11 years (1989-2000).

An **anthem** is a choral composition with a religious text from the Psalms or other parts of the Scriptures or the liturgy. A "full anthem" is sung by an unaccompanied chorus; a "verse anthem" alternates soloist and choir, often instrumentally accompanied.

An **offertory** is generally a short instrumental piece played by the organist or a choral rendition sung while the offering is collected.

Musical offerings include all other renditions not defined above.

[5] *The Faith We Sing* supplement begins with hymn number 2001.

[6] BWV (Bach-Werke-Verzeichnis, Thematic-Systematic Listing of the works of J. S. Bach).

[7] SATB (soprano, alto, tenor, and bass).

Appendix B
Job Descriptions

Job descriptions were introduced in Chapter 9 (page 113) as an essential management tool to establish position responsibilities and guide operations. They are at once both one of the single best methods of promoting effective operations as well as the most neglected. "Job descriptions spell out specifically and concisely, the activities and responsibilities of a job, and the manner and circumstances in which they are to be performed. They include authority, accountability, coordination, and reporting responsibilities." Thus whenever confusion or misunderstandings contribute to deficiencies in any of these areas, job descriptions go a long way in providing a lasting remedy.

Yet despite these exceptional benefits, job descriptions are too often neglected or ignored. The common reasons are two-fold. First, the descriptions themselves are too often vague and insufficiently detailed to provide real guidance and control. Second, new leaders are not instructed on their duties using the descriptions, nor are they informed of their associated accountability. The description instrument is itself sound; the fault typically lies in the failed design and employment.

By way of summary, we list five rules for developing and ensuring the proper use of job descriptions:

1. Descriptions should be written as detailed and comprehensive as possible to provide all necessary guidance to the new position holder. Church job descriptions generally include:
   — desirable personal qualifications including special skills/talents, education and training, and experience.
   — time commitment, meeting attendance, and travel requirements.
   — authority and accountability.
   — leadership responsibilities including recruiting, organizing, directing, coordinating, and reporting.
   — assigned responsibilities spelled out in reasonable detail. This is the *what*, *how*, and *why* of the job.

2. Descriptions should be recognized as an instructional *guide*, one that advises and assists rather than specifically directs. Latitude exercised in interpretation, however, should generally be approved.

3. Descriptions should be understood as a *developing* document to be upgraded and expanded by each succeeding incumbent. Descriptions should be reviewed annually.

A dozen major position descriptions are reported in this appendix:
- Senior Pastor
- Director of Music/Organist
- Congregation Council President

Common Committee Elements
- Parish Life Committee
- Worship, Music, and Arts Committee
- Education Committee
- Stewardship Committee
- Evangelism Committee
- Community Service Committee
- Youth Committee
- Finance Committee
- Property Committee

A number of support positions[1] such as church office, library, and maintenance positions may also warrant descriptions which are not reported here. Large congregations may, in addition, have further need for omnibus positions such as communications coordinator, lay leadership, and director of long-range planning. Such functions, however, are integral to all church activities and consequently often are not separately described.

Non position-specific aspects of employment such as working conditions, salary and benefits, evaluation, grievances and resolution of disputes, and termination are typically detailed in written personnel policy applicable to all staff and consequently not part of job descriptions.

The following descriptions are generic in nature, composites from a number of sources. Individual congregations must, of course, tailor their descriptions to suit the specific situation involved. Descriptions must also be updated to respond to new conditions and challenges.

Senior Pastor

Provide spiritual and shepherding leadership and oversight in developing and implementing the vision and mission of the congregation. Direct and guide the church staff and volunteer leaders in completion of established church missions and goals.

Personal character

The pastor is above all a praying, godly person, fully devoted to Jesus Christ. The pastor seeks with all his/her person to strongly and lovingly communicate God's heart and Word to the congregation, encouraging all in developing their spiritual gifts and discipleship.

Personal qualities sought include:
- a model life of faith and prayer.
- exemplary life style of integrity, humility, authenticity, and openness.
- a heart of love, a caring, shepherding spirit.
- personable with a healthy sense of humor.
- a servant leader who leads by example.

Skills and abilities
- able to preach informative, interesting, expositional messages with relevant application that challenge believers and lead others to Christ.
- a team builder who models, trains, and inspires others in an atmosphere of unity and common purpose.
- an effective communicator from the pulpit and one-on-one.
- capable of casting a compelling vision of all the church's potential.
- knowledgeable of effective management principles and team-based decision-making.

Line of authority

The senior pastor is accountable to God through personal prayer, leading by the Holy Spirit, and looking to Jesus Christ as the head of the Church. He is also responsible and personally accountable to the congregation, reporting to the church council holding ultimate authority. The senior pastor has authority and accountability for leadership of the staff.

RESPONSIBILITIES:
Leadership

- Work with the staff, church council, and committees to provide vision and guidance for church growth and future development of ministries, facilities and resources. Assist in conducting related current and long-range planning, always focused on the church's visions and values.
- Encourage all in the development and exercise of their spiritual gifts and talents.
- Recommend actions and assist council officers in preparing for meetings. Actively participate in council deliberations.
- Commit significant time to renewal, reading, and research for personal growth and health. Attendance at educational and professional conferences is encouraged.

Administration

- Lead and supervise the staff, council, and committees to see that the stated missions of the congregation are effectively and harmoniously accomplished while encouraging creativity and innovation. Hold regular staff meetings and one-on-one sessions, always encouraging open frank discussion of issues.
- Assist in the identification, recruitment, and training of staff and congregational leaders.
- Monitor staff performance and conduct annual performance review.
- Represent the church and work with outside organizations in church related activities.

Worship

Oversee and guide the worship life of the congregation to realize God's calling for all.
- Preach and teach the Word of God in accordance with the Holy Scriptures.
- Set worship service themes and music with the assistance of staff.

- Administer the sacraments.
- Conduct weddings and funerals and provide supportive pastoral care and guidance.

Parish Life

Attend the congregation to see that they receive all needed spiritual care, guidance, and support from the church staff and congregation.
- Encourage true Christian brotherhood among all members.
- Honor and support all church leaders in their roles of striving to be God's disciples.
- Provide pastoral care to all in need by counseling, prayer, crisis intervention, personal visits, and telephone contacts.
- Seek the development of small groups for Christian brotherhood.

Stewardship

Provide guidance and support to secure and develop the time, talents and spiritual gifts, and financial resources of all members of the congregation with special attention to cultivating Christian growth and participation in marginal and new members. Intentionally seeks out venues to utilize the gifts of all.

Evangelism

Oversee and guide the congregation's efforts to reach out to all with the Gospel of Jesus Christ. Demonstrates a passion for the lost.
- Oversee, assist, and participate in all evangelism outreach activities in the neighborhood and surrounding community.
- Help create an inviting and welcoming church environment.
- Assist in the design and oversee the implementation of all welcome training for prospective and new members.

Community service

Work with the social ministry committee to initiate, promote, and support productive social ministry efforts of the congregation.

Christian education

Encourage diligence in study of the Holy Scripture; in use of the means of grace; in prayer and faithful service; and in the manner of holy living. Take every opportunity to personally teach and to challenge and equip all congregants in living as disciples. The pastor's instruction is especially required in the catechumens, new member preparation, youth education, and Bible study.

Finance/administration/property
- Participate fully in the development of the annual church budget, making sure all ministry priorities are funded.
- Work with office holders in preparation and maintenance of job descriptions, personnel policies, and performance evaluations.

Director of Music/Organist

The Director of Music/Organist is the staff person responsible for the church music program including playing the organ and, as proficient, other musical instruments. The Director works under the overall supervision of the senior pastor, in collegial relationship with the church pastors, other staff members, and members of the church's Worship and Music Committee. The Director is the staff liaison to the Worship and Music Committee.

Skills and abilities
— talented instrumentalist.
— broad knowledge of church music repertoire and selection criteria.
— ability to professionally design an attractive, compelling religious service.
— sensitive to the need to provide culturally relevant music and modern instrumentation and arrangements as may arise.[2]
— ability to work independently and effectively with volunteer ensembles to secure their optimal performance.
— ability to compliment the working styles of the pastors, staff, and church council.

RESPONSIBILITIES:
Planning

- Participate with pastors and staff in planning the normal and special worship services of the congregation to ensure their optimal musical enhancement. Attend all designated staff meetings.
- Identify the staffing needs required to support the music program including directors and accompanists.
- Design a strategy for developing and sustaining a full range of opportunities for congregational participation in the music program.
- Assist in the development of alternative worship services as may be sought.
- Work with the Finance Committee in determining the financial resources required to support the music program.
- Maintain a church music resource file.

Operations

- Play the organ and direct the choir at all services as scheduled.
- Conduct weekly and additional rehearsals as required. Seek to develop and enhance member musical talents and skills.
- Work with pastors, staff, and the Stewardship Committee to enlist personnel for membership in the various choirs and ensembles.
- Recruit special music resources as needed.
- Monitor and maintain the church's music resources including the working order of instruments, robes and accessories, and music library.
- Strive to develop new musical skills and maintain currency in liturgical music trends and directions.
- Prepare annual music budget and administer the expenditures of approved items.
- Attend and participate in Worship and Music Committee meetings as an ex-officio member.

Congregation Council President

The Congregation President, together with all Council members, has general oversight of the life, goals, and activities of the congregation to the end that everything is done in accordance with the Word of God. The President is specifically responsible for leading all council and congregational meetings, exercising general administrative responsibility for the entire church organization, and ensuring that all elected and appointed officers and committees function and carry out their assigned duties and responsibilities.

The Congregation President strives to be an example of the life style and ministry of true discipleship.

Primary Responsibilities:
- Ensure that the provisions of the congregation's constitution and its bylaws are carried out.
- Continuously monitor church policies and practices to ensure their effectiveness and consistency with the mission statement and approved plans. Recommend appropriate corrective action.
- Meet with the pastor(s) and selected council and committee members to review past progress and plan future efforts and priorities. This is the president's principal *leadership* function.
- With pastors, staff, and program participants, plan council meeting agendas and prepare advance handout materials.
- Preside at all meetings of the church council. Review previous meetings for lessons learned. Call special council meetings as may be required.
- Communicate council priorities, policies, plans, and approved actions to all congregants.
- Insure proper assignment and implementation of all approved proposals. Provide for means of coordination for joint undertakings.
- Review and secure council approval of all job descriptions.
- Serve as an advisory member of designated committees of the congregation.
- Represent the congregation in matters of business and sign or countersign all legal documents.
- Promote a congregational climate of peace and goodwill, and, as differences and conflicts arise, endeavor to foster mutual understanding.
- Conduct an annual review of the membership roll.
- Present a comprehensive report to the congregation at the annual meeting.

Common Committee Elements[3]

All committees share a large number of common description components such as necessary congregational support, membership, service terms, leadership, and the like. These common elements are reported here a single time in this initial section. They would, of course, be an integral part of each individual committee's job description.

Staff and congregation support
- The pastor(s), staff, council, and congregation members will regularly pray for all committee members and work with the committees to ensure their mission fulfillment.
- The pastor, church officers, and staff will keep the committees informed and provide all necessary assistance and cooperation.
- The leaders of the congregation will provide job descriptions for each committee.
- The congregation will budget appropriate funds to cover the operating needs of each committee.
- The pastor(s) and council will acknowledge and appropriately recognize the services of each committee and its leadership and members.

Committee membership
The committee will consist of at least five members of the congregation, including a chair appointed by the Church Council. The membership should be especially committed to God's requirement to serve with all our talent, strength, and resources. The pastors and any interested congregant will be advisory members of the committee.

In addition to its assigned committee responsibilities to the congregation, committee members have a personal obligation to model the calling of their ministry, exemplifying it to the highest degree...

Service terms
The committee chair's term of office is generally limited to two or three years, thereby extending leadership opportunities. Ex-chairs, with their leadership experience, are strongly encouraged to continue committee membership.

Rank-and-file committee membership can be indefinite, providing it does not interfere with recruiting new enlistments.

Leadership
- The committee chair will exercise the necessary elements of leadership to ensure effective committee operations:

—*Staffing/Organizing/Training.* Democratically seek as broad participation as possible through rigorous recruiting. Systematically arrange the committee for harmonious and unified action. Define and train all members in their assigned responsibilities.

—*Planning* that sets realistic goals and priorities that are in harmony with the missions and capacities of the congregation. Listening to the ideas of all is an important part of early planning.

—*Coordination* of objectives and plans with the church staff and other committees to ensure smooth mutually supporting operations.

—*Directing* that provides the necessary guidance, encouragement, and coordination to accomplish assignments in an effective manner.

—*Evaluating* that rigorously identifies strengths and weaknesses so as to build greater future strength.

- Desirable leadership skills include the ability to determine the essential nature of the topic at hand, a willingness to listen, the skill to

explain clearly and precisely, a sense of humor, and the ability to develop support and enthusiasm.
- Attend all committee, council, and other meetings required of committee leadership.
- Use committee's job description as a guide to the committee's responsibilities, upgrading as experience dictates.

Publicity
- Effectively publicize and promote committee programs and accomplishments with special attention to attracting new membership and support.

Survey and study
- Periodically survey the congregation or special target group, informally and independently or in a unified effort with other committees, to learn member hopes, concerns, and needs relative to the committee's responsibilities.
- Study the committee's field through library research and visits to other churches to improve operating capabilities. Maintain an up-to-date selection of key references in the committee's field.
- Network with other organizations and people beyond the congregation to share mutual concerns, learning experiences, and resources.

Accountability and Reporting
The committee and the chair in particular are accountable to the church council for the effective performance of their assigned duties.
- Prepare as required periodic written reports to the council upon request. The council's approval, for example, is generally required for such undertakings as large inter-committee actions, radical redirection, or substantial resource commitments.
- Prepare an annual *budget request* as part of the congregation's budget development process.
- Prepare an *annual report and review* of its program and achievements to include an evaluation and plans to improve future improvements.
- Constructively participate in the council's *annual review* and evaluation of its effectiveness in fulfilling its responsibilities.

Parish Life Committee
General
"Parish Life," "Christian Community," "In-Reach," and "Nurturing", are all labels referring to how the congregation experiences life together in Christian love for one another and in spiritual growth and fellowship. Parish life involves generous caring for each other, *every* member being important in God's sight and our own. More than any other church activity, achieving a truly loving community is an inherent responsibility of every member as well as the pastors and committees. The ministry contributes many

specifics, but the basic responsibility–to treat everyone as "little Christs"– remains with each congregant.

In the true Christian community we are anxious to be with our congregation friends and trust them always to have our best interests at heart. The Christian congregation, as opposed to any other open access group, continually strives to be "family" to every member. God wills that we love one another. The Parish Life mission is to see this will accomplished.

Mission

To work with the pastors and congregation in developing and sustaining a true Christian community within the church, which provides the love and care to each member as manifested in our Lord Jesus Christ. The committee must be especially sensitive and alert to the needs of individual members.

Responsibilities

- Show love and concern for all members of the congregation by welcoming all, involving all, and treating all with love and dignity to the very least one.
- Monitor the spiritual health of every member by tracking their worship attendance and participation, and detecting inactivity before it becomes a habit. Provide necessary encouragement and counseling assisted by the Stewardship Committee. Note that involvement is often most easily encouraged by invitation to join one of the church's small groups.
- Comfort and provide help in time of hardship and need. This involves working with the pastors and staff to provide a means for identifying the sick, hungry, and lonely within the congregation, and providing appropriate responses. Note: The Community Service Committee (page 391) may help in meeting certain life support needs of members.
- Work with the Stewardship Committee to encourage full involvement of all members in the life and work of the congregation, consistent with individual interests and abilities.
- Canvass and make recommendations regarding the human dimensions of church activities to ensure that member involvement is a personally enriching experience filled with the joy of Christian love and fellowship.
- Establish a place and sense of belonging by fostering a collection of sharing and caring small group communities within the congregation. Each person must feel that he or she belongs to something within the church as a cherished participant. New members especially need to immediately become involved. Small groups must be specifically formed for this purpose. Do not rely on existing structures for these communities invariably have their own overriding missions.
- Ensure that all Sunday service attendees are warmly and individually greeted at the church entrances. Serve as informal hosts during after-service coffee time, engaging all in welcoming conversation especially the apparently neglected. Bring to the attention of assigned Evangelism Committee members any visitors present.

- Conduct welcoming orientation sessions for prospective new members. Train and assign mentors to all individuals and families joining the congregation. Mentors shepherd new families into Christian life within the congregation with special attention to their joining one of the church's "small groups."
- Provide for infant care during the Sunday morning services.
- Provide coffee and appropriate refreshments after each service. Encourage a welcoming, congenial atmosphere.
- Provide convenient display board storage for name tags and encourage their use by all attending members. (Individuals may prefer personal storage in their auto glove compartment.)
- Organize, assign leadership, train, monitor, and support the special function groups, or tasks, within the church community in their respective roles. Examples of such groups typically assigned to the Parish Life Committee are: Sunday Greeters, New Member Sponsorship, Fellowship of Prayer, Lenten Devotional Book, Friends of Shut-Ins, Hostess and Coffee Hour, and Membership Directory.
- Advise the church staff in matters relating to congregational communications to ensure that the importance and involvement of all members is effectively broadcast. Typical church communications include Sunday service bulletin inserts, newsletters, bulletin board announcements, name tags, and website.
- Celebrate the contributions of every member. All volunteer service deserves recognition and we should take every opportunity to show our appreciation and thank all participants.
- Ensure that the pastors and church leaders are accessible to individual members of the congregation.
- Oversee publication of a congregational pictorial-address-telephone directory which vastly aids in everyone knowing each other.
- In addition to the above responsibilities to the congregation, the Parish Life Committee has a special opportunity to develop within its own membership a caring relationship.

Worship, Music, and Arts Committee
General
What happens on Sundays is of major significance in the spiritual lives and well-being of the congregation. It is therefore fitting and proper that the congregation be provided substantial opportunity to contribute to the design and conduct of the religious services in which it partakes. This high responsibility and honor is assigned the Worship and Music Committee, tasked with representing the congregation in all planning and deliberations regarding worship.

Mission
To assist the pastors in planning, supporting, and evaluating the congregation's worship services and festivals, striving in every instance to

provide optimal opportunity to know, love and glorify God and to "bring people into a living relationship with Jesus Christ."

Responsibilities

- With the pastors and music director, assist in planning the design of all services of worship with special attention to securing reverence and glorification of God, true faith, and understanding the saving grace and teachings of Jesus Christ through the Holy Word.

  Further elements of this design include helping the congregation grow in its understanding and appreciation of the seasons of the church year, the lectionary, and the sacraments.

- Assist in developing and introducing new content in existing services and completely new holistic service designs attractive to guests and newcomers.

- Work with the pastor and music director to develop optimal ways music can contribute to the worship experience. Marshall all necessary resources to support the church's choirs. Encourage the participation of instrumentalists.

- Develop ways the performing and visual arts may be used to enhance the congregation's worship, with special attention to using the artistic gifts of congregational members.

- Provide for the recruitment and training of members to serve as lay worship leaders in such capacities as lectors, cantors, and sacrament assistants. Encourage the use of young people as processional cross bearers and acolytes.

- Recruit and train congregational members in supporting worship services by carrying out such tasks as ushering, altar/sacristy care, care of paraments, and the securing and storage of service materials such as candles, wine, palms, ashes, and sanctuary decorations. Work with the Parish Life Committee in securing and training greeters.

- Assist the pastor in developing improved and new ways to strengthen preaching. This may include employment of a "pulpit advisory group" to assist in planning sermons and constructive critiques.

- Promote a children's lesson time with the pastor. (In some instances children of pre-school age are then led to appropriate separate care.)

- Review and selectively use new worship materials including hymn collections, arrangements, and liturgical settings, as they become available. Revive neglected older quality music.

- Encourage periodic invitation of guest preachers.

- Assist in the design of the service bulletin to ensure it is user friendly. Use the insert to publicize future services.

- Develop and oversee the operation and maintenance of the church's audio and visual systems.

- Periodically evaluate the worship service including surveys and interviews with attending members and visitors seeking their input and feedback. Incorporate lessons learned.

- Periodically review the church's sanctuary architecture and acoustics.

- Periodically review the need for a second service.
- Recommend compensation rates for employed clergy engaged in conducting worship services.

Education Committee
General
In no other area of church life is the laity more central, both as leaders and providers, than in Christian education. From church school superintendent to nursery assistant, the program almost exclusively depends on congregational volunteers. This reliance presents both an exceptional opportunity to serve and a great challenge. Meeting all the education needs of a diversified church community requires extensive study, planning, and marshalling. The Education Committee must accordingly be among the strongest of the church's ministries.

Mission
To provide a lifelong program of Christian education opportunities that enables members of all ages to learn the Scriptures and grow in Christian faith and understanding. Much of the day-to-day administration of the church education program may suitably be assigned to a church school superintendent.

Responsibilities
- Provide all planning, direction, and evaluation to effectively conduct ongoing church education programs attractive to and necessary for all segments of the congregation.
- Conduct education needs assessments in the congregation.
- Coordinate recruitment of volunteer teachers for the congregation's education program.
- Conduct fall training workshops for teachers. Maintain suitable orientation instruction materials and incorporate "lessons learned."
- Provide special "introductory" short courses to expand adult participation.
- Plan special events, especially at the beginning of the school year, that promote and encourage participation in the church's education program.
- Communicate with parents regarding the Christian education of their children. Encourage their involvement both in school and at home.
- With the faculty conduct an annual end-of-year review of the education program. Maintain a record of courses taught, course evaluations, and "lessons learned." Adapt and update the school curriculum in the light of available new resource materials and teacher evaluations.
- Provide ways for the congregation to recognize and thank all teachers and volunteer church school leaders.
- Select and introduce periodicals and books of Bible study and Christian living to all church members. Maintain and build the parish library.
- Assist the Stewardship Committee in identifying introductory handout and study materials for spiritual seekers.

- Work with the staff in identifying special instructional needs and inviting guest speakers.
- Effectively announce and promote the church education program.
- Assign classrooms; periodically review the adequacy of employed facilities, furnishings, and equipment.

Stewardship Committee
General
Christian stewardship is management of our assets and talents for God's purposes. It extends to every facet of our being, employing all our skills and resources to serve. We must give ourselves as completely to God as possible, for he has given us the authority to do so and will hold us responsible for our use of his gifts. Think of yourself as simply an administrator of all you are and possess, for we do not even own ourselves. God never relinquishes ownership, only the temporary care. And we must give with true generosity, not hesitantly or with thought of reward. Finally, never tire or be disheartened by any poor response to your service, for through his grace the good work that is possible far exceeds whatever we might envision.

Working with the pastors, the Stewardship Committee has a spiritual mission to encourage and assist members to answer "What shall I render unto the Lord?" This responsibility is never complete, always active. The fullness of the responsibility is nothing less than that of developing Christian lives.

Mission
To provide an ongoing year-round program of stewardship education that invites and encourages all members to participate and share in Christian service and benevolence according to their talents and means. All this is accomplished through the power of the Holy Spirit working for good in us all.

Responsibilities
- Plan and carry out programs to recruit participation and raise funds to support on-going programs and special needs of the congregation and community.
- Provide a year-round contact program through which the hopes and concerns of the congregation are learned and during which members are counseled and encouraged to participate in the church in whatever ways they deem appropriate. Appoint, train, and support a cadre of steward contactors.
- Regularly inform members of the congregation of the many opportunities to serve and participate in the work of the church.
- Select, acquire, and distribute appropriate stewardship resource material.
- Develop educational programs including sermon themes to guide the congregation in furthering their understanding of themselves as stewards of all God's gifts.

- Assist the pastors in interpreting for the congregation the mission and work of the Christian church as a whole and the value of the contribution of each member.
- Maintain a computer record system of the participation of members and of their current interests, abilities, etc., to aid in assisting each individual to find appropriate avenues of involvement.
- Advise the Finance Committee in matters of confidentiality, record keeping, analysis of trends, projections, etc. Work with the committee in conducting the fall "Round-Up" for pledging.
- Advise members of special opportunities for planned charitable giving.
- Work to increase the congregation's understanding of local, national, and world-wide ministries.
- In addition to the above responsibilities to the congregation, the Stewardship Committee has a special opportunity to develop within its own membership a caring, giving, relationship.

Evangelism Committee
General
The members of the Evangelism Committee must fervently believe that scripturally and theologically the first business of our church is evangelism, and this responsibility extends to all members as called by the Spirit; that all aspects of the congregation's life contain the spirit of evangelism; that is, in all things we seek to bring people closer to God. The Evangelism Committee must believe that through training and through the Holy Spirit opportunities for spreading the Good News will be forthcoming.

In no other area is the pastor's support more necessary than in reaching out. Supporting sermons and personal involvement are essential, for going forth is a very difficult task requiring the highest level of leadership and total congregational commitment.

Mission
To lead the congregation in witnessing the gospel of Jesus Christ to people who are not active members of a Christian congregation, and to support the development of faith among this congregation's current members. The committee serves as the conscience and activator of the congregation in reaching out to others who have yet to hear the Good News.

Responsibilities
- Provide a system for identifying *visitors* who attend worship services, engage them in friendly supportive conversation during fellowship time, provide appropriate hand-out materials, and make follow-up contacts to further establish friendship and ascertain ways the congregation may assist. Keep careful records of contacts to ensure adequate attention in every instance.

Support the Parish Life Committee by providing hospitality training to greeters and ushers. Conduct regular audits of the congregation's ability to nurture and cultivate the spirit of hospitality toward guests.

- Maintain a continuing program to educate, encourage, and provide resources to help all congregation members invite *friends, relatives*, and *acquaintances* to worship with them. Use sermons and handouts to teach people *how* to invite others to worship.
- Enlist, train, and support a corps of witnesses whose principal responsibility is to go forth and spread the Good News to the *unchurched*.
- Assist the pastor and lay participants in the development of informal "Friendship Time" instructional sessions for field-contacted individuals seeking faith.
- With the Education Committee, plan and conduct special interest meetings designed to attract community residents. Identify target groups for these outreach efforts and develop specific promotional strategies and invitation communications. Advise church members on how to informally encourage outside participants to join the Christian community.
- Advise the congregation and staff in providing periodic welcoming services that are especially designed to be attractive and "user-friendly" to visitors and newcomers.
- Provide a section in every Sunday service bulletin entitled "Visitor Information."
- Conduct regular audits of the congregation's ethos and practices that nurture and cultivate the spirit of hospitality toward guests and neighbors.
- Work with the Parish Life Committee to ensure sponsorship and encouragement of all new members.
- Train the leaders of all congregation programs to be alert to and responsive to the occasional or indirect participation of non-members in their activities. For example, non-member parents who enroll their children in Sunday school.
- Develop ways to advertise and promote the church services and programs so as to appeal to candidates for the faith. Widen the sphere of church influence via good public relations efforts including advertising. Distribute flyers in the neighborhood and bulk mailings to the surrounding community.
- Maintain records of congregation gains and losses in membership. Discuss with visitors their reasons why they joined or failed to join. Record and convey this information to responsible committees.
- Maintain demographic and other characteristics data of the local community population that will assist in identifying target groups for outreach efforts.

Community Service Committee
General
Unselfish devotion to others is manifestation of the good will of God to all. And there are few actions more personally rewarding. As we help those in need we confront God face-to-face.

No other church program offers such diverse opportunities for involvement, allowing congregations to tailor their participation to best suit members. Major activities include assistance to the poor, homeless, hungry, and sick; remedial tutoring; visits to hospitals, prisons, and retirement homes; house construction and repair; and response to famines, displacements, and natural disasters.

Mission

To organize and provide overall direction of the congregation's efforts to address the social, economic, and emotional needs of the community at large so that quality of life may be improved for all.

Responsibilities

- Study the material and emotional needs of people in the church's service area and alert the congregation to the nature of required assistance.
- Bring to the congregation's attention the special needs of people throughout the world due to natural and other disasters.
- Conduct programs independently, or in conjunction with other organizations, to provide material and emotional assistance to people who are poor, hungry, or victimized.
- Evaluate on-going and new program opportunities in the light of member interests and abilities, and subject need priorities. Modify program involvements accordingly.
- Recognize the unique interests and abilities of members of the congregation and seek to involve each in compatible social ministry efforts. Develop new opportunities as necessary.
- Create awareness of agencies and organizations that seek to alleviate social problems and human needs; develop partnerships with them when feasible; and inform congregational members of their work and the need for financial support.

Youth Committee

General

"And the person who welcomes in my name one such child as this, welcomes me." (Matthew 18:5)

We are so built that in childhood we can more easily come to a knowledge of God in simplicity than in later years. And in those formative years the personal life can be shaped and fitted to God's standard more surely than later on. —Oswald Chambers

Mission

To develop and guide the ministry and programs for children and adolescents so they may grow in Christian faith and service to God and their community. To encourage and nurture the involvement of church youth in all aspects of congregational life. To work closely with the Christian Education Committee in structuring the education and catechism instruction of young people.

Responsibilities

- Develop and oversee programs that provide educational, service, and social opportunities for children, adolescents, and high school age youth of the congregation.

- Structure ways to meaningfully integrate and involve young people into the full ministry of the congregation including leadership roles.
- Provide programs that address the special spiritual growth needs of young people, programs that respond to their social and behavior concerns, and programs that renew and build loving and supportive family ties.
- Develop supportive relationships with the church's young people which may include counseling and visitation.
- Provide guidance to the pastors regarding parental views on the catechism curriculum.
- Develop and oversee ways for young people of high school age to be of service to others.
- Maintain records of young people after they graduate from high school to preserve the congregation's love and concern for their well-being.
- Appoint a member of the committee as Special Events Director responsible for planning, assembling resources, and directing selected traditional yearly youth events. (Note: this responsibility is transferred to a youth ministry director if such a staff position is provided.)
- Be alert to and cultivate the potential future services of youth especially possible callings to the ministry.

Finance Committee

Mission

To provide for the effective management of the financial resources of the congregation to include preparation of an annual budget reflecting realistic anticipated receipts and approved planned expenditures.

Responsibilities

- Provide for a sound financial management system to include bookkeeping, banking, and investment.
- Ensure that all financial matters of the congregation are handled according to professional standards with particular attention to the prompt payment of all obligations.
- Regularly analyze and report to the council the status and trends in church income and expenses together with advisory guidance. Be especially alert and responsive to income shortfalls and expenditure overruns. Assist the Stewardship Committee in broadcasting the budget as informatively as possible and in encouraging financial giving.
- Annually develop and submit to council a yearly draft budget, all components reflecting consultation with the involved staff and committees. Rework as advised.
- Provide for an annual audit of the church's financial record.
- Develop and maintain a long-range financial plan for the congregation.
- Guide the work of an appointed treasurer and financial secretary.

Property Committee
Mission
To provide for the selection, maintenance, improvement, and replacement of the real and personal property of the congregation. To ensure that all selected or designated property meets approved standards of functionality and aesthetics.

Responsibilities
- Provide for the maintenance, repair, and improvement of all real and personal property of the congregation.
- Provide for regular cleaning and maintenance services to ensure proper equipment operation and pleasing surroundings. Advise the involved supervisor regarding the quality of custodial and maintenance services.
- Contract repairs and other services as authorized by the church council.
- Review the need for new equipment, assess options, and make purchase recommendations. The Property Committee should monitor equipment depreciation and obsolescence, make productivity comparisons with new more efficient replacements, and advise accordingly.
- Ensure accessibility and services to people with disabilities.
- Regularly audit the congregation's environmental practices to include energy efficiency, water usage, and environmentally sound waste disposal.
- Review with the Worship Committee the sanctuary sound and visual systems to ensure their adequacy.
- Regularly audit building and property safety elements including fire alarms and extinguisher systems, sidewalks and stair railings, and snow and ice removal.

---

[1] Typical secondary positions generally requiring job descriptions include: business manager; office positions such as church administrator, secretary, receptionist, and office helper; custodial, grounds, and maintenance positions; librarian; Sunday school teacher, daycare coordinator, and nursery attendant; and volunteer coordinator.

[2] The basic instruments of today are the synthesizer, drums, flute, electric guitar, tambourine, bass, and piano.

[3] The content of the job descriptions reported in this text have been derived from many sources including those available on the web. A useful text employed was Michael R. Rothaar, *Developing Effective Committees* (Minneapolis, Augsburg Fortress, 1993), 48 pp.

Appendix C
The Challenge of Seeking Perfection

"Be perfect, therefore, as your heavenly Father is perfect." (Matthew 5:48)

Our heavenly Father does not ask what is beyond our means. So enabled we move forward with confidence knowing we will be guided by the Holy Spirit and strengthened sufficient for any task.

The Commission and Our Enabling Strength

Be shepherds of the church of God, which he made his own through the death of his own Son. (Acts 20:28)

The church is God's spiritual body, commissioned to build his kingdom, strengthened and enabled by the Holy Spirit with all necessary wisdom and power. So aided, we strive for excellence in all church responsibilities—in preserving and enriching worship, in interpreting and teaching the Bible, in serving others, and in extending God's word.

Yet despite this favor, our humanness invariably interferes, leading to misdirection, neglect, and failure. Thus it is incumbent for each of us to strive mightily to serve God to the utmost of our ability, perfecting his church in all ways possible, always humbly and dependent on the Holy Spirit, prayer, and Scripture.

And we know that in all things, God works for the good of those who love him, who have been called according to His purpose. (Romans 8:28)

The Leadership Challenge

Since you are eager to have spiritual gifts, try to excel in gifts that build up the church. (1 Corinthians 14:12)

How well are churches led today? The basic strengths are all in place—our pastors are trained and dedicated, well attending the congregation flock and more often than not leading inspiring worship services. Congregations through elected officers are invariably involved in an array of programs centered on Christian education, youth, and service to others. Visitors are traditionally welcome. And congregations serve as the financial backbone of the church.

On the weakness side, the challenge is overriding complacency, satisfaction with the status quo. In varying degrees, deep-rooted, seemingly intractable, contentment is the bane of modern day congregations. Quite simply, there is little recognition of our deficiencies and basically no call for perfection. Rather than satisfaction and possibly even pride in our accomplishments, we should, of course, be on our knees admitting and attending to our deficiencies while imploring God's help and forgiveness.

There is no greater refuge against change than reliance on current success. Over time congregations tend to gradually accept the status quo as "reasonable under present conditions." This is seldom a deliberate attitude, simply a gradual slide into complacency, lulled by year-to-year consistency. Eventually a sense of well-being evolves, occasionally progressing even to a point of distrust for things "new" or "creative." A shield is erected. "We're doing all we can and we're doing it reasonably well, thank you." This attitude is invariably supported by hesitant, cautious governance. New, possibly "risky" ideas are easily rejected as "untested" or "inappropriate." They may even be interpreted as implied criticism. Thus we find that entrenched, satisfied, and protective leaders are the single most difficult obstacle to church improvement.

Closely allied are the inevitably present naysayers and skeptics who interpret or associate difficulties, obstacles, or pitfalls with seemingly every suggestion, dooming new ideas from the very start. "What are we letting ourselves in for?" The comfort zone of anxious congregations is extremely small compared to the expanded horizons of congregations at the "cutting edge" of Christianity.

Finally, we have the rare but occasional condition of pastoral dominance and the typically associated absence of creative lay leadership. Conservative pastors, especially those on short tours, are inclined to avoid rocking the boat. Others, comfortably entrenched, may be susceptible to running a taut ship with limited allowance for innovation. Elected laity in their brief leadership tenure may also be disappointingly cautious. With such top-level inertia, introducing change can be difficult indeed.

Strategies for Improvement

Therefore, prepare your minds for action . . . (1 Peter 1:13)

Among management consultants there appears consensus that the root causes of organizational reluctance to improve lie deep in the human psyche with no known sure cure. But in contrast, within the church, believing in God's protective care and guidance, all things are possible. Therefore these "strategies for improvement" can be advanced with confidence:

- **Select leaders desiring and capable of rigorous efforts to improve and advance the congregation.** While innovation and improvement should be part of every leader's job description, advancement is not necessarily on the agenda. Too often laity are appointed with the tacit understanding their job is to manage, not lead. This conundrum can only be overcome by either deliberately attempting to appoint real leaders, individuals with the necessary initiative, zeal, and perseverance required; or alternatively, gradually realigning attitudes towards improvement through education and encouragement of the church's management pool. In both instances, appointed leaders must be tasked in no uncertain terms to *lead*. Finally, the pastor's support and encouragement in seeking advancement is essential.

And it should be tacitly understood that leadership requires familiarity with major references in the field and a commitment to seek out informal interaction with the congregation. Members want to converse with their elected officers.

- **Conduct yearly internal audits emphasizing shortcomings and possible advancements as much as accomplishments.** Self-studies without bias and with a real aim toward identifying deficiencies, not only prompt follow-on remedies, but constitute life-renewing therapy in themselves. "We felt good about our potential to improve after this self-study." And the importance of such initiative is underscored by the all too common absence of any real pressure to improve by higher church echelons.

- **Establish a small independent study group to investigate and develop potential opportunities for perfecting the church.** Such "think-tanks," as they may be called, are commissioned to pursue whatever course of investigation that prayer, study, and exploration may prompt, and are exempt from organizational oversight. Nor are they expected to perform an advocacy role which should be left to church officers or possibly an especially appointed lay "advocate."

  Despite the reasonableness of establishing such a study group, the ability to secure participants is likely to be difficult. Seemingly, few individuals believe such self-study is actually necessary nor are they willing to risk their relationships with other members by participating. Amidst such reluctance, considerable attention must be given to the discovery and cultivation of individuals inclined toward such investigation, their number perhaps being no more than one out of a hundred members.

- **Appoint an "advocate" promoter as a point of contact and presenter for member suggestions.** Regular members, questioning their own judgment against the multitude, need an intercessor to knowledgeably express and advance their ideas. Such an appointment must be a trusted, informed, and respected member of the congregation. Advocates must be able to make an impartial yet compelling case for new ideas without distortion or excess. The "why" of every recommendation must always be addressed.

  Throughout the year ideas from the congregation should of course be earnestly sought on a regular basis. And they must all be fairly evaluated and reported if member confidence in the system is to be maintained.

- **Widen the door for innovation by promoting trial-testing of marginal proposals.** Too many proposals are rejected out-of-hand when further consideration and testing might reveal at least some aspects or components worth developing, possibly in an altered form and context. New ideas are generally most easily tested if a discretionary fund for such purposes is available to minimize any financial deterrents.

Proposal Review

So much of what is done to improve the church is initiated and enacted during council meetings that a closing bit of advice regarding the optimal climate for properly reviewing new proposals should be in place.

—Proposals and supporting rationale must be prepared in writing well in advance of meetings to allow deliberate prior study. All important aspects of involved issues must be completely and honestly expressed.

—Meetings must allow sufficient time for extended discussion and debate. Everyone should be encouraged to speak, especially when there are disagreements. Final decisions on controversial issues may properly be postponed to allow time for additional study and reflection.

—The congregation president should not be passive or tolerant of virulent divisions. Emotional and personal grievances should be ironed out.

—The council should practice transparency, transmitting the whole story of their deliberations to the congregation to ensure all are informed of associated concerns and difficulties as well as opportunities and expected rewards.

CHALLENGES

And I heard the voice of the Lord saying, Whom shall I send, and who will go for us? Then I said, Here am I; send me. (Isaiah 6:8)

In the context of the foregoing discussion, we are bold to suggest the following means of caring for and building up God's church. All are well known, all are easily within the capabilities of every church. Some, of course, will be less suitable in a given situation than others, yet all warrant prayerful consideration. And for church members seeking new service, "Is there not an opportunity here for you to be an advocate?"

Note: Each suggestion lists related topic material in the main text.

LEADERSHIP

1. **Extend leadership opportunities to all.** Christian leadership is a singularly rewarding and privileged means of service. Such honor should be extended to as many congregants as possible, even to the very least person.

The church should abound in leadership opportunities. This breadth can be achieved by delegating authority to the lowest possible echelon, reducing terms of service, and by expanding council membership. Delegating authority stimulates leadership, forcing it to surface often in the most unexpected ways. Shorter two rather than three-year terms increase opportunities by 50 percent. Expanding a council of 20 to 30 members does the same. And, of course, no individual member should receive a second high appointment until the entire membership roster has been exhausted. A record of "positions held" can be maintained for this purpose. Previous leaders typically find challenging opportunities wherever positioned, often valuably cultivating leadership in others.

In the rare instances of possible marginal performance, appointments can be augmented by supporting assistants of proven capacity. Better to delegate too broadly and extend leadership, than husband authority and deny such service to the deserving. (Chapter 5, pages 40-42)

2. **Encourage candidacy for major offices, not direct appointment.** "Safe" appointments discourage initiative and creativity. With shorter terms of office, the church ought to be willing occasionally to chance "dynamic potential" as well as "ensured consistency." There are probably few congregations where at least one member has not privately said at one time or another, "If only I could get hold of this church for a year!"

Open positions should be announced and members encouraged to apply. Candidates for council president should expect to be interviewed, and be prepared with their "platform" of plans and proposals. (Chapter 10, pages 119-122)

3. **Train the president-elect and senior officers.** Most elected congregational presidents and senior officers are simply installed, beginning their office with virtually no preparation other than what their own past experience provides. Church offices, however, are unique and of considerable consequence when performed well. Unfortunately, a good share of today's church inertia stems from untrained ultimately marginal lay leadership. Church-specific training will make new presidents and other senior officers much more effective and more comfortable in their position as well. (Chapters 3, 6, 7, 8, 10)

4. **Foster democracy; encourage and fairly attend to criticism and minority positions.** Congregations, foremost among organizations, are accountable to the principles of social equality and respect for the individual. Members are the inherent human element of the church, its mortal foundation. Leaders must consequently extend themselves in soliciting the congregation's advice and opinions. Open and free debate must be encouraged; dissent and the minority position openly recognized and honored. Unanimity and harmony need never be an overriding factor.

A democratic congregation may on occasion appropriately accommodate a conflicting minority position, usually on a trial basis. More often than not such testing proves instructive. Who can say in advance with certainty that one proposal is clearly superior to another? (Chapter 5, pages 39-40 and 42-43; Chapter 7, pages 67-68; Chapter 11, pages 150-153)

5. **Distinguish between the roles of the pastor and congregation president.** The pastor is the congregation's spiritual leader; the elected lay president its chief executive officer. While the exact division between the two positions will vary, congregations should be alert to perceived infringements. The respective roles need to be spelled out in reasonable detail, always recognizing the encompassing nature of pastoral responsibilities. Pastors must be forthright in interpreting and advancing God's will for the congregation. Lay presidents, for their part, should never be hesitant in

rigorously leading; always seeking in every instance pastoral guidance and harmony. (Chapter 4, pages 28-29; Chapter 10, pages 124-129)

6. **Encourage and strengthen the pastor as the spiritual leader.** We love our shepherd pastors and must accordingly treat them as the treasured resource they are. This means supporting and accommodating their special interests and talents, and providing lay augmentation as may be consequentially necessary. Pastors are also strengthened by appreciative congregations, allotting time for prayer, education, and sabbatical leave. (Chapter 10, pages 124-126)

MANAGEMENT

7. **Prepare, broadcast, and observe statements of mission, core values, and operating principles.** After Scripture, prayer, and pastoral counsel, congregational actions are best guided by deliberate founding statements which give shape and definition to the church's ministry. All must be constructed with the greatest of care and reviewed and updated periodically as may be required (see Challenge 10). *Mission* is the central focus of effort and funds (see "Missions" section, page 403, for special opportunities). *Core values* are the standards and qualities the congregation deems essential in focusing behavior. *Operating principles* are the policies and rules that guide action. (Chapter 8, page 77; Chapter 9)

8. **Prepare a written council agenda and distribute to members in advance of scheduled meetings.** Meetings are time-consuming and less productive when attention is devoted to presenting and explaining content that could be communicated earlier. Prepared participants are generally effective participants. Problems to be discussed, the circumstances involved, and the advantages and disadvantages of alternative responses, should all be distributed, whenever possible, in advance. Routine matters need simply be outlined together with recommended action. Such preparation largely frees the meeting for its central purpose, the give-and-take of analysis, debate, and decision. (Chapter 12, pages 167-168)

9. **Employ a trained moderator to conduct council meetings and free the president to actively lead and instruct.** A moderator clarifies issues, facilitates discussion, and effectively sums up, all performed without bias or influence. Selectively freed of these responsibilities allows the president to lead as the position requires, directing and encouraging, not shackled by restrictive presiding duties. Moderating is a full-time task for any congregation member, requiring specialized training. (Chapter 12)

10. **Conduct annual self-audits as a standard year-end responsibility of appointed officers.** Perfection is our goal. A yearly review is an inherent concluding responsibility of elected leadership. The critique typically begins with a re-evaluation of church statements and policy in the light of recent operations. Actual accomplishments may be compared with stated priorities. Effective versus apparently marginal operations may be distinguished. Recommendations are essential. The yearly audit is relatively

brief and perfunctory compared to the more extended work an appointed self-studies team may undertake. (Challenge 11, page 159).

Incumbent officers are generally pleased to report their successes and broaden the responsibility for resolving persistent problems. (Chap. 5, p. 37)

11. **Establish a permanent independent assembly to conduct self-studies and planning.** This group's mission is to strive for excellence in all things by energetically seeking out and responding to advice and recommendations from every available source. The responsibility is largely academic in nature, essentially one of rigorous and impartial investigation, study, and reporting. The group sets its own agenda and timetable. Former church officers are typically good candidates for such a commission, so also are a congregation's "academics." Give them free rein. (Chapter 10, pages 131-133; Chapter 11, pages 156-163)

12. **Prepare and continuously upgrade job descriptions of all key church positions.** Position descriptions establish responsibilities and record proven methodology. They are an essential training device for new appointees. (Chapter 8, pages 77-78; Chapter 9, page 113; Appendix B)

13. **Maintain a reference library of essential works in each church functional area together with required reading lists for elected positions.** No church officer or teacher should be unfamiliar with the literature in their assigned area or field of interest. Required reading is an essential element of good management.

MEMBERSHIP

14. **Maintain records of member qualifications, participation, and attendance.** Detailed member information assists in identifying individuals for leadership positions, training, and as candidates for specific services. The "lost sheep" of the congregation can only be found if their absence is promptly recognized and addressed. The underutilized non-participant can only be "discovered" if such lack of involvement is duly noted and remedied. Computer records with various retrieval parameters are the best means for identifying these conditions for corrective action. (Chapter 5, pages 38-39; Chapter 16)

15. **Maintain a caring personal relationship with all members, especially those marginally attending.** We must treat every member as a treasured individual, continuously reaching out with friendship. Embrace the neglected with the warmth you may now reserve for your personal friends.

Amazingly, a person can be a church member all their lives and never be individually contacted regarding their personal concerns and needs. One observer jokingly referred to the Boy Scouts as more concerned with his involvement than the church.

The self-reliant are sufficiently bold to assert their own way. The non-participant is the one needing our attention. And this mindfulness can be best provided through membership in a small group (Challenge 16). Yet some members will remain isolated, requiring personal contact. Such overtures should be as constructive and convenient as possible, beginning, for example, simply with casual conversation after church. The idea is to recognize and respond to members as *individuals*.

Departing members should also be contacted, not only as a courtesy but, in this instance, for their observations.

16. **Encourage and support every member participation in small groups under trained leadership to foster intimate interaction and a sense of belonging, especially among new and marginal members.** Small groups meet periodically to share their Christian experience and provide mutual support. They have no other mission; no agenda except love and caring. Most church members live their entire lives with no opportunity to speak openly and frankly with others who know them and care. Group action provides this open supportive environment for each participant. (Chapter 17)

17. **Extend a warm personal and sincere greeting and welcome to all visitors.** All are welcome in God's house. Friendship should abound, no visitor unattended, no member neglected. Greeters should be instructed on the breadth and importance of their duties. Name tags greatly ease interaction.

18. **Encourage charitable giving of oneself and one's resources.** The Christian spirit of giving is one of joy, thankfulness, generosity, and anonymity. Yet we all crave a certain amount of tangibility and recognition. Perhaps the best manner of approaching this conundrum is through a personal interview (Challenge 15) with each member, striving to obtain a thoughtful, generous, and balanced contribution, tailored to the individual's circumstances and preferences. Thus a busy executive, for example, may be well satisfied with a large general purpose cash donation while a single parent may only afford limited service in the day-school. Through counseling and prayer each gift is made pleasing in God's sight.

COMMUNICATIONS

19. **Establish the role of ombudsman to encourage and support communication.** Church issues are often sensitive and suppressed. The minority may be cowed by the majority. An ombudsman is an impartial intermediary, trained to receptively listen to problems and effectively convey their nature to appropriate offices. By interceding in difficult matters with patience and understanding, the ombudsman lessens internal conflicts. Most importantly, the ombudsman establishes the value of the individual. (Chapter 11, pages 153-155)

20. **Build and maintain continuous open dialog within the congregation at all levels and among all offices.** Church management is invariably handled by a representative few, with a majority of members out of the loop. This isolation can be countered by keeping the congregation informed regarding pending issues and the responses under consideration. So included, members are more likely to feel part of the process, encouraging active involvement. And leaders can go so far as to ask the opinions of others

regarding current topics. How encouraging that would be, to actually have someone ask your opinion! Yet most parishioners will pass their entire church lifetime without such involvement. On these small things great allegiance is built. (Chapter 5, pages 42-43)

21. Establish a pulpit advisory group to recommend sermon topics. The laity advisory group assists the pastor in assessing the spiritual needs of the congregation and in providing an interactive point of contact. Popularly labeled "market research," identifying the parishioner consumer's needs and preferences should be an automatic input in developing sermon content. Unfortunately, such assistance is seldom sought, possibly from some sense of necessary independence. Yet seeking guidance from *all* sources should be recognized as the height of professionalism. (Chapter 13, pages 184-185; Chapter 15, page 227 "Response")

22. Prepare annual reports to effectively convey both specifics and the totality of church operations. Exclusions and failures should be as evident in the annual report as involvements and successes. Congregations need to be repeatedly aroused to improve, not lulled into complacency. Clarity in all reports is also essential especially regarding finances. Church finances and membership information are best communicated through ratios and trend charts of key measurements. Overall, a one-page annual summary of operational pluses and minus should be provided every member, asking for their commentary. (Chapter 19, pages 305-309; Chapter 23, pages 365-367)

MISSIONS

23. Review and realign mission priorities each year. The church's limited resources should always be focused on their most productive employment. The ratio of returns to costs must be weighed in each instance, transferring resources from marginally less effective programs to those appearing more fruitful. We do this subconsciously every day in making personal decisions. The church on the other hand, as with any major enterprise, requires a more deliberate effort. Yet the process is invariably gradual, with slight shifts each year. When funds decline, however, the action may be quite pronounced, with considerable care taken to cut what appears least required. Steady and increasing budgets on the other hand seldom prompt critical review, each program typically being well defended by its advocates. In such instances the council must take action, requiring and comparing each committee's least productive expenditures, shifting resources accordingly as the evidence suggests. (Chapter 9, pages 102-106)

24. Emphasize evangelism as the great commission. Evangelism is too often fostered off as the mission of sponsored missionaries or neglected altogether due to its inherent difficulty. And there is the self-deceptive defense that social work is, after all, a form of evangelism. Although true to a degree, the core of evangelism is not meeting social and physical needs, it is going forth to persuasively bring God's word into hearts and minds.

No church work is more difficult, seemingly unproductive, and occasionally uncomfortable. Yet the mandate is clear and the potential harvest great. To begin, a few committed leaders must be found, then volunteers gathered and trained. Initial work should be focused on retrieving marginal members, ensuring their nurturing through small group membership. Eventually, field work can be initiated with "lessons learned" a vital tool for improvement. (Chapters 20 and 21)

25. **Experiment in developing new programs and creative approaches to worship.** The opportunities here are beyond measure, but are typically restricted by the congregation's predisposition toward the common and familiar. A little newness seems to go a long way. Thus it is best to introduce changes moderately and temporarily, allowing time for assimilation and possible approval.

Experimentation is the watchword. Never reject anything out-of-hand for God works in mysterious ways. Testing on a trial basis is so little a commitment and so effective in evaluation, it is a pity that such an innocuous tool is not more frequently employed. (Chapters 13 and 14)

26. **Encourage choir membership by allowing limited involvement with reduced rehearsal time.** The idea here is to attract marginally interested or available candidates into the choir by requiring minimal personal commitment. Such involvement is part-time, attendance with the regular choir typically scheduled no more than once a month, commonly at a single service with proportional limited rehearsals. (Chapter 13)

27. **Develop a core Sunday school curriculum for adults**. A carefully designed core curriculum ensures adults the opportunity for a comprehensive Christian education. Essential studies typically require a number of years to complete and are generally offered as the need arises. The core curriculum is not intended to be in competition with current popular studies. Course offerings are provided as the need arises, but it is important to recognize that far too many Christians lack the fundamentals beginning with the Catechism. (Chapter 18, pages 281-283)

28. **Employ short-term courses of a few weeks duration to introduce new topics, update training, and create interest.** Short dynamic courses of four to six weeks are attractive, particularly to congregation members out of the main stream and those unwilling or unable to make a greater commitment. The topics should be as interesting and engaging as possible, taught foremost through discussion. Once enrolled, participants are often "hooked" for continuing involvement. Short-term classes should always be held at the most convenient times and places such as Sunday morning between church services. (Chapter 18, page 282)

29. **Speak out on public issues**. Establish a permanent study group to prepare and distribute brief position papers on selected major public issues such as global warming, crime, gun control, etc. Such papers, signed by

supporting members, can be sent to selected involved officials and organizations as a means of responsible citizenship. (Chapter 22)

30. **Direct the church's humanitarian outreach to those areas that appear most productive in effectively responding to critical needs.** High priority projects typically respond to immediate critical needs or provide lasting returns that far exceed the involved cost. Food to counter starvation is an example of meeting an immediate critical need; immunization is an example of exceptional long-term value relative to cost.

There is also importance in providing close-to-home, direct services. Hands-on field work, for example, is especially suitable for young people as they learn the joys of giving through personal involvement. Office and food service frequently provide the social contacts sought by older members. Such opportunities should be as broad as the congregation's interests.

All "hands-on" volunteer work is immensely valuable in building permanently charitable members. However, catering to individual interests should be balanced by member awareness and response to the larger encompassing set of world and national needs to ensure deliberate knowledgeable choices. (Chapter 22, pages 357-359)

Appendix D
The *Renewal* Reader

*Create in me a clean heart, O God; and renew a right
spirit within me. —Psalms 51:10*

"We patch and tinker more than we renew."
—William James (1842-1910), American psychologist and philosopher.

Perhaps a better term than "Reader" for this appendix title would be *Renewal* "Anthology," for we introduce here the concept of assembling the best of mankind's homage to God, made available each Sunday to service attendees as a take-home handout. "Reader," however, better suggests the informal nature of the involvement sought and the leisurely pace encouraged for its perusal.

The adjacent page will immediately reveal the nature of the subject matter and format intended, saving the need for much further explanation. The purpose of the proposed weekly is simply to bring to the attention of congregations, in systematic memorable fashion, the brilliant eclectic world of Christian oration, art, music, poetry, and quotations relevant to the ecclesiastic date being celebrated. *Renewal* is a reminder of the good works of man to God's glory that transcend time. It refreshes us with the Good News drawn from our heritage of Christian works.

Renewal can be placed with the service bulletin or distributed after the service. Aside from this possible shared timing, *Renewal* is a separate entity from the service, intended to be non–distractive, its scripture lesson unrelated to the Sunday lessons of the church calendar. *Renewal* is intended to be read later, leisurely at home during the week, thus hopefully to extend the reader's knowledge of both scripture and related art and literature in a lasting manner.

One version of the *Renewal* format is a single 5½ by 8½ sheet printed on both sides. The front would present scripture text (unrelated to the church calendar) and associated art work. The back would include prayers, art, poetry, quotations, hymns, history, notables, symbols, definitions, and church calendar notation. If *Renewal* is published on 8½ x 11 inch paper folded cross-wise, the inside would present an abbreviated scripture-related sermon by a noted theologian.

The ten front and back examples presented here are prototype experiments of limited quality and consistency. Future work in this area is tentatively on hold, expected to resume sometime in the near future. Announcements and downloadable copies will be posted on the servant leadership website servantleadershipbook.org.

Renewal

Celebrating the Christian experience

Christ Baptized in the Jordan. Drawing. Rembrandt

JOHN DECLARES JESUS THE SON OF GOD

The Second Sunday after Epiphany

THE CHURCH CALENDAR

The EPIPHANY SEASON serves as a bridge between the birth of Jesus and his passion. The second Sunday is the celebration of the baptism of Jesus and the beginning of His ministry. The color for this second Sunday is green, the church's neutral color for times when festive or penitential colors are not appropriate.

THE GOSPEL: John 1:29-41

On the following day, John saw Jesus coming towards him and said, "Look, there is the Lamb of God Who will take away the sin of the world. This is the Man I meant when I said 'A Man comes after me Who is always in front of me, for He existed before I was born' It is true I have not known Him, yet it was to make Him known to the people of Israel that I came and baptized people with water."

Then John gave this testimony, "I have seen the Spirit come down like a dove from Heaven and rest upon Him. Indeed it is true that I did not recognize Him by myself, but the One Who sent me to baptize with water told me this: 'The One on Whom you will see the Spirit coming down and resting is the Man Who baptizes with the Holy Spirit. Now I have seen this happen and I declare publicly before you all that *He is the Son of God.*"

Translation by J. B. Phillips

Camel's hair coat   *The Luther Rose*

QUOTE

"In baptism, the Christian is born. His old self is buried and the new self emerges. Whether in the case of infants or adults, baptism signifies this more as a promise than as an actually fulfilled fact. The direction is indicated rather than the arrival."

—Friedrich Rest, *Pulpit Preaching*

MUSIC

Lift every voice and sing. Till earth and heaven ring
  Two brothers, James Weldon and J. Rosamond Johnson, collaborated in writing this hymn which has become the official song of the National Association for the Advancement of Colored People.

POEM

  Fall on me like a silent dew,
    Or like those maiden showers,
  Which, by the peep of day, do strew
    A baptism o'er the flowers.
        —Robert Herrick, *To Music, to Becalm His Fever*

PRAYER

  Lord Jesus, we come to Thee now as little children. Dress us again in clean pinafores; make us tidy once more with the tidiness of true remorse and confession. O, wash our hearts, that they may be clean again.
  Make us to know the strengthening joys of the Spirit, and the newness of life which only thou can give. Amen.
        —Peter Marshall, Prayer before United States Senate

LESSER FESTIVALS

  January 5 KAJ MUNK *This Danish pastor, patriot, and playwright was feared by the Nazis because his patriotic articles and sermons helped to strengthen the Danish resistance movement. He was arrested on January 4, 1944; the next day his body was found in a ditch.*

  January 13 GEORGE FOX *Founder of the Society of Friends nicknamed "Quakers." A magnetic personality of great spiritual power, he is an example of selfless devotion, patience in persecution, and ability in organization.*

RENEWAL   2nd Sunday after Epiphany   (Series A, #8)   www.servantleadershipbook.org

Renewal

Celebrating the Christian experience

Christ the Welcome Guest. Von Uhde

WELCOME GOD'S MESSENGER

The Sixth Sunday after Pentecost

THE CHURCH CALENDAR

THE SEASON AFTER PENTECOST is the longest season in the church year. The Sundays after Pentecost represent The Time of the Church–the time between the earthly ministry of Jesus, which is past, and the Advent season of preparation which is ahead. In the pilgrim state in which the church lives and exercises its ministry, it is the Spirit of God who leads and accompanies into all truth. The color green is used for the "after Pentecost" season, a time of growth in the Spirit as the risen Christ is formed in us.

THE GOSPEL Matthew 10:34-42

"Do not think that I have come to bring peace to the world; no, I did not come to bring peace, but a sword. I came to set sons against their fathers, daughters against their mothers, daughters-in-law against their mothers-in-law, a man's worst enemies will be the members of his own family.

"Whoever loves his father or mother more than me is not worthy of me; whoever loves his son or daughter more than me is not worthy of me. Whoever does not take up his cross and follow in my steps is not worthy of me. Whoever tries to gain his own life will lose it; whoever loses his life for my sake will gain it.

"Whoever welcomes you, welcomes me; and whoever welcomes me, welcomes the one who sent me. Whoever welcomes God's messenger because he is God's messenger will share in his reward; and whoever welcomes a truly good man, because he is that, will share in his reward. And remember this! Whoever gives even a drink of cold water to one of the least of these my followers, because he is my follower, will certainly receive his reward."

J. B. Phillips translation

The Season after Pentecost   *St. Matthew*

QUOTE

When home is ruled according to God's word, angels might be asked to stay with us, and they would not find themselves out of their element.
—Charles Haddon Spurgeon

MUSIC

Oh God, Send Heralds   *LBW No. 283*

This hymn was written in 1966 by Elisabeth Havens Burrowes in connection with the celebration of the 100th anniversary of the founding of the Pacific School of Religion in Berkeley, California. The tune, INTERCESSOR, was composed by Charles Hubert Hastings Parry who was a gifted lecturer and teacher at the Royal College of Music.

POEM

Have you had a kindness shown?
  Pass it on;
'Twas not given for thee alone,
  Pass it on,
Let it travel down the years,
Let it wipe another's tears,
'Till in Heaven the deed appears–
  Pass it on.   –Henry Burton: *Pass It On*

PRAYER

Father, who hast made all men in thy likeness and lovest all whom thou hast made, suffer not our family to separate itself from thee by building barriers of race and colour.   –Toc H

CALENDAR

1930 Nathan Soderblom awarded Nobel Peace Prize. *Soderbloom, Archbishop of Sweden, supported the cause of ecumenism, advocated practical cooperation of Christians on social questions, and encouraged the liturgical movement.*

c. 989 Prince Vladimir of Russia baptized. *Previously his life had been brutal, bloodthirsty, and dissolute, but he took his new religion seriously and sought to impose it upon his people. Despite his forced conversions, he was respected for the change in his life, his kindness toward criminals and his generosity toward the poor.*

RENEWAL   6th Sunday after Pentecost   (Series A, #23)   www.servantleadershipbook.org

Renewal

Icon at Vyshorod (12th c.)

Celebrating the Christian experience

MARY, MOTHER OF OUR LORD

11th Sunday after Pentecost

THE CHURCH CALENDAR

According to the Scriptures, Mary was present at all of the important events in her Son's life: in the birth cycle, at the first miracle at Cana, at the cross, at the tomb, with the apostles after the ascension waiting for the Spirit. August 15 has been observed since early times as the day of what the Eastern church calls her "falling asleep," i.e., her death. Luther retained a special affection for Mary and wrote a splendid exposition of the Magnificat. The color is white.

THE GOSPEL Luke 1:46-55

Then Mary said: "My heart is overflowing with praise of my Lord; my soul is full of joy in God my Savior. For he has deigned to notice me, his humble servant and, after this, all the people who ever shall be will call me the happiest of women! The one who can do all things has done great things for me—oh, holy is his Name! Truly, his mercy rests on those who fear him in every generation. He has shown the strength of his arm, he has swept away the high and mighty. He has set kings down from their thrones and lifted up the humble. He has satisfied the hungry with good things and sent the rich away with empty hands. Yes, he has helped Israel, his child: he has remembered the mercy that he promised to our forefathers, to Abraham and his sons for evermore!"

J. B. Phillips translation

The Aureole   *The Annuniciation*

QUOTE

Mother is the name for God in the lips and hearts of little children.
—William Makepeace Thackeray, *Vanity Fair*, Vol II, ch. 12

Honour thy father and thy mother: that thy days may be long upon the land which the Lord thy God giveth thee.   —*Exodus 20: 12*

MUSIC

Immortal, Invisible, God Only Wise   *LBW* No. 526

"Now unto the King eternal, immortal, invisible, the only wise God, be honor and glory forever and ever" (I Timothy 1:17) is the basis for this hymn of pure praise. The rollicking anapestic rhythm of the Welsh melody rushes the singer along to the climactic poetic thought of God being invisible only because He is hidden by the splendor of light.

POEM

The angels . . . singing unto one another,
Can find among their burning terms of love,
None so devotional as that of "mother."
     —Edgar Allan Poe, *To My Mother*

PRAYER

On this day of sacred memories, our Father, we would thank Thee for our mothers who gave us life, who surrounded us early and late with love and care, whose prayers on our behalf still cling around the Throne of Grace, a haunting perfume of love's petitions.

     —Peter Marshall

CALENDAR

1830 Florence Nightingale born in Florence. *She was interested in nursing from an early age and began regular hospital visiting, c. 1844. She studied nursing at Alexandria, and visited Fliedner's deaconesses at Kaiserwerth and trained there in 1851. She headed a hospital in London in 1853, and the following year she went to the Crimea to organize the care of wounded English soldiers. She returned to England in 1856 in weakened health, but continued to advise on health care in the American Civil War and the Franco-Prussian War (1870-71).*

RENEWAL 11th Sunday after Pentecost (Series A, #38) www.servantleadershipbook.org

Renewal

Celebrating the Christian experience

The Ghent Altarpience:
St John the Baptist

GOD SENT HIS MESSENGER, JOHN

The Third Sunday in Advent

THE CHURCH CALENDAR

The church year begins with ADVENT, a season of preparation that looks toward both Bethlehem and the consummation. The traditional color of Advent is purple, the royal color for the coming King. The prayers for the four Sundays in Advent are contemporary versions of historic collects. The familiar phrase "stir up" is retained in two of the prayers, and they all contain a reference to coming.

THE GOSPEL: John 1:6-8, 23-28

God sent his messenger, a man named John, who came to tell people about the light. He came to tell them, so that all should hear the message and believe. He himself was not the light; he came to tell about the light. This was the real light, the light that comes into the world and shines on all men.

[The priests and Levites asked him] "What do you say about yourself?" John answered, "This is what I am: 'The voice of one who shouts in the desert. Make a straight path for the Lord to travel!'"

The messengers had been sent by the Pharisees. They asked John, "If you are not the Messiah, nor Elijah, nor the Prophet, why do you baptize?" John answered: "I baptize with water; among you stands the one you do not know. He comes after me, but I am not good enough even to untie his sandals."

All this happened in Bethany, on the other side of the Jordan river, where John was baptizing.

Good News for Modern Man

St. John, the Baptist

Advent Season

QUOTE

The study of God's word, for the purpose of discovering God's will, is the secret discipline which has formed the greatest characters.
—James W. Alexander

You, then, are to go and make disciples of all the nations and baptize them in the name of the Father and of the Son and of the Holy Spirit. Teach them to observe all that I have commanded you and, remember, I am with you always, even to the end of the world. —Matthew 28: 19-20

MUSIC

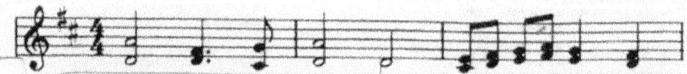

Thine Is the Glory LBW No. 145

Edmond L. Budry wrote the words to this hymn in 1884. He served as pastor of the Free Church at Vevey, Switzerland for over thirty-five years. The tune JUDAS

PERSONAGES

Samuel Johnson asked if a man does not feel trust in God should he try to manufacture it by sheer will-power? Johnson's answer is that he ought to behave as if he did trust God, and that means obeying God. He who obeys God will find sooner or later that he does trust.

PRAYER

O God, who hast bound us together in this bundle of life, give us grace to understand how our lives depend upon the courage, the industry, the honesty, and the integrity of our fellow-men; that we may be mindful of their needs, grateful for their faithfulness, and faithful in our responsibilities to them; through Jesus Christ our Lord.
—Reinhold Niebuhr, 1892-1971

CALENDAR

December 14 THERESA OF AVILA In 1533 Theresa entered a Carmelite monastery but remained without enthusiasm. While praying, she was converted to a life of perfection, and withdrew to form a new spiritual community. A woman of strong character and of great practical ability, her lasting influence as a spiritual writer lay in her enunciation of the states of prayer between meditation ("quiet") and ecstasy ("union").

RENEWAL   3rd Sunday in Advent   (Series B, #3)   www.servantleadershipbook.org

Renewal

The stoning of St. Stephen

Celebrating the Christian experience

SAINT STEPHEN, DEACON AND MARTYR

Lesser Festival

THE CHURCH CALENDAR

The CHRISTMAS SEASON follows as the fulfillment of Advent expectation. Three sets of Propers are provided for The Nativity of Our Lord (Christmas Day) so that the birth of Christ may be seen from several perspectives. The eighth day of Christmas, January 1, emphasizes the naming of the Child Jesus signifying salvation. The color of the Christmas season is white, a color associated with festivals of Christ, traditionally suggesting gladness, light, and joy. The season lasts 12 days, from December 25th through January 5, and throughout, the festive mood should be sustained.

THE SECOND LESSON: Acts 7:54-58

As the members of the Council listened to Stephen they became furious and ground their teeth at him in anger. But Stephen, full of the Holy Spirit, looked up to heaven and saw God's glory, and Jesus standing at the right side of God. "Look!" he said. "I see heaven opened and the Son of Man standing at the right side of God!" With a loud cry they stopped up their ears, and all rushed together at him at once. They threw him out of the city and stoned him.

Good News for Modern Man

COMMISSION

You, then, are to go and make disciples of all the nations and baptize them in the name of the Father and of the Son and of the Holy Spirit. Teach them to observe all that I have commanded you and, remember, I am with you always, even to the end of the world. —Matthew 28: 19-20

Saint Stephen
First Christian martyr

The Phoenix
Symbol of the Resurrection

SONG

I wish for you, my friend, this happiness that I've found
You can depend on Him, it matters not where you're bound
I'll shout it from the mountain top, I want my world to know
The Lord of love has come to me.
I want to pass it on.

—Words and Music by Kurt Kaiser

MUSIC

Battle Hymn of the Republic   *LBW* No. 332
Julia Ward Howe set better words to this Civil War marching song attributed to William Steffe, although in existence long before the war.

PERSONAGE

In regard to this Great Book, I have but this to say, I believe the Bible is the best gift God has given to man. All the good Savior gave to the world is communicated through this Book. But for this Book, we could not know right from wrong. All things most desirable for man's welfare, here and hereafter, are to be found portrayed in it.

—Abraham Lincoln, speech calling for a national
day of prayer, September 5, 1864

BLESSING

May the road rise to meet you.
May the wind be always at your back.
May the sun shine warm upon your face.
May the rains fall softly upon your fields
 until we meet again
May God hold you in the hollow of his hand.

—Old Gaelic blessing

RENEWAL   Saint Stephen   (Series C, Lesser Festival)   www.servantleadershipbook.org

Renewal

Celebrating the Christian experience

Satan Showing Christ the Kingdoms of the World. Drawing. Rembrandt

JESUS TEMPTED IN THE DESERT

The First Sunday in Lent

THE CHURCH CALENDAR

The LENTEN SEASON begins with Ash Wednesday and lasts 40 days (excluding Sundays which are always feasts in celebration of the resurrection). Lent–the word originally meant "spring"–is to be understood as a time to reflect upon baptism, a time for rebirth and renewal in preparation for the celebration of Easter. The traditional color of Lent is purple, to suggest somberness and solemnity.

THE GOSPEL: Mark 1:12-15

At once the Spirit made him go into the desert. He was there forty days, and Satan tempted him. Wild animals were there also, but angels came and helped him.

After John had been put in prison Jesus went to Galilee and preached the Good News from God. "The right time has come," he said, "and the Kingdom of God is near! Turn away from your sins and believe the Good News!"

Good News for Modern Man

"IC XC" Greek for Jesus Christ
"Nika" meaning "conqueror"

Symbol for Saint Mark

QUOTE

"Temptations that find us dwelling in God are to our faith like winds that more firmly root the tree."
—Anonymous

MUSIC

O Lord, throughout These Forty Days   *LBW* No. 99

This hymn is a paraphrase of "Lord, who throughout these forty days," which was written by Claudia Frances Hernaman and included in her Child's Book of Praise, *1873. The tune, Caithness, from the 1635 psalter," represents the high-water mark of the psalmody of the Reformation in Scotland."*

POEM

They took Him to a mountain-top to see
Where earth's fair kingdoms flung their golden net
To snare the feet and trick the souls of men.
—Winfred Ernest Garrison: *Temptation*

PRAYER

From the cowardice that dare not face new truth
From the laziness that is contented with half truth
From the arrogance that thinks it knows all truth,
Good Lord, deliver me.

—Prayer from Kenya

LESSER FESTIVALS

March 1 GEORGE HERBERT *An orphan, Herbert was ordained a priest in 1630 and served as rector near Salisbury. Known as "holy Mr. Herbert," his poems breathe a gentle freshness and grace with a profound love of virtue, and some of his hymns are still sung ("Teach me, my God and King," and "Let all the world in every corner sing").*

March 2 JOHN and CHARLES WESLEY *Gathering around him at Oxford a group of scholarly Christians, John became a central figure in the rise of Methodism. In 1738, hearing a reading from Luther's "Preface to Romans," he had the experience of religious conversion. He spent the rest of his life in evangelistic work, traveling widely. Charles was ordained in 1735 and entered upon an itinerant ministry. A gentle and attractive person, he was a gifted and indefatigable hymn writer.*

RENEWAL   1st Sunday in Lent   (Series B, #14)   www.servantleadershipbook.org

Renewal

Celebrating the Christian experience

Christ and Nicodemus. Drawing. Rembrandt

FOR GOD SO LOVED THE WORLD

The Fourth Sunday in Lent

THE CHURCH CALENDAR

The LENTEN SEASON begins with Ash Wednesday and lasts 40 days (excluding Sundays which are always feasts in celebration of the resurrection). Lent–the word originally meant "spring"–is to be understood as a time to reflect upon baptism, a time for rebirth and renewal in preparation for the celebration of Easter. The traditional color of Lent is purple, to suggest somberness and solemnity.

THE GOSPEL: John 3:14-21

The Son of Man must be lifted above the heads of men–as Moses lifted up that serpent in the desert–so that any man who believes in him may have eternal life. For God loved the world so much that he gave his only Son so that everyone who believes in him should not be lost, but should have eternal life. You must understand that God has not sent his Son into the world to pass sentence upon it, but to save it–through him. Any man who believes in him is not judged at all. It is the one who will not believe who stands already condemned, because he will not believe in the character of God's only Son. This *is* the judgment–that light has entered the world and men have preferred darkness to light because their deeds are evil. Anybody who does wrong hates the light and keeps away from it, for fear his deeds may be exposed. But anybody who is living by truth will come to the light to make it plain that all he has done has been done through God.

New Testament in Modern English

Emblem of Saint John   *The open Bible*

QUOTE

"In all His dispensations God is at work for our good. In prosperity He tries our gratitude; in mediocrity, our contentment; in misfortune, our submission; in darkness, our faith; under temptation, our steadfastness; and at all times, our obedience and trust in Him."   —Anonymous

MUSIC

When I Survey the Wondrous Cross   *LBW* No. 482

Edward Miller wrote part of the melody of this hymn from a tune which remained unidentified for over a century until 1909. Originally titled "Tunbridge," Miller named the tune ROCKINGHAM OLD for the Marquis of Rockingham who was twice prime minister of Great Britain and Edward's friend and patron. Issac Watts was a prominent and influential London minister who wrote over six hundred hymns.

POEM

He sendeth sun, he sendeth shower,
Alike they're needful to the flower;
And joys and tears alike are sent
To give the soul fit nourishment.
As comes to me or cloud or sun,
Father! thy will, not mine, be done.
    —Sarah Flower Adams: *He Sendeth Sun, He Sendeth Shower*

PRAYER

Behold, Lord, an empty vessel that needs to be filled. My Lord, fill it. I am weak in the faith; strengthen thou me. I am cold in love; warm me and make me fervent that my love may go out to my neighbor. I do not have a strong and firm faith; at times I doubt and am unable to trust thee altogether. O Lord, help me.   —Martin Luther, 1483-1546

LESSER FESTIVALS

March 28 JONATHAN EDWARDS *Edwards was one of the most brilliant men America has produced. He was born in 1703 and at age 13 enrolled at Yale. He was a powerful preacher, and a widespread religious revival resulted. In 1757 he was elected president of the College of New Jersey (now Princeton).*

RENEWAL   4th Sunday in Lent   (Series B, #17)   www.servantleadershipbook.org

Renewal

Celebrating the Christian experience

The Incredulity of Saint Thomas. Woodcut. Albrecht Durer

THE INCREDULITY OF SAINT THOMAS

The Second Sunday of Easter

THE CHURCH CALENDAR

The EASTER SEASON is to be understood as the crown of the whole year, the queen of feasts. The Easter Season lasts for seven weeks ending with the Ascension of Our Lord and the following Sunday, which are understood as a continuation of the Easter celebration. The 40-day period of preparation for Easter is thus succeeded by the 50 days of rejoicing. The color of Easter is white. Gold is a possible alternate for The Resurrection of Our Lord (Easter Day), to give special prominence to this highest holy day of the entire year.

THE GOSPEL: John 20:19-31 (verses 19-23 and 30-31 are omitted)

In the evening of that first day of the week, the disciples had met together... But one of the twelve, Thomas (called the twin), was not with them when Jesus came. The other disciples kept on telling him, "We have seen the Lord," but he replied, "Unless I see in his own hands the mark of the nails, and put my finger where the nails were, and put my hand into his side, I will never believe!"

Just over a week later, the disciples were indoors again and Thomas was with them. The doors were shut, but Jesus came and stood in the middle of them and said, "Peace be with you!" Then he said to Thomas, "Put your finger here— look, here are my hands. Take your hand and put it in my side. You must not doubt, but believe." "My Lord and my God!" cried Thomas. "Is it because you have seen me that you believe?" Jesus said to him. "Happy are those who have never seen me and yet have believed."

New Testament in Modern English

Saint Thomas

The Lily, symbol of Easter and immortality

QUOTE

Under the influence of the blessed Spirit, faith produces holiness, and holiness strengthens faith. Faith, like a fruitful parent, is plenteous in all good works; and good works, like dutiful children, confirm and add to the support of faith.   —Juan Valera

MUSIC

Thine Is the Glory   LBW No. 145

Edmond L. Budry wrote the words to this hymn in 1884. He served as pastor of the Free Church at Vevey, Switzerland for over thirty-five years. The tune JUDAS MACCABAEUS is from the chorus, "See, the conquering hero comes," in George F. Handel's oratorio *Judas Maccabaeus*.

POEM

In the darkest night of the year,
    When the stars have all gone out,
That courage is better than fear,
    That faith is truer than doubt.
        —Washington Gladden: *Ultima Veritas, st. 4*

LESSER FESTIVALS

April 19   OLAVUS and LAURENTIUS PETRI   *These brothers were instrumental in the Reformation in Sweden. Both were ordained priests. In 1561 Laurentius, then the Archbishop of Uppsala, preached a sermon setting forth the principles of the Reformation. Together they worked on a Swedish translation of the New Testament with reference to Luther's earlier translation.*

April 21   ANSELM   *Anselm, born in Lombardy about 1033, became a monk, achieving a reputation as a teacher and spiritual director. In a visit to England he was persuaded to become Archbishop of Canterbury. Although caught in the conflict between Church and state, he is considered the leading theologian and philosopher between Augustine and Thomas Acquinas.*

April 23   TOYOHIKO KAGAWA   *Kagawa was disinherited from his wealthy Japanese family when he became a Christian. He spent several years in the slums of Shinkawa, later studying modern social techniques at Princeton. Imprisoned in 1940 as a pacifist, he was a leader in the movement for democracy in Japan after the war.*

RENEWAL   2nd Sunday of Easter   (Series A, #21)   www.servantleadershipbook.org

Renewal

Celebrating the Christian experience

Jesus and His Disciples. Drawing. Rembrandtrist

"I COMMAND YOU, LOVE ONE ANOTHER"

The Sixth Sunday of Easter

THE CHURCH CALENDAR

The EASTER SEASON is to be understood as the crown of the whole year, the queen of feasts. The Easter Season lasts for seven weeks ending with the Ascension of Our Lord and the following Sunday, which are understood as a continuation of the Easter celebration. The 40-day period of preparation for Easter is thus succeeded by the 50 days of rejoicing. The color of Easter is white. Gold is a possible alternate for The Resurrection of Our Lord (Easter Day), to give special prominence to this highest holy day of the entire year.

THE GOSPEL John 15:9-17

"I love you just as the Father loves me; remain in my love. If you obey my commands, you will remain in my love, in the same way that I have obeyed my Father's commands and remain in his love.

"I have told you this so that my joy may be in you, and that your joy may be complete. This is my commandment: love one another, just as I love you. The greatest love a man can have for his friends is to give his life for them. And you are my friends, if you do what I command. I do not call you servants any longer, because a servant does not know what his master is doing. Instead, I call you friends, because I have told you everything I heard from my Father. You did not choose me; I chose you, and appointed you to go and bear much fruit, the kind of fruit that endures. And the Father will give you whatever you ask of him in my name. This, then, is what I command you: love one another."

New Testament in Modern English

 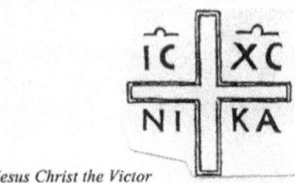

The Easter Cycle   Jesus Christ the Victor

QUOTE

Faith, like light, should always be simple and unbending; while love, like warmth, should beam forth on every side, and bend to every necessity of our brethren.   —Martin Luther

MUSIC

Oh, for a Thousand Tongues to Sing   *LBW* No. 559

This hymn by Charles Wesley is one of twelve in the LBW. He was one of the great hymnwriters of the ages with a total output of over six thousand, the best of which rank with the finest of the English language. The tune AZMON was written in 1828 by Carl Glaser.

POEM

And I know that the hand of God is the
   promise of my own,
And I know that the spirit of God is the
   brother of my own,
And that all the men ever born are also my brothers,
   and the women my sisters and lovers,
And that a kelson of the creation is love.
         —Walt Whitman: *Song of Myself*, sec. 5

LESSER FESTIVALS

May 18 ERIK   *Erik IX of Sweden was a man of great personal goodness. On an expedition to Finland he was accompanied by Henry of Uppsala who founded the church of Finland. Erik has come to be recognized as the principal patron saint of Sweden. He was killed by a Danish pagan prince in 1150.*

May 19 DUNSTAN   *Dunstan became a monk at Glastonbury and was made abbot, c. 943. A strict ascetic, he completely reformed the monastery and made it famous for its learning. He was made Archbishop of Canterbury in 959, and with the king carried out a thorough reform of church and state. He was also known as a musician, an illuminator, and metalworker.*

May 21 JOHN ELIOT   *Eliot came from Cambridge to America in 1631. As an Indian missionary he established 14 villages, inhabited by at least 1100 converted Indians. His Indian translation was the first complete Bible printed in the colonies.*

RENEWAL   6th Sunday of Easter   (Series B, #25)   www.servantleadershipbook.org

Renewal

Celebrating the Christian experience

Cathedral at Rheims

SABBATH MADE FOR THE GOOD OF MAN

The Second Sunday after Pentecost

THE CHURCH CALENDAR

THE SEASON AFTER PENTECOST is the longest season in the church year. The Sundays after Pentecost represent The Time of the Church–the time between the earthly ministry of Jesus, which is past, and the Advent season of preparation which is ahead. In the pilgrim state in which the church lives and exercises its ministry, it is the Spirit of God who leads and accompanies into all truth. The color green is used for the "after Pentecost" season, a time of growth in the Spirit as the risen Christ is formed in us.

THE GOSPEL Mark 2:23-28

Jesus was walking through some wheat fields on a Sabbath day. As his disciples walked along with him, they began to pick the heads of wheat. So the Pharisees said to Jesus, "Look, it is against our Law for your disciples to do this on the Sabbath!" Jesus answered: "Have you never read what David did that time when he needed something to eat? He and his men were hungry, so he went into the house of God and ate the bread offered to God. This happened when Abiathar was the High Priest. According to our Law only the priests may eat this bread– but David ate it, and even gave it to his men." And Jesus said, "The Sabbath was made for the good of man; man was not made for the Sabbath. So the Son of Man is Lord even of the Sabbath."

Good News for Modern Man

The IHS Greek spelling of Jesus

The Church

QUOTE

Sunday, that day so tedious to the triflers of earth, so full of beautiful repose, of calmness and strength for the earnest and heavenly-minded.
—Maria McIntosh

MUSIC

All Hail the Power of Jesus' Name   *LBW* No. 328 and 329

Edward Perronet, writer of the first five stanzas of this hymn, was for many years an ardent worker for Methodism, at times suffering physical abuse for his preaching. The CORONATION tune was written by Oliver Holden, by trade a carpenter. For eight sessions he was a member of the Massachusetts House of Representatives. William Shrubsole wrote the MILES LANE tune in 1779 while a teacher of music in London.

POEM

This solemn pause, the breathing-space of man,
The halt of toil's exhausted caravan,–
Comes sweet with music to thy wearied ear;
Rise with its anthems to a holier sphere!
—Oliver Wendell Holmes, Sr.

PRAYER

Father, in these quiet moments we have caught a glimpse of Thy glory. Inspire us, our Father, to carry into the every-dayness of our lives all to which we aspire at such a moment as this. May our faith have feet and hands, a voice and a heart, that it may minister to others, that the gospel we profess may shine in our faces and be seen in our lives.   —Peter Marshall

LESSER FESTIVALS

June 14   BASIL THE GREAT, GREGORY OF NAZIANZUS AND GREGORY OF NYSSA   *This day commemorates the three Cappadocian fathers. In addition to his eloquence and learning, Basil (born c. 330) was renowned for his great personal holiness and is regarded as the father of Eastern communal monasticism. Gregory of Nazianzus was called to Constantinople in 379 and, by his preaching, restored the Nicene faith. Gregory of Nyssa, a younger brother of Basil, was an eloquent champion of the Nicene faith, he traveled considerably and was in demand as a preacher.*

RENEWAL   2nd Sunday after Pentecost (Series B, #29)   www.servantleadershipbook.org

www.ingramcontent.com/pod-product-compliance
Lightning Source LLC
Chambersburg PA
CBHW031129160426
43193CB00008B/84